Being Elizabethan

Being Elizabethan

Understanding Shakespeare's Neighbors

Norman Jones

WILEY Blackwell

This edition first published 2020
© 2020 John Wiley & Sons, Inc.

The right of Norman Jones to be identified as the author of this work has been asserted in accordance with law.

Registered Office
John Wiley & Sons, Inc., 111 River Street, Hoboken, NJ 07030, USA

Editorial Office
101 Station Landing, Medford, MA 02155, USA

For details of our global editorial offices, customer services, and more information about Wiley products visit us at www.wiley.com.

Wiley also publishes its books in a variety of electronic formats and by print-on-demand. Some content that appears in standard print versions of this book may not be available in other formats.

Library of Congress Cataloging-in-Publication Data

Name: Jones, Norman L. (Norman Leslie), 1951– author.
Title: Being Elizabethan: understanding Shakespeare's neighbors / Norman Jones.
Description: 1st edition. | Hoboken, NJ : Wiley-Blackwell, [2020] |
   Includes bibliographical references and index. |
Identifiers: LCCN 2018056442 (print) | LCCN 2019000726 (ebook) |
   ISBN 9781119168256 (AdobePDF) | ISBN 9781119168263 (ePub) |
   ISBN 9781119168232 (hardcover) | ISBN 9781119168249 (pbk.)
Subjects: LCSH: Great Britain–History–Elizabeth, 1558–1603. |
   England–Social life and customs–16th century. | England–Social
   conditions–16th century. | England–Religious life and customs. |
   Conduct of life–History–16th century. | Faith–Social
   aspects–England–History–16th century. |
   Belief change–England–History–16th century.
Classification: LCC DA356 (ebook) | LCC DA356 .J66 2020 (print) | DDC 942.05/5–dc23
LC record available at https://lccn.loc.gov/2018056442

Cover Design: Wiley
Cover Image: © Art Collection 3/Alamy Stock Photo

Set in 10/12pt Warnock by SPi Global, Pondicherry, India

Printed in the United States of America

V10008784_031319

Contents

List of Abbreviations

BL = British Library, London
BL Lansd. = British Library, Lansdowne Manuscripts
Bodl. = Bodleian Library, Oxford University
CP = The Cecil Papers, the online digital collection of the manuscripts at
   Hatfield House
Doran and Jones, *Elizabethan World* = Susan Doran and Norman Jones,
   eds. *The Elizabethan World* (London: Routledge, 2011)
Hartley, *Proceedings* = T.E. Hartley, ed. *Proceedings in the Parliaments
   of Elizabeth I*, 3 vols. (Leicester: Leicester University Press, 1981–95)
HEH = Henry E. Huntington Library, San Marino, CA
H&L = P.L. Hughes and J.F. Larkin, eds. *Tudor Royal Proclamations*, 3 vols.
   (New Haven: Yale University Press, 1969)
HPT = History of Parliament Trust, *The Commons 1558–1603*. http://www.
   histparl.ac.uk/research/members/members-1558-1603 [Accessed
   November 29, 2018]
Jones, *Birth* = Norman Jones, *The Birth of the Elizabethan Age. England in the
   1560s* (Oxford: Blackwell, 1989)
Jones, *Faith by Statute* = Norman Jones, *Faith by Statute. Parliament and the
   Settlement of Religion, 1559* (London: Royal Historical Society, 1982)
Jones, *God and the Moneylenders* = Norman Jones, *God and the Moneylendes.
   Usury and Law in Early Modern England* (Oxford, Basil Blackwell, 1989)
Jones, *Governing* = Norman Jones, *Governing by Virtue. Lord Burghley and
   the Management of Elizabethan England* (Oxford: Oxford University
   Press, 2015)
Parker Correspondence = John Bruce and Thomas Perowne, eds.
   Correspondence of Matthew Parker, Archbishop of Canterbury (Cambridge:
   Cambridge University Press for the Parker Society, 1853)
Shakespeare = Stephen Greenblatt, Walter Cohen, Suzanne Gossett, Jean E.
   Howard, Katharine Eisaman Maus, and Gordon McMullan, eds. *The
   Norton Shakespeare*, 3rd ed., 4 vols. (New York, London: W.W. Norton and
   Co., 2016)

STC = Pollard & Redgrave's *Short-Title Catalogue of English Books (1475–1640)*, 2nd ed. (1976), digitized as *Early English Books Online* by Chadwyck Healey. https://eebo.chadwyck.com/home [Accessed November 29, 2018]

TNA = The National Archives of the UK, Kew

USTC = Universal Short Title Catalog, a collective database of all books published in Europe from the invention of the printing press until the end of the Sixteenth Century. https://www.ustc.ac.uk/index.php [Accessed November 29, 2018]

List of Figures

Acknowledgments

This book has been in gestation since 1972. When I began studying history professionally, I had a question on my mind. I wanted to understand the relationship between belief and behavior. My lab was the Reformation, in which people openly talked about what they believed and formally altered those beliefs, marking the beginning of early modern culture. Since I began, my work has explored various approaches to this question, and this book is a synthesis of my varied inquests into Elizabethan society.

In 45 years, I have incurred countless debts of gratitude. Many of those are acknowledged in other books, but a few must be recognized again. I have had great mentors: T.H. McDonald, Carl Christensen, Boyd Hill, Wallace MacCaffrey, and, most importantly, Sir Geoffrey Elton. I have benefitted greatly from the generosity of friends who have taught me about early modern England, and sometimes the meaning of life. This list is too long to enumerate, but Robert Tittler, Susan Doran, Glyn Perry, Susan Wabuda, David Dean, and Paulina Kewes are outstanding examples.

This book would not exist without the generosity of the Henry E. Huntington Library in San Marino, California. When Steve Hindle invited me to become the Fletcher Jones Distinguished Fellow for 2015–16, I was delighted at the idea of a year of uninterrupted work in the Huntington, surrounded by a superb group of colleagues. Mary Robertson, Steve Hindle, and Vanessa Wilkie played and continue to play important roles in my education. The first draft of this book was written between walks in the Huntington's gardens and long talks with the other fellows, long- and short-term.

My professional base is Utah State University, which has made my career possible and pleasurable. Our superb librarians have taken good care of me, ensuring access to databases essential for my work. Jennifer Duncan has been endlessly helpful. My colleagues have helped me in many, many ways. Charlie Huenemann and Susan Cogan have read parts of this work and shared their knowledge. Phebe Jensen read the first draft and gave advice that much improved it.

The greatest debt of all is owed to my wife, Cecile Gilmer, who has almost become an Elizabethan, living with my historical musings and journeying with me. She brought her own considerable skills as a writer to the manuscript, serving as the ultimate reader, making it much more accessible. I dedicate this book to Cecile as a tenth anniversary present.

Of all those people and institutions whose generosity has made this book possible, I can confidently declare, like an Elizabethan epitaph, that their virtues will never be forgotten.

Logan, Utah
July 26, 2018

Introduction

In the second half of the sixteenth century—during the reign of Elizabeth I—a new English culture was forming. Far different from the late medieval culture of pre-Reformation England, it was the foundation for a new society whose assumptions, values, and actions were markedly "early modern."

Europeans in the later sixteenth and early seventeenth centuries lived through an era of intense cultural and social dislocation. Across the continent, established ideas about metaphysical and social order were stressed, broken, rejected, confused, and reformed. Outbreaks of religious violence were the most obvious indicators of these tensions, but they were also accompanied with new understandings of social duty and organization. The religious ideologies of the era warred with one another and the governors of their societies struggled to retain control and advance their own visions of what God required of them.

In England, these struggles took peculiar styles, shaped by the nation's history, customs, and unique religious reforms. The generations of Elizabethans fought to live their lives in a culture that was deeply torn over its values, trying out new ways of living and expressing themselves. The results of their battles are celebrated as the "Elizabethan Age," the cultural crucible of the modern English-speaking world.

Hamlet's famous soliloquy, "To be or not to be: That is the question," first heard by theater goers in about 1600, poses a conundrum that had resonances for people of the Elizabethan age.[1] They, in their own rough ways, were all looking for themselves in the welter of old and new ideas and experiences that rushed upon the later sixteenth century. It was a time of particularly rapid change in English society, and it left everyone with puzzles about how to live in

---

1 Shakespeare, *Hamlet*, 3.1.55.

Being Elizabethan: Understanding Shakespeare's Neighbors, First Edition. Norman Jones.
© 2020 John Wiley & Sons, Inc. Published 2020 by John Wiley & Sons, Inc.

a world that was radically conservative and rapidly changing. God, salvation, duty, obedience, pleasure, purpose, domestic roles, and universal absolutes were being questioned by people swimming in the rip currents of conflicting truths.

Everyone was coping with the terror of history, using the tools at hand to understand themselves, their society, and their cosmos. In that sense, they were like us, but they lived in a different reality that gave their universe very different organization, reasons, and options.

This book reflects those reasons, options, beliefs, and experiences. It is about how Elizabethans understood themselves, how they perceived reality and acted on this perception. It is about the negotiations between the presumed static order of a divinely governed world and the rapid changes in thinking, knowing, and doing occurring in the later sixteenth and early seventeenth centuries. Its goal is to make early modern English ways of thinking and behaving understandable, so that its readers can make informed assumptions about how Elizabethans chose the explanations and actions that seemed appropriate to them. *Being Elizabethan* is a portrait of how Elizabethans, as reasonable agents, living in a transformative time, pursued ends determined by their reason in the context of their lives.

Of course, there was no typical Elizabethan. They came in infinite variety. But they shared aspirations, world views, and values that mark them out as people of a particular time and place.

I define "Elizabethans" as those individuals who were fully adult in 1558 and those who, educated in her reign, lived beyond 1603. They incorporate roughly four generations, born between about 1520 and 1590. They shared many events in Elizabeth's reign, but experienced them according to their ages, educations, and social roles.

Trying to capture how people reasoned in their lives is like trying to carry water in a sieve. As soon as you have scooped it up, it leaks out in tiny individualized streams. Historians are challenged to put individuals in context. We know we cannot understand the actions of an individual without understanding the system of values, historical events, and connections within which they lived. But we also recognize that within those contextualizing embraces, there are myriad individual choices defining individual acts and thoughts

No one's choices and expressions in the Elizabethan age were entirely determined by the perceptions sketched in this book, but it is also true that no one's choices and expressions were unconstrained by these perceptions. People were in a negotiation with their society and their God. It was a negotiation inflected by the ideas they shared with one another, and by the experiences they had in common, whether in terms of demographics (e.g., gender, age), occupations, social groups (e.g., families), common modes of expression (e.g., the *Book of Common Prayer*), societal structures (e.g., the legal system), or modes of presentation (e.g., the printing press, the pulpit). Everyone was interacting with institutions and audiences both internally and externally. No one could find self-understanding or engage in social activity without using their shared modes of perception. They lived within a grid of meaning and experience.

The last major attempt to capture the Elizabethan "times" was A.L. Rowse's two volumes, *The Elizabethan Renaissance: The Life of the Society* (1971) and *The Elizabethan Renaissance: The Cultural Achievement* (1972). These took up, he said, "the life of the mind, the values and creative achievements that redeem the record."[2] The first volume ticked the usual boxes of social history—food, lodging, sex, belief—while the second explored the expressions of the "English Renaissance" in drama, music, art, science, and medicine. Accessible, entertaining, and informative, Rowse's books are still in print. Scholarship has advanced far beyond where he left it in 1972, however.

Rowse expressed the rhetorical problem facing attempts to capture the way Elizabethans made sense of their lives. How do you give such a sprawling topic a "vertebrate structure"?[3] How can you create a narrative out of a shapeless, bubbling mass of human values and interchanges? Believing that the "ultimate constituent of history is an individual life," Rowse preferred to tell stories, describing good history as the "Conception of the course of events as a historical, spiritual process—as applied in the philosophy of Hegel."[4]

Being Elizabethan is my attempt to put Elizabethans into the spirit of their age, but with a vertebrate structure much different from Rowse's. I assume that we can only make sense of Elizabethans by listening to how they shaped their choices in the face of historical circumstances. When confronted with a problem, how did they understand its origins? Make sense of its impacts? Conceptualize possible responses? How did they understand good and bad, desirable and undesirable?

Holding my work together is a conviction that has been thrust upon me by the evidence: Elizabethans' perceptions were shaped by a deep belief in God's Word, but they could never agree on the right balance of authority for applying His Word. This accounts for the tension and creativity that marked the era and ushered in the beginning of a secular society based on individualism.

The question animating all my journeys into the Elizabethan world is, "When people believe something, how do they enact their belief?" I have sought to define how Elizabethans perceived the issues confronting them, looking for actions that are predicated on their perceptions. I also want to know how belief is influenced by the experience of actions taken and the realities of life.

---

2 A.L. Rowse, *The Elizabethan Renaissance. The Life of the Society* (London: Macmillan, 1971), ix.

3 A.L. Rowse, *The Elizabethan Renaissance: The Cultural Achievement* (London: Macmillan, 1972), ix.

4 A.L. Rowse, "How to Make History Readable," A Lecture to Henry E. Huntington Trustees, 03/31/1951. HEH 40.8.2.12. This manuscript contains notes on the lecture, so I am not sure if this is a direct quote, or if it is a comment by the note taker.

The goal is to invoke the natural responses of Elizabethans to the world as they met it. To do this, I put down layers of values, virtues, social orders, and education, building up the "base" Elizabethan. I then complicate their enduring values—the sort of "truths" they would give you if you asked them about what should be—with jarring changes that disturbed but did not dethrone those values, creating great social tensions. Attempting to harmonize the disturbances, I explore how Elizabethans understood causation, providence, economics, and politics.

I delineate what they believed in and how they learned those beliefs. I then introduce the challenges to those beliefs. Finally, I explore the adaptations made to accommodate both belief and lived experience. A world, presumed to be static, is disrupted by rapid change, creating new syntheses, placing more emphasis on individual choice, and complicating personal and communal identities.

The book begins by describing the idealized lives of the departed. "Speak nothing but good of the dead" was a sentiment widely held in the early modern period. Believing that ancestors should be models for their successors, Elizabethans portrayed the departed in idealized terms. Funeral sermons, epitaphs, funeral monuments, memorial poems, moralizing verses, and other genres didactically taught the living to prepare for death. They summarized what it meant to be a good man or woman. Most of these models of goodness were biblical and traditional, but they also evolved as religious values changed. In 1558, Queen Mary was an ideal Christian because she, a chaste and honorable woman, had memorized the Psalms in Latin, knew the responses in the mass, and recognized the Pope as her spiritual leader. Katherine Brettergh, who died in 1601, was an equally chaste and honorable lady who read her Bible constantly and hated popes. Both women are contemporarily portrayed as embodying the virtues taught by Christ. The female life well lived could be summed up in the few lines of an epitaph: dutiful, charitable, and pious. But how those virtues were displayed could be distinctly different.

This stability of goodness existed because, despite theological bickering, God was still in His Heaven and the Bible, newly available in English, taught timeless virtues. The dead could be guides to the living because everyone, quick or not, existed in a temporal and social relationship arranged by God. Every individual's beginning and end was a part of the divine plan. God had arranged society hierarchically, assigning each person a role and a station, and history temporally, flowing from The Beginning to The End. In that river of time bobbed the chips of individual lives, all moving with the teleological stream. It was a metaphysical system of meaning within which people paddled in desperate attempts to avoid the rocks of providential chastisement and the whirlpools sucking them toward hell.

God's creation was fixed and unchanging in a way often referred to as the "Elizabethan World View," thanks to a famous book by E.M.W. Tillyard. As

God's creation was constant, so too were social relations. Some people were superior to others, and everyone had a place and a role. Wives who disobeyed husbands had to be disciplined, but husbands who let their wives misbehave also had to be disciplined. All people had to enact their stations, or society would fall apart.

In this "static" society, social disorder was a constant problem. People knew all should be in their place, but there was increasing opportunity to social climb. Lowly merchants might live like lords, making it impossible to know for sure to whom you should doff your cap. God's order was traduced daily, though the law did its best to prevent this.

How did Elizabethans learn their places in the world? Through education in homes, workshops, schools, and churches. The church subjected Elizabethans to enforced instruction in theology and obedience. By law, everyone had to attend every Sunday or be fined, and by law the clergy had to use the *Book of Common Prayer*. English religion and its messages were scripted. So was the religious education of children. Masters and mistresses were required to catechize their children and servants, and there were many catechisms produced for the instruction of children. At home, in church, and in school, children were taught to obey "conscience rightly formed," and Elizabethans had a sincere commitment to the idea that truth would be visible if properly sought. If children were taught correctly, they would self-govern correctly; rather than following the sinful whims of their natural selves, their educated consciences would guide them rightly on the path to virtue and salvation.

Conscience became one of the most important concepts of the era. Its emphasis gave rise to new forms of internal exploration, such as the self-analytical diary and the memoir, and created a tension between obedience to your betters and knowing better than your betters. The Elizabethan educational project created obedience and undermined it, stressed God's fixed plan while urging critical thinking.

Conscience might lead you to question, but community enforced your roles in society. Elizabethans were not isolated individuals; they took much of their identity from their communities. Their roles as Christians, as members of a parish, an occupation, a kinship network, a gender, a neighborhood, an age group, assigned behaviors and costumes. Even the dead were buried in locations according to their social places. The "calculus of esteem" directed people's energies as they fulfilled their roles. But many of these roles were malleable. People might exchange roles, and as they did, they put on new social expectations and put off old ones. They aged, they married, they were widowed, they took on new responsibilities, they got poorer, they got richer. The "string of degree" might not be untuned, as Shakespeare put it, but plenty of Elizabethans plucked higher notes than they were entitled to do, and some played baser tunes. This social mobility was real, though frequently condemned. It had a fruitful dramatic tension to it.

Just as Elizabethans had no word for "unemployment," so they had no words for "inflation," "capitalist," or "self-fashioning." If they had, they might have been better able to describe what was happening around them. Instead, they had the confusion that came from watching people behave in ways in which they were not supposed to behave, ascending and descending as the wheel of fortune turned.

Thus far, much of what I have described suggests a view of the metaphysical that sat uncomfortably with the actual. People did not like to admit that things were not as permanent as they seemed, even though the later sixteenth century saw some profound shifts in self-understanding, even if God was still presumed to have arranged the world. Obviously, the theological reformulations changed individuals' relationships to God, and therefore to God's creation, but Elizabethans' external and internal depictions of divine order were in flux. Their mental and physical worlds were being rearranged. One example of this rearrangement was literal: maps changed. Thanks to the mathematicians, like the Digges family, new ways of displaying physical reality taught them to "see" the physical world differently. Ortelius' *Theatrum Orbis Terrarum* of 1570 showed them a round world, and his techniques allowed flat maps to represent multiple dimension, on the seas and on their surveyed fields.

Mercator's new globe told them that America was to their west, and the experience of America unsettled all sorts of ideas about food, about God, and about themselves. Race and culture needed new definitions. Cosmography changed, too. Galileo had English counterparts who were using telescopic observation to chart the heavens, and, as John Donne's poetry reminds us, people began to talk about their interior and exterior universe as a place on a map. Purgatory, which had been a place on the Catholic metaphysical map, was abolished, slowly turning heaven and hell into metaphors rather than physical places that could be located by geographers.

All this learning from observation turned toward humans, too. Vesalius produced the first map of the human body in 1543, and English anatomists quickly followed his lead. Dr. Caius required his students in Cambridge to dissect executed felons and then attend their proper, respectful Christian burials. Traditional Galenic medicine, which did not need anatomy, was being challenged by different diagnostic methods, so by the early seventeenth century it was possible to have the same doctor see illness from multiple pathologies at once, providing Galenic, Paracelsian, and astrological diagnoses of a single patient.

Earlier concepts of physical reality were unsteady in the face of all the new learning. Even time became relative. When Catholic Europe abandoned the Julian calendar for the Gregorian in 1582, the English would not go along. But ways of thinking about time were shaken, bringing into question the order of divine and human history. If there were pharaohs in Egypt before the date of the biblical creation, what did time mean?

In history, as in religion, there was a revolution happening under the influence of the *ad fontes* principles of humanism. Elizabethans had to remodel their past because they were destroying the relics of medieval religion and reinterpreting the history of Catholic England. Shakespeare's "bare ruined choirs" described the remains of the rejected past; in its place came a more nationalist, more secular, more humanist history that pondered individuals' choices in historical context, and the evidence for them. Elizabethans were reading, writing, and viewing history as a part of this new dialogue about the individual's place in community and creation. Their reconceptualizations of the past help us understand them. After all, if there had been no history of the primitive church, would there have been Presbyterians? And if Elizabethan gentlemen had not been taught the history of the Roman Republic, weaned on Ciceronian Latin, would they have thought about their state and responsibilities in the same way? Would the King James Bible have been possible if English scholars had not accepted the necessity of understanding God's Word by learning ancient languages?

Historical events in motion tested Elizabethans' understanding of the world. When they encountered a plague, or good fortune, the Spanish Armada, or the ever-present Spanish Inquisition, how did they react? If we want to understand how they used their perceptions, we must look for their application.

Divine providence was a key explanation of causation: once you have identified the cause of a thing, you have a chance to amend your life. Interpreting historical events through this lens made it possible to understand what was happening and why. When God smites you, you can repent, and God will relent. But if you are weak, Satan sees his chance and bad things happen. Responding to frightening events, Elizabethans knew God was warning them to return His static system to balance.

The most pragmatic thing you could do in the face of misfortune was to address the metaphysical sources of it. Pray, repent, and love God—but loving Him was like loving your own father; it was a matter of duty, and you could be walloped if you failed to obey either of them. "Our Father who art in Heaven, Thy will be done…"

Theirs was a grimly loving God. In such a world, where were the "Renaissance Faire" Elizabethans? Was no one having a good time? How did popular culture "perform" in the face of strict ideas of virtue?

Taking Philip Stubbes' famous Jeremiad, *The Anatomy of Abuses*, as a guide to sinful behavior and its providential consequences, there is a surprising level of congruence between his perception of their behaviors, which he saw as lewd, and what they were doing in daily life. There is plenty of evidence of cakes and ale. The scene between Sir Toby Belch and Feste in *Twelfth Night*, when the former asks, "Dost thou think because thou art virtuous there shall be no more cakes and ale?" sums up a raging debate about the propriety of community socializing. The virtuous were against cakes and ale and communal sociability that involved alcohol and dancing. But they were against lots of other things, too, including usury, greed, lust, and popular pastimes like plays and maypole dances. Traditional ways of relating to one another were under pressure, and the "virtue" so stressed in their educations was harder to define or find. As Queen Elizabeth observed late in her reign, all men had become "virtueless foxes." It provoked some to assert traditional values more loudly, and others to call for them to be abandoned. All the debates displayed conflicting ideas about what God required, what might trigger providential wrath, and what was good in conscience. Conscience, informed by Scripture, became the battleground of behavior. There were strong adherents on all sides.

Stubbes was concerned about incipient capitalism, too. Of course, Elizabethans had no capitalism, because they did not have a word for it (it is a nineteenth-century coinage). It was not one of their analytical categories. They expressed their economic ideas in the ethics of exchange, worrying about mutuality, fairness, greed, oppression, and legality. Living in an era of rapid inflation, huge population growth, economic displacement, and globalizing trade, earlier Elizabethans thought more about the visible effects than the causes. Poverty and unemployed were assumed to be freely chosen by the healthy, a sign of their sinful natures, provoking increasingly punitive ways of controlling the needy.

When they thought of the causes of what we would call inflation and increases in real prices, they used mechanical explanations. Human greed and sinful impulses caused economic troubles. Greedy rulers debased the coins, which had a static value, so if coins (and people) were purified, econ-omies would be healthy. These models, however, were insufficient, and the cultural roots of "capitalism" are to be found in Elizabethans' reframing of economic exchanges with new tools like double-entry book keeping and in how they believed the law could be used to regulate the economy—for moral and self-interested reasons. Were their changing business practices forcing ideological redefinitions of economic categories, or were Protestant ideas producing capitalist rationales, encouraging changing economic behavior? Naturally, ideas and activities worked together. New kinds of economic activities, including joint stock companies and monopolies, forced new questions about money, morality, and the state to be asked. Once they had been, the Elizabethans adapted their modes of explanation to answer them. By the early seventeenth century, modern ideas of eco-nomics, divorced from Christian ethics, were emerging. Phillip Stubbes raged against the new global economy, but he could not prevent his compa-triots from developing it.

All this agonizing about change and choice, conscience and fear of God, had deep interior dimensions hardly visible to the historians. Everyone needed ways of feeling the emotions of divine fear and hope, imagining themselves and God. But England's options for expressing emotion, for stirring the soul, were few and focused on words, thanks to its Protestant phobia about images. The later Elizabethans could only express their emotional beings in oral and aural ways.

Across Europe, religion was moving toward the emotional interiority of Baroque art and architecture; in England, that interiority focused on words. Something distinct was happening in the use of language in pulpits, on the page, and in theaters. For Elizabethans, words formed their cultural landscape, while sermons and meditations on the Holy Word gave them their mystical connections to God. The English experienced the intellectual changes of the early Baroque, but generally expressed them differently than their continental neighbors. They became connoisseurs of poetic performances, and of emotional words set to music performed in congregations and in small groups. Across the era, they inclined to an internalized individualism, an empirical religion of the heart, sharpened by the drama of Anglican liturgical worship.

By the time the last Elizabethans were adults, English society had been profoundly reformulated. The fixed, hierarchical creation remained, in theory, but it was badly dented in ways that would lead, by the mid-seventeenth century, to the radical social reformulations of the Civil War era of the 1640s. This static universe had been attacked from multiple angles by the Elizabethans, whose science, global voyages, historical explorations, changing economic lives, sense of self, and Protestant ideas all demanded reformed understandings. The Elizabethan age was the crucible in which the dross of the older world view was cooked off, forming a new cultural amalgam that made 1620 immeasurably different from 1520. The richness of Elizabethan life sprang from the terrible, fruitful contradictions of the time, as they struggled with the collapse of an older order and the creation of a new one.

And that is the irony of the Elizabethan era, the English Renaissance. For most people alive at the time, it had its glorious moments, but it was also a time of great discomfort. Religious tension was a fact of daily life. Theological disagreements turned constantly into political and social tensions, splitting families and communities. Angst about economic behavior and the genuine misery of adapting to a changing economy, inflation, and population growth were equally divisive. Religious disagreement and economic disputes became intertwined—all part of the conversation about morality. Politically, England was generally stable, but it was a very uncertain time on the world stage. War was a constant part of later Elizabethan life, and, though James I resolved the succession crisis and ended the wars (for a few years), he did not bring concord. He united two kingdoms that neither liked nor trusted each other, prompting questions about political identity and allegiance that added one more brick to the load of confusion already toted by Elizabethans. All this made attempts to puzzle out the organization of reality very important to the age, in which even those most certain about God's plan were uncertain about its daily interpretation.

Confusion made the age one of the most culturally productive in English history. Crisis and confusion gave point to the nation's dialogue with itself about who it was and how it ought to live.

When William Shakespeare died in 1616, he was set to become a part of the bedrock of the new English culture, an inextricable part of the curriculum in English-speaking schools. But when he retired to Stratford to live off his revenues as a landed gentleman, he would not have known the fame in store for him. His experience was of a world that was still trying its wings, attempting to make sense of demographic change, economic difficulty, moral confusion, theological gridlock, political tension, and social displacement. When a consensus had been reached, much later, his words would embody the debated views that came of that confusion.

1

Idealized Lives: Speak Nothing but Good of the Dead

On December 10, 1558, Bishop White of Winchester preached at the funeral of Queen Mary Tudor. He took as his theme the Biblical text, *"ladudam mortuas magis quam viventes"*—"it is better to praise the dead than the living."

By praising Mary's exemplary life, White was trying to convince the clergy and magistracy of England to resist the pestilential wolves of heresy coming out of Geneva and Germany, at the new Queen Elizabeth's invitation, full of blasphemy and heresy. Their duty called them to be faithful dogs who barked to protect England from heresy and rebellion. Better a lively dog than a dead lion![1]

He extolled Mary's godly virtues. He told of how, as she was dying, she received the Eucharistic *viaticum*, the passport into heaven. While receiving the sacrament of Extreme Unction, she was saying the Psalms from memory as the priest read them. At the elevation of the host, she, weak as she was, lifted up her eyes with a devout heart. Then, bowing her head at the benediction, she surrendered "a mild and glorious spirit into the hands of her maker."[2] "I verily believe," he said, "the poorest creature in all this city feared not God more than she did." All the bishop's hearers were urged to be careful not to die "without charity, without devotion, without good works, murmuring and blaspheming against Jesus Christ and his church."[3]

This was a brave sermon, barking at the new queen, but it took a familiar form. The dead queen was a model of Christian virtue, leading the way to heaven. Mary would have agreed with William Peryn, the newly restored Prior

---

1 BL, Cotton, Vespasian D.18, fo. 97. See Carolyn Colbert, "'Mary hath chosen the best part': The Bishop of Winchester's Funeral Sermon for Mary Tudor," in Elizabeth Evenden and Vivienne Westbrook, eds. *Catholic Renewal and Protestant Resistance in Marian England* (Farnham: Ashgate, 2015), 273–92.
2 BL, Cotton, Vespasian D. 18, fos. 102v–3v.
3 Ibid., fo. 105.

Being Elizabethan: Understanding Shakespeare's Neighbors, First Edition. Norman Jones.
© 2020 John Wiley & Sons, Inc. Published 2020 by John Wiley & Sons, Inc.

of the Dominican house at Blackfriars, who confessed his sins as defined by the Roman Catholic Church in 1554:

> I confess my innumerable iniquities wherein I have continued and offended the chief in breaking of the holy ten commandments, in the 12 articles of the Catholic faith, the statutes and commandments of holy Church, in the 12 counsels of the gospel, in breaking such private vows as I have promised, in the 7 mortal sins, omitting the 7 works of mercy ghostly, and in not doing the 7 works of the holy inspirations. I have misused the gift of grace lent unto me[4]

As he says elsewhere, we should all admit, "I am the most wicked wretch and unkind sinner."[5]

Later, Elizabeth's Protestant preachers were not interceding for the souls of the dead or keeping the commandments of the Roman Catholic Church. But they were still celebrating the departed as role models for the living. When Mistress Katherine Brettergh died in June of 1601, she was praised as an ideally godly woman, able to reject Satan on her deathbed and accept her salvation. The proofs of her ideal Christian life were very different from those of Mary Tudor.

Born late in Elizabeth's reign, Katherine Brettergh had taken her faith into her own hands, reading and meditating on scripture, keeping her mind and heart oriented toward God. She needed no priest; nor did she need Peryn's list of mortal sins and works of mercy. As William Harrison said in her funeral sermon:

> The Scriptures she knew from a child, and by reading thereof, gained such knowledge, that she was able readily to apply them when occasion was offered, as we may see at the time of her death, and that so fitly, and effectually, that she seemed to have made them her daily meditation. For the things of this world she was moderate, and sober, and by her Christian life and death, she might teach many Gentlewomen, how vain the pleasures and fashions of this world are, and how far unable to bring that peace to a distressed heart, that the embracing of true Religion can.[6]

Katherine was celebrated as a paragon among women. In an age when many thought women too dim to read and understand scripture, she was living the

---

4 London, Guildhall Ms. 20,845, fo. 33.
5 Ibid., fo. 30v.
6 William Harrison, *Deaths aduantage little regarded, and The soules solace against sorrow Preached in two funerall sermons at Childwal in Lancashire at the buriall of Mistris Katherin Brettergh...* (1602), 1–2. STC (2nd ed.)/12866.

ideal for all Christians. As Thomas Gattaker said when he published the funeral sermon of Rebecca Crisp,

> Examples of this sex are in some respect of the twain the more needful. That Popish conceit sticketh still in the minds of many: that knowledge and book-learning is for great Clerks only; mean men, and women much more then, have no need of it, neither indeed can attain unto it. Yet God telleth us, that they must all know him from the highest to the lowest, whom he showeth mercy unto in remission of their sins. And surely, if to know God in Christ be life eternal; then to be ignorant of him, cannot be, or bring but eternal destruction. Besides that, Christianity worketh no distinction of Sex. The same common salvation is propounded to both Sexes; the same means of attaining it are likewise common to either.[7]

In the world into which Mary Tudor was born in 1516, it was unexpected—even heretical—for common folk of either sex to read and comprehend the Bible in the common tongue. Good people did not need to know the Bible to be good, but they had to act in accord with Christian virtue taught by their priests. Henry VIII put the Bible in English in every parish, but in 1540 he and his parliament had second thoughts. They concluded that the holy book was too dangerous for uneducated men and all women to read.[8]

Nonetheless, by the time Katherine Brettergh was born in the 1580's, popular access to the Bible was highly desirable, and Katherine could demonstrate her godliness by being a Bible-reading Christian. She was thought capable of wrestling with sin and salvation personally. Her ideas of virtue were very different from Queen Mary's, but Mary Tudor and Katherine Brettergh were both ideals of the good Christian life for their times.

All women and men were challenged by the question of what it means to be a good person; to live virtuously; to be a model for your associates and your descendants. It was universally agreed that "We should in our lifetimes, when fit occasion is offered, perform all good duties which are commanded in the word of God." This makes the précises of lives found in wills, funerals, and tombs excellent descriptions of lives ideally lived, the departed modeling for the edification of the living. As Robert Pricke said at the funeral of Sir Edward and Lady Susan Lewknor, there was "no greater comfort under heaven, nor security in all desperate temptations of Satan; than the conscience of a life

7 Thomas Gattaker, *Certain Sermons*, quoted in Eric Josef Carlson, "Funeral Sermons as Sources: The Example of Female Piety in Pre-1640 Sermons." *Albion: A Quarterly Journal Concerned with British Studies* 2000: 32(4), 584. http://www.jstor.org/stable/4053628 [Accessed November 29, 2018].
8 34 &35 Hen. VIII, c. 1.

well led." Moments when Elizabethans confronted death stirred them to thoughts of their eternal salvation or damnation, and moved them to lead good lives.[9]

Elizabethans spent a great deal of energy trying to be good, or at least appearing to be good, and their efforts are indicators of how they saw the purpose and value of their lives. According to their generation, gender, and station, they participated in the great debate over how one ought to live. Evolving conceptions of the individual's relationship to God and society across the century meant there were tensions between generations and individuals over the virtuous life, though the tendency was toward greater emphasis on personal intentions and less on the communal values.[10]

Between the ideas of personal virtue displayed by Mary Tudor and William Peryn in the 1550's, and those exemplified by Katherine Brettergh and Rebecca Crisp in the early seventeenth century, there were many versions of personal virtue, generationally attuned.

William Holcot described himself in his 1573 will as "the vilest and wickedest worm of the western world and island of England." Like Father Peryn, he recognized his sinful nature and his need for repentance, but unlike Peryn, Holcot was a minister in Elizabeth's newly Protestant church. Nonetheless, Holcot, though a Protestant, used older, Catholic, language in describing his relationship to God. He bequeathed his soul to God his maker, asking God not to judge him according to his sins, "but only through the free merits of his dearly beloved son Jesus Christ, our inestimable jewel and ineffable joy, our sole savior and blessed brother ... whose only begotten son Jesus Christ is my only perpetual chantry priest ordained of God, which priest by his only sacrifice on the cross, once offered for all hath purchased for me (amongst others) a perpetual free pardon for all my offences and the punishment therefore."[11]

Holcot's will is fulsome in piety, and he was clearly a committed Protestant, but some Catholic habits died hard. Assured of his salvation by his "chantry priest" Jesus, he still wanted the sort of commemoration and prayers that came from an obit (endowed prayers for the departed), and he recognized the importance of acts of alms-giving. Willing books and money to University and Queen's Colleges at Oxford, he wanted their prayers. He left £20 in gold to Queen's, to be put into their buttery book of battells and used to pay sixpence toward the meals for two scholars. In return, the scholars were required to

---

9 Robert Pricke, *A verie godlie and learned sermon... Preached at... the celebration of the solemne and mournfull funerals of the right orshipfull Sir Edward Lewknor Knight, and of the vertuous Ladie Susan...* (1608), Sig.B2v., B3–3v, [D3]. STC (2nd ed.)/20338.
10 Norman Jones, *The English Reformation. Religion and Cultural Adaptation* (Oxford: Blackwell, 2002) explores generational tensions.
11 TNA, PROB 11, 57, #15, fo. 190.

recite, while at the Master's table, "after the last grace there said at dinner," as follows:

> Lift up your hearts to God.
> *Response:* We lift them up unto the Lord.
> Let us give thanks to the Lord our God for William Holcot.
> *Response:* It is meet and right so to do.

Then they were to say from memory the twenty-two verses of Psalm 119, "beginning with the first and so every day in order, ending daily with this St. Jerome's hymn 'Glory to the Father.'"

Holcot made similar bequests of meat for Sunday dinners, with an expectation of thanks for his life. Anyone familiar with the rhythms of the *Book of Common Prayer* recognizes the prayer and response as taken from the anaphora of the Anglican communion service. He apparently owned more than one *Book of Common Prayer*, leaving his largest copy, along with Erasmus' *Paraphrases* on the New Testament, a buckram cloth for the communion table, and money to buy a new hearse cloth, to his parish. His gifts mimic older traditions of funeral charity, but in a Protestant form. His will adds a warning to his parishioners to avoid excommunicated or outlawed people, who might tempt them to Satan.[12]

Matching his generous works, he humbly asked for his body to be buried in the shroud he had already provided, and if he died far away, his heart was to be removed from his body and returned to his Buckland parish church.[13] He died in June 1575, and his heart resides today in a niche in the church's wall.

Clearly, William Holcot's idea of being a "good" Christian included actions that harked back to pre-Reformation definition of goodness, but they were expressed in Protestant ways. This is not surprising, given his checkered religious past. It was the sort of history shared by many early Elizabethans, full of religious zigzags.

Holcot was a Protestant, but his religious convictions had wandered. He told John Foxe the story of how he, an evangelical trying to get a book to Archbishop Cranmer, when Cranmer was imprisoned in Oxford's Bocardo, was arrested. Accused of heresy and threatened with expulsion from the university and perhaps death, Holcot, through "frailty of flesh," had subscribed to the Catholic articles. Foxe said of him, "though then an *Apostata*, [he] is yet now a penitent preacher."[14] This sort of conflict between his religious worlds might account for

---

12 Ibid., fo. 191.
13 Ibid., fo. 190.
14 John Foxe, *The Unabridged Acts and Monuments Online* or *TAMO* (1583 edition) (Sheffield: HRI Online Publications, 2011). http://www.johnfoxe.org/index.php?realm=text&edition=1583& pageid=2158&gototype=modern#top [Accessed November 29, 2018].

the emphases in his will on a life lived according to the *Book of Common Prayer*. Christ was his only "chantry priest and savior," but his frame of virtue contained a strong sense of the importance of obedience to the Queen's church, and a heightened sense of the dangers Satan posed for the faithful.

The next generation of Elizabethans had less connection to Holcot's world, modeling virtues more emphatically Protestant. Sir Francis Hastings recalled the death of his devoutly Protestant brother Henry Hastings, Third Earl of Huntingdon, in 1595. Born about 1536, Henry was raised as a companion to Edward VI. Sir Francis remembered his brother's goodness and praised his godly virtues:

> He was a sincere professor of God's truth and therein most zealous. A loyal servant to his sovereign, and for her service would spare neither purse nor pains. A careful man for his country, being in public causes most provident, and in private most upright, loathing and detesting to seek gain by either. A most loving and tender hearted man to his kindred, for whom he held nothing that he had too dear. A most pitiful man to the poor, and devising continually how to do them good. A true friend to his friends, and ready always to perform the true part of an honorable friend to them. And an honest man to all men in all actions. Here have you the portraiture of as perfect a man as flesh and blood can afford ... His affection to religion I set down to be sincere and zealous; ... as he showed ever in his own person a love to religion, by frequenting the word preached, and presenting himself often to the holy table of the Lord ... [He] endeavored by all possible means that he could to season them [his kin] with a true taste of these sweet comforts that the Holy Gospel of God doth offer to all them that from their hearts embrace it and believe it.[15]

As for his sister-in-law, Lady Katherine Dudley Hastings, Sir Francis declared she learned from the Book of God to love true religion and hate papistry in her heart. Sir Francis commemorated her godliness with a poem:

> When pangs grew great, she found but little rest;
> Yet faith was strong in God, her father dear,
> And from this faith she found it always best
> To praise her God, and pray to him in fear;
> And to this end the preachers she would call
> To come to her, who fail'd her not at all.[16]

---

15 Claire Cross, ed. *The Letters of Sir Francis Hastings 1574–1609*. Somerset Record Society LXIX (1969), 58–9. HEH HA 5099.

16 Ibid., 63–4.

By the time Henry and Katherine died, the marks, if not the goals, of proper behavior had changed, and so had their justifications. When they were children—they had married when she was a child—good behavior was displayed through obedient, good actions. Bad behavior was known by its disobedient, negative actions. God awarded and punished according to the quality of the action. In the war between God and Satan, people were tempted on the spot, prompted to choose between good and bad. Endowed by God with inborn knowledge of right and wrong, conscience could be their guide to choosing correctly; those who refused to do the right thing did so voluntarily.

By the late sixteenth century, however, many thought good and bad behaviors were not, in themselves, worthy of reward or punishment. Instead, they became the signs of faith, and God judged consistency of faith over time rather than counting individual sins. Those who had accepted God's grace were prompted by faith to make virtuous choices.

Satan worked to counter these promptings, abusing each person's "particular" weaknesses to prevent good choices. Devilishly disguising his misleading messages with poor reason, Satan undermined people's will to obey God. Only those who actively sought God's help would escape hell. But God had given each individual enough awareness to know it was possible to serve Him and to resist Satan. Once this desire to serve was awakened in a person, God would help.[17] This awakened conscience, aided by God, sought to follow God using the tools of Bible reading, prayer, and introspection.

Mrs. Katherine Stubbes, dying after giving birth, modeled the awakened conscience in combat with the Devil. Married at fifteen, she was nineteen and a half when she died in 1590. Her husband, Phillip Stubbes, celebrated her as a role model for Christians. About fifteen years her senior, Phillip idealized her as a fervently devout teenager, always reading the Bible and other proper books and asking him to explain passages. She seldom left the house, only learned from her husband, was totally obedient to him, and refused to tolerate swearing or loose talk under her roof. She was sober, in every sense of the word. When her neighbors chastised her for always reading, she said a friend of the world was no friend of God.

When she became pregnant with a "man child," she prophesied that she would die. A week or so after her easy delivery, she was struck by a fever, lingering for six weeks. Hardly sleeping, she heartily prayed that she could die and be with Christ. Her child, she bequeathed to her husband and God, asking that he be raised in good letters and in true religion.

Fixing her mind on God, she rejected secular things. When her puppy, "which in her lifetime she loved well," got on her bed, she kicked it away. Piously, she told Phillip that they must repent of having loved the dog more than fellow

---

17 Kenneth Parker and Eric C. Carlson, *"Practical Divinity." The Works and Life of Revd Richard Greenham* (Aldershot: Ashgate, 1998), 103–4.

Christians. When she had put away worldly things, she made a confession of faith, prefacing it with clear statement of her belief in double predestination and her certainty of election to salvation:

> I would not have you think, that it is I that speak unto you, but the spirit of God which dwelleth in me, and in all the elect of God, unless they be reprobates: for Paul saith, Rom. 8 If any one have not the spirit of Christ dwelling in him, he is none of his. This blessed spirit hath knocked at the door of my heart and God hath given me grace to open the door unto him, and he dwelleth in me plentifully.[18]

Like an operatic heroine, her deathbed confession goes on and on, covering all major points of the Creed, denouncing papists and purgatory, and confirming predestination. She rejects transubstantiation, denying that sacraments confer grace. With her last breaths, she was quoting chapter and verse like a preacher in his pulpit. But just as she was finishing, Satan appeared to her. During her confession, she bore a sweet, lovely, amiable countenance, "red as a rose and most beautiful to behold," but suddenly the look on her face changed: "she frowned and looking (as it were) with an angry, stern, and fierce countenance, as though she saw some filthy, ugly-some, and displeasant thing: she burst forth" scornfully and disdainfully, in contempt of the Devil. She gave Satan such a tongue lashing that he fled "like a beaten cock."

She sang a psalm, gave instructions for her funeral, ordered her husband not to mourn for her since she was going to Heaven, and welcomed death. Sitting up in bed, she stretched out her arms to embrace the "sweet messenger" of everlasting life. Committing her soul and body into the hands of the Lord, she died, a model for all Christians.[19]

Skeptical people might suspect Phillip Stubbes of embellishing his wife's holiness—he did make his living writing hyperbolic religious tracts—but his account of her death sold very well. She taught her contemporaries about how to live virtuous lives and die good Christian deaths, in accord with scriptural principals.

Of course, most people fell between these extremes. They might be Protestants, but they also believed that they could, using their consciences rightly formed by reason, make choices between good and bad. They were neither entirely free to choose, nor so weak that choice was impossible.

In fact, it is probable that nearly everyone had to take that line, since there were more choices than ever between how to know good and how to know bad. For most people, of all kinds, being good was a matter of actions more than intentions.

---

18 Phillip Stubbes, *A christal glasse for christian vvomen containing, a most excellent discourse, of the godly life and Christian death of Mistresse Katherine Stubs...* (1592). STC (2nd ed.)/23382.
19 Ibid.

Thomas Buttes, writing in his commonplace book about 1580, made prescription for himself, encapsulating his desire to live a virtuous life aimed
toward salvation:

> T he longer life, that men on earth enjoys,
> H is body, so much the more he doth offend,
> O ffending God, man's soul no doubt destroys,
> M an's soul destroyed, his torments hath no end,
> S yth sin, God's wrath against us doth procure.
> B eware therefore, O wretched sinful wight
> U se well thy tongue, doo well, think not amiss,
> T o God pray thou, to guide thee by his sprite,
> T hat thou mayst tread, the path of perfect bliss,
> E mbrace thou Christ, by faith, and servant love,
> S o shalt thou reign, with him in heaven above.[20]

Buttes was a Protestant gentleman who did his Christian his duty according to
his station, giving a gilt communion cup to his parish, paying for glazing its
windows, and generally acting as a good steward to his parish church at Great
Ryburgh, Norfolk. He once sued the parish's minister for not catechizing the
youth, giving alms to the poor, or offering public prayers of thanksgiving for
the accession of Queen Elizabeth on November 17. Born in 1513, he was of that
first generation of Cambridge students who followed the reformed faith.[21]

Thomas Buttes lost his wife Brigette in 1571 when she was thirty-nine. A
collection of Latin obituary poems translated in his commonplace book
imputed to her all the standard female virtues, but some of the poems strike an
ironic note. Fletcher, Buttes' friend from Cambridge days, wrote:

> She ought have lived, for her virtue passed all,
> Apt was she for the world but yet more apt for God withall.

Bernard Carter wrote of her:

> Her Godliness and virtues rare did profit her but small,
> Nor yet the liberal hand where with she fed the poor withall.
> Nor that which is the woman's prize, the chaste unspoiled bed,
> Which she as firm as life did hold, stood her in any stead.[22]

---

20 HEH HM 8 Thomas Buttes commonplace book "A Boke of Verses named Aurum e Stercore.
Collectore R.O. Talbott," fo. 159v.
21 Historical Manuscripts Commission, *The Manuscripts of Rye and Hereford Corporations*,
13, Part 4, 413.
22 HEH HM 8 Thomas Buttes commonplace book "A Boke of Verses names Aurum e Stercore.
Collectore R.O. Talbott," fos. 20v–1v.

If Thomas' acrostic is anything to judge by, he did not take such an ironic stand about what was required to lead the good life.

Francis Wilsforde, who was in religious exile with his parents in Mary's reign, was a Prayer Book user of Calvinist leanings. Much younger than Buttes, he also mapped his moral universe in his commonplace book. The book opens with an injunction to himself: "Look upon these notes and gatherings, and where ye find them consonant wth the Scriptures, receive them, and where the contrary then reject them. Try all things wth the true touchstone which is God's word."[23] In 1587, Wilsforde created an acrostic on his name:

> **F** .1. Fear God, believe his word,
> **R** Rebuke the evil, commend the good.
> **A** .2. Amend your life, in time of grace
> **N** No better way, whilst thou have space,
> **C** .3. Cast care on God, that cares for all,
> **I** In duty & love, yet work thou still,
> **S** So God will rid thee from all thrall
> **W** .4. Well ward way wise, but not too late
> **I** In matters doubtful, refaineth speech,
> **L** Leave them to other, that truth can teach
> **S** .5. Speak not unasked, then answer right,
> **F** For, better silent, then rash in talk,
> **O** .6. Open yet the truth, if thou it know,
> **R** Reprove all such as discord sow,
> **D** .7. Do good to all thy self that lack,
> **E** Even for our Christ, & savior's sake.

Set out in a box beside the poem is this exhortation to himself: "Well warned, way wise q[uo]d Wylsforde. Way not weary of doing well, q[uo]d Wylsforde." Why did he need to warn himself to do well? He was very aware of the fleshly lust of youth, the pride and ambition of middle age, and the greed of old age, and he hoped to live in ways that avoided them.[24]

These sorts of sobering personal reflections on virtue were expressed in many ways. Women might display them in needlework adorning their stools, chairs, and walls. Elizabeth, Countess of Shrewsbury, known as "Bess of Hardwick" after the show house she built there, illustrated lessons about female virtue in wall hangings produced by professionals under her direction. This series of hangings tells the stories of great women of mythology and classical history. Referred to as the "Noble Ladies Series," they represent

---

23 CUL, Luard 179a,1. Common-Place book of Francis Wilsford, c. 1581–88.
24 CUL, Luard 179a, 184.

Figure 1.1 Set of wall hangings depicting noble women of the ancient world, Lady Penelope flanked by Perseverans and Paciens, the Hardwick Embroideries at Hardwick Hall, Derbyshire. Courtesy of the National Trust.

Penelope, Artemisia, Lucretia, Cleopatra, and Zenobia. Penelope, patiently awaiting the return of her husband Ulysses from the Trojan War, is flanked by the virtues of Patience and Perseverance (Figure 1.1). Artemisia, Queen of Halicarnassus and ruler of the Persian satrapy of Caria, commanded part of the Persian fleet at the battle of Salamis. In her hand, she holds the chalice containing wine and her husband's ashes. She is about to drink them, making her his living tomb. Her loyalty associated her with the virtues of Constancy and Piety. Lucretia is the Roman woman whose rape and subsequent suicide, restoring her family's honor, brought down the monarchy of Tarquin the Proud and caused the foundation of the Roman Republic. Naturally, she is supported by the female figures of Chastity and Liberality. Zenobia, Queen of Palmyra, who saved the Roman Empire by attacking Persia, is flanked by a spear-carrying Magnanimity and Prudence. The Cleopatra panel is missing, but those that remain stress female goodness—self-sacrifice for one's family and nation.[25]

---

25 Nicole LaBouff, "An Unlikely Christian Humanist: How Bess of Hardwick (c. 1527–1608) Answered the 'Woman Question." *The Sixteenth Century Journal* 2016: 47(4), 847–82.

Alive, Elizabethans were bombarded by messages about their moral duties. Dead, their lives became didactic examples of how the living ought to conduct themselves. There was an enthusiasm for commemorative poetry that recounted the godly virtues of the dead in often florid detail. Robert Greene, for instance, published an obituary poem honoring Sir Christopher Hatton. In *The Maidens Dreame*, the virtues, beautiful women all, takes turns sighing and praising his liberality, justice, prudence, fortitude, religion, temperance, bounty, and hospitality. Hospitality, crippled by Hatton's death, speaks of how well he fulfilled his role as steward of the poor, sighing:

> Ay me... my love is lorn by death,
> He that his alms frankly did bequeath,
> And fed the poor with store of food: the same
> Even he is dead, and vanisht is his name.
> Whose gates were open, and whose alms deed
> Supplied the fatherless and widows need.
>
> He kept no Christmas house for once a year,
> Each day his boards were filled with lordly fare:
> He fed a route of yeomen with his cheer,
> Nor was his bread and beef kept in with care,
> His wine and beer to strangers were not spare.
> And yet beside to all that hunger grieved,
> His gates were ope, and they were there relieved.
> Well could the poor tell where to fetch their bread[26]

Naturally, only the rich and powerful were commemorated in print, and there was a snobbish tendency to write poems in Latin and Greek rather than in English, but everyone understood the tropes to use when praising the dead. When Robert Dudley, Earl of Leicester, was buried in Oxford in 1588, he was mourned with a single broadsheet of Latin poetry, which, presumably, was appreciated by all the Latinate scholars of the city.[27]

The virtues of men and women were sometimes encapsulated in the portraits that became popular in Elizabeth's reign. The image of the person was frequently joined with text making them into a role model. A wonderful example is the panel portraits of John and Dorothy Kaye painted about 1567, to grace their home at Woodsome, Yorkshire. Dorothy's portrait (Figure 1.2),

---

26 Robert Green, *A maidens dreame upon the death of the Right Honorable Sir Christopher Hatton knight, late Lord Chancellor of England* (1591). STC (2nd ed.)/1227.

27 Thomas Holland, *Carmen funebre in mortem illustrissimi Comitis Leicestrensis, qui Corneburiae in agro Oxoniensi 4. Sept. 1588. vita defunctus est* (1588). STC (2nd ed.)/13595.5.

Figure 1.2 Portrait of Dorothy Kaye. Courtesy of Kirklees Museums and Galleries.

done when she was 44, has texts, nearly overwhelming her picture, that explain the virtues of the good wife:

> To live at home in housewifery
> To order well my family
> To see they live not Idly

> To bring up children virtuously
> To relieve poor folks willingly
> This is my care with modesty
> To lead my life in honesty

Her husband, John, who declared his portrait (Figure 1.3) to be a reminder to those who came after him, described his life thus:

> I Live at home in husbandry/Without office or fee truly
> As servyth mine ability/I maintain hospitality
> Teaching to these humanity/By rules of Christianity
> In cause of ambiguity/I never shew extremity
> Where malice is I pacify/Where just cause is I gratify
> My promise ready to fulfill/Thus have I lived & will do still
> Hoping by like to have such gain/As after death to live again

John, who wrote autobiographical poems his whole life, probably wrote these. His rent book opens with another poem that describes the qualities of the gentleman he aspired to be:

> Four Points for a gentleman
> A cleanly house, lodging, meat, drink, & fire,
> provide for the friend, he hath his desire.
> Then armor & weapon fit for thy degree
> to defend thy king, thyself, & thy country.
> Thirdly in stable a Byard or steed
> that will go thy Journey & serve thee at need.
> But chiefly a closet or some secret place
> to observe God in daily,
> and call for his grace.
> Who hath these things ready,
> his needs must I scan
> to know well the duty
> of a right gentleman.[28]

John and Dorothy Kaye expressed their ideal virtues in 1567; subsequent generations shared these with them. When Lionel Tollemache was designing

---

28 Robert Tittler, "Social Aspiration and the Malleability of Portraiture in Post-Reformation England: the Kaye Panels of Woodsome, Yorkshire, c. 1567." *Northern History* 2015: 52(2), 182–99.

Figure 1.3 Portrait of John Kaye. Courtesy of Kirklees Museums and Galleries.

his tomb in Helmingham, Suffolk, in the second decade of the seventeenth century, he telegraphed his values:

> My many Virtues, Moral and Divine,
> My liberal Hand, my Loving Heart to mine,
> My Piety, My pity, Pains and Care,
> My neighbors, Tenants, Servants yet declare.[29]

Virtues were often expressed on funeral monuments inside churches, like Tollemache's, in the later sixteenth and early seventeenth centuries. Before the Reformation, monument art had been heavily religious in focus, begging the parishioners to remember Christ's passion and pray for the souls of the departed. After the Reformation, "idolatry" was banned and people became very cautious about artistic expressions that were obviously religious. No more crucifixes, Pietas, saints, symbols of the passion, or *"ora pro nobis."* In their places came images of the defunct, lines about their genealogy and good lives, and classical representations of the virtues that embodied the characteristics of lives well led: piety, chastity, wisdom, justice, perseverance, temperance, fortitude, prudence.

The huge tomb of Sir Anthony and Lady Grace Mildmay exemplified all this (Figure 1.4). Lying side by side, the two are surrounded by life-size statues of classical virtues. The inscriptions remember their lineage, their virtues, and the duties they performed. Sir Anthony's reads:

> Here sleepth in the Lord with certain hope of resurrection Sir Anthony Mildmay Knt. Eldest son to Sir Walter Mildmay knt. Chancellor of the Exchequer and Privy Councilor to Queen Elizabeth. He was ambassador from Queen Eliza: to the most Christian King of France Henry the 4th Ano. 1596. He was to Prince and Country faithful and serviceable in peace and war, to friends constant, to enemies reconcilable, bountiful and loved hospitality. He died September 11th 1617.[30]

His wife's says:

> Here also lieth Grace Lady Mildmay the only wife of the said Sir Anthony Mildmay ... who lived 50 years married to him and 3 years a widow after him. She was most devout, unspottedly chaste maid, wife, and widow.

29 Nigel Llewellyn, *Funeral Monuments in Post-Reformation England* (Cambridge: Cambridge University Press, 2000), 347.
30 Sir Anthony Mildmay and Lady Grace Mildmay—St Leonard's Church, Apethorpe, Northamptonshire, UK. http://www.waymarking.com/gallery/image.aspx?f=1&guid=16c2f15b-99a4-4e9a-b7b2-15c72e55bdf1 [Accessed November 29, 2018].

Figure 1.4 The Mildmay tomb, St. Leonards' Church, Apethorpe, Northamptonshire. In each corner of the monument stands a female figure representing one of the four virtues – Piety, Charity, Wisdom and Justice. C B Newham / Alamy Stock Photo.

> Compassionate in heart and charitably helpful with physic, clothes, nourishment or counsels to any in misery. She was most careful and wise in managing worldly estate, so as her life was a blessing to hers and in her death she blessed them...[31]

In keeping with St. Augustine's reminder that tombs are for the living, not the dead, monuments became didactic. They were worthy of contemplation because the men and women commemorated were exemplary Christians. Their tombs helped people remember their excellent virtues, moving them to pious imitation.[32]

The tomb was a sly way of bragging about the importance of the deceased while at the same time teaching the living. In Harrington, Northamptonshire, for instance, the Saunders family erected a tomb in 1588, probably for William

---

31 Ibid. http://www.waymarking.com/waymarks/WM44KF_Sir_Anthony_Mildmay_and_Lady_Grace_Mildmay_St_Leonards_Church_Apethorpe_Northamptonshire_UK [Accessed November 29, 2018].
32 Llewellyn, *Funeral Monuments*, 346–8.

Saunders, who died in 1584. It commemorated two women and four men, flanked by Hope and Faith. The epitaph reads:

> Known to the world by virtue and desert
> Renown of life true honor of his mind
> Faith to his friend his free and princely heart
> His country's love which yet remains behind
> See here the fruits of everlasting fame
> A body dead but not a dying name
> Saunders.[33]

The dead had become instructors in piety to the living.

Sir Robert Cecil, Earl of Salisbury, son of Lord Treasurer Burghley and principle secretary to Queen Elizabeth and King James, enjoys a tomb that represents his two bodies, the public and the private. He lies in state on top, and below is his skeleton, carved to remind the viewer of Death, the great leveler. Supporting his earthy glory are the female figures of the virtues of Faith, Justice, Fortitude, and Prudence. The tomb was designed to participate in the spiritual lives of its viewers as a reminder of earthly impermanence and duty.[34]

An epitaph for Sir Thomas Scott, a Kentish gentleman who died in 1594, sums his virtues in more homely verses, but they echo all the others:

> He kept tall men, he ride great horse,
>   He did write most finely;
> He used few words, but could discourse
>   Both wisely and divinely.
>
> His living mean, his charges great,
>   His daughters well bestowed;
> Although that he were left in debt,
>   In fine he nothing owed.
> ...
> In justice he did much excel,
>   In law he never wrangled:
> He loved religion wondrous well,
>   But he was not new-fangled[35]

33 Quoted in Peter Sherlock, *Monuments and Memory in Early Modern England* (Aldershot: Ashgate, 2008), 157–8.
34 Llewellyn, *Funeral Monuments*, 340.
35 Brinsely Nicholson, ed. *The Discoverie of Witchcraft by Reginald Scot* (London: Elliot Stock, 1886), xvi–xvii.

Chief Justice Sir James Dyer (d. 1582) was remembered in poetry and in a tomb epitaph in Great Staunton for his good deeds and adherence to duty. Praised as a stout doer of justice, merciful, charitable, a mirror to the virtuous, generous, caring for his servants and family, and always concerned about the welfare of his country, he died in faith. His epitaph declares all this, and reminds the reader, "*Vivit post funera virtus*"—"Virtue outlives death."[36]

And so the dead of high degree taught the living how to succeed in life, exemplifying, if not by actually embodying, the virtues of good men and women. Turning away from Satan and sin, good Elizabethans were supposed to be charitable members of their communities, seeking the common good, loving their neighbors, and living the virtues taught by Christ.

Their conceptions of what made a proper life did not change radically through Elizabeth's era, but their sense of themselves in relation to God and their earthly community did. No longer needing prayers from others for their souls, later Elizabethans sought to guide their lives by the Bible, good thoughts, and attention to honor and virtue. The Elizabethan life well lived could be summed up in the few lines of an epitaph: dutiful, charitable, pious.

---

36 George Whetstone, *A Remembraunce of the Precious Vertues of the Right Honourable and Reuerend Iudge, Sir Iames Dier, Knight, Lord cheefe Iustice of the Common Pleas who disseased at great Stawghton, in Huntingdon shire, the 24. of Marche, anno. 1582* [1582]. STC (2nd ed.)/25345.

2

Divine Social and Political Orders

Divinely Ordered Hierarchy

Elizabethans lived in an ordered world, created by God. To grasp the way they organized it requires an understanding of how they saw themselves in the social and political order.

God arranged His creation hierarchically, assigning each person and thing a place, a part, and a station. All of it, from hell to dirt to the angels, was linked together in a "great chain of being" (Figure 2.1). Classically described by the scholar E.M.W. Tillyard, it was a Neoplatonic ordering in which people were in exactly the middle. They therefore had "correspondence" with the orders above and below them, influenced by them and capable of influencing them. They had the unique ability to either rise toward heaven or descend toward hell according to their behavior. When the proper correspondences were not observed, things became disordered and chaotic.[1]

All human society was likewise ordered, with the monarch at the top and the poorest wretches on the bottom. Every person, therefore, had a superior and an inferior, and was expected to behave according to his or her place in the rankings.

This orderly universe was the perfect work of God: a chain, a series of corresponding planes, a harmony. Within that perfection resided human history, which, according to the Bible, was flowing from The Beginning, in the Garden of Eden, toward The End, the Apocalypse as described in the Book of Revelation.

God's hand was on history, which was moving toward the moment when Christ would return to earth and reign for a thousand years, joined by the 40 000 martyrs who merited early resurrection. At the end of that millennium, there would be a general resurrection and all time would end. After the final judgment, the saved would live with God in heaven for eternity, and the damned would suffer in hell.

---

1 E.M.W. Tillyard, *The Elizabethan World Picture* (London: Chatto and Windus, 1943).

Being Elizabethan: Understanding Shakespeare's Neighbors, First Edition. Norman Jones.
© 2020 John Wiley & Sons, Inc. Published 2020 by John Wiley & Sons, Inc.

Figure 2.1 The "Great Chain of Being" from Diego Valades, *Rhetorica christiana* …. (1579), 220. Plate b. Courtesy of the Getty Research Institute.

Each person was expected to prepare for this final judgment, determining his or her eternal destination. But the nature of their preparation was dictated by their place in God's hierarchy. Women and men had different roles assigned to them, and so each played a different part; masters differed from servants, rulers differed from the ruled. Every man could be master of someone if he was a husband and a father. In the little economy of the household, the merest man had authority over his wife, children, and servants. In turn, every woman could be mistress of someone, if there were children or servants, when her husband was not present. Widowed women could be mistresses over their households but had no master in the immediate sense, though their eldest son might have a great deal of power over them.

The 1559 homily on "Good Order and Obedience to Rulers and Magistrates" summed up the official understanding of Biblical harmony, making it clear that God demanded obedience: "In earth [God] hath assigned and appointed kings, princes, with other governors under them, in all good and necessary order." Everything in creation had its proper place and time. Rain and sun, fishes and beasts, women and men had assigned roles. Each created thing had to perform its function for the world to work. It was a divine ecology. "Every degree of people in their vocation, calling, and office, hath appointed to them their duty and order ... and every one have need of other: so that in all things to be lauded and praised the goodly order of God."[2]

This conception of divinely crafted organic relationships between people assumed that everyone had a place and recognized the duties of their place. Everyone had a master, and disorder in society came when people disobeyed their masters or sought to rise about their stations. These boundaries were expected to be observed, and the Elizabethans spent lots of time worrying about those who trespassed beyond their God-given place.

But knowing a person's place presented difficulties. The most obvious marker was costume. People often dressed better than they were, impersonating their superiors, to whom more deference was due. The category of "gentleman" was especially problematic, since this was in the eye of the beholder. A man with wealth, or who had attended a university, or who lived without manual labor could be expected to be called "mister" as long as he dressed the part. Whereas other social degrees were a matter of blood, this one was a matter of virtue expressed in apparel. As the Cambridge theologian William Perkins explained in his popular work on "cases of conscience," people should dress

> in respect of place, calling, and condition, for the upholding and mainte-
> nance thereof. Now we call that necessary raiment, which is necessary
> both these ways. For example, that apparel is necessary for the scholar,

---

2 "An Exhortation concerning Good Order and Obedience to Rulers and Magistrates," in *Certayne sermons appoynted by the Quenes Maiestie...* (1559). STC (2nd ed.)/13648.5.

the tradesman, the countryman, the gentlemen; which serveth not only to defend their bodies from cold, but which belongs also to the place, degree, calling, and condition of them all.[3]

Laws dictating how people dressed were frequently enacted in Elizabeth's reign. Justices of the peace were expected to enforce them, with the goal of preventing disorder in the commonweal. Lord Keeper Bacon, chief legal officer of the realm, explained why justices had to be encouraged to look for people dressing above themselves:

> And touching confusion of degrees, who can now know a yeoman from a gentleman or a mean gentleman from a knight or a knight from a baron. Yea I am sure, ye all think that it is very hard many times to know a serving man from a noble man by his apparel and all for want of executing of this law ... And to the better observing of the statutes of apparel me thinks it were a good advice to give you that if in your open assemblies you shall see any man that shall seem appareled contrary to the statute to enquire of such of the justices as you may best trust whether he may justify the wearing of it or no or what he paid in the last subsidy. And such as you find faulty to see severally punished ... So doubtless if any such offenders should be present before you in such great assemblies and nothing said to them, that example must needs do great hurt[4]

Bacon's linking of clothing, social degree, and social responsibility is key to Elizabethan thinking about hierarchy. Early in Elizabeth's reign, Principal Secretary Sir William Cecil had a list of all laws concerning "ordinate apparel" drawn up, to discover what needed enforcing.[5] The complexity of these laws must have been baffling to everyone, but the key to them lies in the word "ordinate," with its meaning of "keeping within order." Dress marked your place in the divine social order, representing your duties and defining your social relations.

It was presumed that the law would ensure people dressed according to their rank. A handbook for officers of Courts Leet and Courts Baron, the local courts presided over by the landlords and their appointees, makes this plain. The book, printed again and again, has a nice chart showing who may wear what, according to income. Written in Law French, the eccentric blend of French and English used by lawyers, it states that people without £100 a year in income from lands could not use velvet in jackets, doublets, and purses. Nor could they

---

3 William Perkins, *The Second and Third Bookes of the Cases of Conscience...* (1608). 97. *STC* (2nd ed.)/19670.
4 HEH Ms. HM 1340, fos. 26v–7v, 30–30v.
5 TNA SP 12/23, fo. 20.

use damask, silk, camlet, or taffeta in cloaks, coats, and outermost garments. It goes on to delineate what kinds of furs can be used by whom, and it concludes with a discussion of gold chains with the "S" design that indicated you were an administrative officer. These chains could be draped over members of the Queen's council, mayors, barons of the Exchequer, recorders, serjeants at law, apprentices at law, physicians of the Queen, and others who filled those offices. Offenders against these rules were to be punished by these local courts.[6]

If a person was dressed above his or her social station, he or she might be honored inappropriately—an offense to God and a corruption of good order. Men were expected to doff their hats to those of higher station. As in the modern military, the rank was saluted, not the person. But there were nuances to these salutes, including the depth of the bow that went with the doffing of the cap. One man was reported to the Queen for failing to show proper "reverence" to Sir Robert Dudley. The accused explained, "we put off our caps ... for myself I knew him not ... me knew not it was he ..."[7]

Official costumes were everywhere. Gowns, chains, staffs, badges, blazons, hats, ruffs, colors, fabrics, numbers of pleats, length of sleeve, all spoke the language of place and occupation. As Elizabeth's reign wore on, the battle continued against social climbing in the secular world.

In the church, there was a different sort of fighting over "orderly" dress. Catholic priests had been known by their gowns, their square hats, their tonsured heads, and their shaven faces, and were therefore accorded the honorific "sir," which recognized their special place in society. After the Reformation, this costume was a bone of contention between those who wished to prove their Protestant Biblicism and those who still believed servants of God should be distinguished by their dress. Catholic priests, the more radical Protestants contended, were magicians in league with the Devil, and to dress as they did was to honor "popish rags." Ministers—they rejected the word "priest" because they did not believe in the Catholic sacrifice of the mass or transubstantiation—should wear "sober" street gowns and might grow beards and wear long hair, unlike the "shavling" Catholic priests. Queen Elizabeth had different ideas, wanting them to be honorably dressed so they could be recognized and receive the deference that servants of God deserved.

Attacking "popish trumpery," students at Cambridge rebelled against wearing the traditional white surplice and clerical cap in chapel. Students entering St. John's College chapel properly attired were hissed and mocked, and the Vice-Chancellor found his horse had been tonsured like a monk, its tail cut short like a cleric's hair, and a priest's square hat affixed to its head. Curbing these "surplice and hat fanatics," Sir William Cecil, the chancellor, drew the

---

6 John Kitchin, *Le Court Leete, et Court Baron ... et les cases et matters necessaries pur Seneshcals de ceux courts a scier...* (1580), 15–17. STC (2nd ed.)/15017.
7 BL Add. 48023, fo. 353.

university up short, forcing some recantations.[8] In March 1566, Bishop Grindal of London did the same for his diocese, holding a clerical fashion show to teach his clergy how to dress and demanding that they subscribe to the order or lose their jobs.

Thomas Earle, the vicar of St. Mildred's, Bread Street, London, was one of those who refused at first but later conformed enough to keep his church. He reported he and his colleagues felt "killed in the soul of our souls" by having to dress like Catholics. He fought the battle of dress all his life, and, though he kept his parish, refused to dress as Elizabeth expected the clergy to dress. He was presented by his churchwardens as late as 1597 for refusing to wear the required surplice. He died in 1604 after 43 years of obstinate ministry.[9] For men like Earle, dress still denoted role and station, so it was imperative their clothing not send a confusing message.

Earle fought for his right to dress as he believed God wanted him to dress. By the end of Elizabeth's reign, many in the rising generation agreed. After the deaths of Burghley and Elizabeth, who had so believed in orderly apparel, Parliament spent a great deal of time debating apparel. In 1604 the House of Lords proposed the repeal of all the laws about dress, handing the authority to regulate it to the new king. The Commons, however, were deeply offended by something in the bill—perhaps the King's assertion of his authority over what had been a parliamentary matter—and rejected it, startlingly, on the first reading, after a division of the House.[10] Consequently, the deregulation was stealthily included in a long list of laws being repealed and continued, marking the end of the systematic enforcement of sumptuary laws, though not the end of concerns over disorder in dress.[11]

Dress was about order, and order was about your physical place in the world. Processions, civil and ecclesiastical, were a constant part of Elizabethan life, and each person was carefully placed in relation to all other people. If you wanted to understand the hierarchy, all you had to do was to see who walked where behind the Queen, the mayor, the sheriff, the bishop, or the corpses of the dead. Great energy went into planning these displays of order, and people had to have the clothes for their places.

Keeping people dressed according to their station, walking and sitting in the appropriate order, and all other "ordering," was an affirmation of the way God

---

8 H.C. Porter, *Reformation and Reaction in Tudor Cambridge* (Hamden, Conn.: 1972), 114–27. John Strype, *Annals of the Reformation and the Establishment of Religion* (Oxford, 1824), I.2, 153–6.
9 CUL Mm.1.29, fos. 3–3v, 49–49v.
10 "House of Commons Journal Volume 1: 24 March 1604," in *Journal of the House of Commons: Volume 1, 1547–1629* (London, 1802), 152. British History Online http://www.british-history.ac.uk/commons-jrnl/vol1/p152 [accessed November 29, 2018].
11 Frances Elizabeth Baldwin, *Sumptuary Legislation and Personal Regulation in England* (Baltimore: Johns Hopkins Press, 1926), 249.

had aligned His creation. That creation was harmonious, and people should act in harmony to please God and make society work. An essential part of a child's education was to understand people's places, to read the text of dress and deference, and to behave accordingly.

Richard Mulcaster, writing in 1582 about elementary education, portrayed the purpose of schooling as ensuring that the "young fry" may be brought up to "prove good in the end, and serve well in that place, whereunto they shalbe loted [allotted] for the benefit of their country."[12] It was the perfection of natural abilities through education that taught children the beauty of concord, and the danger of dissension in the body politic.[13]

This idea that people had been allocated their places by God for the benefit of England was behind the 1563 Statute of Artificers, codifying concerns about those who were "disordered" and "masterless." A major piece of legislation, the statute clarified and unified the treatment of apprentices, husbandmen, and various sorts of servants according to their roles. Firmly placed under the authority of their masters and mistresses, apprentices could not leave their employment before the end of their contracts without permission of the justices of the peace. Mistreatment by a master or mistress was no excuse for running away, though the aggrieved party could complain to the justices. A masterless young person could not refuse to be an apprentice if a householder demanded it, and the justices could imprison youths who refused to serve. To maintain proper social boundaries, the statute also forbad apprenticing people of the wrong social classes in skilled trades. If the parents of a would-be apprentice were worth less than £3 a year, they could not apprentice the child in a market town. Informers were empowered to snoop, looking for illegal apprentices.[14]

Attempting to regulate access to trades and keep people properly controlled, this statute embodies the assumption that the role of the state was the enforcement of divinely decreed order, as each person performed a distinct role like an instrument in an orchestra. Society was supposed to harmonize, performing as directed by the divine composer.[15] That social harmony, like an individual's life, was deeply interconnected with the rest of God's creation. As the Propeht Esdras in the biblical Apocrypha put it: "Upon the fourth day thou [God]

---

12 Richard Mulcaster, *The First Part of the Elementarie which Entreateth Chefelie of the right Writing of our Enlgish tung* (1582), 28. STC 18250.

13 Jacqueline Cousin-Desjobert, *La théorie et la pratique d'un éducateur élisabéthain. Richard Mulcaster c. 1531–1611* (Paris: Èditions SPM, 2003), 205.

14 5 Eliz. I, c.4.

15 Christopher Marsh, *Music and Society in Early Modern England* (Cambridge: Cambridge University Press, 2010), 59. Richard Mulcaster, *Positions vvherin those primitiue circumstances be examined, which are necessarie for the training vp of children, either for skill in their booke, or health in their bodie* (1581), 36. STC (2nd ed.)/18253.

created the light of the sun, and of the moon, and the order of the stars, and gave them a charge, to do service even unto man."[16]

The importance of God's starry messengers in individual lives is shown in a two-sided portrait of Sir Christopher Hatton done sometime around 1580 (Figure 2.2). On the one side is his face; on the other are allegories of time and a poem on the subject. Surrounding his face is a horoscope of four concentric rings. The innermost is divided into thirty-six parts, each governed by a planet. The next ring contains representations of the seven planets; the one after that, the twelve signs of the zodiac. The fourth ring has seventy-two divisions and is linked to an astronomer in the lower right, using an armillary pointing to what may be Hatton's birth date in late August 1540. The armillary is labeled ambiguously, in Latin, with a phrase that might mean "destined to" and might mean "destined from" eternity. Another phrase, again in Latin, says, "born, raised up, buried"; it is presented alongside arms and the motto "*me spes*," "my hope."

The images and poetry on the rear of Hatton's portrait state a philosophy of life as well as a warning. Little paintings depict him lively—he was famous for having enchanted Elizabeth with his dancing—and dead. Clearly, time is to be seized "by its hair" before it turns the bald back of its head. If, it warns, you do not seize it, you cannot catch it. The Latin poem, paraphrasing a famous Greek poem on time, says as much.[17]

What exactly Hatton's portrait was meant to convey, or even how it was displayed, is hard to know, but clearly, he expected the astrological message to be delivered. His short time on earth was dominated by the stars, he seems to say, even though he was also a devout Christian.

Astrology was a respected science that, when used correctly, could explain disease, predict the future, and ensure success. Based on a linear conception of time, and on the conviction that there as an ordered celestial influence on human lives, it was fodder for almanacs and popular manuals of prognostication. Astrology communicated the influence of nature and reinforced prophecy for Christians, making it useful, popular, and dangerous.

As they were with many things, Protestants were bothered by astrology because it smacked of Satanic powers. In fact, judicial astrology, which was used to foretell the future and explain portents like earthquakes and eclipses, was frowned on by most theologians. It is easy to see why these practices were a threat to good order, since they foretold happenings that threatened the establishment. At the beginning of Elizabeth's reign, judicial astrologers Michel Nostradamus and Lewis Vaughan foresaw trouble. Vaughan averred that a partial eclipse of the moon in 1558 indicated that 1559 was would be a year of strife, contention, murder, disease, and religious tumult. Vaughan knew that late 1559 would see rebellion

---

16 2 Esdras 6:45–6. Geneva Bible.
17 C.W.R.D. Moseley, "A Portrait of Sir Christopher Hatton, Erasmus and an Emblem of Alciato: Some Questions." *The Antiquaries Journal* 2006: 86, 373–9.

Figure 2.2 Lord Chancellor Sir Christopher Hatton, ca. 1580. NPG L256. Reproduced by permission of the Northampton Borough Council.

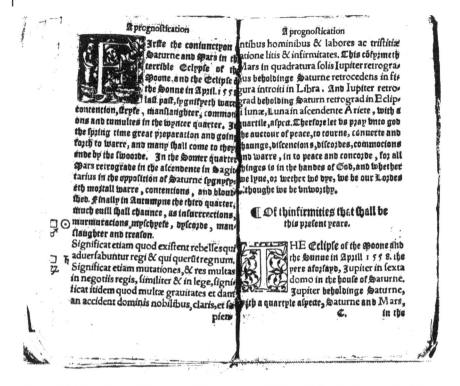

Figure 2.3 The eclipses of the sun and the moon predict trouble for the kings and noble lords. Lewes Vaughn, *A new almanacke and prognostication, collected for the yeare of our Lord God. M.D.L.IX. Wherein is expressed the chaunge and full of the moone, with theyr quarters. The varietie of the ayre, and also of the windes throughout the whole yeare, with infortunate times to bie and sell, take medycine, sowe, plante, and iourney in, both by lande and by water, and other necessarye thinges, as heareafter shall appeare. Made from the merydian of Gloucestre, and Poole Articke, there mounted. LIII. degrees, seruynge for all Englande.* (1559), Sig. c. STC (2nd ed.) 520. Henry E. Huntington Library and Art Gallery.

and the overthrow of the monarch, so he put his prophecy into Latin to keep it from the knowledge of the rebellious commoners (Figure 2.3).[18]

Nostradamus, whose prophecies are still popular today, received a similar message from the heavens. 1559 and 1560, he said, would see calamity, misery, and trouble that affected bishops and priests more than any others, with difference of sects, murmuring against ceremonies, feuds, noise, and discontinuance of solemnities. Bishops would be robbed of their dioceses and new ones would be created in their places.[19] This was so well known that when Matthew Parker,

18 Lewis Vaughan, *A new almanacke and prognostication, collected for the yeare of our Lord God. M.D.L.IX...* (1558), unpaginated. STC (2nd ed.)/520

19 Michel Nostradamus, *The prognostication of maister Michael Nostredamus, doctour in phisick. In prouince for the yeare of our Lorde, 1559: With the predictions and presages of euery moneth* (1559), unpaginated. STC/2259:04. The threat against bishops comes in April.

offered the position of Elizabeth's first Archbishop of Canterbury, was reluctant to accept, he had to explain that it was not because "the prognostications of Mr. Michael Nostradame reigns in my head."[20]

This caused so much concern that the works of Nostradamus were banned, and booksellers were fined for selling translations of them. The Privy Council agreed with John Calvin, who argued that foretelling the fates of nations and churches was not permissible to Christians, even though it was ok to use astrology for personal understanding.[21]

Since all creation could be used to deliver messages from Heaven, there were other ways of learning about the disorders in the world. Nostradamus warned that there would be many monstrous births in the disordered times, and Elizabethans paid careful attention to them. There is an illustration of the prodigies born "contrary to the course of nature" in 1562 sketched on to the probate copy of Margaret Lane's will in the Probate records for that year.[22] Pigs with men's noses were God's way of warning against sin; sickness might be, too, but more often it was caused by astral influences on the individual.

Judicial astrology was forbidden by church and state because it was dangerous, but that did not mean the stars were without power that could be used for good. Medical astrology was a useful scientific tool. A person's exact time and place of birth could be triangulated with an exact astronomical moment to diagnose disease without examining the patient. The influences of the heavens shaped people's personal destinies, and an expert could help them deal with their problems.

Simon Forman and Richard Napier, physicians practicing astrological medicine in London later in Elizabeth's reign, left a huge collection of casebooks containing hundreds of horoscopes, with notes placed into "houses" allowing them to discover the pattern of celestial influences and answer patients' questions (Figure 2.4). They did not have to see the patients, or even examine their urine (standard medical practice of the day), to know what was wrong. The astrologer physician mapped the positions of the planets, sun, and moon at the moment of a patient's query. The chart or horoscope was a square divided into twelve "celestial houses," and the movements of the planets were calculated from a book of planetary motions. With everything plotted, the practitioner read the results according to rules about the positions of the planets in relation to those of other heavenly bodies.[23]

---

20 *Parker Correspondence*, 59–60.

21 Jean Calvin, *An admonicion against astrology iudiciall and other curiosities, that raigne now in the world: translated into English, by G.G.* (1561). STC (2nd ed.)/4372.

22 TNA, PROB 11/45/fo. 58.

23 Lauren Kassell, Michael Hawkins, Robert Ralley, John Young, Joanne Edge, Janet Yvonne Martin-Portugues, and Natalie Kaoukji (eds.), 'Casebooks', The casebooks of Simon Forman and Richard Napier, 1596–1634: a digital edition, https://casebooks.lib.cam.ac.uk, accessed 26 January 2019.

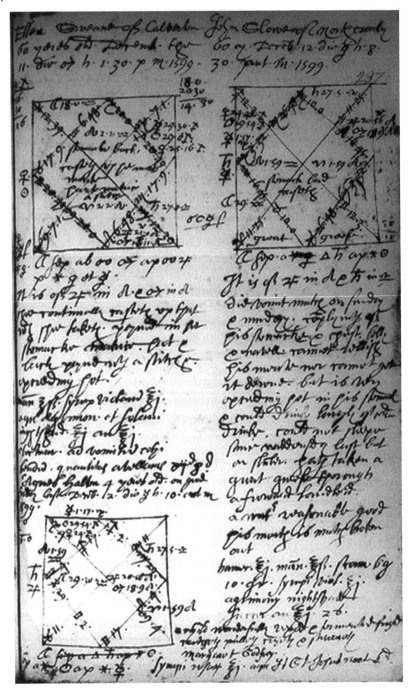

Figure 2.4 A page from Richard Napier's casebook for 11–12 December 1599. MS Ashmole 228, fo. 237r. Reproduced by permission of the Bodleian Libraries, Oxford.

From these readings, the astrologer could provide answers to questions about disease, pregnancy, business affairs, and other things. However, he sometimes refused a patient if he determined that the affliction was from God, and he sometimes prescribed no medicine if he determined that the disease was fatal or could not be cured. As Simon Forman noted of one woman's genetic illness in 1597, "the sickness comes from God. And it is entailed the seed of the party and the offspring shall have the same disease, and there is no way but prayer unto God and repentance first. That the finger of God may be taken from her, or else no medicine will prevail."[24]

The sun, moon, and stars were visible manifestations of the order God imposed on creation. Invisible, but real, were a variety of metaphysical beings that influenced humanity. God was served by angels and archangels; Satan by demons. Spirits and ghosts were all about. Their interactions with humans were common, and as the sixteenth century wore on, there was more and more interest in witchcraft as a cause of disease and misfortune. As *The Book of Homilies* puts it, "if we stand in necessity of corporal health, whither go the common people, but to charms, witchcrafts, and other delusions of the devil?"[25]

Satan caused illness, which could only be overcome by God's strength, when called upon with faith. God could overcome all the influences of demonic spirits causing human suffering, sometimes sending His angels. Simon Forman used them in his medical practice. Following the instructions in a book, delivered by the Angel Panphilius to King Solomon on golden plates, he could put questions about pregnancies, virginity, and other things to angels, who would inspire him with an answer.[26]

When an illness was caused by a demon, divine intervention was necessary. The "Maiden of Chester," Anne Milner, who was cured of an epileptic disease in 1564, learned this as Master John Lane, a minister, held her down and blew vinegar up her nose while calling on God and invoking the blood of Christ. This went on for hours, until she could repeat the Lord's Prayer and *Te Deum* with those around her. And so she was cured.[27]

In 1599, seven people suffered demonic possession in Lancashire. To drive out the demons, more than thirty people gathered in a room with the afflicted, praying as they writhed, contorted, and blasphemed against the "Bible babble." One by one, the spirits came out, each taking a different form. Mistress Byrom

---

24 Lauren Kassell, *Medicine and Magic in Elizabethan London* (Oxford: Oxford University Press, 2005), 148–9.

25 "The Second Part of the Sermon for Rogation Week," in *Certain Sermons or Homilies Appointed to be Read in Churches in the Time of Queen Elizabeth* (London: Society for Promoting Christian Knowledge, 1846), 514.

26 Ibid., 218–21.

27 John Fisher, *The copy of a letter describing the wonderful woorke of God in deliuering a mayden within the city of Chester, from an horrible kinde of torment and sicknes...* (1565). STC (2nd ed.)/10910.

felt hers rise from her belly and come out of her mouth, leaving her with a sore throat. Shaped like a crow's head, the demon flew into a corner of the parlor "with darkness about it," where it lingered until it suddenly disappeared in a flash of fire.[28] Since these sorts of possession were well attested in the Bible—Christ himself had cast out demons who behaved in similar ways—everyone knew they were possible, even if there were always skeptics ready to doubt that it was demons or witches in particular cases.

Some were skeptical about Satanic forces, but skeptics were not well received. Reginald Scott was a polymath whose greatest distinction came from his engineering work on a dam for Dover harbor. A member of parliament and an expert on hop growing, Scott took it upon himself to refute Jean Bodin's book of 1582 explaining how sorcerers used demons.[29] Having attended witchcraft trials and interviewed self-proclaimed witches, he concluded they did not exist. In his 1584 book *The Discoverie of Witchcraft*, he argued against witchcraft and other superstitions, including Catholicism, astrology, and alchemy, using Biblical arguments, physics, and a sense of humor. His research was thorough and heavily documented. It led him to some dangerous conclusions. He denied the existence of devils and demons, finding them to be metaphors for our internal promptings.

His book was well known but not well received. James VI of Scotland (soon to be James I of England) repudiated him in his *Daemonology* (1597). Deeply impressed by the witch trials going on around him, the Scottish king wrote that "the fearful abounding at this time in this country, of these detestable slaves of the Devil, the Witches or enchanters" had prompted him "to resolve the doubting hearts of many; both that such assaults of Satan are most certainly practiced, and that the instruments thereof, merits most severely to be punished: against the damnable opinions ... of one called *SCOT* an Englishman."[30]

Leading English theologians, such as William Perkins, attacked Scott too. His skepticism attracted some support, but he clearly did not speak for most of his compatriots when he suggested they were fooled into believing mere spells could influence things.[31] He was denying the order of the universe.

The hunt for witches in England was mitigated by English law, which made it a secular crime. Harm had to be proved before a prosecution could succeed. Moreover, the apparent power of witches contradicted the power of divine providence, making some theologians, even Perkins, less interested in

---

28 John Darel, *A true narration of the strange and greuous vexation by the Devil, of 7. persons in Lancashire...* (1600), 10–11. STC (2nd ed.)/6288.

29 Jean Bodin, *De la demonomanie des sorciers* (Paris: 1582). USTC 1699.

30 James VI & I, *Daemonologie in forme of a dialogue...* (1597), fos. 2–2v. STC (2nd ed.)/14364.

31 David Wootton, "Scott, Reginald (*d.* 1599)," *Oxford Dictionary of National Biography* (Oxford: Oxford University Press, 2004). http://www.oxforddnb.com.huntington.idm.oclc.org/view/article/24905 [Accessed November 29, 2018].

it than many on the Continent and in Scotland, where it was tried by church courts as a crime against God.

You did not have to be a witch to conjure ghosts, but those who did were suspect. Henry Cesar, a minister in Cornwall, was reported to the justices of the peace for claiming Sir Walter Mildmay (or maybe Principle Secretary Walsingham) had a conjuror summon the ghost of Cardinal Pole. Cesar was interrogated about this. It came out that he had only heard the story, not seen the event, and he was no conjurer himself—but it was also discovered that he owned papist books, perhaps proving the use of Pole's ghost for malicious intent.[32] The appearance of the Cardinal's ghost was treated matter-of-factly; the question of why it appeared was what mattered. Was it, like Hamlet's father, come from the grave to deliver a message?

If the metaphysical world was filled with beings and messages, so too was the physical one. Genesis 1:26–30 said man was created in God's image and given dominion over the fish, the fowl, the animals, all creeping things, trees, green herbs, and seeds. Humanity was to subdue them all, taking dominion over the creatures of the earth for its own use. Since all things were created by God for people, it behooved them to catalog creation and determine the divine purpose behind it.

With this assumption driving the effort, Elizabeth's reign saw the publication of the first herbals in English, all of them produced for medical purposes and all assuming plants were put on earth for human use.

William Turner, the pugnaciously Protestant Dean of Wells, spent his time attacking papists and expounding God's creation. He published herbals as a young Cambridge don, but his exile during Mary's reign gave him a chance to research his much larger *Herbal*. Drawing on the continental herbalists and adding English plants and his own observations, he recorded how God's plants could be used to cure humans. He not only cataloged the plants, he wrote on the medical virtues of various spas and of wines. He was determined, he told Sir William Cecil, "seeing that God hath also endued me with the knowledge of bodily Physic, after that I had sought to promote the kingdom of GOD, to communicate some part of my knowledge that God hath given unto me in natural knowledge, unto my brethren that had need thereof."[33]

Turner doubted Dioscorides' "doctrine of signatures," the popular assumption that God made plants to look like the body part that was suffering, indicating their curative powers.[34] Turner's skepticism was fueled by new medical theories circulating in Europe that held that the chemical essence of a thing

---

32 TNA SP 12/173/1, fo. 90; SP 12/176/1, fos. 150v–151.
33 William Turner, *A new boke of the natures and properties of all wines that are commonly vsed here in England...* (1568). Dedication. STC (2nd ed.)/24360.
34 William Turner, *The first and seconde partes of the herbal ... with the properties, degrees, and naturall places of the same...* (1568). STC (2nd ed.)/24367.

was more important than its outward form. This theory, Paracelsianism, presumed that the powers of stones and plants could be distilled and used for human good. First translated into English in 1580, the work of Theophrastus Paracelsus taught how carefully distilled essences like "Oil of Gold" would "with the help of Nature" cure nearly everything that was not genetic in origin.[35] By late in Elizabeth's reign, there were many Paracelsian physicians, chemically compounding oils and ointments.

So, Elizabethans believed they lived in a world that was ordered in hierarchies in the "Great Chain of Being." Humanity, God's special creation, sat in the center of creation, and all things above and below related to human lives. People should be obedient, knowing their place in this order and keeping to it, living in a universe in which God gave them a clear role to play. Rulers and nations, too, had to know and keep their place. In the Reformation, that was hard to do.

Political Order

Elizabethans knew God created government to ensure He was properly worshipped and social order was maintained. Just as He put all creation into hierarchical order, so He gave human authority to the ruler, who was expected to align human law with God's law. God's presumed purpose for government created defined expectations, guiding English discussions of political order.

St. Paul was clear about it: "Let every soul be subject unto the higher powers. The powers that be are ordained of God. Whosoever therefore resisteth the power, resisteth the ordinance of God: and they that resist, shall receive to themselves judgement [damnation]." He went on to explain that "princes are not to be feared for good works, but for evil." The prince is the "minister of God for thy wealth," given the sword of the state to take vengeance on evildoers. Therefore, a person must be subject to the ruler for conscience sake, paying taxes and giving honor to the prince as to God. Paul connects the duty of the ruler to the enforcement of the "though shalt nots" of the Ten Commandments, preventing blaspheme, murder, theft, and adultery, while promoting love of one's neighbor.[36]

This expectation that the prince was God's minister against secular evil was common to Protestant and Catholic states alike. They all sought to force people to be good, but the definition of "good" was increasingly uncertain in the sixteenth century. Protestants had denounced some sorts of "good deeds" done

---

35 John Hester, *The first part of the key of philosophie. Wherein is contained moste ex-* [sic] *excellent secretes of phisicke and philosophie...* (1580). STC (2nd ed.)/19181.5
36 Romans 13:1–10. Quoting the Geneva Bible. Where the Geneva Bible, with its Calvinist leanings, used "judgement," both Tyndale and the King James Bible used "damnation" in verse 2.

by Catholics, such as prayers for the dead, monasticism, pilgrimages, and even witnessing the repeated sacrifice of Christ in the mass as bad, even damnable. Late medieval Catholicism's insistence on doing works that pleased God— requiring individuals to do good, repent evil, and perform spiritual works— was rebuffed. Nonetheless, Protestants still insisted people must fulfill God's expectations about worshiping, giving alms, obeying one's betters, and keeping the Ten Commandments. The differences between Catholics and Protestants turned around which things had to be done and, most importantly, why. Were you earning points toward salvation, or thankfully working to please God, who had already saved you?

This debate over what sorts of "goodness" had to be enforced by church and state created deep political problems. If the prince had the duty of enforcing God's law, making people behave as God wanted, then the definition of righteous behavior had to be resolved. Unfortunately, as princes changed, so did definitions of goodness. Differing theologies had complex political implications, as Elizabethans knew well. They remembered when Henry VIII seized the property of the monasteries and Queen Mary burned heretics alive to ensure obedience to God's law.

The traditional belief that the body politic must conform to divine will started to present intellectual difficulties in the early sixteenth century. Theologians began to overthrow the idea that order descended in a line from God to the church, to the king, to the male head of the family. For Elizabethans, it was possible to imagine their individual relationships to God in new ways, believing that God's plans had been misunderstood and corrupted. The goal of the Reformation was to return to the primitive purity of the original Christian society ruled by God's Word, and the first generation of Elizabethan adults were immersed as youngsters in debates over individual salvation and proper church order. How God communicated to His people was a challenging question, and they debated whether worship should be in English, and the Bible made available in English translation. They chose, or refused to choose, between salvation through their own efforts, salvation by faith alone, and salvation by absolute election. They chose, or had imposed upon them at various times, obedience to the Pope and the Roman Catholic Church, obedience to the Supreme Head of God's Church in England, and obedience to God's Supreme Governor in England: Elizabeth.

The theological debates cracking open the static model of civic order centered on soteriology—the process of salvation—and ecclesiology—the structure of the church. They went together, since to be saved, one must follow the church, which mirrored God's model for proper worship. Salvation required pursuit of the right path to heaven, but different paths demanded different life styles. What the right path—the True Church—was, and how one behaved on that path, was debated intensely in Europe in the sixteenth century.

To comprehend sixteenth-century religion, we must understand how Protestantism redefined the relationship between God and His people, leading to the interiorization and personalization of faith. In the period between 1520 and 1560, various models of reformed Christianity were advanced by theologians and communities in Western Europe, culminating, in England, in the "Elizabethan Settlement of Religion."

The key issues were established in the 1520's, when Martin Luther wrote lively, clear expositions of his core theology. His reform was built on three axioms that utterly rejected the soteriology and ecclesiology of the papal Roman Catholic Church. First, he declared the central paradox of Christianity: a Christian is truly free, lord of all, and subject to none; a Christian is the most dutiful servant of all, and subject to everyone. This paradox is resolved by understanding the effect of faith on the Christian. Faith, when accepted from God, makes the free Christian into a voluntary servant of God, and therefore the Christian does the good things God expects of those who are faithful to His covenants. The believing soul, through faith in Christ, becomes free from all sin, fearless of death, safe from hell, and endowed with eternal righteousness, life, and salvation thanks to Christ.

Second, the soul, married to Christ, needs no one to intervene on its behalf with God. Every believer can go directly to Christ for help, acting as his or her own priest. This concept of the "priesthood of the believer" made the Catholic clergy and the Pope unnecessary middlemen.

Third, the only necessary guide for a Christian was the Bible, as instruction on how to obey God was provided by the Bible alone. It was the job of all Christians to find the core of Christian doctrine in Scripture: "that without any merit, as a gift of God's pure grace in Christ, we attain righteousness, life and salvation."[37]

The combination of salvation by faith alone, the priesthood of every believer, and the complete authority of the Bible meant that the Catholic Church was perverting Christianity by claiming to stand between the believer and God. Luther rejected the ecclesiastical authority of the Pope and his priests, refusing to believe that people had to do good works to earn their way into heaven

Looking closely at the Bible, Luther could not find evidence that Jesus had instituted the seven sacraments claimed by the Church of Rome. All believers, said the Romanists, approached God through His sacraments, which could only be performed by the priests of the church. These seven were the Eucharist, baptism, confirmation, marriage, ordination, penance, and extreme unction (the last rites).

---

37 Martin Luther, *Luther's Works, XIV: Selected Psalms III*, 36. Quoted in Alec Ryrie, "'Protestantism' as a Historical Category," *Transactions of the Royal Historical Society, Sixth Series*, 2016; 26, 74.

Luther argued that since Christ himself was baptized, and Christ commanded Christians to partake of the Eucharistic meal of bread and wine in memory of his crucifixion, these two sacraments had to be used. The other five he rejected as unbiblical.

This was radical, disordering, and heretical, but Luther went even further. Addressing a letter to the nobility of Germany, he declared that the secular princes had the duty to purify worship of God. Luther urged them to declare themselves "emergency bishops," throw out the Pope and his minions, take control of the church, oversee the clergy, and seize and destroy the tools of superstitious "papal" religion such as monasteries and shrines.

Luther piously explained all this in a letter to Pope Leo X, emphatically denouncing the evils of the papal curia. Naturally, Leo X was not persuaded. Luther was excommunicated, and his duke, Frederick of Saxony, hid him to keep him from being burned as a heretic. While in hiding, Luther translated the New Testament into German, insisting the Bible had to be available in the common tongues of all believers. He was breaking the stranglehold on biblical access by taking it out of the learned Latin and putting it in the people's tongue.

Leo X took some consolation from the fact that young Henry VIII of England, rebuffing Luther's assertion that there were only two sacraments, wrote a *Defense of the Seven Sacraments* in 1521. Leo was so pleased he granted Henry the title—still used today by the monarchs of the United Kingdom—*Defensor Fidei*, Defender of the Faith.

The irony of Henry VIII's new title was not lost on those who watched him renounce his marriage to Catherine of Aragon, marry Anne Boleyn, and break with the papacy in the early 1530's. In the *Defense of the Seven Sacraments*, Henry demonstrated that marriage was a sacrament, and that the union of a man and a woman was indissoluble, like that of Christ and His church. A man must love his wife as he loves his own body, said the King. Henry found no irony in this, because he had a scriptural defense that justified annulment, remarriage, and nationalizing the church. In 1534, Henry took control of his own church and began a remodeling that drew on continental examples.

Henry's reformation occurred in a very creative time for Protestantism. In all its forms, the reformed movement was wrestling with the relation of the individual to God, and the church to the state. The Elizabethans were heirs to these debates about soteriology and ecclesiology.

Luther, depending on Duke Frederick of Saxony for his preservation, taught that God and the prince deserved deference and obedience. The prince was to ensure that God was worshipped properly and that the church was conducted properly. He allied himself with Duke Frederick, who chose state-appointed superintendents to oversee churches.

In the Holy Roman Empire, imperial cities, too, were busy reforming religion in the 1520's and 30's. Huldrich Zwingli in Zurich thought Luther was wrong in keeping so much of the old mass, convincing the city council to reform its churches. The order of his worship stressed daily preaching. Ministers recited texts that had once been sung, and there was no music. The Eucharist was celebrated by clergy in street clothes, the congregants seated around a table in the center of the church as if at a meal. Zwingli's Eucharist was a memorial, nothing more. Christ was in Heaven, and the faithful gathered around the table to recall his instruction to "do this in memory of me." This interpretation deeply offended Luther, who believed that when Christ said, "This is my body which is broken for you, do this in remembrance of me," holding up the bread, he meant it literally, not in a memorial sense.

In Strasbourg, Martin Bucer blended Lutheran and Zwinglian ideas about worship. His German-language services used congregational psalm singing, Bible readings and sermons, and communal prayers for forgiveness. The form of Bucer's Eucharist, however, was much closer to Luther's than to Zwingli's. As in Zurich, the Strasbourg city council took control of the church in 1534, in part because of the Anabaptist revolt in Münster.

Münster's "radicals" refused to join with the secular state, insisting that the individual was free to follow God no matter what religion the prince preferred. Generally lumped together as "Anabaptists," their 1534–35 attempt to create a Davidic Kingdom in Münster, ruled by a prophet king who reinstituted polygamy and governed through a council of twelve apostles, frightened rulers everywhere. Münster's theocracy was crushed, but the movement continued. Anabaptists sought freedom to follow God in conscience. They separated from established churches, practicing adult conversion and baptism, seeking to convert others, and covenanting together in believer communities. By the late 1530's, the Anabaptist followers of Menno Simmons were established in the Low Countries as separatists, pacifists, and rigorously moralist communities. Henry VIII banned them, but treated them with less rigor than most European rulers if they agreed to leave England.

In Geneva in the 1540's, John Calvin created a powerful branch of the reformed movement that deeply influenced Elizabethan religion. Calvin, a lawyer, concluded God knew who was going to be saved before they had been born. Some, he declared, were "elected"—chosen—for salvation, and others were "elected" for damnation. Nothing an individual could do would affect God's eternal decree of election. The "goodness" or "badness" of works did not influence God's decision.

Like Luther and Bucer, Calvin associated the reformed church with the political community, but his version of the magisterial reformation separated church and state while insisting that the state should enforce the church's teachings. In Geneva, the secular government was deeply responsive to the theological advice of the Company of Pastors. At the same time, authority in this community came from the people. Seeing no need for top-down bishops, Calvin stressed the biblical office of the *presbyteroi*—the "elders" elected by the congregations through the prompting of the Holy Spirit. Rather than having a bishop or a king lead the church, the church led itself through the action of the Holy Spirit.

The varieties of reform that emerged in the first half of the sixteenth century were never fully reconciled. Protestants commonly accepted the Bible as self-authenticating, believing grace allowed all people access to God through it, without priestly mediation.[38] They disagreed about how this worked, however, and about the relationship of the church and the state.

When Henry VIII broke with the Roman Catholic Church in 1534, he chose a vaguely Lutheran position—using his authority to "renew" the national church by cleansing it of superstition, rather than opting for the wholesale reformation undertaken in some communities on the Continent.

The Act of Supremacy of 1534 declared that the King was the Supreme Head of the Church in England, nullifying the authority of the Pope and placing religion under Henry VIII's direct control. Over the next six years, he rooted out "superstitious uses," closing the monasteries and seizing their assets, pensioning off the monks and nuns, and eradicating the shrines to saints like St. Thomas á Becket at Canterbury, Our Lady of Walsingham in Norfolk, and the Holy Blood at Hailes Abbey. Clearly influenced by Lutheran denunciations of earned salvation, Henry was equally attracted by the wealth of the dissolved monastic houses. Structurally, Henry's church looked just like the Pope's, but stripped of the Pope and the monastic orders.

Notably, the English were given the Bible in their own language. William Tyndale's New Testament, with its deeply Lutheran prefaces, became available in all the churches in England, in an edition known as the Great Bible, in 1539. Ironically, Archbishop Cranmer's preface to this Bible warned its readers not to argue about what it meant, leaving that to learned men. Reading the Bible was good, he said, but just as eating too much honey can make you sick, so too can too much puzzling about scripture: "I forbid not to read, but I forbid to reason."[39] This forbidding was in vain. Once the Word of God was in the hands of the laity and the learned alike, questions were bound to arise.

The earliest English handbooks for instructing youth in religion tried to answer those questions. Catechisms help us see the confusion early Elizabethans had over how to please God. These were the books teaching them what God required them to do.

In 1539, Richard Taverner, humanist, reformer, Bible translator, and close associate of Thomas Cromwell, published the first English catechism. It was aimed at parents who needed to teach their children the rudiments of the faith, and in its preface it praises Henry VIII for abolishing idolatry and the Pope, "our archenemy and the most pestilent overthrower of all godliness, but also his devilish laws, constitutions and superstitious things which have heretofore entangled our consciences contrary to the Evangelical liberty and truth of

---

38 Ryrie, "Protestantism," 77.
39 Thomas Cranmer, "A Prologue or Preface Made by the Most Reverend Father in God Thomas Archbishop of Canterbury Metropolitan and Primate of England," *The Byble in Englyshe...* (1540). STC (2nd ed.)/2071.

God's word."[40] It clearly was an anti-papal catechism, but it retained very Catholic concepts of the role of God's law and God's expectations about human behavior. Those who keep God's law, grounded in the Ten Commandments, will be rewarded, Taverner taught, with prosperity and eternal life.[41] Of course, since all people are sinners, the acceptance of Christ through faith is required of them to make up for lapses in their obedience.

Taverner's 1539 catechism, though it rejects the Pope, teaches children the "good" works, obedience to God's law in faith, and the participation in the seven sacraments of the Catholic faith. Luther had reduced the number of required sacraments to two—baptism and the Eucharist—but Tavener had not, though he called baptism and the Eucharist the "principal sacraments." For Tavener, works of penance still earned forgiveness by the church: "By penance we attain the high benefit of absolution, neither ought we to neglect the power or keys of the church, since to it Christ saith, whose sins so ever you forgive shalbe forgiven, and whose sins you retain shalbe retained."[42]

Taverner's conservatism about the sacraments was appropriate, since in the 1540's Henry tried to claw back some reforms, approving the 1540 Act of Six Articles, which condemned a number of Protestant doctrines. People who denied transubstantiation were prosecuted and burned, and English evangelicals once nurtured by Henry had to flee for their lives, moving to Swiss cities like Basel, Strasbourg, and Geneva, where they were introduced to the next waves of reformed theology.

Those catechized in the later 1540's heard a more Protestant message than Taverner or Henry VIII would have liked. Robert Legate's 1545 spousal catechism, used by husbands to teach their wives so they could teach their children, dropped discussion of penance and the sacraments of the church and became much more evangelical, saying, "God makes only all men righteous and good. For when a man hears the Gospel of Christ and believes it, the same belief makes him good and righteous."[43] Asked if "the law can make any man good," the wife is to respond, "as little as the glass can make him fair that looks in it ... for the law indeed demands perfection and righteousness of us, but it gives no man power to do it."[44] The wife—and therefore the children—was taught the Ten Commandments and the Lord's Prayer, but not the sacraments.

For Taverner in 1539, penitential good works were still expected and required. Six years later, Legate stressed Christ's imputed grace, which made

---

40 Richard Taverner, *A catechisme or institution of the christen religion* (1539), "To the Christian Reader." STC (2nd ed.)/23709.

41 Ibid., fo. 23.

42 Ibid., fo. 65.

43 Robert Legate, *A briefe catechisme and dialogue betwene the husbande and his wife...* (1545), Sig. Bii.v. STC (2nd ed.)/4797.3.

44 Ibid., Sig. B[vi].

up for humanity's imperfection. In 1547, in the new air of Edward VI's reign, Archbishop Thomas Cranmer published a collection of homilies—canned sermons—to be read in churches. Cranmer absolutely embraced the three pillars of Protestant theology: salvation by faith alone, justification by grace not works, and the priesthood of the believer.[45] In his homily on justification, he explained how faith justifies (acquits) a sinner without requiring penitential works.[46]

This theological debate stirred the nation. Many of Elizabeth's future councilors and bishops were teenagers in the 1530's and 40's, and witnessed this conflict as it played out. When young Edward VI took the throne on January 28, 1547, these young people, like William Cecil, came into their own, helping his council make England fully Protestant. First legally abolishing purgatory, they went on to abolish the Latin mass. Archbishop Cranmer produced the first *Book of Common Prayer*, providing worship in English, which Edward imposed on the nation by the Act of Uniformity of 1549.[47]

As fortune's wheel turned, Martin Bucer and Peter Martyr Vermigli, fleeing Strasbourg because of Charles V's attempt to impose Catholic worship on the city, became exiles in England. In 1547, Bucer was appointed Regius Professor of Divinity at Cambridge by Edward VI, while Martyr was appointed to the same position at Oxford. Together, the two deeply influenced Edward's Protestant Church. Bucer presented Edward with a handbook, *de Regno Christi*, for installing a reformed Christian state in Edwardian England, setting out principles for the monarch to follow. He gave a copy to Princess Elizabeth, too.[48] Bucer and Martyr would make a deep impact on Elizabethan leaders of state and church.[49]

By 1552, claims that the1549 *Book of Common Prayer* was too Catholic led to the production of a new prayer book, put into place by the second Act of Uniformity. Hardly had it been enacted than English religion began reversing its course. When Edward died in July 1553, his half-sister Mary defeated his attempt to change the succession to keep England Protestant. She returned the nation to the Latin mass and the jurisdiction of the papacy in 1554.

---

45 Dairmaid MacCulloch, *Thomas Cranmer* (New Haven: Yale University Press, 1996), 372–4.
46 "The First Part of the Sermon of Salvation," in *Homilies*, 26–7.
47 Norman Jones, "The Cambridge Connection and the Shaping of the Elizabethan State," in John McDiarmid, ed. *The Cambridge Connection in Tudor England: Humanism, Reform, Rhetoric, Politics* (Leiden: Brill, forthcoming).
48 Benjamin Pohl and Leah Tether, "Books Fit for a King: The Presentation Copies of Martin Bucer's *De regno Christi* (London, British Library, Royal MS. 8 B. VII) and Johannes Sturm's *De periodis* (Cambridge, Trinity College, II.12.21 and London, British Library, C.24.e.5)." *The Electronic British Library Journal* 2015, Article 7, 1–35. https://www.bl.uk/eblj/2015articles/pdf/ebljarticle72015.pdf [Accessed November 29, 2018].
49 Patrick Collinson, *Archbishop Grindal 1519–1583: The Struggle for a Reformed Church* (Berkeley: University of California Press, 1979), 49–56.

A stream of English Protestants fled Mary's religious persecution. These "Marian Exiles" gravitated to Strasbourg, Frankfurt-am-Main, and Geneva. In Strasbourg, the English community, which included many leaders of Edward's church, worshiped according to the 1552 *Book of Common Prayer*. In Frankfurt, they followed a less structured form devised by William Whittingham (who had studied in Geneva), in which deacons were expected to preach, and the laity had more authority in the congregation, electing ministers. There, "our brethren of the Purity," as John Bale called them, met the *Book of Common Prayer* with "despisings and cursed speakings." In Geneva, an English exile community led by John Knox developed its own form of worship in keeping with the Calvinist model, rejecting both the *Book of Common Prayer* and episcopal government.

The exile community in Frankfurt dissolved into divisive arguments about whether the *Book of Common Prayer* had to be used, could be modified, or could even be rejected outright. John Knox came from Geneva to join the debate, clashing angrily with future bishops of Elizabeth's church like Richard Cox and Edmund Grindal. Knox drew John Calvin into the conversation, eliciting from him some critical comments about the *Book of Common Prayer*. Calvin rejected the idea, pushed by many English, that variations in worship were acceptable if they did not deny the essentials of the faith, known as "adiaphora." He thought they permitted too much latitude for retaining superstitious Catholic ways. Elizabeth would disagree.

Ultimately, these exile communities were in a battle over whether worship had to be legally established and uniform, as in Edward VI's time, or congregations that conformed to biblical principles could be freely formed, needing no king to make them devout.[50] The dispute was never resolved in exile, because Queen Mary died on November 17, 1558. Assuming Elizabeth would return England to Protestantism, the exiles began to go home, carrying their grudges with them.

Meanwhile, most English people conformed to Mary's reestablished Catholicism. Princess Elizabeth, Sir William Cecil, and their colleagues recognized the biblical principle that the authority of the magistrate is greater than the right of an individual to think or worship for himself, though the individual may rest secure in the knowledge that God sees the secrets of the faithful heart. Accepting Queen Mary's authority, they outwardly acted like Catholics, while inwardly remaining Protestants.[51]

What their conformity implied was spelled out in another catechism. With papal authority and Catholic worship restored, Bishop Edmund Bonner of

---

50 Collinson, *Archbishop Grindal*, 72–9.
51 Norman Jones. *Governing by Virtue. Lord Burghley and the Management of Elizabethan England* (Oxford: Oxford University Press, 2015), 200–13.

London wrote a new Catholic catechism that once more taught good works. He broke the required good acts into works of bodily mercy, works of spiritual mercy, the seven gifts of the Holy Spirit, the seven sacraments of the church, and the beatitudes. Works of bodily mercy included feeding the hungry, watering the thirsty, clothing the naked, visiting the sick, receiving needy strangers, and redeeming captives. Works of spiritual mercy were things like correcting sinners, teaching the ignorant, counseling the doubting, praying for one's neighbor, comforting the sorrowing, suffering injuries patiently, and forgiving those who cause offense. These offset the Seven Deadly Sins. In Bonner's system, required to be taught to every child in London during Mary's reign, the Christian life was one of doing—of works—that proved you were following God's command to obey Him and love your neighbor as yourself. By doing them in obedience to God, salvation would follow.[52]

No Protestant would disagree with Bonner's belief that God wanted these good things done for their neighbors, but they were no longer "good" in themselves. This Protestant theology was powerful and liberating, but it was hard to separate what was done because of an informed conscience and what was done as a saving work, since they looked the same. Feeding the hungry looked like feeding the hungry. Only the intention behind the action was unclear. This made room for the Nicodemites, who conformed and were seen to do righteous works, but who did not accept the Catholic sacramental theology.

English people like Bishop Bonner were glad to have Catholicism reestablished, returning happily to the old worship—though they, too, found their certainties shaken. Their cheer turned to confusion with the deaths of Cardinal Pole and Queen Mary within a day of each other in November 1558.

Princess Elizabeth, literally a cause of the English Reformation, because of her father's desire for her mother, grew up in this welter of theological arguments, in which the English state religion was a shakily defined thing, dependent on royal preference. That may be why she never vocalized her own theology.

The disputes over proper worship and church governance in the 1530's, 40's, and 50's were attempts to make religious practice harmonize with God's plan. It was assumed God, having created one true church, expected everyone to worship accordingly or suffer the consequences. As God had created queens to rule the nation, maintaining divine order, they had to be obeyed. Elizabeth, refusing to define her own theology, accepted God's mandate, insisting that she be obeyed, not challenged, about God's will. To maintain harmony, the hierarchical order established by God required obedience to her.

Consequently, after a quarter century of religious confusion, the twenty-five-year-old Elizabeth stabilized England's religion soon after she took the throne

---

52 Edmund Bonner. *An honest godlye instruction* (1556). STC (2nd ed.)/3281.

on November 17, 1558. The so-called "Elizabethan Settlement of Religion" was enacted by parliament in early 1559, taking effect on June 11 that year. Once again, England abolished the foreign power of the papacy, and national worship was performed according to the *Book of Common Prayer* of 1552. In almost every way, the Elizabethan church was a continuation of the Edwardian church.

The Elizabethan Act of Supremacy did make one important concession. Rather than naming Elizabeth Supreme Head of the Church, as Henry VIII, Edward VI, and Mary had been, she was declared to be the Supreme Governor of the Church. Apparently, this was a concession to religious sensitivities on all sides, since most agreed that a woman could not be the head of the church.

The Act of Uniformity made two edits to the *Book of Common Prayer*, removing the denunciation of the "detestable enormities" of the Bishop of Rome and modifying the language of consecration in the Eucharist, obfuscating its theological intentions. Otherwise, it retained the Edwardian text of 1552.

Monasteries opened under Mary were closed. Churches were cleansed of "idolatrous" images, and purgatory was abolished, yet again. However, the Settlement left in place things like the "ornaments rubric" that required clergy to dress like Catholic priests, and failed to reenact some reforms, like clerical marriage—setting the stage for conflicts that continued across the reign. Soon, debates over these issues would turn into arguments about obedience to the Queen.[53]

The English church was still led by bishops. Mary's Catholic bishops were legally removed from office and Elizabeth slowly appointed Protestants in their places. Unsurprisingly, these new bishops soon ran into trouble, because Elizabeth would not allow them to use parliament to enact Protestant articles of faith or reform the church discipline. England retained the canon law of the Roman Church, except in those cases in which the Queen's prerogative was threatened.[54] The church became a department of Elizabeth's state.

Elizabeth's religious intentions are debated, but it appears she was trying to prevent the sort of religious conflict that was then boiling up across Europe. Inclined toward Lutheran ideas of worship and authority, she did not want to drive any sect into revolt.

Knowing God had given her responsibility, as His Handmaiden, to keep order and punish evil, she undertook to do the job in a new way. Avoiding divisive religious demands, she expected everyone to obey her as they obeyed God in conscience. As she told the heads of the Oxford colleges in 1592: "For indeed, you do not have a prince who teaches you anything that ought to be

---

53 Norman Jones. *Faith by Statute. Parliament and the Settlement of Religion 1559* (London: Royal Historical Society, 1982).
54 1 Eliz. I, c.1; c. 2.

contrary to a true Christian conscience. Know that I would be dead before I command you to do anything that is forbidden by the Holy Scriptures." Therefore, they were not to dispute about what scripture meant, but to obey her, doing "what the divine law commands and ours compels." Every person was to obey his superior in rank, knowing God would punish superiors who erred.[55]

Obedience to Elizabeth was demanded, but what did the Elizabethan Settlement expect in terms of obedience to God's law? It did not cancel divine law, but it interpreted it with nuance. Alexander Nowell's long catechism, published in English in 1570, tried hard to explain the distinctions that made the law of God more of a guideline in conscience, turning good works into mere proofs of goodness and introducing a situational ethics that depended on intention more than action.

For Nowell, the laws in the Old Testament were not always literal. Rather than stoning adulterers or marrying your brother's widow as the letter of the law required, he taught that your responses were to be filtered through Christ's injunction to love God and your neighbor. The law requires, he taught, "to give to everyman his own, it doth in sum comprise all the parts and duties of every man privately in his degree and trade of life." This guide to life is summarized in the Ten Commandments and the law, but each person will live them according with his or her own situation.[56]

Thus, works—those things traditionally believed to influence God's willingness to save or damn—have nothing to do with eternal destiny. God prompts good works, but He does not reward them. Salvation comes from the bountifulness of God; justification, Christ's payment of the debt of sin on our behalf, is God's free gift of His love. But, though they do not influence our access to Heaven, good works are not bad. They are evidence of our love of God and our neighbor, as God requires. Because, "we, being redeemed with the blood of Christ ... and having beside received innumerable and infinite benefits of God, should live and wholly frame ourselves after the will and appointment of our redeemer." People prove their gratitude by "good endeavors and works."[57]

Therefore, "good" works in official Elizabethan theology were good only if done with a "good conscience." External actions were dismissed in favor of right intentions. Thomas Norton's clear 1574 translation of Calvin's *Institutes* says:

> Therefore, taking away all mention of the law, and laying aside all thinking upon works, we must embrace the only mercy of God, when we entreat of justification: and turning away our sight from ourselves, we must

55 Leah S. Marcus, Janel Mueller, and Marty Beth Rose, eds. *Elizabeth I. Collected Works* (Chicago: University of Chicago, 2000), 327–8.
56 Nowell, *A Catechisme*, fo. 20. STC (2nd ed.)/18708.
57 Ibid., fo. 52.

behold Christ alone. For there the question is not how we be righteous: but how although we be unrighteous and unworthy, we be taken for worthy. Of which thing if consciences will attain any certainty, they must give no place to the law ... before the judgement seat of God it hath no place in their consciences ... The whole life of Christians ought to be a certain meditation of godliness[58]

The Old Testament law "pricks us to goodness," but doing the works required by God's law does not save us. Christ saves us, which is why we try to obey his law inscribed on our consciences.

In a world created by a providential God with clear intentions, these debates about what sort of godliness the church and state must promote were troubling. They undermined constituted authority and emphasized individual vocation and conscience. People should be good, but good was in the eyes of the beholder, or only in the eyes of God. God expected you to obey the monarch, but what divine rules were monarchs to enforce?

This theology meant that the Elizabethan Settlement of Religion was inherently theologically unstable, and that Elizabethans engaged in sometimes violent disputes over godly government.

---

58 John Calvin, "On Christian Liberty," *The Institution of the Christian Religion*, Thomas Norton, trans. (1574), III, c. 19, π 2, fo. 342v. STC (2nd ed.)/4418.

3

Roles

Disputes over what it meant to obey God took concrete form in the roles people were expected to play. Everyone was a part of an extended community, with multiple duties, depending upon age, gender, social status, occupation, and other variables.

We can see these roles spelled out in wills. When he died in 1559, Thomas Nicolson left significant gifts to the communities to which he belonged. A member of the Cordwainer's Company in London, Nicolson donated for "relief of the poor of the craft." Having provided for the elderly members of his trade, he gave support for the Company to purchase a new "common house or hall," nurturing his guild's ongoing community. Thinking of the future of the Cordwainers, he provided £40 "to be lent on good security to poor young men of the mystery to occupy withal, those that have been his apprentices to have the preferment." Financing young men to set up shop as cordwainers, and preferring his own apprentices over the rest, he was making it possible for a new generation to succeed in the trade. Remembering his kin, Nicolson left money to his wife, his daughter, and his grandsons. Thinking of his home parish, St. Clement Eastcheap in London, he made a gift to his poor neighbors there. Then he added the City of London's orphans to his will, leaving money to educate them in the "newly erected" (1546) Christ's Hospital.[1] At the end of his life, Nicolson was playing his roles as head of his family, a leader in his "mystery," his parish, and his city.

In the twenty-first year of Elizabeth's reign, Richard Pelter, a brewer, died. In his will, he made his social networks clear. He instructed his executor to put a marble slab on his tomb, engraved with the arms of the Brewers' Company and pictures of himself, his two wives, and his five children. Besides supporting his

---

1 "Wills: 1–10 Elizabeth I (1558–68)," in *Calendar of Wills Proved and Enrolled in the Court of Husting, London: Part 2, 1358–1688*, ed. R. R. Sharpe (London: Her Majesty's Stationery Office, 1890), 673. Accessed September 22, 2015. https://www.british-history.ac.uk/court-husting-wills/vol2/pp668-682 [Accessed November 29, 2018].

Being Elizabethan: Understanding Shakespeare's Neighbors, First Edition. Norman Jones.
© 2020 John Wiley & Sons, Inc. Published 2020 by John Wiley & Sons, Inc.

family and his trade, he gave money to the poor in multiple London parishes, to poor maidens needing dowries, and to poor prisoners in several London prisons. Most interestingly, he left a barrel of ale to each of his customers, recognizing his relationship with the taverns he had supplied during his life as a brewer.[2]

In 1614, William Jones, a Monmouthshire man who became a London merchant trading in Hamburg, left £9000 to endow a school, an almshouse, and preaching in Monmouth. Five miles from Monmouth, he endowed another preacher and more poor relief in Newland, Gloucestershire. He tied his home in Monmouthshire to his London occupation by making the London Company of Haberdashers the executor of his will. For his London community, he provided £1600 for a preacher, and a similar amount to set up pensions for decayed haberdashers. He left £1000 to aid poor preachers in England. As a godly man, Jones was taking care of his communities by blessing them with education in Protestant godliness. As a wealthy London merchant, he expressed his sense of community in far-off Wales, in London, and among the godly.[3] By including impoverished preachers, Jones was also identifying with people who were his ideological compatriots, not his kin or his neighbors.

Nicolson, Pelter, and Jones were thinking of themselves within their localities and social networks. Their identities were shaped by their community roles. Though schools, the prayer book, and other institutionalized forms of instruction shaped the way Elizabethans intellectualized their world, they modeled their living by imitating family members and neighbors, elders in their trades, peers in parishes, villages, and towns. Within these, people were sorted by gender, age, and status in complex frameworks of social relations. Young people, enmeshed in these networks, acquired an understanding of their roles in their overlapping communities. They learned propriety and deference, how to read the descriptors of place and rank in clothes, manners, and language, how to dress, and how to behave themselves accordingly.

In cities and towns where male civic participation was controlled through membership in guilds or city companies, apprenticeship to a master in the trade was the usual way of acquiring an occupation, and of becoming "free" of a city. Being raised in the guild, apprentices learned a mesh of overlapping identities according to gender, age, trade, parish, town, county, and family. You owed duty to all, and all owed duty to you. Charity, for instance, began at home, with each parish taking care of its own "deserving poor," and each guild looking after members who fell on hard times. They would take care of

---

2 Ibid., 693.
3 Joseph P. Ward, *Culture, Faith, and Philanthropy. Londoners and Provincial Reform in Early Modern England* (New York: Palgrave Macmillan, 2013), 97–8.

you, and you had to take care of them. These same organizations mediated conflicts within the communities, often in the name of good fellowship and neighborliness. They were all designed to put you in your place and keep you there, since the continuation of the hierarchical system, economic stability, and God required it.[4]

Richard Thornhill, newly elected Warden of the London Grocers' Company in 1574, explained this social reality to the assembled Grocers. His speech is summarized breathlessly in the Company records:

> Wherein he declared the carefulness of our forefathers of this company toward us that in providing us a place to assemble in, and how they did not spare to bereave their children and kin folk of goods and lands for the conservation and maintenance of this worshipful company, and being moved ... by the word of God did for our better continuance devise good government of this company, but also to keep and guide the same in brotherly love and unity which is one especial mean to preserve and continue all companies and common weals, declaring also very pithily the contrary being contention and disagreement to be always the dissolution and overthrow of all as well companies as commonwealths ... to persuade the company to obedience and order, wherein he declared his great zeal which he bears toward this company's good government and continuance in worship which God grant.[5]

It was a history lesson, a stimulant to benefaction, a call for donations, and a warning about the necessity of cooperative behavior. This is what members of these small commonwealths were expected to learn and exemplify.

Other social knowledge was delivered in ceremony and decoration. The Carpenters' Company of London hung in their guildhall their "story," a four-panel, eleven-yard canvas portraying the importance of carpenters in Biblical history. Carpenters, it should be remembered, built Noah's Ark and the Temple in Jerusalem. But most importantly, Christ himself had apprenticed as a carpenter, and gone on to teach in the synagogue (Figure 3.1).[6] Clearly, God liked carpenters!

Companies, colleges, and towns had rituals bonding their members and providing sites of memory. Elections and commemoration dinners were a formal part of the members' lives. Before the Reformation, corporate religious worship was a part of it too, though across Elizabeth's reign worship began to disappear as a group act. At the beginning of the reign, the Grocers attended

---

4 Ian Archer, *The Pursuit of Stability. Social Relations in Elizabethan England* (Cambridge: Cambridge University Press, 1991), 58–9.
5 London, Guildhall Library, MS 11588/1, fo. 256.
6 Robert Tittler, *The Face of the City. Civic Portraiture and Civic Identity in Early Modern England* (Manchester: Manchester University Press, 2007), 56.

Figure 3.1 A 19th c. copy of the Four Scriptural Paintings, Carpenters' Hall, London. Artokoloro Quint Lox Limited / Alamy Stock Photo.

evening prayer as a body, and then had a feast before an election. They, like most companies and colleges, had endowed feasts that included prayers and masses for their benefactors. But by its middle, these exercises were changing. The Grocers eventually abandoned their patron saint, St. Antholyn, whose feast had been a time to pray for the departed members, remembering benefactors in a new way: "It was moved … that the names of such as have been benefactors to this company in lands money plate or other ornaments necessary for this house to be read at some open quarter day for a memory of their good wills. Whereupon it was now agreed that their names shalbe rehearsed once in a year at the least."[7] These commemorations of benefactors, practiced in universities and colleges as well as towns and guilds, recognized shared responsibility for the institutional community over time.

Members of guilds and companies were also members of parishes, like Nicholson's St. Clement Eastcheap. The parish was a basic unit of local government, encompassing the physical boundaries assigned to a parish church community. There were thousands of them, each with clergy who provided baptisms and the Eucharist, marriages and funerals. The Reformation had deeply disturbed these communities, without erasing them. Local people were heavily invested in their parish churches and the services they provided, including burial in the churchyard, so when royal reformers had them cleansed of "superstitious" decorations and practices, community emotional and fiscal

---

7 London, Guildhall Library, MS 11588/1, fo. 179.

investments were wiped out. But the Elizabethan state maintained the parish community that focused on the church.[8]

Though they were told they could no longer pray for the dead, since purgatory was a popish fiction, Elizabethan parishioners remained in communion with their communities, living and dead. In the *Book of Common Prayer*, the dead were seen as part of the mystical Body of Christ to which all Christians belonged. Now, rather than praying for the dead to be delivered from purgatory, the parish was remembering its dead as role models: "Let us praise God for all those that are departed out of this life in the faith of Christ, and pray unto God that we have grace for to direct our lives after their good example, that after his life we with them may be made partakers of the glorious resurrection the life ever-lasting."[9] Plaques in churches that listed parish benefactors helped shape ideas about what the good example of the dead might be.

To be a worthy member of Christ's mystical body required that Christians put aside all contention and strife with their neighbors, living in charity with one another. Christ had died a horrible death for us; the least we could do was to love our neighbors as He had loved us. The Eucharist should "stir up in us the love of God, and our neighbor." That love found expression in charity toward one's neighbors—individually, and, if one was wealthy, to the whole parish.[10] That is why people were expected to publicly exchange the "peace" before taking communion—those who were out of charity with others should have made up with them beforehand. Neighborliness was an important concept, derived from older forms of social organization that were under attack religiously, economically, and demographically. But it was highly valued, and it was reciprocal. People were expected to perform their social status in the community, and, living and dead, members of the parish were carefully graded by their neighbors.

In the little community of Swallowfield, the "chief inhabitants" met in December of 1596 to draw up a set of articles governing their community. Famous as an example of the "reformation of manners," these articles stressed the Christian nature of community:

> [6] And that no man shall do anything one against another nor against any man,
>> by word nor deed upon affection, or malice, in our meeting nor to be discontented, one with another, since none of us is ruler of himself, but the whole

---

8 Jones, *English Reformation*, 58–133.
9 W.H. Frere, ed. *Visitation Articles and Injunctions of the Reformation Period*, 3 vols (London, New York, Bombay, Calcutta: Longmans, Green, & Co., 1910), III, 29.
10 Lucy Wooding, "Remembrance in the Eucharist," in Andrew Gordon and Thomas Rist, eds. *The Arts of Remembrance in Early Modern England. Memorial Cultures of the Post Reformation* (Farnham: Ashgate, 2013), 32–3.

company or the most parte is ruler of us all.

[7] And that none of us shall disdain one another, nor seek to hinder one another

neither by words nor deeds, But Rather to be helpers, assisters & counselors of one another, And all our doings to be good, honest, loving and just one to another.

Of course, the "chief inhabitants" were very concerned with maintaining proper godly order in Swallowfield, making certain that the poor knew their duty to their betters. Article 15 says:

And every one promises to do his best to end all strifes which shall happen

between neighbor & neighbor be they poor or rich, And that such as be poor

& will malapertly compare with their betters & set them at naught, shalbe warned

to live & behave themselves as becomes them, if such amend not, then no man to

make any other account of them [but] of common disturbers of peace & quietness[11]

Within these little commonwealths, social conventions placed people in their roles. When they addressed or described one another as "Goodman" or "Goodwife," "Mother," "Old," "Master," "knave," and other such things, familiar and loving or alienating and harsh, they were recognizing local social standing. There were formal and informal addresses. The formal included "Master" and "Mistress," while the informal included "Old," "Mother," "Father," and "Widow," "Dame," either alone or in combination. "Goodman," "Goodwife," and "Goodie" lay somewhere in between. All but the most formal were local in application and indicated a recognition by the speaker of the qualities of the person named within their known community.

To be called "Master" or "Mistress" was recognition of elite social and economic standing. By plotting the burials of people so described in parish registers, we can see that they were demonstrating their wealth and power through prime tomb locations, often within the church. On the other hand, to be called "Goodman" or "Goodwoman" did not require gentility or a formal office. It was reserved for social peers and the "middling sort."[12] Their tombs mingled with the whole community in the churchyard.

---

11 Steve Hindle, "Hierarchy and Community in the Elizabethan Parish: The Swallowfield Articles of 1596," *The Historical Journal* 1999; 42 (3), 849–50.

12 David A. Postles, *Social Proprieties Social Relations in Early-Modern England (1500–1680)* (Washington, D.C.: New Academia Publishing, 2006), 22–46.

Emotive expressions, both affectionate and dis-affectionate, come into the mix, too. People addressed as "friends" and "loving friends" were often called upon for service or advice, the title evoking neighborliness. "Railing" and "reviling" included a wide range of insulting words that were aimed at dishonoring their targets, as when the churchwardens of Romford were called "gentlemen beggerlie knaves."[13] Naturally, the written records are most eloquent about the insults offered to the authorities.

In a society as hierarchical as Elizabethan England, familiarity was rare. You would not think of addressing your social superior, or parent, or perhaps even your spouse, informally. Even Lord Burghley addressed his brother-in-law and old friend, Sir Nicholas Bacon, Lord Keeper of the Privy Seal, formally as "Your Lordship."[14]

One possible evidence of the impact of the Reformation on social identities is found in names chosen by godparents for children. Forenames might well be associated with confessional identities. Elizabethans would have been sensitive to the ideological weight of the names given to children, choosing intentionally and finding meaning in the names people bore. Some communities were known for their religious naming patterns. Banbury in Oxfordshire became noted for "grace names" that mirrored the puritanical values of the town. There, Biblical names were popular for boys, such as Zachary and Job. Hopestill, Obedience, Patience, Justice, Prudence, Makepeace, and Silence were names given to girls there in the early seventeenth century. It was this sort of pious naming that Ben Jonson was mocking when he created the character Zeal-of-the-Land-Busy, a "Banbury man," in his play *Bartholomew Fair*.[15]

Catholics may have had their equivalents. Cuthbert, around Durham, and Frideswide, near Oxford, continued to be popular where those saints' cults were traditionally practiced.

Bastards were sometimes given names—perhaps by the community—that marked their status. Identity as a *filius/a populi* (son or daughter of the people) or *filius/a spuria* (illegitimate son or daughter) in the baptismal record might result in a name that fit the crime, like "Transgression," "Charity," or some other unusual word that set the bearer apart as one who had to be supported by the parish.[16] In Swallowfield, two articles were aimed at controlling the costs of supporting bastards, declaring that anyone who took in a "Wife or other woman with child, & suffer her to be brought a bed in his house that thereby the parish shalbe charged with a child or children there borne" had to be reported to the churchwardens who controlled the money for the poor. They also declared that the paternity of such a child had to be established so the

---

13 Ibid., 93.
14 BL Lansd. 94, fo. 195.
15 Postles, *Social Proprieties*, 118–21.
16 Ibid., 128.

father could be made to pay.[17] Given these attitudes, it is not surprising that bastards might be vindictively christened.

As illegitimate births remind us, standing in the community was tied to the status of a person's family, and families recognized—though sometimes did not act on—the mutual duties of solidarity and support. Then as now, they varied widely in affection, but who your family was mattered. Since you were born into a social station, you deserved deference according to your family's status. This hierarchy is most obvious within the ranks of the nobility, though everyone recognized and honored it.

For instance, in discussing a proposed Lord Lieutenancy for the Scottish Borders, it was clear that the command structure had to be based on family standing, with each grade of military authority predicated upon birth. As the Privy Council said to the Lord President of the North, trained bands of militia should be "committed to the leading of knights and gentlemen."[18] There could be no effective shared governance among men of equal rank, "for when two at one time remain in one country in authority any while together, equal in birth and estimation, they cannot but have some secret inclination to disdain each at other, and think the well doing of them to be derogation to the other's honor and renown."[19]

In 1595, Archbishop Matthew Hutton of York advised Lord Burghley that the new Lord President of the North and Lord Lieutenant should be a nobleman. "This country, albeit most willing to obey whomsoever her Majesty shall appoint, yet wisheth that one may be sent hither that is *ex antiqua nobilitated* [from the ancient nobility]."[20]

Shakespeare summarized the importance of degrees and order in his society, speaking through his character Ulysses in *Troilus and Cressida*:

> O, when degree is shaked,
> Which is the ladder to all high designs,
> Then enterprise is sick. How could communities
> Degrees in schools, and brotherhoods in cities,
> Peaceful commerce from dividable shores,
> The primogenitive and due of birth,
> Prerogative of age, crowns, sceptres, laurels,
> But by degree stand in authentic place?
> Take but degree away, untune that string,
> And, hark, what discord follows: each thing meets
> In mere oppugnancy[21]

17 Hindle, "Swallowfield Articles," 849–50.
18 HEH, HM 30881, fo. 2.
19 TNA, SP 59/1, 53–53v.
20 CP 36/97.
21 Shakespeare, *Troilus and Cressida*, I,3,Ll.100–10.

But standing in "authentic place" was hard to ensure. It was tied to wealth and other forms of power and influence. Across Elizabeth's reign and into the seventeenth century, there was a growing disparity of wealth between various groups of people. They were not, in our modern way of thinking, classes so much as what the Elizabethans called "sorts." A lieutenant, whose service was honorable, was disparaged from promotion to captain with the observation, "although he be a gentleman of birth, yet is he but a mean man to supply a place of such credit."[22]

Being well born was important, but if you were "mean"—too poor—you could not afford to carry the social weight necessary to do the job. It was also possible to become wealthier than your "sort" should be. This was confusing, and Elizabethans' ability to talk about people who crept out of their places was limited by their imagination. For instance, Richard Mulcaster divided the "commonality" into merchants and manual laborers, but the only way to tell them apart, he said, was by their wealth. Rich merchants were not gentlemen, though they could be the "chiefest inhabitants" of their towns and take on all sorts of civic responsibility. But people who belonged to the civic elite often shaded into gentlemen, and defining a "gentleman" was very hard. If a person carried himself like a gentleman, spent money like a gentleman, and had the attitudes and speech of a gentleman, he might pass, and so might his wife—but was he truly a gentleman?[23]

A 1597 manuscript entitled "A Collection of Arms in Blazon" encapsulated the confusion between antiquity of birth, fortune, and virtuous service. Could wealth and service make a person gentle? "I know there are some," it says, "which condemn nobility derived from elders, for say they that often times of horses are born mules." However, citing Cicero, it points out that if you want a good hunting dog, you look at its pedigree. Both breeding and fortune are like clothes: if you beat the clothes a man wears, you are not beating the man. And yet breeding is more likely to hunt together with virtue.[24] In short, good birth helps ensure that a person will serve the commonwealth well, though it is true that many men make their own fortunes and serve virtuously, becoming gentle through service.

Mental calculations of wealth and social worth were performed constantly. A study of the people asked to give evidence in church courts in the sixteenth and seventeenth centuries suggests they could easily estimate the worth of others, in goods, and could describe their personal value, too.[25] They

---

22 TNA, SP 12/241, fo. 136.
23 Laura Stevenson, *Praise and Paradox. Merchants and Craftsmen in Elizabethan Popular Literature* (Cambridge: Cambridge University Press, 1984), 79–91.
24 Folger Shakespeare Library, Ms. V.b.375, 141.
25 Alexandra Shepard, *Accounting for Oneself. Worth, Status and the Social Order in Early Modern England* (Oxford: Oxford University Press, 2015), 82–113.

quantified status, and with that quantification went social expectations. If you were worth the part, you should play it—unless, of course, you used your wealth to misrepresent yourself. When taxes were levied, gentlemen of the neighborhood were expected to estimate their neighbors' wealth and determine what they might pay. The national tax of fifteenths and tenths was a property tax, and many other sorts of rates used the same neighborly method of assessment, whether levying troops and horses for the militia or repairing a road.

The Privy Council often complained about how the commissions for taxes, loans, and the militia underrated themselves and their friends. It especially galled the Council that "aspiring knights" and office holders with known fees were being rated for taxation at fictitious values. If you aspired to be accepted as a gentleman, you should pay taxes like a gentleman.

Of course, a person could be overestimated as well as underestimated. This led to legal confusions, like the case in Devon in which John Hewes, though accounted a yeoman by his neighbors, turned out to only have copyhold land, not freehold, which meant he could not claim the status. This made him a mere "farmer" who rented others' lands.[26]

Ironically, therefore, the ways in which people understood their roles included the certainty that it was possible to alter them. One could become a gentleman, take on the title of esquire, and perhaps even buy a crest from the College of Arms. Marrying up or down might change one's social value, too. So, though roles were conceived as static, people did not behave entirely as if they were. There was a negotiation going on in the gray spaces between roles and status, deference and patriarchy.

The starkest example of the confusion caused by failure to perform a role allotted by birth and status is Elizabeth Tudor's refusal to marry. As soon as she inherited the throne, intense speculation began about her husband. It was unthinkable that she would not marry, and the security of the dynasty—the very fate of the nation—hinged on her marriage and the children that would spring from it. In her first parliament, the members petitioned her to marry. She replied that she would, if God pleased to incline her to do it, but "in the end, this shall be for me sufficient, that a marble stone shall declare that a Queen, having reigned such a time, lived and died a virgin."[27] But no one believed her.

Instead, they had long arguments about whether she should marry a subject (the chief candidate being Sir Robert Dudley) or a foreigner (such as the Archduke of Austria, Charles—or perhaps Eric XIV of Sweden, if one preferred

---

26 Mildred Campbell, *The English Yeoman under Elizabeth and the early Stuarts* (New Haven: Yale University Press, 1942), 23–4. Citing HEH EL 2123.
27 T.E. Hartley, *Proceedings in the Parliaments of Elizabeth I*, 3 vols. (Leicester: Leicester University Press, 1981–95), I, 44–5.

a Protestant king). Whoever he was, he would determine the future of the nation, because it was a wife's role to honor and obey her husband. And a husband there must be. As the Spanish Bishop of Aquila told the Emperor Ferdinand, England was united in the opinion that the realm "would rather ... come under the sway of any man than that it should be ruled as it is at present."[28] Sir William Cecil prayed: "God send our mistress a husband, and by him a son, that we may hope our posterity shall have a masculine succession. This matter is too big for weak folks and too deep for simple."[29]

Elizabeth spent her life dealing with gendered assumptions about what she was supposed to do, how she was supposed to behave, to whom she was supposed to listen. Deflecting them, she deployed intransigence and a very clever sense of how to play the gender card in her own favor, trapping the governing classes in their own expectations.

Elizabeth knew that the divinely created system of status between generations, spouses, and extended kin created expectations of patriarchy, deference, and obedience, just as God's order created them in the larger world. As queen, she could turn into a prince when necessary—a trick especially visible in Latin, with its gendered endings. Her subjects were expected to be who they were born to be, as God placed them in the hierarchy. A female monarch, given the role of king, had two bodies. Physically female, she, when assuming her princely persona, performed a masculine role.

Men were expected to play their superior roles, and their wives were expected to show proper deference to them. When this "natural" order was overturned, the community took it upon itself to reassert it. Henry Machyn, whose diary is a rich source of information about mid-Tudor London, tells of how, on Shrove Monday in 1563, a man was carried through Charing Cross on the shoulders of four of his peers. Before them went a bagpiper, a sham player, and a drummer, surrounded by twenty men carrying lighted torches. This was done "because his next door neighbor's wife did beat her husband; therefore it is ordered that his next neighbor shall ride about the place" for failing to step in and uphold the local order.[30]

This "rough music," a cacophonous noise, demonstrated that the moral harmony had been turned into a squawking outrage.[31] The community would not tolerate domineering women, or milksop men who could not rule their wives.

---

28 Victor von Klarwill, ed., T.H. Nash, trans. *Queen Elizabeth and Some Foreigners. Being a series of hitherto unpublished letters from the archives of the Hapsburg family* (London: John Lane the Bodley Head, 1928), 171.

29 BL, Add. 35830, fo. 159v.

30 Diary: 1563 (Jan–July)," in J.G. Nichols, ed. *The Diary of Henry Machyn Citizen and Merchant-Taylor of London (1550–1563)* (London: Camden Society, 1848), 298–312. http://www.british-history.ac.uk/camden-record-soc/vol42/pp298-312 [Accessed November 29, 2018].

31 Christopher Marsh, *Music and Society in Early Modern England* (Cambridge: Cambridge University Press, 2010), 45–6.

It was most often used on men whose wives had abused them verbally, beaten them, or betrayed them sexually.

Extended family communities placed other responsibilities on their members. Writing to his wife's cousin, Sir Thomas Copley, Lord Burghley caught the presumed duties of kinship neatly. Sir Thomas was a Catholic who had fled from England to find freedom of worship; Lord Burghley was, in Copley's eyes, the chief prosecutor of Catholics. But Burghley told Copley he was "forced to conceive well of you because I knew you were of blood and kindred to my wife, so as your children and mine by her were to be knit in love and acquaintance by blood, and in deed as I have good cause to love my wife well, so have I always taken comfort in loving her kindred, showing to them as I might all good friendship."[32]

Thomas Wotton wrote a letter to Maximilian Brooke, whom he described as his "very loving cousin." In it, Wotton, a leading figure in the administration of Kent with strong Protestant preferences, explained to the seventeen-year-old that he was offering him words of encouragement about his studies. As one of Brooke's kinsmen, Wotton loved and esteemed him. Therefore, he presumed to exhort him to study well: "Your parents, your friends, your country, all which have interest in you, look duly for it."[33]

Children had to be prepared to behave according to their gender and station. Lady Grace Sherington Mildmay, writing for her granddaughter in the early seventeenth century, tells us that, as the daughter of a knight, she was given the education of a lady, preparing her for her role as mistress of a large household.

Grace Mildmay underscored the place of daughters in their fathers' homes. A daughter did not choose her husband. A wise father chose a husband for her, ensuring she was properly placed. Lord Burghley reminded his son Robert that this should be done in a timely way, "lest they marry themselves."[34] This entailed negotiations between the families of the betrothed, and, though it is assumed that sons had some choice, the selection process was deadly serious. Sir Walter Raleigh was full of wisdom on this issue, suggesting that his son marry a pretty woman to beget handsome children, since their beauty was a part of their inheritance. "If thou have care for thy races of horses and other beasts, value the shape and comeliness of thy children." However, when choosing a wife for breeding good progeny, men should not be blinded by beauty. They must consider the woman's honor and credit in calculating the safety of their choice. It was better, he said ironically, to have a mistress than to marry for beauty.[35] Daughters were expected to accept their fathers' choices.

32 TNA SP 12/99, fo. 30v.
33 G. Eland, ed. *Thomas Wotton's Letter-Book 1574–1586* (London: Oxford University Press, 1960), 19.
34 Ibid.
35 Ibid., 21.

Children in the long Elizabethan age were prepared for life by learning obedience to God and their betters so they could fulfill their appointed roles in their communities. Those who did not have obvious roles, who did not play their assigned parts, were considered dangerous. During an outbreak of rabbit poaching in County Durham in 1596, the justices at the Quarter Sessions heard charges against two men whose crime was defined as "not having lands, degree, license, or trade." Being "Masterless," they were assumed to be vagrants.[36] In 1598, the same Quarter Session, dealing with burglary, murder, theft, and assault, also heard a charge that Robert Bee of Monkwearmouth was "a common brawler and oppressor of his neighbors and reputed a common malefactor, sower of strife."[37] His crime was unneighborliness that required the authorities to chastise him. In both these cases, Bishop Matthew and his fellow justices were dealing with people who lacked a controlling social better. Masterless men were assumed to be criminal and lazy; common brawlers disturbed community values and acted "out of place."

On the other hand, people who were recognized as neighbors might expect community support, even when they had not earned it. In 1602, for instance, forty-five Staffordshire men petitioned the justices to "bind over … our neighbor," a known thief. They were willing to take responsibility for him because they believed, now that he was married, he would mend his ways, "hoping that this small public punishment might have wrought some shame and repentance."[38]

But why should they stay "in" their places, since there was no effective way of keeping people from creeping up the social ladder? People were conditioned by their social networks and required by law to stay where they were put.

Robert Miller, an apprentice tanner for three years, got into a fight with his master's wife. Aged fifteen or sixteen, Miller told her he wanted to be released from his apprenticeship and allowed to "provide me of a service in some place." His master, urged by his wife, told him that if he could not work quietly with her, he was free to depart. Up to this point, the story sounds vaguely modern, but what happened next suggests how large the gap was between "servants," masters, and mistresses. His master agreed to release him, but he used the law to forbid him to leave the Hundred and, essentially, turned him over to two local farmers to be bound to them as an apprentice. Young Miller complained, "Master, I have served these three years in your occupation and ken no skill in husbandry and will be loath to lose all this time"—the time he had served as an apprentice tanner. Those three years, however, did him little good. Tricked by

---

36 C.M. Fraser, ed. *Durham Quarter* Session *Rolls 1471–1625. Surtees Society* 1991; 199, 99.
37 Ibid., 103.
38 Keith Wrightson, "The 'Decline of Neighborliness' Revisited," in Norman Jones and Daniel Woolf, eds. *Local Identities in Late Medieval and Early Modern England* (Basingstoke, New York: Palgrave Macmillan, 2007), 28.

his master into waiting until a new pair of shoes was ready for him, he discovered that a warrant had been issued by the justices of the peace to force him to work on the farms. Fleeing to Norwich, he apprenticed himself to another tanner, but he had to start over again, with another seven-year apprenticeship. His old master sneered at him for being so foolish.[39] He had used the law to put Miller in his place, which was one of subservience.

Early in the reign of Elizabeth, a landmark law, entitled *An Act Containing divers orders for Artificers, Laborers, Servants of Husbandry and Apprentices* (usually called the "Statute of Artificers"), set the parameters of English labor regulation for generations to come, allowing us a glimpse at the ways in which Elizabethans idealized relationships between workers and their masters, mistresses, and dames. At the heart of the law was the desire to banish idleness, advance husbandry, and ensure reasonable wages to the workers. It sounds benign, but the very first clause took up the question of who could be compelled to work in skilled trades. Unmarried people under the age of thirty who had experience in a trade could be forced to work in that trade at the request of any master. On the other hand, masters could not dismiss their servants before the end of their agreed term of service without permission from a justice of the peace. If permission to dismiss was given, the master had to give three months' notice before termination. Nor could servants just quit. Anyone leaving the service of his or her master, mistress, or dame had to give a quarter year's notice or suffer imprisonment.

The Act began setting wages, too, and it regulated the parameters of service. Adolescents were to be apprenticed for at least seven years in skilled trades, and they might not marry until they had finished their training. Beginning in the middle teens, the apprenticeship might last into a person's mid-twenties. This, in theory, prevents the "riotous and licentious life" young men would normally live. Even on the farm or the sheepfold, where apprenticeships began as early as ten, they could not end until the child was twenty-one. The riotous apprentice was a stock character of Elizabethan social concern, and this law addressed that, along with the idea that laziness—not unemployment—produced beggars.[40]

The apprentice was expected to do obey his master, and the master owed a living to his servants and apprentices. The statute tried to put everyone in their places, regulating the freedom of all parties for the prosperity of all. Under the watchful eyes of master and mistress, youngsters were tamed and taught skills that were economically useful. Many of them were also taught to read and write as requisite skills for their trades. But it all fell on the master and mistress to control them, to catechize them, to send them to church, to train them, and to keep their youthful urges suppressed.

---

39 R.H. Tawney and Eileen Power, *Tudor Economic Documents*, 3 vols. (London: Longman, 1924), I, 350–1.
40 5 Eliz. I, c. 4.

Though mostly boys were apprenticed, girls—especially orphaned girls—could be, too. Their range of occupations was limited by their gender. "Housewife [housekeeping] and seamstress" and "seamstress and tailor" were the most common female apprenticeships in the mid-sixteenth century, with manual crafts and food services following far behind.[41] Bound to a master and his wife for seven years or more, they were trained by the latter.

It was much more common, however, for girls to learn their social place and station through being put out to domestic service without any formal legal arrangement. At ten or so, they entered the households of other women as servants, learning the domestic sciences through participation in them. This employment was unstable, and many servants moved, either because they chose to or because they were discharged.[42]

This fluidity of employment characterized male apprenticeship, too. Though apprentices were formally bound to serve for at least seven years, and legally could not leave until they were over twenty-four, a majority did not finish their apprenticeships. Some died, some were dismissed, some were traded to other masters, some ran away, and some failed to learn. The more fluid the system, the more the masters and apprentices benefited, since it allowed for contraction of trade on the one hand, and for seizure of opportunity on the other.[43]

Most young people received on-the-job training. Their elders were sure that this had to happen in their teen years, when they were thought to be malleable. If they were not set on the right path then, there was little hope for them.[44] These attempts to imprint job skills and virtue on young people were not always welcomed, and the court records bear lively evidence of youthful indiscretions. As the effort to make the young into godly adults increased, so, too, did the fear of youth. By the late sixteenth century, the civic clampdown on youthful misbehavior combined with the new punitive poor laws, which incarcerated the masterless and forced them into service.[45]

Because of the nature of the training in apprenticeship, there is very little direct evidence of how it worked. We can only catch glimpses in the writings of a few Elizabethans.

Thomas Whythorne (Figure 3.2), the first person to write an autobiography in English (with spelling he made up himself), spent a great deal of time thinking about his life and how he came to be who he was. His work was entitled,

---

41 Ilana Krausman Ben-Amos, *Adolescence and Youth in Early Modern England* (New Haven: Yale University Press, 1994), 137.

42 Ibid., 152.

43 Patrick Wallis, "Apprenticeship and Training in Premodern England." *The Journal of Economic History* 2008; 68(3), 832–61.

44 Paul Griffiths, *Youth and Authority. Formative Experiences in England 1560–1640* (Oxford: Clarendon Press, 1996), 49–54.

45 Ibid., 383.

Figure 3.2 Thomas Whythorne (Whithorne), by Unknown artist, woodcut, 1571, published 1590. NPG D8321. Reproduced by permission of the National Portrait Gallery.

A Book of Songs and Sonnets, with long discourses set with them of the child's life, together with the young man's life, and entering into the old man's life. He made lyrics out of his life, and then wrote the book to explain them. Born in 1528, he was raised in his father's house until he was ten, and then sent to live with an uncle near Oxford. Asked by his uncle whether he would become a priest, a physician, or a lawyer, he declared his love of music, and so his uncle sent him to Magdalen College Music School for six years. At about seventeen, he moved to London and became the "servant and scholar" of John Heywood, a professional musician and playwright. Heywood had deep family ties to Sir Thomas More and was a conservative Catholic who had barely escaped execution in the Prebendaries Plot of 1543. But by the time Whythorne joined him, he was living quietly, composing books of proverbs, epigrams, and poetry that sold well. In 1564, after flourishing under Queen Mary, Heywood went into religious exile on the Continent. Young Thomas Whythorne learned a great deal from him as he copied proverbs and plays, though it does not appear that he learned to be a Catholic.

In keeping with his new profession of musician and librettist, Whythorne wrote a pedantic poem that summarized his life and education up to that point (proving he had not yet learned to be a poet).

> Whereas a friend of me placed with the master
> That now I serve, and Master John Heywood
> His name it is, of whom I hear this good,
> That he of poets of England in this time
> Is most famous for writing English rhyme...
> Beside all this, my said master, even he,
> In music sweet can frame sweet notes t'agree;
> And instruments belonging to the same
> He can aptly and cunningly them frame.
> The which to learn I ply myself daily
> Thereto, that I may reap some fruit thereby.
> Also to write in rhythm I do practice;
> And the first fruit of that I did devise
> I here do write, and it to thee do send.
> And thus of this my rhythm I make an end.

Whythorne, when he was about twenty, left life as a "scholar and a servant," in which he had been "troubled with fear of tutors and masters," and became his own man, and "therewith a master." Hanging a painting of Terpsichore, the muse of music and dancing, in his London chamber, he began teaching music.[46] He served in great houses (probably including the Earl of Warwick's) as a personal tutor in the early 1560's.

As a musician, he had a strong identity with his trade. A recent study says that "the correct understanding and application of the rules of composition was the foundation of Whythorne's own definition of 'musician.'"[47] Devoting many pages of his memoir to the discussion of the history, antiquity, value, and importance of music, Whythorne asserted its healing powers, its ability to produce harmony among people, and even its power over animals. He tells a charming story of how bagpipes can drive away wolves. But music was a serious business, not to be left to minstrels and amateurs who were insufficiently trained to practice it. Citing the Bible, Aristotle, Cicero, the Greek and Roman myths, and contemporary authors, English and Italian, Whythorne

---

46 James M. Osborn, ed. *The Autobiography of Thomas Whythorne* (Oxford: Oxford University Press, 1961), 17–20.
47 Katie M. Nelson, "Thomas Whythorne and Tudor Musicians," (Unpublished PhD Dissertation, University of Warwick, 2010), 82.

demonstrated its ancient pedigree and insisted "the science" of music be left to professionals. "Pettifoggers of music," such as schoolmasters and minstrels, were ignorantly and spitefully dragging it down from its previously exalted status. "Blockheads and dolts," meaning the puritanical, were condemning it, and the professional musicians' trade had been damaged by the Reformation.[48] Clearly, part of Whythorne's self-identity was wrapped up in his occupation.

Whythorne's mid-Elizabethan memoir shows he was obsessed with his social status. He saw himself as a gentleman, but as a music tutor he mostly found himself among his "betters." This meant he had to put up with insults that he would not have borne in other company. "I have been," he said, sorting his detractors by rank,

> in the companies of those who be worshipful, right worshipful, and also honorable, and saw that the meaner sort (in comparison with their estates) were driven to put up quietly with some injuries at their hands; also how such things, which the inferior sort either said or did in the presence of their greaters or betters was but to be allowed of as I pleased their superiors to take it

After meditating on passages from the apocryphal book of Ecclesiasticus, he resolved: "I should not keep company with my greaters."[49]

To avoid depending on arrogant patrons, he pioneered the publication of part music for private performances around a table, seeking fame as quickly as possible so that he could live without an employer. He was attempting to "self-fashion" his image so he could find a happier way of living.[50] As a part of this self-invention, he added "gentleman" to his name and "discovered" an old coat of arms belonging to his family.[51] Living in London, far from his paternal home in Ilminster, he had promoted himself to a new social status.

Whythorne was busy rising in a world that lacked an approving moral language to celebrate the hard-working, thrifty person who improved through effort. Elizabethan preachers, like William Perkins, made it clear that riches, if you had them, were God's gift and had to be used for God's purposes. There was no theology that approved social climbing, and, though some people did succeed in changing their stations, they were not praised for it. If they got money, they were expected to act as if they were born to it. God's idea of how to use money was not to make more money. He required a person to spend it virtuously on alms, schools, and other causes outlined in the Sermon on the Mount.

Elizabethan playwrights and novelists capture this conundrum of describing self-made men as those whose natural virtues explain their wealth, and whose

---

48 Ibid., 232–45.
49 Osborne, *Whythorne*, 172.
50 Nelson, "Whythorne," 255.
51 Ibid., 258.

virtuous generosity proves their gentility. Sir Thomas Gresham, the very rich merchant who built the Royal Exchange, featured in Thomas Heywood's two-part play, *If You Know Me Not, You Know No Body*. The first part, written just after Queen Elizabeth died, is about her troubles during the reign of Queen Mary, and involves Gresham foiling a plot to have Elizabeth executed. In the second part, Gresham himself is the hero. In the first scene, one of his factors is conversing with a Barbary merchant, who asks him about his master:

> *Factor:* He is a merchant of good estimate:
> Care how to get, and forecast to increase,
> (If so they be accounted) be his faults.
> *Merchant:* They are especial virtues, being clear
> From avarice and base extortion.[52]

The drama is about how Gresham built the Royal Exchange, and it shows his inspiration as being the other great men and women of London, whose portraits hung in a gallery in St. Paul's. Dean Nowell gives him the tour, describing each one's virtuous use of wealth in founding schools and alms houses, and doing other good deeds that earned them "widows orisons, lazars prayers, orphans thanks." Moved to tears, Gresham swears to do good while he lives.[53]

Gresham founds the Exchange (and gets knighted for it, along with the right to call it the "Royal Exchange"), but he does not care for money. He laughs when the new King of Barbary breaks a contract made with the old king, sending him a pair of slippers instead of the £60 000 he is owed. To prove his devotion to Queen Elizabeth before the Russian ambassador, he buys a pearl for £1500, has it ground up, and drinks the powder in a cup of wine as a toast to her. Then, he invites the ambassador to tour his school of the seven liberal sciences, "a university within itself." "We are not like those that are not liberal, till they be dying," he declares. "[W]hat we mean to give, we will bestow and see done whilst we live."[54]

Though Gresham was a real person, his generosity did not play out in the real world as easily as it did in the theater. He built the Exchange, but his school did not get opened until long after he was dead. Nonetheless, he was a figure well known in later sixteenth-century London and was used as a type for the way a rich merchant ought to act, careless of present gain, but careful of the good of his community. How he got his money was glossed over in favor of his virtuous use of it. His spending made him gentle. The character Gresham in the play is surprised to hear that the famous Mayor of London, Richard Whittington, was gently born. He had thought Whittington had "raised himself by a venture of

---

52 Thomas Heywood, *The Dramatic Works of Thomas Heywood… in six volumes* (London: 1874), 193.
53 Ibid., 276–9.
54 Ibid., 301.

cat." But nobility will out, and Whittington was hereditarily destined to be the Lord Mayor he became.[55]

In Thomas Deloney's novel *The Pleasant Historie of John Winchcombe, otherwise called Jacke of Newberrie*, written in the 1590's, we see these tensions between station and spending played out. The hero, Henry, "so good a companion, he was called of old and young Jack of Newbury," is a broad cloth weaver who, through diligence and cleverness, rises until he can provide, as the title page declares, work for 500 poor men. What is praiseworthy, however, is his generosity, not his job creation. Deloney tells us that Jack would "spend his money with the best, and was not at any time found a churl of his purse." Whenever he had money, he spent it; he kept himself in comely and decent clothes; he did not get drunk. He behaved discreetly, with honest mirth and "pleasant conceits," so he was "every gentleman's companion."[56]

In short, late Elizabethans found it hard to describe those who changed social status through effort, but they knew people who did it, and some—like Thomas Whythorne—aspired to do it themselves. In a world of God-made men, bourgeois virtues like thrift and hard work were invisible.[57] Just as they had no word for "unemployment," they had no words for "capitalist" or "self-fashioning." They just had the confusion that came from watching people behave in ways in which they were not supposed to behave, changing roles in life as the wheel of fortune turned.

Ambition, they understood, but to "aspire" was a negative virtue. As Sir Francis Walsingham mused, ambition was as commendable in men as beauty was in women. Men of ambition sought honor the natural way, by doing good and honorable acts. But ambition became offensive when it sought to gain titles and power, "which at the first, were, or at least should be the mark whereby to distinguish men according to the rate of their virtues and sufficiencies; but are now only arguments of a man's good fortune, and effects of the Prince's favor."[58]

Promotion through hollow ambition was frowned upon as dangerous to ordered communities based on well-defined roles. Allocated by family status, gender, and age, they held society together and kept it working. Which was why defying the social hierarchy was thought to be a form of impiety.[59] But changing conditions in society meant that many were adjusting their social status, and that ambition had opportunity. Those changing conditions were the

55 Ibid., 277.
56 Francis Oscar Mann, ed. *The Works of Thomas Deloney* (Oxford: Clarendon Press, 1912), 1, 3.
57 Stevenson, *Praise and Paradox*, 6–7.
58 John Somers, "Sir Francis Walsingham Anatomizing of Honesty of Ambition and Fortitude Written in the year 1590," in *A Collection of Tracts* (London: 1748), IV, 391.
59 Anthony Esler, *The Aspiring Mind of the Elizabethan Younger Generation* (Durham: Duke University Press, 1966), 40.

product of the vast economic and geopolitical alterations in the later sixteenth century. Society had never really been static, but it was becoming much harder to insist that it was immutable.

The people who lived in Elizabeth's England were experiencing the world in new ways. In the reigns of Henry VII and VIII, England watched the discovery of the Americas and the Iberian expansion from afar, but Mary Tudor's marriage to Philip II had drawn it into the worldwide conflicts of the era: first the Habsburg-Valois wars, and then wars with Spain, the French civil wars, the Dutch Revolt, and the Irish rebellions. England was also drawn into the global economy by some of the same forces. Inflation was rampant, as was population growth. English merchants spread over the world, looking for markets to replace those lost in the continental wars. The vast religious revolution that took part in the first half of the century was, by Elizabeth's reign, beginning to settle into a permanent new faith in England, changing the way people thought of God and the past, just as they were mapping their world for the first time.

By the 1590's, the world was known to be a very different place than it had been even fifty years before. The stability people had been taught to depend upon had turned into a house built on sand. New roles, new social understandings, were necessary. Elizabethans had the hard job of making sense of it all.

4

Taming the Natural Child: Preparations for Living

Elizabethan children were not innocent or good. They were "natural," wild creatures who had to be tamed through discipline and an education in duty and virtue. As Bishop Bonner said in the preface to his 1555 *Catechism*, "youth, of itself is propense and ready, without any teacher, to take, and embrace vice, unthriftiness, and all manner naughtiness."[1]

Children's natural naughtiness started with Adam and Eve. If Eve had not shared the fruit of the Tree of Wisdom with Adam, there would have been no children in the world. God, out for His evening stroll in the Garden of Eden, discovered what they had done, and cursed them for breaking His rules. That curse doomed them to have children, to work, and to die. According to Genesis 3:

> And God unto the woman said
> Thy sorrows shall increase
> And oft with child I will thee make
> Thy pain shall never cease.[2]

To Adam was given the punishment of supporting a family by the "sweat of his brow." And then he and they would die. The children of Adam and Eve inherited their original sin, so all humanity was inclined to choose evil over good. Only because of God's grace was there any hope for sinful humanity.

Those punished with parenthood, though loving, knew that their wild children needed to be tamed, and beating was an important tool for purging them of sin and reducing their natural pride to obedience. It was hard for a parent to do this, so they often bound their children over to others as servants, apprentices, and students to be strictly raised and taught a trade. All of this was in the name of preservation of the family estate and for the good of the community.

---

1 Edmund Bonner, *An honest godlye instruction...* (1556), Sig. Aii. STC (2nd ed.)/3281
2 William Hunnis, *A hyue full of hunnye contayning the firste booke of Moses, called Genesis...* (1578), fo. 5v. STC (2nd ed.)/13974.

Being Elizabethan: Understanding Shakespeare's Neighbors, First Edition. Norman Jones.
© 2020 John Wiley & Sons, Inc. Published 2020 by John Wiley & Sons, Inc.

Children were not so much valued for themselves—though they were loved—as for their roles in perpetuating and serving families and communities.[3]

Thus, children learned virtue, the root of which was biblically enjoined obedience to their superiors and to God. St. Paul declared, echoing the Fifth Commandment: "Children, obey your parents in the Lord: for this is right. Honor thy father and mother (which is the first commandment with promise) that it may be well with thee, and that thou may live long on earth." Ecclesiasticus, that wise book of the Old Testament Apocrypha, taught: "Who so honors his father, shall have joy of his own children; ... My son, help thy father in his age, and grieve him not so long as he lives; ... Who fears God, honors his parents."[4]

In his 1561 instructions to his eldest son Thomas, who was setting off for a year of educational travel and language study on the Continent, Sir William Cecil, First Baron Burghley, summed up the theology of childrearing. His role as father was to bring his children "from ignorance to knowledge, to the hands of God ... And if you shall please him and serve him in fear, I shall take comfort of you, otherwise I shall take you as no blessing of God, but a burden of grief and decay of my age."[5]

Sir William's son Robert received his own paternal advice around 1580. Still pious, it contained only ten precepts, to which Robert was to add the Ten Commandments. Burghley was especially clear about teaching a child to understand his or her place in the divine order of things. "Towards thy superiors," he wrote, "be humble yet generous; with thy equals familiar yet respective; towards inferiors show much humility and some familiarity, as to bow thy body, stretch forth thy hand, and to uncover thy head, and suchlike popular compliments." This gentility prepared the way for advancement, showing people you were well-bred and making them think well of you.[6] This was a common and important element in childrearing, since everyone had to know how to "do their duty" to their betters, their peers, and their inferiors. Bowing, cap doffing, and proper forms of address had to be learned as a child.

Parental advice tended to follow this pattern: be Godly, keep God's law, prosper through obedience to God, marry carefully (as instructed), be frugal and thoughtful, keep hospitality proper to your station but no more, and watch your tongue. Do not oppress the poor and remember who you are. If you were successful in these things, you would be a virtuous person. Elizabethans' goals in childrearing echoed the language of virtue written on their tombs.

---

3 Anthony Fletcher, "Prescription and Practice: Protestantism and the Upbringing of Children, 1560–1700." *Studies in Church History* 1994; 31, 325–7.

4 Ephesians 6:1–3; Ecclesiasticus 3:8–6; 13.

5 BL Harelian 3638, fo. 106v. Louis B. Wright, ed. *Advice to a Son. Precepts of Lord Burghley, Sir Walter Raleigh, and Francis Osborne* (Ithaca: Cornell University Press for Folger Shakespeare Library, 1962), 5.

6 Wright, *Advice*, 12.

Because everyone agreed that the key to making virtuous adults was true religion, they invested in religious education. This was formal, in the sense that catechisms were written and taught, and large parts of schooling used religious texts and contexts. It was also informal, in that children were naturally incorporated in settings where they learned by observation and imitation.

When it came to God, Elizabeth was concerned that children learn the right things. If being a good citizen was about obeying God's Handmaiden the Queen, she could not leave religion to chance. Nor could she fail God by allowing her people to live in ignorance of their duty to Him. Consequently, the royal injunctions enforcing the Elizabethan Settlement of Religion in 1559 had provisions for education. Most importantly, they required catechizing every Sunday before evening prayers and on holy days.

The cathechism used for preparing children for confirmation in the church was printed in the prayer books beginning in 1549. There, it was short and to the point, ensuring everyone knew the basics: the Apostles' Creed and what it meant; the Ten Commandments; the Lord's Prayer; and dependence upon God. It also asked them to define their duty to God and their duty to their neighors. Asked what it meant to love one's neighbor as one self, the catechumen was taught to say:

> To submit myself to all my governors, teachers, spiritual Pastors and Masters. To order myself lowly and reverently to all my betters. To hurt no body by word, nor deed. To be true and just in all my dealing. To bear no malice nor hatred in my heart. To keep my hands from picking and stealing, and my tongue from evil speaking, lyng and slaundering. To keep my body in temperance, soberness, and chastity. Not to covet nor desire other men's goods. But learn and labour truely to get mine own living, and to do my duty in that state of life, unto which it shall please God to call me.[7]

The catechism guaranteed all members of the church knew the key beliefs and duties, and it was learned by rote. Literate and illiterate alike were expected to know it, and it was short enough to be learned as a mechanical exercise. Some cathechisms were written for mothers to use with their children, such as the one produced by Dorcas Martin, the wife of the Lord Mayor of London. Asked, "My child, art thou a Christian?", the child sweetly replies,"Yea, by the grace of God, whereas of nature I was a child of wrath."[8]

---

7 John Booty, ed. *The Book of Common Prayer 1559. The Elizabethan Prayer Book* (Washington, D.C.: Folger Shakespeare Library, 1976), 286.
8 Dorcas Martin, "An instruction for Christians, conteining a fruitfull and godlie exercise, as well in wholesome and fruitfull praiers..." in Thomas Bentley, ed. *The monument of matrones conteining seuen seuerall lamps of virginitie, or distinct treatises...* (1582), 233. STC (2nd ed.)/1892.

For the older and better educated, there were more complicated catechisms that required explication beyond memorization. In print, they were expanded for use as teaching tools. They provided a way to learn religion, and when taught in Latin they helped students master that essential tongue. That is why the first Elizabethan catechism was in Latin.[9] Written by the Dean of St. Paul's, Alexander Nowell, around 1562, it went through extensive review by Sir William Cecil, the Lower House of Convocation, and the bishops before it was printed in 1570. An English version quickly followed, and both were popular, shaping generations of English youth.[10]

In Nowell's catechism, the master informs his student that his first duty is to teach him true religion. "For this age of childhood," he lectures, "ought no less, yea, also much more, to be trained with good lessons to godliness, than with good arts to humanity." "Wherefore," he ominously adds, he is going to examine the student to see how well he has studied.

The first question is easy. "What religion it is that thou professes?" The student, who has clearly studied very, very hard, replies it is the religion "whereof the Lord Christ is the author and teacher." And are you, the master demands, "a scholar of our Lord and schoolmaster Christ?"[11] Naturally, the student says, "Yes," and then the really hard questions begin. Sections on "Obedience, which the law requireth," "faith," "invocation and thanksgiving," and "the sacraments and mysteries of God" follow one after another. It ends with the master's valediction. Observing that the servant who knows the master's will and does not follow it will be beaten harder than the one who is ignorant, he commands: "Go to therefore, my child, bend all thy care and thought hereunto [godliness], that thou fail not in thy duty, or swerve at any time from this rule and prescribed form of godly life."[12]

Though there were frequent complaints that catechizing was not happening, and it is almost certain that no one was held to the standard of Nowell's examination, a great deal of effort went into education. Statutes of the schools that were blooming across England suggest that they aspired to be places of religious instruction. As every catechized child knew, the Bible was God's word, so there was an imperative for everyone, even girls, to learn how to read. They were preparing to read and learn God's Word and do His will. Education was structured around that goal.

At Westminster School, for instance, the boys rose at 5 a.m. daily, praying on their knees beside their beds, before beginning classes at 6. Their workday

---

9 Ian Green, *The Christian ABC. Catechisms and Catechizing in England c. 1530–1740* (Oxford: Clarendon Press, 1996), 93–8.
10 BL Lansd. 7, fos. 18–18v. TNA SP 12/71, fo. 34.
11 G.E. Corrie, ed. *A Catechism written in Latin by Alexander Nowell, Dean of St. Paul's; together with the Same Catechism translated in English by Thomas Norton* (Cambridge: Cambridge University Press, 1853), 113.
12 Ibid., 219.

began with the headmaster, on his knees, leading his kneeling students in prayer. Students took turns saying grace at meals, and their colleagues recited the psalms appointed. On saints' days, the mornings were devoted to a sermon, the catechism, and scripture. After these, the boys had to write a summary of the sermon in Latin poetry or prose, or, for the youngest, in English.[13]

Though God was expected to be at the heart of human life, what did Elizabethans think formal education was for? Certainly, the ability to read the Bible was valued, but it was more a matter of practicality. The deeply classical form of their liberal education belies its utility. Latin was the language of learned communication, making a boy ready for university and for life among the elites. Though theoretically static, the hierarchical structures of Elizabethan society was an "open elite," where talent could lead to opportunity through education.

For many children not of the elite, education was necessary for the trades they were entering. Merchants, for instance, had to know how to read, write, and cipher, and they needed enough foreign language to deal, at the least, with French- and Italian-speaking colleagues. This meant that the schools were open to boys who demonstrated intelligence, regardless of their social status.

Beside all the language instruction, with its beatings and parsing, there was something else going on. Children were learning the virtues that made them self-governing individuals and prepared them to be good masters. The combination of Christianity and the classics made it possible for them to join the magisterial classes, who, thanks to their education in virtue and honor, accepted the duty of running a nation that had no bureaucracy or standing army. Education provided moral discipline and furnished a didactic warehouse of examples for students to apply when confronting the world's troubles. The examples of great men were part of their rationale apparatus. England needed men who were educated to participate in ruling the nation.[14]

An order from the Privy Council to the churchwardens of St. Savior's Parish in London expresses this baldly. It describes Thomas Clement, "a poor scholar born and brought up amongst [them], and likely to prove an able man to do service unto his country if he might have convenient exhibition to maintain him to his learning in one of the universities." Therefore, the parish was ordered to supply money to support him. They knew, said the Council, that the parish had revenue "sufficient and fit to be bestowed on such charitable intents, as heretofore in like cases had formerly been used."[15]

The Edward VI grammar schools established across the country on the ruins of monasteries and chantries created increased opportunities for all boys and

---

13 Arthur Francis Leach, *Educational Charters and Documents 598 to 1909* (Cambridge: Cambridge University Press, 1911), 506–19.
14 Jones, *Governing*, 27–43.
15 TNA PC 2/18, fo. 317.

were part of a national movement. Westminster School, the Merchant Taylors' School, and many others joined them. In 1562, the inhabitants of the Isle of Guernsey petitioned the Queen to grant them wheat, owed from dissolved obits and friaries, to support the creation of "Queen Elizabeth's School" in a disused chapel.[16] The grant was made and, though the schoolmaster complained in 1565 that the inhabitants were savages, a *"gens barbara"* who hated literature, by 1570 Sir Thomas Leighton was petitioning for support for the school's two top students to go to Cambridge and Oxford. They, being of "poor parentage," did not have the means.[17]

Explicit in many of the grammar schools was the idea of education as a competitive meritocracy. As a 1570 proposal to create free schools in Hertford, Tewksbury, Bourne, Market Deeping, and other places conceived it, in each school the four best scholars would receive 12d a quarter. However, if any other boy excelled the top four, he would get the 12d, displacing one of them. This competitive scholarship was matched with another grant to the four best-behaved boys, "not given to swearing." They, too, got 12d a quarter. (One wonders if a boy who used even gentler language could bump them down, too?) A separate part of this proposed endowment took care of girls' advancement by making money available for dowries to ensure good marriages.[18]

Though there were "free schools," students still had to find a way to live. Simon Forman tells us in his autobiography how he kept trying to attend lessons but work prevented him. Having been apprenticed at age eleven, he was taken from school and set to "keep sheep and to plough, and gathering of sticks and such like." At fourteen, he ran away and apprenticed himself, while still trying to learn. His master complained about how much time he spent with his books and eventually took them all away. He desperately tried to keep his Latin going by questioning a boy who was boarding there about his lessons at the free school in Salisbury. Then he got a job as a servant to two Oxford students, hoping that being in the university, he could learn. Instead, he spent his days fetching and carrying, with little time to attend the Magdalene College free school. Yet, in the end, he became a schoolmaster himself, and went on, through many vicissitudes, to a learned career as physician and astrologer.[19]

Then, as now, higher purposes were motivations for schools and universities. Richard Mulcaster, the founding headmaster of the Merchant Taylor's

16 CP 2/97; CP 186/57.
17 TNA SP 15/12, fo. 92. TNA SP 15/19, fo. 72
18 Bodl., Ms. Jones 17, fo. 11.
19 James Orchard Haliwell, ed. *The Autobiography and Personal diary of Dr. Simon Forman, the celebrated astrologer, from A. D. 1552, to A. D. 1602, from the unpublished manuscripts in the Ashmolean museum, Oxford* (1849), 4–12. http://babel.hathitrust.org/cgi/pt?id=mdp.3901508213 9711;view=1up;seq=22 [Accessed November 29, 2018].

School, thought deeply about education and wrote influential books on how schools and curricula should be organized for boys and girls. But he understood that learning, in and of itself, was not the point of education. A teacher had to ensure a child could think critically about any issue that arose: "he must bend his wits to weigh the particularities, whereby both the general conclusions be brought to be profitable, and his own judgement to be thought discrete." It was this ability to apply what had been learned to circumstances in life that made an individual virtuous, according to Aristotle. Mulcaster confirmed that this was the point and proof of education. It was, he said, "the line to live by, the guide to all our doings, the touchstone" that distinguished "a contemplative creature from an active courage."[20] Only active, educated people were useful to the commonwealth. Education created good leaders and subjects, giving them the virtues and skills needed for daily life.

The virtues were learned from reading ancient authors, as much as from Bible stories. Roman literature and history taught by example. In his *Apologie for Poetrie*, Sir Philip Sidney explained that the poet's job was "feigning notable images of virtues, vices, or what else, with that delightful teaching." He knew that everyone, child and adult, preferred to learn through stories, and that great poetry could teach good behavior. "Glad they will be to hear the tales of Hercules, Achilles, Cyrus, Aeneas, and hearing them, must needs hear the right description of wisdom, value, and justice."[21]

Youngsters were taught how to govern themselves and others by reading rhetoric, history, and cosmology. This learning prepared them to give counsel and to speak in assemblies. At about the age of seventeen, when his reason was developed enough to bridle his "courage," a youth would enter the most important part of the curriculum. According to Sir Thomas Elyot, whose 1531 *The Book Named the Governor* was reprinted nine times in the sixteenth century, the student should begin with Aristotle's *Ethics*, going on to Plato and to Cicero's *De officiis*:

> Lord God, what incomparable sweetness of words and matter shall he find in the ... works of Plato and Cicero; wherein is joined gravity with delectation, excellent wisdom with divine eloquence, absolute virtue with pleasure incredible, and every place is so enfarced with profitable counsel joined with honesty, that those three books be almost sufficient to make a perfect and excellent governor.[22]

---

20 Richard Mulcaster, *Positions wherin those primitive circumstances be examined, which are necessarie for the training vp of children either for skill in their booke, or health in their bodie* (1581), 130–31. STC (2nd ed.)/18253a.

21 Phillip Sidney, *Apologie for Poetrie* (1595), sig. C. [4]; E[4v]. STC (2nd ed.)/904:16.

22 Thomas Elyot, *The Book Named the Governor*, ed. S.E. Lehmberg (New York: Dutton, 1970), 39.

Cicero, Caesar, Livy, and Sallust were mainstays, joined by the poets Ovid, Vergil, and Horace and the comedies of Terrence. Authors of late Republican and early Imperial Rome, they taught Roman ideals and civic virtue. By late in Elizabeth's reign, the usual pedagogical practice was for boys to translate from Cicero much more than from the Bible, since the Latin of the Vulgate Bible was much poorer than Cicero's. The whole curriculum focused on virtue, modeled on Roman ideas but inflected by Christian teachings.[23]

This created some tension between the curriculum and life outside of school. Richard Mulcaster noted that Athenian and Roman rhetorical traditions were for use in democratic assemblies. In England, eloquence was now "half drowned" for want of democracy, or "half doubted" for "discredit of divinity."[24] England was a Christian monarchy, not a pagan republic.

Sir Thomas Wilson disagreed. Demosthenes, the great Greek rhetorician, was worth studying because he provided such a good rhetorical example "that none ever was more fit to make an English man tell his tale praise worthily in any open hearing, either in parliament or in pulpit, or otherwise."[25]

Clearly, this curriculum provided young men with ideas to use when speaking in public, their minds well stocked with apposite references. It gave them a verbal shorthand, quotes to employ to make a point. In parliament, for instance, Francis Alford could toss out the Roman Fabius Maximus' comment to the Roman Senate, "*nunquam quicquam dictum inconsideratius*," "never was a subject introduced at a more unseasonable time," knowing most of his colleagues would recognize the senatorial precedent for censuring members.[26] His opponent could toss back the example of Zenocrates, who, according to Livy, said it was a dishonor to protect a lying ambassador, "*dignitas no[n] tuetur legatum mendacem*."[27] Invoking classical examples was standard practice, made possible by the way boys were taught their Latin—though they were reminded by Cicero, "*lege vivimus, non exemplis*," "we live by law, not examples."

Grammar school boys learned rhetoric and wit by practicing it. John Stow, in his survey of London in the 1590's, recalled how boys and masters from the London schools would gather on a "bank boarded about under a tree" near St. Bartholomew the Great for disputational sport. The boys "apposed and answered" questions, one arguing until overcome by another. Of course, boys being boys, these rhetorical rivalries could turn violent. Stow says

---

23 Freyja Cox Jensen, *Reading the Roman Republic in Early Modern England* (Leiden, Boston: Brill, 2012), 26–32.

24 Mulcaster, *Positions*, 240.

25 Thomas Wilson, trans. *The Three Orations of Demosthenes Chiefe Orator among the Grecians...* (1570), dedication. STC (2nd ed.)/6578.

26 Hartley, *Proceedings*, I, 327.

27 Ibid., 329.

"the children ... disorderly in the open streets, provoke one another with '*salve tu quoque, placet tibi mecum disputare, placet*': [*Hello, would you like to dispute with me, please*?]" and so, proceeding from questions of grammar, "they usually fell from that to blows, many times in so great heaps that they troubled the streets, and passengers."[28]

It was a vigorous form of rhetorical training that excluded all those who did not have a humanist education—almost all women and most men—but it was the ideal preparation for magisterial participation. The ruling orders had their own way of communicating that united them and excluded those beneath them.

Richard Rainolde, dedicating his *Foundations of Rhetoric*, explained rhetoric was the capstone of learning. "For the end of all arts and sciences, and of all noble acts and enterprises is virtue ... Who so is adorned with nobility and virtue ... will," with good rhetoric, "move and allure the favor and support of virtue in any other," as Cicero says, "even to love those whom we never saw, but by good fame and bruit beautified to us."[29]

The impact of this training is obvious when we look at addresses to justices, juries, special commissions, and other groups charged with governing. We could cite dozens, if not hundreds of speeches in the courts, to parliament, at public celebrations, and in churches that used the tools of rhetoric, following a cursus that proceeded from ancients to moderns, and finally to the greatest truths in the Bible. Most speakers took virtue as a text or subtext.

All grammar schools and universities provided a Latin-based education using classical texts and incorporating a "liberal education" that included mathematics. If "tongues" were the path to all knowledge and the road to the Bible, mathematics molded rational minds, while being essential for trades and for sciences such as navigation, astronomy, and astrology.[30] Elizabethan school children learned arithmetic and some algebra. University students were expected to study geometry, arithmetic, and cosmology. Sir Thomas Smith left money to Queen's College, Cambridge to found two mathematical lectureships in 1573, one in geometry and the other in arithmetic (which included algebra). Strikingly, these lectures were not read "as of a preacher out of a pulpit," but taught with pen and paper, or a stick and compass in sand or dust, so the students could understand by doing it themselves.[31] This mathematical literacy, with its utility, created a strong demand for books and instruments for

---

28 John Stow, *A Survay of London...* (1599), 55–6. STC (2nd ed.)/23342.
29 Richard Rainolde, *A Booke Called the Foundacion of Rhetorike* (1563), dedication. STC (2nd ed.)/20925a.5.
30 Mulcaster, *Positions*, 241–2.
31 Quoted in Mordechai Feingold, *The Mathematician's Apprenticeship. Science, Universities, and Society in England 1560–1640* (Cambridge: Cambridge University Press, 1984), 39.

navigation, surveying, cartography, and other mathematical sciences among the educated classes.[32]

Ironically, all this development of analytical skill undermined traditional received authority, teaching students to question. The idea of primacy of conscience undercut the primacy of obedience. Analytical thinking became an acceptable reason to embrace conflicting ideas. Graduates knew God elected everyone to a future determined before time. Each person had a destiny. And each person had the duty to use his or her conscience "rightly formed" in fulfilling it. It made it very hard to put community before individual, law before conscience. If the wild wills of the young had been bridled by education, was it only to empower their willful consciences?

Putting it more concretely, Richard Mulcaster worried that England was educating too many people, and of the wrong sort. Since the Reformation, he said, there had been less need for "bookmen," and "wits" now had to be sorted so that only the most civil were educated. The signs of civil wits were quietness, concord, agreement, fellowship, and friendship. Uncivil wits were the opposite. "How then," he asked, "can civil society be preserved, where wits of unfit humors for service, are in places of service … ?" Wits misplaced, he said, were "unquiet and seditious."[33]

Mulcaster was prescient, noting the effects of Reformation values on educated people. The hopeful Erasmian humanism taught in schools assumed that children would be better adults if they were properly educated. This ideal combined with the Protestant doctrines of *sola scriptura, sola fide*, and priesthood of the believer to exult the individual conscience over tradition and civil authority. If you could not trust the received biblical text, or the authority of a church encrusted with relics of superstition, you could not respect your inherited religion. As an apologetic commissioned by Lord Burghley said, "The faith of our fathers is not always true."[34] And if you believed everyone was empowered by God to read the Bible as a guide to his or her personal life, you did not value conformity to any authority whose understanding departed from your own informed certainty. Education in later sixteenth-century Europe was preparing students to question the values of their betters. Mulcaster was right to notice that too many educated people might be a bad thing.

But the tenor of the times ran against him. The ability to read and understand the Bible was increasingly important to Elizabethans, and as that emphasis strengthened, so too did the argument for letting conscience be your guide. Lord Burghley made the argument for conscience—linked, of course, to

---

32 Eric H. Ash, *Power, Knowledge and Expertise in Elizabethan England* (Baltimore: Johns Hopkins University Press, 2004), 137–9.

33 Mulcaster, *Positions*, 137–8.

34 Thomas Bilson, *The true difference betweene Christian subiection and vnchristian rebellion...* (1586), 303. STC (2nd ed.)/3072.

proper obedience to the Queen—in his 1583 *The Execution of Justice in England*. He then commissioned Thomas Bilson to flesh it out for him. Bilson wrote 686 octavo pages of dialogue between Philander the Jesuit and Theophilus the Christian, in which the right of the Queen to execute traitors, who sometimes happened to be Catholics, was proved. It was an academic argument—entertaining and humorous in spots—that used church history as its primary ground of dispute. Bilson, in asserting the right of the Queen to rule her God-given country, nonetheless maintained the primacy of conscience:

> THEOPHILUS: If every man shall answer for himself, good reason he be master of his own conscience in that which toucheth him so near, and no man shall excuse him for.
> PHILANDER: This is to make every private man supreme judge of religion.
> THEOPHILUS: The poorest wretch that is may be supreme governor of his own heart: princes rule the public and external actions of their countries, but not the consciences of men.

The gloss of this read: "The magistrate no governor of the conscience."[35]

By the later 1580's, this argument giving conscience authority was turning up in many places, frustrating the divinely established authorities of state and church. People's exalted consciences, fed by religious and political propaganda, were asserting themselves in the ways Philander the Jesuit said they would. The Jesuits, in fact, seized on the argument and refined it with their own casuistry, making it possible, in good conscience, to lie about their papal allegiance. Other Catholics argued a clear conscience was their license to live peacefully in England.

The proper exercise of conscience in obedience to God's word required that believers be rightly instructed by men who had received a liberal education. No man could preach in Elizabeth's church unless he had a university degree, which meant that the clergy were trained in the formal logic, rhetoric, and history that made biblical interpretations and sermons possible.

Thus, liberal education was practical education. Sir Walter Mildmay explained this when creating Emmanuel College, Cambridge. It was an ancient practice in God's church, he said, to found schools and colleges for the education of young men in piety, good letters, the Bible, and theology. Being thus instructed, they could teach "true religion and pure theology, refute all errors and heresies, and by the shining example of blameless life excite all men to virtue." Colleges and universities, he described as "seed plots of those most noble plants of Theology and right good learning." These gardens of learning ought to be "opened like fountains, that, arising out of the Paradise of God,

---

35 Ibid., 297–8.

they may as with a river of gold water all regions of our land."[36] Graduates of his college were expected to leave Cambridge and take up pastoral work once they had achieved the degree of Doctor of Divinity.[37]

Sir Walter's daughter-in-law, Lady Grace, did not attend a university, since her role was to be the wife of a man of rank, managing his extended household. Her governess taught her arithmetic, letter writing, herbalism, anatomy, singing, and needlework. As a moral education, she had Grace compose poetry mocking married people who flirted with others' spouses. She instructed her not to gossip, not to be a busybody, not to talk much when she knew little. Overall, Grace was told, "I should ever carry with me, a modest eye, and a chaste ear, a silent tongue, and a considerate heart, wary and heedful of myself in all my words and actions."[38] This governess demanded she do nothing against her conscience. She was to eschew ribaldry, idleness, and people who were of "undermining dispositions," full of questions and subtlety, "lest the innocence, and virginity of our tender hearts should be stained."[39]

Grace told her granddaughter, Mary Fane, to examine everything she saw, heard, thought, loved, or desired in the light of God's word. She wrote: "This book of my Meditations is the consolation of my soul, the joy of my heart and the stability of my mind. As they are approved by the word of God, and as I do approve them in mine own conscience by the same word." Though her learning was "rude," she had spent her life meditating on scripture as it applied to her daily experiences, learning to depend wholly on God "with good conscience."[40]

Her education in deportment and faith was suitable for girls of all ranks. The catechism taught similar lessons about avoiding lewdness and lightness, keeping the Ten Commandments, obeying one's betters, and performing one's feminine roles righteously. As Grace recorded in her autobiographical "pilgrimage," she was the good wife and manager she was trained to be. Married to Sir Anthony Mildmay, she ran their household, and she took a special interest in the poor, providing medical aid through her own study of "physic."

A godly woman who saw her troubles as providential, she nonetheless wrote an unflattering portrait of her father-in-law Sir Walter. Pious though he was, he cheated his son out of his proper inheritance. When he had forced Anthony to marry her, he had promised "before God" that "if thou marry with this woman

---

36 Frank Stubbings, trans. & ed. *The Statutes of Sir Walter Mildmay Kt Chancellor of the Exchequer and one of Her Majesty's Privy Councillors; authorized by him for the government of Emmanuel College founded by him* (Cambridge: Cambridge University Press, 1983), 25–6.
37 "De Mora Sociorum." Ibid., 95–6.
38 "Lady Mildmay's Meditations," Northampton, Northamptonshire Libraries, Phillipps Ms. 2569, 11–13.
39 Ibid., 10.
40 Ibid., 30–31. Linda Pollock, *With Faith and Physic. The life of a Tudor Gentlewoman Lady Grace Mildmay* (London: 1993), 42.

I will give thee all that I have, and whatsoever else I can procure, shall be thine."[41] After Sir Walter died, they discovered he had left half his estate to Anthony's brother, and founded Emmanuel College, Cambridge with much of the rest.

Emmanuel College was what Queen Elizabeth correctly termed a "Puritan Foundation" to evangelize the nation. Other collegiate founders had other intentions. When Dr. David Lewis, Dr. Hugh Price, Dr. William Aubrey, and others convinced Lord Burghley to get a patent from Elizabeth to create a new college at Oxford in June 1571, they seemed less interested in theology than in civil law. All Welshmen, and all civil lawyers, they proposed to use money provided by Price, whose will gave £60 a year for the purpose, to found Jesus College.[42] It may have been the intention of these founders to create a college for students from the diocese of St. David's in Wales. However, in the wake of Elizabeth's excommunication by the Pope in 1570, the patent founding Jesus College declared it was to propagate the true Christian faith, combat abuses, and end heresies. The number of Welsh lawyers among the foundation's future principals makes one suspect that they preferred to provide education in civil law for Welshmen. Certainly, by the early seventeenth century, that was the character of the college.[43]

The Welsh lawyers of Jesus College may have been told to dedicate it to repressing religious ignorance, but the universities were more relaxed about religion than might be imagined, at least in the beginning of the reign. After all, the right education was presumed to lead to the right outcomes, so it is expected that it took more than a decade to reform the curriulcum. The faculty was purged of Catholics, but Oxford did not have a list of approved religious texts for undergraduates until 1570. Though colleges were expected to catechize their students, the students themselves were not expected to take the oath of supremacy, accepting Elizabeth as Supreme Governor of the Church, until 1580.[44]

Because the oath of supremacy was not administered until a student graduated, Catholic boys could attend the universities, though they did not take degrees. They tended to concentrate in places like Oxford's Hart Hall, whose principal, Philip Rondell, a "papist in his heart," created a safe place for teachers

---

41 "Mildmay's Meditations," 37–8.
42 TNA, PROB 11/56, fo. 270v.
43 William P. Griffith, "Jesus College, Oxford, and Wales: the first half-century." *Transactions of the Honourable Society of Cymmrodorion, 1996.* New Series, 1997; 3, 21–5, 29. http://welshjournals.llgc.org.uk/browse/viewpage/llgc-id:1386666/llgc-id:1424937/llgc-id:1424962/getText [Accessed November 29, 2018]. Norman Jones, "David Lewis Founding Principal of Jesus College." *Jesus College Record* 2009; 33–42.
44 S.L. Greenslade, "The Faculty of Theology," in James McConica, ed. *The History of the University of Oxford. III. The Collegiate University* (Oxford: Oxford University Press, 1986), 296–7.

and students who disagreed with the puritanical bent of some of the colleges. As dependencies of other colleges, these halls did not have chapels, conveniently making the students' nonconformity invisible, since they had no church to attend. Rondell, who was not only the principal but also owned the lease of the hall, ran it for all of Elizabeth's reign, until he died in 1599. Hart Hall (now Hertford College) educated several men who became Jesuits and Catholic martyrs.[45]

The purpose of education was to develop students' critical faculties and skills, often in preparation for advanced degrees in theology, medicine, or law. All of these were based in Latin learning and humanism, helping their practitioners become expert in their technical disciplines. For instance, Dr. Lewis, the first principal of Jesus College, Oxford, had very clear ideas about how an education in civil law was to be conducted. He believed that students should know the primary texts before studying the secondary commentaries and theoretical works. Writing to his protégé, Julius Caesar, who was studying law at Paris, Lewis said he was "very glad that you have taken that course of study whereby you may con over the text before you enter into the labyrinth of the doctors or interpreters, for I would not have you cumber yourself ... before you come to practice." Caesar, when he became an active lawyer, would find the commentaries useful as needed. Trained in the humanities himself, Lewis belonged to the school that applied philology and history to legal texts, and he was pleased Caesar was doing the same.[46]

Lawyers often did not graduate from a university. They took a year or two of work in Oxford or Cambridge and then moved to one of the Inns of Court, to learn the common or the civil law by instruction and apprenticeship. They had to know Latin and be educated in it before they arrived, or else enroll in one of the Inns of Chancery, institutions which provided basic education and fed men into the Inns of Court. At the Inns of Court, they learned Law French, the language of the common law courts, and the arcane formal system of writs and forms used in litigation. There was a heavy demand for legal education, both for gentlemen who had no intention of practicing and for the expanding market in lawyers. Litigation increased rapidly in Elizabeth's reign, but by the end of it there was not enough work for all of the lawyers.[47]

Once they had learned the "Frenglish" of the courts, students could use textbooks like John Kitchin's handbook for "apprentices" in Chancery, *les cases et matters necessaries*. Kitchin excoriated the "serving men ignorant in the law" appointed by lords to oversee their local courts, whose ignorance could only be

45 Sidney Graves Hamilton, *Hertford College* (London: F.E. Robinson, 1903), 14–23.
46 BL Add. 11406, fos. 150–150v.
47 Craig Muldrew, *The Economy of Obligation: The Culture of Credit and Social Relations in Early Modern England* (London: Macmillan, 1998), 2–3.

cured by going to an Inn and learning Law French. Education was the only road to that service, Kitchin insisted.[48]

That same apprenticeship model created a demand for handbooks, each in the language of the appropriate court. For the Court of Admiralty, where Dr. Lewis, and later Sir Julius Caesar, were judges, or the Court of Arches, the ecclesiastical court of the Archbishop of Canterbury, the language was Legal Latin, a tongue as eccentric as Law French. A gentleman who was involved in an action in one of these courts needed both Latin and a civil lawyer who could navigate its thickets. In Francis Clerke's unpublished guide to the Court of Arches, there is a case that asks the hard question of whether it is an extenuating plea if the accused, having received a summons in Latin, cannot understand it.[49] Guides for practitioners were popular for all courts, because in all courts both lawyers and gentlemen going to law needed them. Those without legal training or a lawyer could buy "law for dummies" books that contained all the forms required for most legal actions, such as William West's *Symbolaeography*.[50] It was never too late to learn.

Youth during the Elizabethan age were prepared for life by institutions that taught obedience to God and their betters, readying them for their appointed roles. Ideally, they were taught to worry about how their lives should be shaped by God in an active engagement with His will as expressed in the Bible. As the reign went on, more and more children came of age uncomfortable with the traditional ideas of simple obedience and static roles. Not remembering the "old days," they were impatient with their elders, shaping a new conversation about the individual's relationship with God and society. This new conversation, embodied in theater as much as in theology, focused on conscience rightly used.

Since children were born as wild savages in need of correction and domestication, they had to be prepared to live their assigned roles, transformed into members of God's community in England. That transformation required struggle to overcome Satan and learn habits that made them good citizens of God's commonwealth. As they learned and lived, they were expected to conform to a hierarchical world in which they had a clear place in their community. Though the natural order had been disturbed by the Reformation, it was still assumed that their compass should be pointing the way to the New Jerusalem.

---

48 Kitchin, *Le Court Leete*.

49 Francis Clerk, "Practica celeberrima ac quotidiana observat[a] ac usitata in Curijs Reverendissim[i] Cantuariensis Archiepiscopi edita per egrigium virum Franciscum Clark unum Procur[ator]um de Archubus." HEH HM 35072, fo. 4v.

50 William West, *Symbolaeography which may be termed the art, description or image of instruments, extra-iudicial, as couenants, contracts, obligations, conditions, feffements, graunts, wills, &c. Or the paterne of praesidents. Or the notarie or scriuener* (1592). STC (2nd. ed.)/25267a.

5

Seeing the World Anew

In November of 1579, Thomas Stevens, a Jesuit from Wiltshire, sent his father in England a letter describing his seven-month voyage to Goa. Perhaps the first Englishman to set foot on the Indian subcontinent, Stevens recounted adventures with sharks and other strange sea creatures. The Portuguese pilot, though always sure of latitude, had to guess where they were "touching longitude," so they were lost for part of the voyage. They were nearly wrecked on the Cape of Good Hope because of a navigational error. The Cape was a land "so full of tigers and people that are savage, and killers of all strangers" that they had no hope "but only in God and a good conscience" if they were forced ashore. Arriving in India, he saw a people, nearly naked, who lived in a strange landscape. The fruits and trees were alien. "Hitherto," he said, "I have not seen a tree here, whose like I have seen in Europe." Even their beverages were unheard of—the wine of the palm tree and of a "fruit called cocos."[1] Stevens became famous in England for this letter; in India, he became famous as the father of Indian Christian literature, dying there in 1619. He was reporting a world unimaginable to his father's generation.

Though Elizabethans knew the world to be an unchanging, ordered place carefully built by God, they were experiencing intellectual and social changes that forced them to adapt their conceptions of reality. They did not give up on the models they believed in, but they had to reinterpret God's design.

Terrestrial Space

Elizabethans accepted their determined positions in social and metaphysical space, but their grasp of geographical space was much less precise. Most early mid-Tudor people had never seen a map. They could not have described the

---

1 "The voyage of Thomas Stevens about the Cape of Buona Esperanza unto Goa in the East India, Anno 1579" in Richard Hakulyt, ed. *The Principal Navigations, Voyages, Traffiques and Discoveries of the English Nation* (Cambridge: Cambridge University Press, 2014), VI, 377–84.

Being Elizabethan: Understanding Shakespeare's Neighbors, First Edition. Norman Jones.
© 2020 John Wiley & Sons, Inc. Published 2020 by John Wiley & Sons, Inc.

shape of the place they called England with any accuracy, and, though very aware of the seas that surrounded them, they could not have accurately sketched the shores of the English Channel or the Irish Sea. Nor could they accurately depict their village or manor. Their understanding of the heavens was equally fuzzy. From the 1540's onward, that began to change rapidly. New places were being discovered or described to the English for the first time. There were people alive in Elizabeth's reign who might have remembered the news of Columbus' discoveries, but English people were just getting their first glimpses of American, East Asian, and African peoples, animals, and plants. Geographical knowledge would improve across the century as modern mapping techniques were invented, surveying got better, and printing disseminated geographical depictions and descriptions, but most people's sense of geography would remain fuzzy, like their conception of the "outside" world in general.

In the 1550's, Thomas Butler, an Essex merchant, had to draw his own map of Britain as he collected information about distances, tides, and other things important to the movement of his wool. The one drawn in his commonplace book was based on the thirteenth-century Gough Map, which was the model for printed maps of Britain until the late 1550's. He may have known it from a version done by George Lily in 1546, later printed in London by Butler's friend Thomas Gemini (Figure 5.1).[2]

Butler's map has no fine details, and none too close a relationship to cartographic reality. It shows nothing of the newly developing world of mathematical mensuration that Gemini was to bring to London. It was not a tool for travels, but he had to make do with it. Had he lived just a few years beyond 1555, he would have seen a revolution in mapping that produced newer, more accurate, and much more varied maps of Britain, its regions, and its locales, down to the level of manors and towns. His children would have a much more precise knowledge of where they were on the globe, as well as on the island. The whole earth became a more expansive, better defined place.

This was caused by a mathematical revolution with a very practical bent. Richard Cortés, Gerard Mercator, and Abraham Ortelius on the Continent, and their colleagues Leonard and Thomas Digges, William Cunningham, John Dee, and others in England, were applying geometry to surfaces, trying to find ways to represent space. Mercator was a globe maker, naturally concerned about how to project the lines of latitude on to the curved surface of the earth, giving us the Mercator Projection that defined the world for Europeans through the late twentieth century. First published in 1569, Mercator's maps used a rectangular grid that allowed navigators to follow rhumb lines representing

---

2 Daniel Birkholz, "The Gough Map Revisited: Thomas Butler's 'The Mape off Ynglonnd,' c.1547–1554," *Imago Mundi* 2006;58(1), 23–47.

Figure 5.1 George Lily, *Britanniae Insulae Quae Nunc Angliae et Scotiae Regna Continenet Cum Hebernia Adiacente Nova Descriptio* (1546). BL K.Top.V, item 2. Credit: British Library, London, UK © British Library Board. All Rights Reserved/Bridgeman Images.

constant compass bearings. This let captains "plot a course" from England to America, or anywhere else, using compass bearings and sailing along latitudes. Sailing charts commonly showed compass headings, but getting one's bearings at sea was a complex job, backed up with dead reckoning based on expert knowledge of winds, tides, and currents. The lack of good charts for the British Isles before the 1580's meant that even the most informed navigators could make spectacular mistakes, like those that led much of the Spanish Armada on to the rocks of Ireland.[3]

Mercator encouraged his friend Abraham Ortelius in Antwerp to use his technique in the production of the first world atlas in 1570. With the publication of his *Theatrum Orbis Terrarum*, it became possible to see the known continents and their relationship with one another—including the fact that Ortelius believed there was a Northwest Passage permitting traveling west to China from Europe. The atlas' title page hinted at the new vision of the world it contained, since its allegorical figures of the five continents included a Native American (shown holding a European's head) and the rumored Magellanica (also known as *Terra Australis*), whose existence Aristotle had theorized, and whose whereabouts had been confirmed by Magellan's voyage around Tierra del Fuego.[4]

These maps and globes were extremely popular among those who could afford them. The inventory of the Earl of Leicester's London house after his death in 1588 showed a large selection of maps, globes, and pictures (the distinction between maps and pictures was unclear), including a chart of the world "made in fashion of a book" bound in vellum, and a "Globe of the whole word in a frame of wood."[5] Elizabethans were projecting themselves on to a round globe with defined continents, islands, rivers, nations, and towns. In the early 1590's, Emery Molyneux, who had sailed around the world with Sir Francis Drake, began producing globes for sale in London. Some, like the one now at Petworth House, had the circumnavigations of Drake and Sir Henry Cavendish marked on them. Molyneux wrote a work entitled *The Globes Celestial and Terrestrial Set Forth in plano*, which is now lost, but there is plenty of evidence for the impact of his handiwork on English conceptions of the world.[6]

---

3 Ken Douglas, "Navigation: The Key to the Armada Disaster." *Journal for Maritime Research* 2003; 5(1), 74–120.

4 Rodney Shirley, "Allegorical images of Europe in some atlas titlepages, frontispieces, and map cartouches," *BelGeo [Online]*, 2008; 3–4, 341–54.

5 Elizabeth Goldring, *Robert Dudley Earl of Leicester and the World of Elizabethan Art* (New Haven: Yale University Press), 306–11.

6 Susan M. Maxwell, "Molyneux, Emery (*d.* 1598)," in *Oxford Dictionary of National Biography* (Oxford: Oxford University Press, 2004). http://www.oxforddnb.com/view/article/50911 [Accessed November 29, 2018].

Christopher Marlowe beautifully evoked the influence of maps when, in *Tamburlaine Part II*, the bloody king was brought a map on which he traced his conquest to that point. But there was more: "Look here, my boys; see, what a world of ground list westward from the midst of Cancer's line, Unto the rising of this earthly globe." Dying, he laments, "And shall I die, and this unconquered?"[7]

It was an understanding that gave meaning to Puck's brag in *A Midsummer Night's Dream*, "I'll put a girdle round about the earth in forty minutes."[8] The audience, perhaps seated or standing in a round theater named The Globe, could imagine the earth as Ortelius, Mercator, and Molyneux had portrayed it.[9]

In 1556, Leonard Digges produced a book introducing measurement and instrumentation to an English-reading audience. It was clearly titled:

> *A book named Tectonicon, briefly showing the exact measuring, and speedy reckoning all manner land, squared timber, stone, steeples, pillars, globes &c. Further, declaring the perfect making and large use of the carpenters ruler, containing a quadrant geometrical: comprehending also the rare use of the squire [square]. And in the end a little treatise adjoined, opening the composition and appliances of an instrument called the profitable staff*

Digges' publisher was Thomas Gemini, the Italian instrument maker and map engraver living in Black Friars in London. Making sure the title page fully informed the customers of what the book would do for them, Gemini announced that he was in his shop, "ready exactly to make all the instruments appertaining to this book."[10]

The book's first half covered the geometry needed to make maps and survey land, using the tools of two poles (a.k.a rods or pearches[11]) and cords, but stressing Digges' newly invented "instrument geometrical." With it, you could measure mountains, valleys, fields, buildings, trees, rocks, or any other thing. Digges and Gemini were contributing to the new science of cosmography, with its emphasis on measuring for accuracy. As Digges said of this little book, it was now possible to measure anything accurately—if you used a long enough

---

7 Christopher Marlowe, *Tamburlaine Part II*, 5.3,ll. 147–48, 159.
8 Shakespeare, *A Midsummer Night's Dream*, II.1.l.175.
9 Victor Morgan, "The Literary Image of Globes and Maps in Early Modern England," in Sarah Tyacke, ed. *English Map-Making 1500–1650* (London: The British Library, 1983), 46.
10 Leonard Digges, *A boke named Tectonicon... conteynynge a quadrant geometricall...* (1556). STC (2nd ed.)/6849.5.
11 Pearche: a rod of a definite length used for measuring land, etc. Later: a measure of length used esp. for land, fences, walls, etc., varying locally but later standardized at $5^1/_2$ yards, $16^1/_2$ ft (approx. 5.03 m). Also called *lug, rod, pole. Oxford English Dictionary.* The "rod" became a standard in measuring land in England and America.

measuring rod to allow for nuances, since a tiny mistake multiplied many times over distance.

In 1559, William Cunningham, a medical doctor when he was not watching the stars, published *The Cosmological Glass*. Taking the form of a merry conversation between friends—Spoudeus, listening to Philonicus on how to correct compass headings using astronomical observation, says, "I thank you sir, for this, your gentleness, in beating these things into my gross, and dull head"—it illustrated the geometry and the instruments used for measuring the earth and the waters, and thus making a "mirror of the world."[12]

A useful part of this dialogue was the naming and explaining of the disciplines of cosmography, geography, and chorography. Cosmography mapped the universe, geography the earth. Chorography, a very popular Elizabethan genre, showed the parts of the earth "divided in themselves," describing the ports, rivers, havens, floods, hills, mountains, cities, villages, buildings, fortresses, walls, and other distinctive features. It was as if a painter did a detailed study of an eye or an ear, rather than the whole body.[13] To explain his point, Cunningham reproduced a chorography of the city of Norwich as it was in 1558, measured from a pasture outside of the town (Figure 5.2). On it, every building, bridge, church, and other feature, right down to sheep, was represented, along with the chorographer and his instruments.

These chorographic maps suited people who navigated by landmarks rather than by street names or grids. They gave visual form to knowledge they already had.

On the seas, you could not give places a visual form, so the market for texts on navigation was lively. At the beginning of Elizabeth's reign, the best navigators in the world were the Spaniards trained to guide their fleets to America and back. Their handbook, published in Spanish in 1551 by Martin Cortés, was known to the English merchant community. Translated into English, it was published in 1561 by Richard Eden as *The Art of Navigation*. Eden enthused in the preface about the possibilities in the undiscovered world—the mountains of ice in the frozen seas of the Hyperborean region, the rocks, islands, and rich lands yet unfound.[14]

At the same time, another Londoner, John Dee, was thinking deeply about geometry and maps. In 1558, Dee published a Latin book on astrology with the unrevealing title of *Aphoristic Introduction Concerning Certain Powers of Nature*. With a dedication to Gerard Mercator, seemingly associating the work with the great geometer, Dee's book called for the mathematical observation of the celestial forces that act on the earth. Using geometric optics, he argued for

---

12 William Cunningham, *The cosmographical glasse...* (1559), fo. 88. STC (2nd ed.)/6119.
13 Ibid., fo. 7.
14 Richard Eden, trans. *The arte of nauigation...* (1561), preface. STC (2nd ed.)/5798.

Figure 5.2 "The City of Norwich in England, 1558," William Cunningham, *The cosmographical glasse conteinyng the pleasant principles of cosmographie, geographie, hydrographie, or nauigation* (1559), between fo. 8 and 9. STC (2nd ed.) / 6119. Henry E. Huntington Library and Art Gallery.

a Euclidian astrology.[15] Dee would go on to be the great Elizabethan master of the arts of navigation, via astrology.

Richard Eden felt compelled in the preface to his *Navigation* to remind his readers that Dee's astrology had been wittily described by Sir Thomas Smith as "*Ingeniosissimam artem mentiendi*"—"the most ingenious art of lying."[16] However, since astrologers studied the motion of the heavens just as navigators and astronomers did, it was hard to distinguish between them.

Eden may have been right about astrology, but Dee was making important contributions to navigation and mapping. Odd as John Dee was, and as crazed about secrecy, it is not clear who knew of his work on what he called his

15 John Dee, *Propaedeumata aphoristica...* (1558). STC (2nd ed.)/6463.
16 Eden, *Navigation*, preface.

"paradoxal compass," invented in the late 1550's but not revealed until 1577.[17] Using this compass, he was solving the problem of navigation among the ice mountains of the north, supporting expeditions like that of Martin Frobisher, who was searching for the Northwest Passage shown on Ortelius' maps. The further north one sailed, the less accurate the plane charts showing divisions of latitude were, since the compass bearings were no longer accurate. Dee, thinking of imperial expansion, developed his compass to allow mathematical extension of a line infinitely. His stereographic polar projection showing the pole at the center and latitudinal lines as concentric circles, allowing navigators to use the radiating rhumb lines to plot a course.[18]

Elizabeth's realm was getting similar attentions. By the early 1560's, Lawrence Nowell, Anglo-Saxon expert and tutor to the Earl of Oxford, had proposed to Principal Secretary Cecil a national mapping project.[19] This resulted in the Nowell-Burghley Atlas, containing maps of England, Wales, Ireland, and part of Scotland for Cecil's personal use (Figure 5.3). Cecil annotated it with his itineraries in 1564–70. It had sketches of Cecil and Nowell on the cover.[20]

The public had to wait until the 1570's to get a clearer picture of the physical form of the realm, when Christopher Saxton began publishing his maps of all the counties in England and Wales. Using methods like those outlined in Digges' *Tectonicon,* Saxton, his surveyors, and his engravers produced a series of county maps, gathering them together in 1579 to create an atlas of England and Wales, the first published national map in the world. For the first time, an inhabitant of Leicestershire could mentally picture the shape of his county and see where boundaries were. He could even know where Wales began and England ended. Saxton decided that Monmouthshire was an English county, rather than a Welsh one—forgivable because the borders of the principality had never been established. Though people could now "see" England and Wales, only a few could read the captions. Perversely, Saxton's maps of England were in Latin, while his maps of Wales were in English.[21]

Saxton had created what they called flat maps: hills, rivers, and valleys represented on a piece of paper. It was a new, artificial way of comprehending what John Donne described as the "round earth's imagined corners."[22]

---

17 John Dee, *General and rare memorials pertayning to the perfect arte of nauigation annexed to the paradoxal cumpas...* (1577). STC (2nd ed.)/6459.

18 Lesley B. Cormack, *Charting an Empire: Geography at English Universities 1580–1620* (Chicago: University of Chicago Press, 1997), 98–9.

19 BL, Lansd. 6, fo. 135.

20 BL Add 62540, fos. 3, 4v, 5.

21 J.H. Andrews, "A Saxton Miscellany." *Imago Mundi* 2013; 65(1), 87–96.

22 John Donne, "Holy Sonnets," in Helen Gardner, ed. *John Donne. The Divine Poems* (Oxford: Clarendon Press, 1978), 8.

Figure 5.3 Map of Great Britain. HEH, HM 160, William Bowyer, *Heroica Eulogia*, 1567, fo. 141. Henry E. Huntington Library and Art Gallery.

Most people had little use for a map of a large place, but surveying was giving them maps of their possessions, and those were valuable. The period between 1558 and 1598 saw the evolution of estate mapping from rare and crude to commonplace and sophisticated. When Elizabeth began her reign, land holdings were described in written form, based on square measures of acres (of indeterminate scale) and relationships to adjacent properties. Sometimes there were panoramas, too, but nothing like scale maps. By the end of the century, maps provided representations of measured spaces. Under the patronage of Sir William Cecil, Master of the Court of Wards and responsible for leases of property all over the nation, surveying was strongly encouraged.[23]

These estate maps were important legal documents. At first, both parties in a legal dispute might produce a sketch map, and the local elders would be called on to say which was "truthiest." But by the 1580's, professional surveyors like John Lane were expected to produce accurate and impartial maps for the law court, rather than maps that represented what others took to be correct. Measurements were not partisan.[24]

The space in which English people had their being had become more "real," visible, and demarcated between the 1540's and the 1620's. It was, as Shakespeare put it, a "brave new world," but only because they could now "see" it.

Ethnography

Shakespeare's lines from *The Tempest* evoke another reality:

> Oh wonder!
> How many goodly creatures are there here!
> How beauteous mankind is! O brave new world,
> That has such people in't![25]

All the mapping crystalized ideas about people, too. Identity could be tied to an ever more complex map of ethnicity and cultural identity as knowledge of the world grew. Most Tudor people had no concept of race as a category. Race for them meant the genealogy from whence a person came, without being sorted by color. By the same token, their concepts of nationality were much less political than cultural and linguistic.

---

23 Peter Eden, "Three Elizabethan estate Surveyors: Peter Kempe, Thomas Clerke, and Thomas Langdon," in Tyacke, *English Map-Making*, 68–9.

24 Rose Mitchell, "Maps in Sixteenth-Century English Law Courts." *Imago Mundi* 2006; 58(2), 212–19.

25 Shakespeare, *The Tempest*, V.1.183–4.

When confronted by people of differing pigmentation, they reached for their Bibles and asked from whom these people descended after The Flood. Noah had three sons, Ham, Shem, and Japheth, and their children populated the then known world. Ham, cursed by Noah, and forced to serve the others, was considered the father of the peoples of Africa. Shem was the first Semite, father of the Jews and all the other Middle Eastern peoples. Japheth was the progenitor of the Europeans. The awareness that there were peoples who did not fit into these genealogies was disturbing to sixteenth-century Christians. Bartolomé de las Casas, however, relieved their anxiety by locating the American indigenes within Shem's children, the "lost" tribes of Israel. He was convinced the indigenous Americans originated in Ancient Israel, proving from the Bible that they were the ten lost tribes. It made them Jews, and therefore people favored by God and capable of conversion. They, unlike the children of Ham, should not be enslaved. He suggested that slave labor could be imported from Africa to replace the freed Indians. Pope Paul III confirmed this in a papal bull in 1538, but de las Casas was denounced as a heretic later because his writings detailed the violent conquest of the Americans. Elizabethans, who hated the Catholic Spaniards, approved of de las Casas' attacks on the Spanish empire. In 1583, his history of the conquest of the Indies was translated into English. Dedicated to the provinces of the Low Countries, then suffering the Spanish tyranny, it was subtitled, "Spanish cruelties and tyrannies, perpetrated in the West Indies, commonly termed the newe found world."[26] De las Casas informed the "Black Legend" popular in England, portraying the Spanish Catholics as diabolic.

In 1576, Martin Frobisher went searching for the Northwest Passage to Cathay via the Arctic marked on Ortelius' maps. At a first meeting with the Inuit, Frobisher's company gave them gifts and practiced a rudimentary anthropology, writing down words in their language and describing the Inuit as "like to Tartars." Relations quickly deteriorated, however, and the Inuit abducted five of the English crew. In response, Frobisher abducted an Inuit man— referred to by one of the Englishmen as "our new prey"—and took him back to England, where he died within days of his arrival. He was buried in hallowed ground in St. Olave's churchyard, London, after portraits and a death mask had been taken. He was, perhaps, the first Native American ever seen on English soil.[27] Unfortunately for everyone involved, Frobisher also brought back a rock that was believed to contain gold, sending him on further fruitless expeditions to the Arctic and causing endless law suits.

---

26 Bartolomé de las Casas, *The Spanish colonie, or Briefe chronicle of the acts and gestes of the Spaniardes in the West Indies, called the newe world...* (1583), "To the Reader." STC (2nd ed.)/4739.

27 James McDermott, *Martin Frobisher, Elizabethan Privateer* (Oxford: Oxford University Press, 2001), 143–9.

Africans were, of course, known. Unlike the Native Americans, they were the descendants of Ham, and therefore subject to enslavement. Few English people could have seen a black person, but they understood there was a market for them. In the 1560's, John Hawkins led voyages to West Africa, where they raided the coastal towns, filling their ships with "prey," and selling them into slavery in the West Indies. Hawkins made a great deal of money for his investors, including Queen Elizabeth and Sir William Cecil. His third voyage, however, was a disaster. Attempting to sell his captives in the port of Vercruz, he was attacked by the Spanish fleet and lost four of his six ships. Only he and Francis Drake got their ships home to England, in 1568.[28]

By late in Elizabeth's life, there is evidence that the African slave trade had entered popular consciousness, and that a few black slaves had been brought from abroad into England. The Court of Requests in 1587 heard an appeal from Hector Nunes, a Portuguese *converso* doctor living in London, who had purchased an "Ethiopian" slave from an English sailor. The Ethiopian refused to "tarry and serve him," and Nunes wanted his enslavement enforced by the court, or a refund. The court concluded that Nunes had no remedy in common law, since it did not recognize slavery.

Elizabethans did not have a concept of pigmentation as a racial divide, even though "blackmoors" and "niggers" were a known commodity.[29] It happened that the "sons of Japheth" were European Christians, the children of Shem were Jews and Muslims (and apparently Native Americans), and the family of Ham was cursed by blackness and given to idolatry. These religious distinctions functioned in ways that race might now. This made the categories of people fluid and confusing in the sixteenth century. People of all colors could be slaves in the Spanish and Ottoman empires, where religion and criminality—not race—were the categories associated with slaves.

This had the odd effect of giving early modern Protestants the impression that papists had never really been children of Japheth; they were Muslims *manqué* and the children of Shem.[30] No wonder the categorization system began to break down.

In the same way, ethnicity and nationality were not yet based on maps and political allegiances so much as on caricatures drawn from accents, foods, suntans, and eccentric customs. People were formed the way they were because of the effect of the environment on them. Rather than being racists, Elizabethans were geohumoralists.

---

28 Richard Hakluyt, Voyages (London: Everyman, 1962), VII, 53–62.
29 Emily Weissbourd, "'Those in Their Possession': Race, Slavery, and Queen Elizabeth's 'Edicts of Expulsion." *Huntington Library Quarterly* 2015; 78(1), 1–19.
30 Norman Jones, "The Adaptation of Tradition: The Image of the Turk in Protestant England." *East European Quarterly* 1978; XII(2), 161–75.

Influenced by the classical science of Hippocrates, English ideas about ethnography and race presumed that the Galenic humors expressed in a geographic location—moist, cold, hot, dry—shaped the people who lived there. Good-tempered people, according to this model, live in temperate climates where the sun's heat is moderate. In the cold north, said Aristotle, the peoples' distemper is caused by moisture trapped in their cold bodies, closing their pores and dulling their wits. It makes them large people, with deep voices, and whitens their complexions. Their thickened blood makes northerners as courageous as they are dim. Inversely, southern peoples are smaller, darker, and wilier.[31]

In 1576, these ideas were popularized by Jean Bodin in his *Six Books of the Republic*, published in Latin and French. Bodin became popular reading among England's learned community, though he was not translated into English until 1606. He had already endorsed "geohumoralism" in his *Method for the Easy Comprehension of History* (1566), and his compound of Aristotle and Hippocrates became common currency. Gabriel Harvey reported the popularity of Bodin in Cambridge: "You cannot step into a scholar's study but (ten to one) you shall litely [sic] find open either Bodin *de Republica* or Le Royes' *Exposition upon Aristotle's Politics*."[32]

All of this roughly made sense to Tudor people, whose prejudices against the Scots and the Irish fitted neatly into the model. But their use of classical authors, who placed the English, too, into the class of cold and doltish peoples, forced them to construct a way to turn themselves into "Mediterranean" types. The Romans, they believed, had "civilized" England, and England was now "civilizing" the Irish. Edmund Spenser considered the Irish to be, as Bodin and the ancients taught, Scythians. Northern people possessed of barbaric but sometimes admirable traits, they were hard to civilize, and, in fact, English people who lived long among them often reverted to barbarity. Since the English, before they were civilized by the Romans, were like the Irish, it was possible for English people living in Ireland to "return to their natural dispositions."[33]

This notion that the "natural disposition" of a people could be changed through civilization into something better would be applied by Elizabethans and their descendants to peoples all over the world. Wherever the climate was not temperate, there was an opportunity for improving civilization.

---

31 Mary Floyd-Wilson, *English Ethnicity and Race in Early Modern Drama* (Cambridge: Cambridge University Press, 2003), 23–66.
32 Edward John Lang Scott, ed. *The Letter Book of Gabriel Harvey* (London; Camden Society n.s., 33, 1884), 79. Despite his reputation as an anti-Aristotelian, Bodin (and Le Roy) kept Aristotelian ideas about politics and peoples common into the eighteenth century. Anna Becker, "Jean Bodin on Oeconomics and Politics." *History of European Ideas* 2013; 3.
33 Floyd-Wilson, *English Ethnicity and Race*, 59.

By the time English exploration of the New World got underway in the 1580's, it was deemed appropriate that a "scientist" and an artist join expeditions to record the discoveries and map the royal claims. Thomas Harriot was the mathematician chosen to go to Virginia by Sir Walter Raleigh.

Harriot, deemed one of the best mathematicians and instrument makers of the day, was hired by Raleigh to teach his captains the science of navigation before setting out on the first Roanoke voyage. Harriot sailed with them in 1584, spending a year in Virginia before returning to England with Sir Francis Drake in 1586. Though more interested in conic sections and algebra, Harriot wrote about what he learned of America on the voyage, publishing in 1588 *A Brief and True Report of the New Found Land of Virginia.* As a reward, Raleigh gave him land in Ireland, where he and Raleigh may have grown the first Virginia potatoes in Europe.

John White illustrated Harriot's *Brief and True Report*, giving English readers some of their first visual depictions of the New World (Figure 5.4). White, who became the governor of Roanoke Colony, painted a watercolor of the village of Secoton. Strikingly, he carefully depicted gardens growing Indian corn, pumpkins, sunflowers, and tobacco.[34] Those looking at the illustration in 1588 might not have been able to name these plants, but they shortly became very important to everyone in Europe.

Culinary Landscape

The introduction of alien foods from the Americas altered the way people ate, how they thought about eating, how well they could eat, and what addictions they had. Those Virginian foods and tobacco portrayed by White were the beginning of a transformative change in diet and land use in Europe.

It was a rare English person who tasted a potato, a tomato, or corn (maize) in Elizabeth's reign. These foods were American in origin and were just becoming known to Europeans. The Spanish and Portuguese began importing some of them in the earlier sixteenth century, but they took a long time reaching Britain.

John Gerard recognized the rarity of American plants, and the confusion about what they were good for, when he wrote his *Great Herbal*. Published in 1597, after years of research, Gerard, who "borrowed" much of its contents from continental herbalists, specifically set out to include the plants of the Americas in his book. He knew little about them, and had to fall back on his own research as gardener to Lord Burghley, whose great gardens were Gerard's laboratory. Gerard reported that he knew of "sweet potatoes" because he had

---

34 "Indian Village of Secoton," Plates 38 A & B, with commentary. http://www.virtualjamestown. org/images/white_debry_html/white.html#s38 [Accessed November 29, 2018].

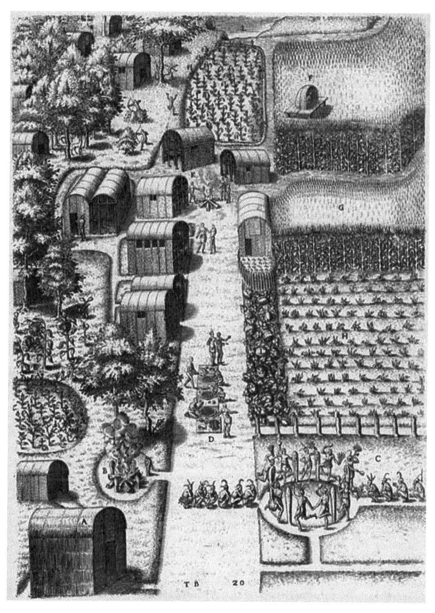

Figure 5.4 John White, "XX The Town of Secota" in Thomas Harriot, *A briefe and true report of the new found land of Virginia*…. (1590), np. STC (2nd ed.) / 12786. Henry E. Huntington Library and Art Gallery.

bought them in the Exchange in London, but that this "potato" had not yet been described by an herbalist. Another unknown variety of potato he recorded as recently received from Virginia, perhaps brought by Harriot. But were these alien tubers edible? He found that if they were roasted in embers and flavored with oil, vinegar, and salt, or boiled in wine, they were good.[35]

Gerard described another plant from the Americas that would take much longer to gain acceptance in England, *Frumentum indicum.* Also called "Turkey wheat," or maize, he noted this corn was less nourishing than the wheat, rye, barley, and oats eaten by Europeans, so it was a better pig food than human food. A good scientist, Gerard commented that there was no certain evidence of the "virtue" of this corn, but that "barbarous Indians," making the best of what they had, thought it was a good food.[36]

No one before the reign of Elizabeth had ever smoked a pipe of tobacco or cocaine. However, examination of chemical residue in the bowls of pipes excavated in Stratford-upon-Avon show tobacco, cocaine, and cannabis were all in use there in the late sixteenth and early seventeenth centuries.[37] John Gerard described all, explaining how tobacco had come from the West Indies.[38]

Far from Gerard's garden on Lord Burghley's estate, other Englishmen's minds were expanding as they encountered societies, people, animals, plants, and diseases new and foreign. Richard Hakluyt celebrated them in a series of publications that came together in his *The principal navigations, voiages, traffiques and discoveries of the English nation, made by sea or over-land, to the remote and farthest distant quarters of the earth,* which began appearing in 1589. Before that, he had published other books on America, and it was Hakluyt who arranged for Thomas Harriot's book on Virginia to be published in 1590.[39]

Hakluyt collected all sorts of information about the widening world, passing it to interested scholars. A major European publishing effort was devoted to describing natural history. As we have seen in Gerard's case, the English often appropriated the works of continental scholars and published an English version. Edward Topsell, a clergyman who wrote popular theology, got into the natural history business in the late sixteenth century, "borrowing" and publishing on four-legged animals. By the early seventeenth century, Topsell, though often paralytic in his right arm, was writing *The Fowles of Heaven or The History of Birds* for the popular market.[40] Lifting the content

---

35 John Gerard, *The herball or Generall historie of plantes. Gathered by Iohn Gerarde of London Master in Chirurgerie* (1597), 780–82. STC (2nd ed.)/11750.

36 Ibid.

37 Francis Thackeray, "Shakespeare, plants, and chemical analysis of early 17th century clay 'tobacco' pipes from Europe." *South African Journal of Science* 2015; 111.7/8, Art. #a0115, 2 pages.

38 John Gerard, *The Herball or Generall historie of plantes* (1633), 357–8. STC (2nd ed.)/11751.

39 ODNB, sub Richard Hakluyt.

40 HEH Mss EL 1142, fo. 3.

of continental authors, he added American birds to his book, making it unique. But how did he know about these species? In his description of the "Chuwheeo," he explained it was a "Virginia bird whose picture I received from that worthy industrious and learned compiler of navigations, whose praises will remain to the worlds end in the monument of his own labors, I mean Mr Hakluyt."[41]

Perhaps Hakluyt made money from his publications, but Topsell claims not to have profited. His histories of beasts and serpents, he said, were divulged to the world "to the Stationers great profit and my own impoverishing ... They are the men which are rich by making scholars poor: and scholars are poor by making them rich." But Topsell's hopes sprang eternal. He was optimistic for his book on birds, which was not finished or published before his death in 1625: "The swan singeth sweetest when he is old, and whitest, and peradventure my last labors will be sweeter than the former."[42]

Topsell's cosmography, by the time he was old and gray, must have been very different than that of his youth. People had learned to place themselves geographically; they were coming to grips with extra-biblical lands and peoples, confusing their ideas about creation and revelation. Even the heavens were being mapped, with disturbing implications.

Astronomy

There was a demand for astrological maps as working tools for astronomers, but astrology and medicine were the primary reason for mapping the stars. Simon Forman, long practiced in the science of medical astrology, "set down by experience" a 1603 table "To know in what place of the body every planet doth cause distemperatur [sic] or diseases and what part they rule."[43]

Whatever its purpose, observational astronomy was shifting the earth out of the center of creation. In 1543, Nicolaus Copernicus published his heliocentric theory of the universe in Lutheran Nuremberg, setting off a debate among astronomers across Europe. Many, like Tycho Brahe, tried to square the heliocentric theory with the Bible by positing a "geoheliostatic" system, which gave the sun two satellites and let the earth remain the center for the rest. Christoph Clavius, the Jesuit who led the creation of the new Gregorian calendar, liked Copernicus but stopped short of accepting his contradiction of the Bible, which says, in Genesis 1, that God made the sun and moon to give light to the earth, which was centrally placed in the vault of heaven. Moreover, the Israelite King

---

41 Ibid., fo. 85v.
42 Ibid., fos. 3v–4v.
43 Reproduced in Kassell, *Medicine and Magic*, 135.

Joshua had asked God to make the sun stand still, prolonging daylight for the massacre of the Amorites. God obliged, "so the sun abode in the midst of the heaven," proving it orbited the earth.[44]

In England, scholars were interested in the sun-centered model, and Thomas Harriot and Thomas Digges worked separately on the issue, perhaps with primitive telescopes. Digges, building off an older work of his father Lawrence, added a translation of Copernicus and a "perfect description" of the heavens that showed the sun in the middle, with the earth (a.k.a. "this globe of mortality") orbiting it, in 1576 (Figure 5.5).[45] Strikingly, Digges' map of the heavens shows the "orb of stars fixed infinitely up." It was an unbordered heaven of the sort known to people who had looked through telescopes and been astonished by the vastness of space.[46]

Harriot, who had publicized the Virginia project of Sir Walter Raleigh and developed a sophisticated algebraic system for navigational purposes, was making telescopic observations and sketching the moon. He became convinced that Copernicus was right in his heliocentric theory, and he theorized the elliptical motion of the planets. Many of his observations were done using a huge astronomer's cross staff. By the early seventeenth century, he had seen what Galileo saw and became a heliocentric.[47]

Luckily for Harriot, English churchmen did not find the Copernican theory worrisome, but they were bothered by the presumption that common men might learn more secrets of nature than learned scholars. Archbishop Whitgift understood that all this astronomy tended toward Presbyterianism. It was unnatural—too "popular"—to think mere Christians could have scientific authority.[48]

Most people, of course, knew of these geographical and cosmic explorations only vaguely, thanks to publishers who saw that the outlandish would sell. Matthew Dimmock sums up how the Elizabethans knew the world: "The combination of a contemporary cosmographical template, underpinned by a medieval system of categorization, with an obsessive interested in commercial possibilities, all qualified by an English Protestant sensibility, formed the dominant approach to both new and old worlds by Elizabethan writers."[49]

---

44 Joshua 10:12–13. Geneva Bible.
45 Leonard Digges and Thomas Digges, *A prognostication euerlastinge of right good effecte...* (1576), fo. 43. STC/288.03.
46 My thanks to Glyn Parry and Charlie Huenemann for teaching me about these issues.
47 J.J. Roche, "Harriot, Thomas (c.1560–1621)," in *Oxford Dictionary of National Biography* (Oxford: Oxford University Press, 2004); online edn., October 2006. http://www.oxforddnb.com/view/article/12379 [Accessed November 29, 2018].
48 John Whitgift, "The Defence of the Answer to the Admonition," in John Ayre, ed. *Works* (Cambridge: Parker Society, 1853), III, 273–5. My thanks to Glyn. Parry for pointing this out.
49 Matthew Dimmock, "Awareness of the Outside World," in Susan Doran and Norman Jones, eds. *The Elizabethan World* (London: Routledge, 2011), 668.

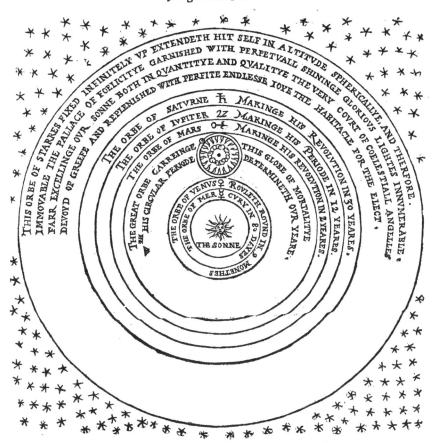

Figure 5.5 Thomas Digges' Copernican map of the heavens, 1576. From Leonard and Thomas Digges, *A prognostication euerlastinge of right good effecte…* (1576), fo. 43. STC / 435.51. Henry E Huntington Library and Art Gallery.

Dimmock is saying that Elizabethan knowledge of the world was predicated on preexisting ways of seeing, imagining, and defining. The natural way of making sense of new experiences was to put them into already labeled boxes constructed by the ancients. When meeting a new plant, for instance, John Gerard's scientific method demanded he ask if the Roman botanist Pliny the Elder had described it. The knowledge of "barbarous" people was discounted, while that of Roman authorities was always respected. But he also compared it to known plants. The tomato, he noted rightly, is in the poisonous night-shade family, and not to be trusted.

The discovery of the Americas and the un-biblical, un-classical people who lived there forced a rethinking of histories both natural and divine by European intellectuals. The newly found additions to nature had to be fitted into the creation described in the Book of Genesis. The existence of places, animals, plants, and indigenes not described in the Bible provoked biblical criticism on behalf of natural science. Clearly, all the peoples of the world had to have descended from Adam and Eve, so which of the sons of Adam had started the bloodline that populated the Americas?

Time

This sort of criticism encouraged historical research. As already mentioned, the most likely candidates for the Americans were the ten lost tribes of Israel, a solution proposed by Spanish theologians that put them into a known chronology, within a dating system that began either with Creation or with the Incarnation of Christ. This annual calendar was paralleled by the church calendar, which was based on the life of Christ and punctuated by holy days, feasts, and fasts honoring saints and important theological moments. Most English institutions used the church calendar within the year, so the legal and academic terms were tied to it. The law divided the year into terms that began with the feasts of St. Hilary, Easter, Holy Trinity, and St. Michael (Michaelmas). In theory, the Reformation should have undone this Catholic system.

The medieval liturgical calendar had been full of saints' days that Protestants rejected. Surprisingly, the English church kept some of them. However, the calendars in various versions of the *Book of Common Prayer* were never consistent. The 1559 prayer book had twenty-four saints' days. Some, like that in the Latin edition of the 1560 *Liber Preces Publicarum*—made for the universities and schools where Latin was the official tongue—included more holy days than contemporary Catholic liturgies. The 1561 version of the calendar, by Archbishop Parker, was different again, with fifty-five saints commemorated on black letter days. Though the list of 1561 became standard in later printing of the prayer book, the other lists remained in circulation. Of course, many

Protestants wished to reduce the number of holy days to just a few, such as Christmas and Easter.[50]

This same confusion reigned in the world of almanacs. Widely available in cheap editions, these annuals were used for all sorts of purposes, such as knowing when to plant, for calculating when bills were due, for legal reasons, or for religious reasons. Of course, there were also Catholic almanacs in circulation, so the calculation of days, times, and seasons was a muddle.[51]

The church calendar remained useful because it was seasonal. Counting by the number of days after a major feast, its commemorations generally fell in the right spot. For instance, the feast of St. John the Baptist always coincided, by a day or two, with the summer solstice, marking the longest day of the year. If you used the Julian calendar, that feast fell on June 11, not modern June 21, when the solstice occurred. For those who watched the seasons, the church calendar was more accurate.

The research of the astrologers and astronomers, led by Copernicus, had demonstrated that the calendar in use in Europe, the Julian calendar, was flawed. Over the centuries, it had become more and more inaccurate, making the true date of Easter further and further out of line with the seasons. The Council of Trent had authorized a correction, and Pope Gregory XIII declared that in October 1582, a new, more accurate calendar would take effect. The error accumulated in the twelve centuries since the Council of Nicaea was corrected by a deletion of ten days. The last day of the Julian calendar, Thursday October 4, 1582, was followed by the first of the Gregorian, Friday October 15 1582. Roman Catholic countries fell into line with the papal bull *Inter gravissimas*, and Protestants found their calendar differing from that of the rest of Europe.

Naturally, being Protestants, they had no desire to grant the pope authority over anything. In London, John Dee was summoned by the Privy Council to advise them on the issue, and he proposed an alternative, more accurate, solution to the calendar problem. The papal calendar, he claimed, was a recognition of the corruption of the Roman Church, so a good Christian like Elizabeth should lead Europe to true calendar reform by using Dee's calculations to get the date of the incarnation right, creating "Queen Elizabeth's Calendar," which corrected by eleven days instead of ten. At first, Elizabeth seemed ready to bring English dating into line with the Gregorian, but her bishops objected, there was political foot dragging, and in the end, it was not done. England's official calendar remained out of sync with Catholic Europe until 1752.[52]

---

50 Norman Jones, "Elizabeth, Edification and the Latin Prayer Book of 1560." *Church History* 1984; 53(3), 174–86. Phebe Jensen, Religion and Revelry in *Shakespeare's Festive World* (Cambridge: Cambridge University Press, 2008), 65–70.
51 Jensen, *Religion and Revelry*, 71–5.
52 Glyn Parry, *The Arch-Conjuror of England, John Dee* (New Haven: Yale University Press, 2011), 147–59.

As dates within years were disputed, so too was numeration of the years themselves. The Gregorian calendar fixed the beginning of the new year as January 1. England continued to date its years from Lady Day, March 25, so that historians must be aware of the difference between Old Style dates and New Style dates when determining when documents were written. Thus, March 1, 1590 in the Old Style becomes March 1, 1591 in the New Style. Though the papal mathematicians and astronomers were right, and English mathematicians and astronomers knew it, Protestant English people located themselves incorrectly in time because of theological hatred.

Of course, many of them expected the end of time very soon, and debates about time and calendar were intimately linked to estimates of when the end of the world would take place. One reason Lord Burghley liked Dee's calendrical calculations was that "he maketh his root from the very point of the nativity of Christ in the meridian of Bethlem [sic]; and the Romans have made their root from the time of the Council of Nicaea."[53] If you divide sacred history into fixed amounts of time, leading to the expected thousand-year reign of Christ on earth, it is important to know as accurately as possible where on the divine timeline you are.

Lord Burghley's assessment of Dee's calendrical work was based on research. He had studied the issue carefully in 1582, filling several folios with notes on different ways of calculating the lengths of years and days. Lunar months and solar months, months "natural," "legal," and "papisticall," civil years and sacred years were all compared. Historical methods of dating were studied, too. He noted all systems were subject to change because none exactly matched the "natural" year. Romulus, or Tarquin, established a Roman year, which was replaced by the Julian year of Augustus. Those years were not the same as Egyptian, Greek, or Hebrew years. The Egyptian year and the Gregorian "papisticall" year were 360 days long, while the Julian was 365.[54]

This sort of sophisticated thinking about time presented growing problems as scholars explored the history of the ancient world. Biblical time presumed a known date of creation that could be calculated by counting back the generations of Adam listed in Genesis. Unfortunately, the humanist enthusiasm for the history of the ancient world had led some to notice that Egyptian lists of kings extended much further back than the generations of Adam. This caused calendrical gymnastics by scholars, such as Joseph Scaliger in Leiden, to get the dating of the Bible to square with historical evidence. In 1583, Scaliger proposed a resolution in his *New Work on the Rectification of the Epochs*, which attempted to reconcile the calendars of all the ancient civilizations, creating a common dating system for everything that was independent of Christian time. When he had done that, however, he was faced with the problem that his scale

---

53 BL Lansd. 39, fo. 28.
54 BL Lansd. 103, fos. 29–40.

had to extend to a time before the calculated date of Biblical creation. Eventually, he posited an artificial scale of what he called "proleptic time." From the Greek, this meant "time before time," a seeming logical impossibility, but one which, Scaliger insisted, made Biblical time reconcilable with "Gentile" time.

James Ussher, a late Elizabethan scholar and cleric, took up Scaliger's work and carried it forward. Through painstaking biblical analysis, Ussher concluded that the date of creation was 4004 BC, on the evening of October 23.[55]

The Elizabethan sense of historical time and space was being overhauled in another way as England became alienated from Catholic Europe. Once, Europe was united as Christendom, open to the members of the common, Catholic faith. The Reformation had changed that freedom of movement as borders and minds closed. In the physical sense, no Protestant wanted to be found in the Spanish and Italian territories of the Inquisitions that kept Catholicism pure. As Elizabeth came to her throne, Pope Paul IV issued the *Index auctorum et librorum prohibitorum*. A guide to censors about what authors and books should be forbidden to the faithful, it was followed in 1564 by a Tridentine list.[56] Catholics were forbidden to read or print books by all heretics, including Luther, Calvin, and the English Protestant martyrs Thomas Cranmer, William Tyndale, Nicholas Ridley, and Hugh Latimer. The English responded in kind, attempting to stop intellectual intercourse with Catholics. As Lord Keeper Bacon told the Privy Council, justifying the proclamation against importing seditious books and libels, they made "men's minds to be at variance with one another, and diversity of minds maketh sedition, seditions bring in tumults, tumults make insurrections and rebellion. Insurrections make depopulations and bring in utter ruin and destruction of men's bodies, goods, and lands."[57]

Because many English Catholics fled to Catholic countries in search of religious freedom, and some returned to England as missionaries, there were efforts made to prevent free travel to Catholic areas. The map of Europe was being redrawn. To paraphrase Winston Churchill, a religious iron curtain was coming down across Europe. Though classical Latin culture continued among the learned, cities like Rome, once recognized as the goal of every educated traveler, had been made suspect and unsafe. Just as people could see maps that showed borders, some were becoming dangerous to cross.

---

55 Arthur McCalla, The Creationist Debate. *The Encounter between the Bible and the Historical Mind* (London, New York: T&C Clark, 2006), 29–33.

56 *Index Auctorum et Librorum QVI AB OFFICIO S. Rom. & vniuerfalis inquisitionis caueri ab omnibus et singulis in universa Christiana Republica mandatur... Romae 1559.* http://daten.digitale-sammlungen.de/~db/bsb00001444/images/index.html?id=00001444&fip=72.234.51.142 &no=7&seite=6 [Accessed November 29, 2018]. *Index Auctorum et Librorum cum Regulis Confectis per Patres Tridentina Synodo delectos... Coloniae 1564.* http://daten.digitale-sammlungen.de/~db/0003/bsb00031795/images/[Accessed November 29, 2018].

57 TNA SP 12/44, fo. 109v.

Anatomical Maps

The remeasuring of space and time was accompanied by observational mapping of anatomy. In 1543, the same year Copernicus announced that the earth orbited the sun, Andreas Vesalius published his astonishing seven-volume De *humani corporus fabrica*, with its detailed illustrations of the parts of the human body based upon dissections conducted in Padua. In 1545, Thomas Geminus pirated an edition of Vesalius and published it in England.[58] He did another edition in 1553, dedicated to Queen Mary.[59] Then, in 1559, he brought out a new compendium of anatomy, dedicated to Elizabeth. Published in English, complete with plates pirated from another source, it had the same name, but it was not Vesalius' work at all. His introduction explains delicately how we need to know our bodies because we are created in God's image.

Geminus' first illustration is of a nude man and a nude woman, both modestly draped (Figure 5.6). She is holding a little sign that proclaims "*nosce te ispsum*" ("know thyself"). In following illustrations, the flesh is stripped from them, and their entire anatomy is displayed.[60]

When Vesalius was working on his anatomy book, John Caius, re-founder of Gonville and Caius College, Cambridge, was living with him in Padua. Not surprisingly, Caius brought an interest in detailed anatomy home to England. A dedicated student of Galen, Caius wanted medicine taught through observation. In 1546, he began a lecture series at the Company of Barber-Surgeons that lasted for twenty years. Granted permission by Queen Mary to recreate Gonville Hall, Cambridge as a new college called Gonville and Caius in 1557, Caius asserted his belief in medical training based on empirical experience. His new statutes required his medical students to attend an annual human dissection. In 1564, Caius got a license from Elizabeth allowing the college two executed felons a year for dissection. The felons, after being "anatomized," were to be honorably buried in St. Michael's Church, with the principal and fellows of Gonville and Caius in attendance.

Thomas Lorkyn, Regius Professor of Physic at Cambridge from 1564 until 1591, was leading these dissections in the 1560's, as we know from annotations in his copy of Loys Vasse's 1541 anatomy book, *In anatomen coporis humani*:

> Anno domini 1565 the xxviii of March I did make anatomy of Richard [overwritten with the name "Rauffe"] Tiple at Magdalene College

---

58 *Compendiosa totius anatomie delineatio, aere exarata: per Thomam Geminum* (1545). STC (2nd ed.)/11714.

59 *Compendios a totius anatomie 20 elineation, aere exarata: per Thomam Geminum.* STC (2nd ed.)/11715.5.

60 *Compendios a totius anatomie 20 elineation, aere exarata: per Thomam Geminum* (1559), 7. STC (2nd ed.)/11718.

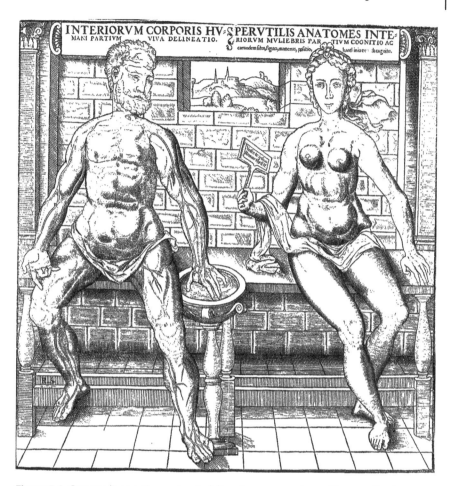

Figure 5.6 *Compendios a totius anatomie delineatio, aere exarata: per Thomam Geminum.* (1559), 7. STC (2nd ed.) / 11718. Henry E. Huntington Library and Art Gallery.

continuing Wednesday Thursday & Friday. forenoon and afternoon. from 8 til 11 & from 1 to 6 & on Saturday morning buried him chested [i.e. in a box] at 8 a clock being the 5th Day after his hanging.[61]

Present at Lorkyn's dissections, and presumably at the feasts that generally followed an "anatomizing," were several young men who would become leaders of Elizabethan medical circles. William Gilbert was there, probably fulfilling one of his requirements for his doctorate in medicine, before going on to a

---

61 Peter Murray Jones, "Thomas Lorkyn's Dissections, 1564/5 and 1566/7." *Transactions of the Cambridge Bibliographical Society* 1988; 9(3), 214.

brilliant career not only as Burghley's and Elizabeth's personal physician and President of the Royal College of Physicians, but also as a natural scientist. His *De magnete, magneticisique corporibus* (1600) became a seminal text on magnetism, making the first uses of the terms "electric force," "magnetic pole," and "electric attraction." All the time he was practicing medicine in London during the 1570's and 80's, he was making meteorological observations that would go into work posthumously published by his brother, *De Mundo nostro sublunary philosophia nova* (*A New Philosophy of our Sublunary World*). In his observations are notes on the positions of the heavens during the "great cold" of 1564, the hottest points of the summers of 1566, 1567, and 1568, and the humid cold summer of 1574.[62]

Gilbert's fellow medical student Thomas Hall was at the dissection because he was being educated at the expense of the Company of Barber-Surgeons. They had sent him to Magdalen College in 1566, and after he graduated, he returned to take up the post of Dissector at Barber-Surgeon's Hall.

The need for a dissector tells us a great deal about the way barber-surgeons thought of their job. They were not medical doctors, they were practitioners who (unlike doctors) touched the wounded and broken bodies of their patients. Surgery was defined as cures undertaken through the "right use and application of the hand." Thomas Gale, who was Master of the Company twice in the 1560's, remarked: "Surgery, for the greater part, consists in right use of profitable experiments: which require both long time in finding of them out, and also in obtaining their right use."[63] In his lectures to the company, Gale taught the treatment of wounds of all sorts, including his long experience, acquired during Henry VIII's wars in France, with wounds caused by the new firearms, which crushed and shattered bodies, frequently requiring amputation.

Gale had dressed those shattered limbs, and cut many of them off, cheerfully reassuring his patients that the fear hurt more than the amputation. His descriptions of surgery demonstrate that he learned by experience. When cutting off a leg, he reminded his colleagues, you must not let your saw fray the nerve between the tibia and the fibia. You should cut the nerve first, he warned, lest you cause spasms and even the death of the patient. He went on to describe the need to quickly stop the bleeding. White-hot iron applied to the stump of the limb often killed the patient with shock, so he urged the use of a cauterizing powder he himself had invented.[64] Gale's *Certain Works of Surgery* of 1563 was the first manual of surgery in English.

---

62 Suzanne Kelly, *The De Mundo of William Gilbert* (Amsterdam: Menno Hertzberger & co., 1965), 18–19. William Gilbert, *De Mundo nosto sublunary philosophia nova* (Amsterdam: 1641), 268–9.

63 Thomas Gale, *Certaine vvorkes of chirurgerie, nevvly compiled and published* (1563), 3 vols.; preface. STC (2nd ed.)/11529.

64 Gale, *Enchiridion*, in *Works*, fos. 51v–57.

Though Elizabethans were not at the forefront of those who were mapping the human body, they were in that generation of Europeans who, for the first time, got a good look at its mechanics. The Regius Professor of Physic, Thomas Lorkyn, left his large library to Cambridge University in 1591. It was to be housed in a special cupboard with two locks and only two keys. One was for the Librarian and the other for the Reader in Physic. In that intact personal library, we find Latin books from Leiden, Basel, Paris, Venice, and other centers of publishing and anatomy. Lorkyn was keeping up with the anatomical publications and disputes of the leading anatomists of his day, using their books to guide his dissections and teaching.[65]

Elizabethans were learning what the *microcosmos* of man looked like inside. Their ideas about the causes of disease and natural processes would change very slowly, but some of them, through their empiricism, led a reshaping of people's ways of locating themselves terrestrially, metaphysically, temporally, and internally. John Donne, born in 1574, brought all these senses of "mapping" together in a poem he wrote during an illness in the 1620's:

> Since I am coming to that holy room,
>> Where, with thy choir of saints for evermore,
> I shall be made thy music; as I come
>> I tune the instrument here at the door,
>> And what I must do then, think here before.
>
> Whilst my physicians by their love are grown
>> Cosmographers, and I their map, who lie
> Flat on this bed, that by them may be shown
>> That this is my south-west discovery,
>> *Per fretum febris*, by these straits to die,
>
> I joy, that in these straits I see my west;
>> For, though their currents yield return to none,
> What shall my west hurt me? As west and east
>> In all flat maps (and I am one) are one,
>> So death doth touch the resurrection.
>
> Is the Pacific Sea my home? Or are
>> The eastern riches? Is Jerusalem?
> Anyan, and Magellan, and Gibraltar,
>> All straits, and none but straits, are ways to them,
>> Whether where Japhet dwelt, or Cham, or Shem.

---

65 Jones, "Lorkyn's Dissections," 223.

We think that Paradise and Calvary,
Christ's cross, and Adam's tree, stood in one place;
Look, Lord, and find both Adams met in me;
As the first Adam's sweat surrounds my face,
May the last Adam's blood my soul embrace.

So, in his purple wrapp'd, receive me, Lord;
By these his thorns, give me his other crown;
And as to others' souls I preach'd thy word,
Be this my text, my sermon to mine own:
"Therefore that he may raise, the Lord throws down."[66]

Donne's poem evokes how the understanding of the physical world was changing for Elizabethans. God the creator is still in charge, salvation through the sacrifice of Christ is real, and the journey toward salvation is mapped on to the globe, the progress marked by the names on its surface.

All of this means that later Elizabethans were understanding themselves and their place in the world in ways unimaginable to their forbearers. Those born at the beginning of the reign, who came of age in the 1570's and 80's, knew a world in which their physical location could be calculated and displayed on a map; one in which their place could be surveyed and platted, just as they could see their insides laid open in a book by Vesalius or Dr. Caius. Their past was not their parents' past, and the purpose of their state was God's purpose in ways early generations would have found puzzling. Most of all, they were seeing themselves as microcosms in God's plan, each with a vocation and a conscience capable of discerning for itself right from wrong, true church from false. Individual conscience was becoming the standard, and was creating inescapable tensions over social positions and communal values. It was this debate over identity and propriety that drove the Elizabethan social machine.

---

66 John Donne, "Hymn to God, My God, in My Sickness," in Gardner, *John Donne*, 50.

6

Reimagining England's Past

Shakespeare's seventy-third sonnet, picturing "Bare Ruined Choirs, where late the sweet birds sang," evokes the monastic ruins that were scattered all over England—intentional ruins, stripped or repurposed by his parents' generation. The dissolution of the monasteries was a massive rejection of a past that reformers construed as a time of error and ignorance, best destroyed. The rejection of the papacy and Catholic theology after nearly a thousand years of English worship required a retelling of the national history to justify it. The Protestant re-creation of the Primitive Church demanded a new history for the True Church. Ideological divides within families, and new forms of social climbing, prompted retellings of family histories. Elizabethans invented new historical narratives to fit their changing society.

Elizabeth's reign opened with historical arguments about God, the right of succession, and the legitimacy of female rule. In 1558, John Knox published an ill-timed diatribe against the governance of Mary Tudor, Mary Queen of Scots, and Mary de Guise (the French regent in Scotland). Titling it *The First Blast of the Trumpet Against the Monstrous Regiment of Women*, Knox soon found himself barred from returning to England by its new queen, Elizabeth, for saying that "no woman can presume to reign above a man," and "the authority of all women is a wall without a foundation." He had proved it scripturally with the help of the Fathers of the Church, but Elizabeth was not impressed.[1]

Knox's title page declared, "Truth is the Daughter of Time." Fellow exile and Greek scholar John Aylmer, defending the new queen, took Knox at his word and shot back with a historical argument. Elizabeth was God's instrument, he asserted, declaring "God is English" and therefore would fight at her side. He maintained that Christ "as it were" had enjoyed a second birth in England thanks to Elizabeth, requiring all to obey him through obedience to her. Moreover, there were many precedents for happy reigns by women. He argued

---

1 John Knox, *The first blast of the trumpet against the monstruous regiment of women* (Geneva, 1558), fos. 15, 56v. STC/253:09.

Being Elizabethan: Understanding Shakespeare's Neighbors, First Edition. Norman Jones.
© 2020 John Wiley & Sons, Inc. Published 2020 by John Wiley & Sons, Inc.

with proofs from the biblical, classical, and English past, proving the power of history in battles over the truth. "If men will decide weighty matters," he asserted, "they must not only counsel with the Bible, but exercise themselves in ancient stories ... Wherefore, let no man disdain histories, or find fault with us, though we travail in histories about this controversy, for nothing better openeth it, nothing more confirmeth it, nor nothing sooner bringeth out of doubt, that is now brought into question."[2] In short, Elizabethan England had a past that could be used to defend the present and guide the future of what Aylmer declared to be a mixed polity in which monarch and parliament ruled together under law.

That English past was written employing the tools and models learned from Roman and Greek historians and now being applied to church history. The rigor of historical arguments based on evidence prompted Elizabethan scholars to gather records as ammunition in their fights over the meaning and trajectory of history. For the first generation of Elizabethan Protestants, history proved the papacy was the embodiment of the Antichrist. The task of Protestant historians was to uncover the pure, true form of religion practiced in the apostolic age so that superstitious accretions could be removed and the Antichrist defeated.

Over time, however, historical study contributed to the skepticism and confusion people felt about the old certainties. History became a tool evoking allegiances, feeding nostalgia, and providing entertainment. National history, in the hands of historians like John Foxe and Raphael Holinshed, came to the fore, and the Englishs' understanding of themselves, as seen in the mirror of their history, began to change.

History was important to Elizabethans because it could reveal the truth. Or, to put it another way, absolute truth could be found in the past. In a world in which everyone agreed that the Bible was true but disagreed about what truths it contained, history became the referee in theological disputes. Only by recovering the practices of the first, "primitive" Christians could the Bible be properly interpreted.

William Whitaker, Master of St. John's College, Cambridge, claimed history could redeem the Primitive Church. If the historical accuracy of the Scriptures was recovered, he claimed, "the truth itself, which we profess, would rise above suspicion ... and establish itself in the light and conscience of the world."[3] This truth, based on Scripture and recorded history, not on traditional customs or human ecclesiastical authority, used arguments about sources and chronology

---

2 John Aylmer, *An harborovve for faithfull and trevve subiectes, agaynst the late blowne blaste, concerninge the gouernme[n]t of vvemen...* (1559), Sig. [P.4v]; [R1v]; [E.4v]. STC (2nd ed)/1005.

3 William Whitaker, *A Disputation on Holy Scripture: Against the Papists, especially Bellarmine and Stapleton.* William Fitzgerald, ed. (Cambridge: Parker Society, 1849), 11.

to make its points. "History and the books of the holy fathers" were Whitaker's proofs.[4]

Whitaker was starting with the truth he knew to be true and reinforcing his testimony with historical "evidences." He was using a methodology established by the Lutheran theologians Matthias Flacius Illyricus and Matthias Judex, whose *Magdeburg Centuries* used historical evidence showing the persistence of the True Church in the face of papal corruption. Arguing for the necessity of church history, Flacius Illyricus set out a research project for himself and his co-religionist: to write the history of the church from the time of Christ's birth until the present, a history that would defeat the corrupt papists.[5] Aided by English scholars such as John Bale, Matthew Parker, and William Cecil, the German Lutherans had collected evidence from English history, dedicating their fourth volume to Elizabeth in 1560.[6]

Their idea of historical testimonies to the Truth was echoed by John Foxe in his *Acts and Monuments of these latter and perilous days, touching matters of the Church, wherein are comprehended and describe the great persecutions and horrible troubles, that have been wrought and practiced by the Romish prelates, specially in this realm of England and Scotland, from the year of our Lord a thousand, unto the time now present* (Figure 6.1). Foxe assured his readers of the accuracy of the history recounted, claiming the evidence was "gathered and collected according to the true copies and writings certificatory as well of the parties themselves that suffered, as also out of the bishops' registers, which were the doers thereof."[7]

Foxe's first edition appeared in 1563, becoming a best-selling defense of the English reformation, inventing the idea of "Bloody Mary," and giving the nation new heroes. These works of historical national justification were met by English Catholic historians with more history, struggling for the same effect. Knowing their Church was True, they, too, took historical evidence as proof.

Thomas Stapleton was a prolific Catholic historian in English and Latin, writing of the conversion of England to Christianity in *A fortress of the faith first planted among us Englishmen, and continued hitherto in the Universal Church of Christ. The faith of which time protestants call, papistry* (1565). In it, he provided a translation of Bede's eighth-century *History of the English Church and People*, arguing, forcefully, that Bede's evidence demonstrated that the

---

4 Ibid., 244, for example.
5 Matthias Flacius Illyricus, *Catalogus testivm Veritatis, Qvi ante nostram ætatem reclamarunt Papæ...* (Basil: 1556), "Epistola," images 13–14. USTC 619735. http://diglib.hab.de/drucke/alv-v-598/start.htm?image=00014 [Accessed November 29, 2018].
6 Norman Jones, "Matthew Parker, John Bale, and the Magdeburg Centuriators." *The Sixteenth Century Journal* 1981; 12(3), 35–49.
7 Quoting the title page of the 1563 first edition. https://www.johnfoxe.org/1563_titlepage.jpg [Accessed November 29, 2018].

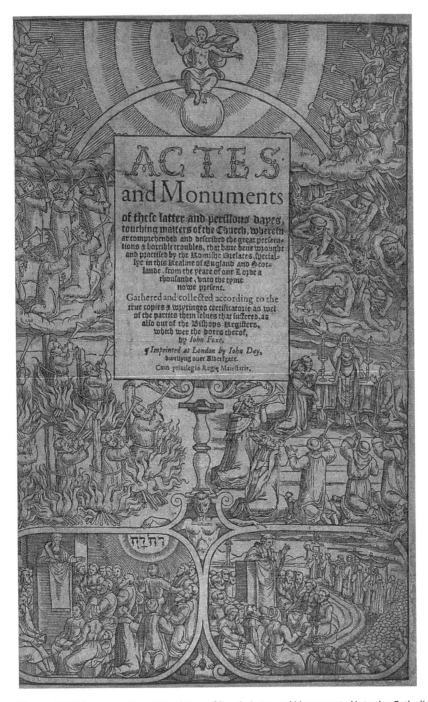

Figure 6.1 Title page of the 1563 edition of Foxe's *Actes and Monuments*. Note the Catholics on the right worshipping the Devil. The Protestants on the left are worshipping God. John Foxe, *Actes and monuments of these latter and perillous dayes touching matters of the Church, wherein ar comprehended and decribed the great persecutions [and] horrible troubles, that haue bene wrought and practised by the Romishe prelates, speciallye in this realme of England and Scotlande, from the yeare of our Lorde a thousande, vnto the tyme nowe present*….(1563) STC (2nd ed.) / 11222. Henry E Huntington Library and Art Gallery.

"corruptions" Protestants denounced were, in fact, the true practice of the Catholic Church in England. For the past 900 years, he asserted, English people had followed the true religion. Lying cold and indigestible in Protestants' stomachs, this history, he said, proved that "papistry" was true Christianity, and, therefore, Protestantism was heresy. The history of the church was the true fortress of the faith.[8]

Good theology rested on good history, and Catholic and Protestant scholars shared an unshakeable conviction that their party possessed "our truth." Thus, they needed detailed histories making that truth visible. As the Catholic scholar Caesare Baronio said in 1583, writing history was like making a mosaic. Just as an artist glued together stones and marble to create a picture of a saint, so historians glue together evidence to make visible the truth of theology.[9] This meant, however, that they immediately began to argue about whose historical account was most accurate. Catholics and Protestants accused each other of bad history. Conrad Bruno, a Catholic, insisted that the Lutheran Magdeburg Centuriators, to make their case, had betrayed the historical truth. Historians, said Bruno, were to describe and narrate what happened, not judge or declare what was false or true in the past. That, he said, was the method of doctrine, not history.[10] But the reason for writing history was to confirm doctrinal truth.

Responding to Onofrio Panvinio's reasoned historical arguments about whether St. Peter had been Bishop of Rome, someone—probably the book's owner, Tobie Matthew, Vice-Chancellor of Oxford and later Bishop of Durham and Archbishop of York—pithily summed up the polarity of historical debate: "*Immo inter verum et falsum non est medium*" ("On the contrary, there is no middle way between true and false").[11]

In these historical debates, there was one tie breaker: the Bible itself. It had to be translated correctly; if it was, then God's Word could be properly understood, and dissent would cease. By late in Elizabeth's reign, there was great scholarly and public interest in putting the Bible into proper historical and linguistic contexts.

---

8 Thomas Stapleton, *A fortresse of the faith...* (Antwerp, 1565), 3. STC (2nd ed.)/23232
9 Stefania Tutino, *Shadows of Doubt. Language and Truth in Post-Reformation Catholic Culture* (Oxford: Oxford University Press, 2014), 85–7.
10 Conrad Bruno, *Adversus Novam Historiam Ecclesiasticarum, quam Matthias Illyricus et eius Collegae Magdeburgici per centurias nuper ediderunt, ne quisque illis male fidei historicis novis fidat, admonitio Catholics.* (Dillingen, 1565), Sig. B5.
11 Onofrio Panvinio, *De primatu Petri et Apostolicae Sedis potestate libri tres ... contra Centuriarum auctores* (Venice, 1591), 210. USTC 846557. The book comes from Matthew's personal library in York Minster, XIII.L.30. It was featured in the exhibition curated by Stefan Bauer and Bethany Hume, "The Art of Disagreeing Badly: Religious Dispute in Early Modern Europe," The Old Palace, York Minster, November 15–December 15, 2016. https://social. shorthand.com/DisagreeBadly/uCUKGM1tKT/the-art-of-disagreeing-badly [Accessed November 29, 2018].

Biblical translation and history were a matter of national importance, and Lord Burghley pursued them. For his own edification, he wrote a complex genealogical table of the Kings of Judea, beginning with David, tracing the Maccabeans, the Assyrians, the Persians, the Egyptians, the Romans, and listing the members of the Sanhedrin. More than a set of family trees, this list contains a running historical commentary, adding notes such as the one that says that in the thirty-fifth year of Herod's reign, Christ was born, and in the same year, Herod murdered 40 000 innocents.[12]

Burghley was fluent in Greek and Latin, but his study of Bible history was hindered by his lack of Hebrew—though he was not sure Hebrew was necessary for a Christian Bible scholar. After all, if Jesus and the Apostles had quoted the Old Testament in the Septuagint Greek translation, was not Greek good enough for the English? In the mid-1580's, he summoned the Hebraicist Hugh Broughton from Cambridge to the Court for a three-hour discussion on difficult points of Greek and Hebrew. It was clear to both that some Bible translations favored papist interpretations of theology, and so a new translation of the Old Testament would be a good thing—but did it have to be based on Hebrew texts?

Broughton, a good academic, got patrons to pay for a new translation from the Hebrew. He claimed that many influential people, including Queen Elizabeth herself, had encouraged him to do it. Elizabeth, he said, had dispatched a footman to inform Sir Francis Walsingham that "some clearing of the Bible's translation" must be done. Broughton told Burghley that he thought the books of Moses needed little work but that "Job, and the prophets may be brought to speak far better unto us." To help clarify everything, a new Bible must have maps and chronological tables.[13] Broughton did not get the money.

Nonetheless, Elizabethan scholars took his argument to heart, seeking the kernel of Truth through the study of ancient languages. Lancelot Andrewes (1555–1626), for instance, made it his goal to learn one language every year.

Andrewes studied under Richard Mulcaster at the Merchant Taylors' School in the 1560's, and then went up to Pembroke Hall in Cambridge in 1571. A serious scholar, he became one of the greatest linguists in Europe. Having arrived at Cambridge with Latin and Greek, he added Hebrew, Chaldee (Aramaic), Syriac, Arabic, and fifteen modern languages to the list of those he could read.

As Dean of Westminster in the 1590's, he took a special interest in the school, personally instructing boys in Hebrew. In 1604, James I appointed Andrewes head of the Westminster Company of Bible translators, assigning his team Genesis, Exodus, Leviticus, Deuteronomy, and First and Second Kings. Four

---

12 TNA SP 12/255, fos. 116–30.
13 BL, Lansd. 75, fo. 8.

additional companies were created, with a total intended membership of fifty-four scholars.

Though the number of translators may never have reached fifty-four, it is telling that there were that many learned men available for the effort. Most of those appointed were born in the 1550's and 60's, coming to adulthood midway through Elizabeth's rein. Educated at Cambridge and Oxford, they were ordained clergy. They were learned in the various ancient tongues in which the biblical texts existed. Among them were scholars like William Bedwell, one of Europe's leading Arabic experts. A friend of Andrewes from their Pembroke College days, he spent much of his life preparing an Arabic–Latin dictionary. The number of scholars like Bedwell and Andrewes tells of the commitment of Elizabethans to the importance of words, historically understood, as a guide to God's intentions.[14]

The work of these learned committees produced the first edition of the King James Bible in 1611. "Building upon their foundations that went before us, and being holpen by their labors," the authors endeavored "to make that better which they left so good; no man, we are sure, hath cause to mislike us." Out of many good translations, they had produced one principal good one. One that would deeply influence English-speaking cultures.[15]

As Bible translations and historical research change people's perceptions, they became part of the national armory against heresy and papistry. Another very important part of the armory was the retelling of English history with a Protestant spin, stressing how the English nation came to follow God's truth.

Elizabethan historians knew printed books could create new historical memories, laying new truth over folk memory. John Aubrey, collecting English biographies in the second half of the seventeenth century, lamented: "Before women were readers, the history was handed down from mother to daughter ... when they sat up late by the fire telling tales."[16] Once they began to read books, the oral tradition died. And that is exactly what the polemical historians of Christianity wanted to happen: memory had to be changed, the "good old times" remembered as a period of ignorant superstition or glorious piety, depending on the theological position of the historian.

As a part of this process, English Protestants had to destroy the memories as well as the physical reminders of Catholic worship. Tradition, and therefore history, had to be eradicated. Superstitious remnants had to be removed from minds, ceremonies, and buildings, preventing idolatry. When Elizabeth came

---

14 David Norton, *The King James Bible. A Short History form Tyndale to Today* (Cambridge: Cambridge University Press, 2011), 54–62.
15 "The translatours to the reader." *The Holy Bible conteyning the Old Testament, and the New: newly translated out of the originall tongues...* (1611). STC (2nd ed.)/2216.
16 Quoted in Adam Fox, "Remembering the Past in Early Modern England: Oral and Written Tradition." *Transactions of the Royal Historical Society* 1999; 6(9), 236.

to the throne, all adults could remember the destructive see-saw of religious change. They knew how Henry VIII closed the monasteries and dispersed their books and treasures. They recalled the "cleansing" of their parish churches in the time of Edward VI, when stained glass, statues, rood screens, paintings, and embroidered vestments and altar clothes were destroyed. They remembered the cost of repairing that damage under Mary, when they were expected to put it all back. They witnessed another round of iconoclasm in the early 1560's as the Elizabethan church once more erased visual reminders of Catholic worship, and paid the cost of another set of physical alterations.

Much historical evidence was destroyed in these purges. Statues of saints, painted glass images of holy figures, rood screens, altars, and other things were removed, making it impossible to practice traditional worship in the churches. Books were destroyed as monasteries fell, and cathedral and university libraries were purged of the records of a pious, Catholic past.

The earliest leaders of Elizabeth's church were anxious to erase the faith of their fathers. Dramatic scenes of destruction were supervised by the royal visitors who toured the country enforcing the Injunctions of 1559, binging the churches into conformity with the restored faith. Henry Machyn, a draper in London, recorded how the Injunctions changed worship in the summer of 1559, putting the emphasis on the sermons, not the mass. Paul's Cross, the open-air pulpit attached to St. Paul's Cathedral, was central to the anti-Catholic propaganda. Machyn reported that on September 17, 1559, "Veron, a new preacher"—meaning a Protestant preacher—delivered a sermon to the Lord Mayor and a "great audience" on the theme, "Where are the bishops [and] old preachers? Now they hide their heads." That same month, he noted that the new form of morning prayer was being used, Geneva fashion, with congregational singing.[17]

Across Elizabeth's reign, students were catechized into knowing that the old ways of serving God were wrong, and congregations heard sermons and homilies against the worship practiced by their forebearers. As Thomas Bilson's character Theophilus the Christian tells Philander the Jesuit, "The faith of Christ we be bound to keep, the faith of our fathers we be not … The faith of our fathers is not always truth."[18]

The iconoclasm unleashed by the visitations encouraged destruction of tombs and other secular monuments within churches. People with hammers and crowbars smashed and pulled down all sorts of images, probably on the assumption that they were all superstitious—but also to sell the spoil. In the fall of 1560, Elizabeth issued a proclamation prohibiting the destruction of church

---

17 "Diary: 1559 (July–Dec)," in Nichols, *The Diary of Henry Machyn*, 202–221. http://www.british-history.ac.uk/camden-record-soc/vol42/pp202-221 [Accessed November 29, 2018].
18 Thomas Bilson, *The true difference betweene Christian subiection and unchristian rebellion…* (1585), 537. STC (2nd ed.)/3071.

monuments and demanding that the historical memories enshrined in churches be preserved. If they had been destroyed, the proclamation ordered that they be restored. People, "partly ignorant, partly malicious or covetous," it declared, had been breaking ancient monuments of metal and stone that had been erected "only to show a memory to the posterity of the persons there buried, or that had been benefactors to the buildings or donations of the same churches or public places, and not to nourish any kind of superstition."

This destruction of monuments and plaques erased knowledge of descent and inheritance. The tombs, statues, and brasses maintained the memory of heritage, and ensured the true course of inheritance. Therefore, it was forbidden to deface any monument, tomb, or grave "or to break any image of Kings, princes, or noble estates" set up in their memory. Sir William Cecil amended the draft of the proclamation to ensure it included a ban on breaking images in glass windows. As an afterthought, the proclamation also tried to stop church bells and lead from church roofs being sold, "making a hideous desolation of the places of prayer."[19]

William Harrison summed up the changes in the physical spaces of worship, designed to erase the old forms and put the emphasis on God's Word properly preached:

> As for our churches themselves, bells and times of Morning and evening prayer remain as in times past, but all images, shrines, tabernacles, rood lofts, and monuments of idolatry are removed, taken down, and defaced; only the stories in glass windows excepted, which, for want of sufficient store of new stuff and by reason of extreme charge that should grow by the alteration of the same into white panes throughout the realm, are not altogether abolished in most places at once but by little and little suffered to decay … Finally, whereas there was wont to be a great partition between the choir and the body of the church [the rood screen], now it is either very small or none at all and, to say the truth, altogether needless, since the minister saith his service commonly in the body of the church with his face toward the people, in a little tabernacle of wainscot [pulpit] provided for the purpose.[20]

As the churches were stripped of their Catholic worship aids and their spaces altered for preaching instead of Eucharistic liturgy, one of the whitewashed walls in each was devoted to a new decoration: the text of the Ten Commandments. Reminders of superstitious traditions were replaced by God's immutable Word.

---

19 TNA SP 12/13, fos. 77–79v.
20 William Harrison, *The Description of England*, Georges Edelen, ed. (Washington, D.C.: Folger Shakespeare Library, 1994), 35–6.

Reformers were obsessed with erasing "superstitious" worship, but their efforts were also destroying local history and identity. Closing a monastery, converting a holy well into a spa, erasing a saint's feast, or ending a pilgrimage had deep effects on the local populace. The community narrative was being intentionally disrupted, setting up a religious divide between the "time of ignorance," in which their forbearers lived, and the enlightened present, when God's Word was "more clearly revealed here in England than it had been many years before."[21]

The first half of Elizabeth's reign was spent forgetting and rewriting corporate and community histories. If there were no saints and no purgatory, the many guilds in English cities had to either close or change the way they explained their purposes. Community solidarity was traditionally maintained through veneration of a common saint and prayers for the dead members of the company. In this new era, the solidarity was needed more than ever, but it had to be repackaged so that earlier communal histories were deleted, and new ones formulated.

The London Grocers' Company, for instance, had St. Anthonin as its patron saint. Since the fourteenth century, they had venerated him on his feast day, May 18, maintaining an altar in his honor, where they held a requiem mass and dirge for departed members. By the 1570's, the Grocers had changed the feast into a dinner. They had changed the prayers for their dead brethren into a commemoration of departed benefactors. Noticeably, they had removed the old religious symbols from their company hearse cloth. Company corporate life went on as before, but by late in the reign, all echoes of its Catholic history had dissipated.

The Grocers' brethren in the Pewterers Company kept part of their historical memory, while changing the way it was celebrated. Administering a benefaction for prayers for the soul of Lawrence Ashlyn, a former master who died in 1546, the company performed a legal trick. Though his will required them to pray for his soul—to offer an obit or requiem mass—they wanted to keep the gift even if they could not fulfil the contract. So, they transformed his mass into another form of remembering. They struck out the word "obit" from their record and wrote in "bequest" in 1562. They carefully spent exactly the amount that had been previously used for the requiem mass to pay for a dinner for the master and two wardens in memory of Master Ashlyn.

One of the ways of telling the "new" history of these communities was through civic portraiture, celebrating the leading members over time as a way of recasting the history of guild, town, and college communities. As these institutions removed the relics of their earlier history and built new halls, they commissioned or were given portraits of their leaders and benefactors. Sometimes

---

21 Will of William Cecil Lord Burghley. TNA PROB PRO/11/92, March 1, 1597, fo. 241v.

commissioned in bulk, and often of low artistic quality, they taught a didactic history. As Francis Little explained in 1627, the portraits in the hall of Christ's Hospital in Abingdon preserved the memories of past governors, "whose precedent posterity should do well to imitate and follow, doing the like for those benefactors that shall come after, preserving also those that be already made, keeping also still their names and works upon record."[22]

Christ's Hospital in Abingdon was founded in 1553 upon the property of the Fraternity of the Holy Cross, a religious guild endowed in the early fifteenth century. It kept the town's bridges in repair and built an alms house for twelve "decayed" people. Sir John Mason, a local man educated by the Abbot of Abingdon who went on to be a councilor to four monarchs, oversaw the dissolution in Abingdon, and he and fellow townsmen converted the property from "superstitious use"—the inhabitants of the alms house had prayed for the dead—into a hospital doing what it had always done: housing the elderly and caring for the bridges, but without the prayers for souls in purgatory. Mason and Little saw Christ's Hospital as a continuation of a history of local charity. "It were to be wished that so many of the [governors] as God hath enabled would be good examples themselves to draw upon others, by extending and giving of their estates ... imitating and following therein the good examples of many that ... was in the like place of the Holy Cross as they are now in the Hospital of Christ."[23]

Because there were land titles involved, even the most ardent Protestants had to recall the days when Catholicism flourished. But remembering could be selective and done with thoughtful spins on history. A brilliant example of this is a strange manuscript entitled *Heroica eulogia*, produced by William Bowyer for the Earl of Leicester in 1567. Bowyer, Keeper of the Records in the Tower of London, was what amounted to the national archivist, so he had calendared the great mass of royal records. From that collection, he prepared a treatise proving historically Leicester's rights, promising "sometimes the truth comes to light unsought."[24] Bowyer's belief in the power of historical evidence led him to create new kinds of historical arguments, built around the factual evidence in patents, grants, charters, extents, and other legal records, in combination with poetry, painting, and coats of arms.[25] Like historians of the church, he believed that history, properly documented, told the truth.

Of course, historical research was important, because there were many issues concerning pedigrees, inheritance, and land roiling Elizabethan life that could be resolved with "evidences." Bowyer, as royal archivist, was competing with

---

22 Robert Tittler, *The Face of the City. Civic Portraiture and Civic Identity in early Modern England* (Manchester: Manchester University Press, 2007), 159–60.
23 Ibid.
24 HEH HM 160, title page.
25 HM 160, letter of dedication.

the College of Arms in the battle over documents. The College asserted a monopoly on family pedigrees, demanding all records be transferred to it. Serving social climbers who hoped to discover some reason to receive a coat of arms, the College sought a patent that allowed it to claim it was the place "where unto shall be presently brought all books and rolls of arms, writings and pedigrees and other records or precedents whatsoever they be in any wise touching or concerning the office of arms, being in the several hands and custody of all and every of the officers of arms, or any other, to the use, persons as they may conveniently be gotten."[26] Bowyer, of course, was not about to give up the records under his control in the Tower.

As the heralds of the College knew well, memories of local and personal history were selective. Families "rewrote" their memories according to their ideological preferences and political expediency. Catholics, now excluded from royal service in ways that made their gentle status suspect, constructed family histories that glorified their exclusion as proof of their faith. Portraying themselves as martyrs who resisted the Satanic decay around them, they created family folklore based on faithful suffering and duty. They also celebrated service to past monarchs and crusading ancestors.

The Shirley family history, as recorded by Sir Thomas Shirley, was one of pious Catholic sacrifices. Sir Thomas' uncle died fighting in defense of the Catholic Church against the Dutch and English. An aunt became a nun. His mother, dying in 1595, instructed that her five children should be raised Catholic. They all suffered financial losses and imprisonment.[27] Their family history was written to prove them to be good Catholics.

Other families celebrated stories about their ancestors' loyalty to Protestantism. James Whitelocke's father, a merchant, had died in Bordeaux in 1570. Refusing extreme unction from a Catholic priest, he was denied burial in hallowed ground. Outraged, the English merchants in Bordeaux loaded their guns and escorted his body to a decent burial in an olive grove. By recording the story, his son was reminding his family of their inherited duty to testify to and sacrifice for the true Protestant faith.[28]

But all families descended from Catholics, so family histories sometimes took odd twists, preserving important tales but cleansing them of their Catholic meanings. In 1607, Sir William Wentworth recorded the providences God had vouchsafed his family, including the story of how he came to be born in 1561.

Sir William, a Protestant, told how his parents had four daughters in eleven years, but no son. Suffering from a burning fever in 1560, his father, another Sir

---

26 TNA SP 12/42, fo. 135.

27 Richard Cust, "Catholicism, Antiquarianism and Gentry Honour: The Writings of Sir Thomas Shirley," *Midland History* 1988; 23, 40–4.

28 James Whitelocke, *Liber Famelicus of Sir James Whitelocke*, John Bruce, ed. Camden Society OS (1858), 5.

William, was visited by an apparition of a "well favored gentlewoman of a middle age in apparel and countenance decent and very demur." "Wentworth," she said, "I come from God." She told him he had many more years to live (he would die in 1588) and that he would have a son. Putting her hand into the bed, she anointed his privates and said "when thou are well, go to the well of St. Anne of Buxton and there wash thyself and thank God." Accordingly, he recovered, bathed at the well of St. Anne (which by then was Buxton Spa), and immediately begot his son William.

It was a story that both his father and mother liked to tell, but what was not included in William's 1607 account was that this seemed to be the intervention of St. Anne herself. St. Anne had answered their prayers and given them a son. The story remained, but St. Anne became an unnamed gentlewoman, and prayers to her went unmentioned.[29]

It is hard to know how English people got what historical and biblical literacy they had, but there are hints that even the illiterate had some. Nehemiah Wallington's mother, who died in 1603, was, he said, "rife in all the stories of the Bible, likewise in all the stories of the martyrs, and could readily turn to them; she was also perfect and well seen in the English Chronicles and the Descents of the Kings."[30]

That Wallington, a London joiner, could tell this story indicates the presence of new sources of popular knowledge about the Bible and the past. With the Bible now in English, with literacy increasing, and with biblical knowledge coming to everyone in the nation thanks to the *Book of Common Prayer*, biblical literacy skyrocketed.

So, too, did knowledge of English history, and publishers rushed to meet the demand for it. Edward Hall's *Union of two noble and Illustrious families of Lancaster and York* detailed the Wars of the Roses. Hall's printer, Richard Grafton, produced his own history in 1569, *A chronicle at large and meere history of the affayres of Englande and kinges ... from the Creation of the worlde, unto the ... first yere of the reigne of our most deere and sovereigne Lady Queene Elizabeth*. It saw multiple editions (Figure 6.2).

Raphael Holinshed's *Chronicles of England, Scotland and Ireland* was popular, too. First printed in 1577, it grew to three volumes by 1586. Though Holinshed died in 1580, his *Chronicles* expanded over time under the editorship of John Hooker, alias Vowell. It was a team effort, and included things like William Harrison's *Description of England*. Many of the leading historians of the era worked on "Holinshed," including John Stow.

---

29 Oxford, Bodleian, MS Top, C.14, fos. 83–4. J.P. Cooper, ed. *The Wentworth Papers 1597–1628.* Camden Society 4th ser., 1973; 12, 26–7.
30 Quoted in Ian W. Archer, "Discourses of History in Elizabethan and Early Stuart London," in Paulina Kewes, ed. *The Uses of History in Early Modern England* (San Marino: Huntington Library, 2006), 210.

Figure 6.2 Richard Grafton, *A chronicle at large and meere history of the affayres of England....* (1569), Frontispiece. STC (2nd ed.) / 12147. Henry E. Huntington Library and Art Gallery.

Stow, son of a tallow chandler, begin publishing summaries of chronicles in English in 1561. Prolific, his best seller was the *Survey of London Containing the original, antiquity, increase, modern estate, and description of that city, written in the year 1598.*

Beyond the history of Britain, universal histories laid out the chronology of the world, and biblical history was popular. But how did the illiterate learn them?

Some knowledge came from the pulpit, some from hearing books read, and some, perhaps, from common talk. But broader literacy in biblical and historical things came from the plays done at Corpus Christi Day or Whitsunday, when communities reenacted them. In Chester, the Chester Plays "were the history of the Bible, composed ... that the simple might understand the scripture."[31] These old plays came under attack in Elizabeth's reign, as did the maypoles and church ales, since they were associated with both idolatry and misrule.

In Coventry, the fifteenth-century Hock Tuesday play remembered the defeat of the Danish by the women of Coventry on St. Bride's Night, 1021. When they staged it before the Queen at Kenilworth in 1575, the players took the opportunity to beg Elizabeth permission to go on performing it. It had been yearly played without ill manners, papistry, or superstition, until recently, they said, when it had been put down by their preachers, who, though learned and sweet in their sermons, were "too sour in preaching away their pastime." They asked her to tell the preachers to stay out of the city's policy, and to permit them their historical commemoration again.[32]

As the miracle and mystery plays that had taught Bible stories and history to the illiterate slowly declined and died, they were replaced by performances with historical themes. Christopher Marlowe wrote plays that ranged throughout history, from classical, to high medieval, to contemporary. *Dido Queen of Carthage* reworked Virgil's *Aenied*; *Tamburlaine* told the tragic tale of the great Turkic conqueror; and *The Massacre at Paris* recounted the 1572 slaughter of French Protestants, including the philosopher Ramus.

Shakespeare did the same, putting classical lives based on Plutarch, such as *Julius Caesar*, on to the stage, as well as a string of plays about British kings, such as *Richard II*, *Henry V*, and *Macbeth*.

This kind of history grew from the humanism that had arrived in schools in the early sixteenth century. In the first humanist era, the history was didactic, teaching by example. An educated person learned Roman history straight from the Latin sources, reading Caesar and Cicero, Livy and Sallust. The great Romans were joined by other heroes of the classical world, such as the Persian

---

31 Quoted in Martin Ingram, "Who Killed Robin Hood? Transformations in Popular Culture," in Doran and Jones, *Elizabethan World*, 467.
32 Robert Laneham, *A letter whearin part of the entertainment vntoo the Queenz Maiesty at Killingwoorth Castl in Warwik sheer in this soomerz progress 1575 is signified...* (1575), 32–4. STC (2nd ed.)/15190.5.

king Cyrus the Great, known from Xenophon's *Cyropaedia*. This history taught children models for virtuous lives, gave them stoic philosophy, and provided a shorthand for orators. As Sir Henry Billingsley unexpectedly told readers of his translation of Euclid's *Geometry*, history is essential because it

> teaches us rules and precepts of virtue, how, in common life amongst men, we ought to walk uprightly: what duties pertain to ourselves, what pertain to the government or good order both of an household, and also of a city or common wealth. The reading likewise of histories, conduces not a little, to the adorning of the soul and mind of man, a study of all men commended: by it are seen and known the arts and doings of infinite wise men gone before us. In histories are contained infinite examples of heroical virtues to be of us followed, and horrible examples of vices to be of us eschewed.[33]

The rising tide of popular historical consciousness was accelerated by the reading of educated people across Europe. They, in turn, deployed historical analogies in relation to their local contexts. Thus, English people could talk as if England were a Roman republic and a monarchy, or the Roman Empire and a monarchy. But they were talking as Christians, with a distinct religious value system, and as members of a decaying feudal society whose political structures were far removed from those of Rome.

Reading Livy and Cicero, Plutarch and Tacitus, provided perspective on contemporary society. As Richard Rainolde explained to the readers of his *A Chronicle of all the Noble Emperors*, history taught how to rule. Quoting Cicero, he argued that good rulers attained great wisdom by reading history, just as Queen Zenobia—a special model for Elizabeth—had.

For Rainolde, the reading of history was "a spur to virtue, a bridle to repress vice in all that fear God. An history is the glass of princes, the image most lively both of virtue and vice, the learned theatre or spectacle of all the world, the council house of princes, the trier of all truths, a witness of all times and ages." History threatened evil rulers with infamy, and offered perpetual fame for their noble acts, making it "a bit and snaffle to the proud and ambitious, the learned school of princes, the book of princes, and their quiet and soft pillow to sleep on, the perfect description of the marvellous works of God, in the preserving of princes and common wealths, a pattern of all common wealths laid before our eyes ... He knoweth nothing that knoweth not histories."[34]

In talking of Elizabeth's divine mandate, Rainolde employed the Latin of the Roman republic, calling the book's dedicatee, Lord Burghley, "Senator." Ironically,

---

33 Henry Billingsley, trans. *The elements of geometrie of the most auncient philosopher Euclide...* (1570), "The Translator to the Reader." STC (2nd ed.)/10560.
34 Richard Rainolde, *A chronicle of all the noble emperours of the Romaines...* (1571), "Epistle to the Reader." STC/393:05.

in a book praising Elizabeth's providential authority, the dedication declares that her imperial commonwealth was blessed with wise senators—better protectors than walls and towers.[35]

John Smith, a young man who acquired a copy of Rainolde's history in 1625, shows us how the book was used. He annotated it, carefully inserting Christian dates into the lives of the Roman emperors, noting when Jerusalem appeared in the text. He indicated in the margins any mentions of Britain. He marked the appearance of "Mahomet" in the story, and noted "this is that Antichrist that denieth Christ to come in the flesh," adding references to the Gospel of John in the margin.[36] He wrote that it was a "practice of prelates to poison princes," showing how far bishops were removed from the doctrine of the Gospel, which teaches men to obey princes "even to the death."[37] It was clear that John Smith had absorbed the lessons that Protestant historians like John Aylmer were teaching. History amplified theological truth.

Elizabethans were using history as a source of moral models, but they used it as an analytical tool, too. Gabriel Harvey was employed by Sir Philip Sidney as a "discourser," teaching Livy as a model of political analysis. When young Thomas Smith was preparing to establish a plantation in Ireland in the early 1570's, he read Livy on the military operations of Hannibal and Scipio Africanus to learn how to command troops.[38]

History provided models and precedents, and so was critical in the great debates in law courts and among social-climbing families. In the 1580's, a group composed of lawyers, members of the College of Arms, and others who had legal concerns founded a Society of Antiquaries. It included professional "archivists," such as Robert Bowyer, Keeper of the Records in the Tower; Lord Burghley; Sir William Fleetwood, Recorder of London; William Camden; John Stow; and John Selden. They began reading papers on assigned historical topics to the club, delving into the records at their disposal, sharing books, and pooling knowledge. For about twenty years, they presented papers on things like the office of the Earl Marshall, the history of coinage, parishes, the laws of England, the Heralds, mottoes, lawful combats, the office of the High Steward, constables, the history of parliament, and other very English topics. Many of them were interested in ancient history, too, but in the Society, they concentrated on English history and institutions.[39]

---

35 Ibid., "Epistola Decidatoria."
36 Ibid., fos. 68v, 69, 168v–169. The marginal annotations are in the copy in the Henry E. Huntington Library.
37 Ibid., fos. 197–197v.
38 Anthony Grafton, What Was History? *The Art of History in Early Modern Europe* (Cambridge: Cambridge University Press, 2007), 65, n. 6.
39 Michael Stuckey, "'...this Society tendeth...': Elite Prosopography in Elizabethan Legal History," *Prosopon: The Journal of Prosopography* 2006; 1, 1–58.

The antiquaries' researches in legal history bore fruits that spilled over into their activities in parliament. They were building a sense of English historical identity based on documentation. Just as historical understanding of the Bible led to criticism of the historically evolved Roman Church, so history was useful in disputes about policy, precedent, and polity. Recognition of change over time made the present less sacred, less sure of its providential trajectory. Historical research eroded certainty and stimulated a faith in critical analysis.[40] As the translators of the King James Bible so clearly understood, historical context even affected the Word of God, requiring translations suited to time, place, and language.[41]

In politics, learning of the dark misdeeds of Roman emperors and decayed Roman morals gave people lots to think about. Beginning in the 1580's, Europeans became enamored of the histories written by Tacitus, the Roman historian who wrote the *Annales*, detailing the corruption of the early emperors. In his *Germania,* he praised German society as purer than Roman. In his biography of Julius Agricola, he described the geography and ethnography of ancient Britain, praising the virtue of the Britons over the corrupt habits of the Romans. Tacitus' books dwelt on the ways of corrupt fawning and flattering courtiers, as encapsulated by Tiberius' evil, scheming, favorite Sejanus. Tacitus provided a shorthand for talking about tyranny and corruption.

Tacitus' accounts of Roman operations on the edges of their empire fascinated Elizabethan military men in the detail they provided about how Romans and non-Romans fought, and the virtues of officers serving abroad. Campaigning in Ireland and the Low Countries, Robert Dudley, Earl of Leicester, and Robert Devereux, Earl of Essex, read Tacitus for his insights, and learned the value of decisive leadership.

When Henry Savile published translations of *Agricola* and *Germania* in 1591, he argued that military strength and a knowledge of history went hand in hand. At the same time, he drew parallels between the tyranny of the decadent Roman emperors and that of Spain's Phillip II. Tacitus was providing a historical way of talking about the enemies of Protestantism and the glories of great soldiers that made reading him very interesting to later Elizabethans. The Earl of Essex filled a notebook with observations drawn from his works.

For men who sought glory and felt the corrupt Court did not appreciate their virtue, Tacitus' Rome mirrored the world they saw around them. The Earl of Leicester, aggrieved at Elizabeth for not supporting his bid to be the Governor General of the Netherlands, and the Earl of Essex, smarting under her rebukes

---

40 Nicholas Popper, Walter Ralegh's History of the World and the Historical Culture of the Late Renaissance (Chicago: University of Chicago Press, 2012), 3–5.
41 "The translatours to the reader." *The Holy Bible* (1611). STC (2nd ed.)/2216.

for his conduct in Ireland, found Tacitean explanations for their troubles.[42] Their enemies, likewise, drew on the same Roman history to attack them. Later, at his treason trial, Essex was denounced through historical comparisons as "a Catiline, popish, dissolute, and desperate." William Fulbecke turned Roman history into an extended metaphor for Essex's treason in his *Collection of the Continual Factions, Tumults, and Massacres of the Romans and Italians* (1601). The Roman past was an accepted shorthand with which to talk about current affairs.[43]

The accession of James VI of Scotland as James I of England in 1603 created new historical enthusiasms. History was mobilized in arguments over his authority and in efforts to make a union of the two nations possible. The presence of a foreigner who did not respect "traditional" ways of ruling roused defenders of English custom, who invoked history in support of their cause. James, of course, came bearing a Scottish national past, too, with different origin myths that promoted differing understandings of the rights of a king. All of this had to be either squared or rejected, depending on the politics of the thinker.

William Camden, Clarenceux King of Arms in the College of Arms, envisioned the possibilities of a British union in a revised edition of his *Britannia*, a chorographical description of England, Scotland, and Ireland based on their antiquities. He had been working on it since Ortelius urged him to write it in 1577. In 1607, he added a justification of England as the leader of a composite British empire, headquartered in Roman London, embodying a pure episcopal religion older than the papacy, and culturally superior to the Gothic peoples of Wales and Scotland. Supplemented with maps, the book asserted England's superiority over the other peoples of Great Britain.[44]

Camden caught the eye of King James, who liked his description of how his poor mother, Mary Queen of Scots, was led astray by evil counselors rather than being bad herself. James asked him to write a history of England and Scotland in the reign of Elizabeth using Tacitus' *Annales* as a model. The year-by-year account allowed Camden to describe the things done without interpreting them too much, presenting the "facts." Lord Burghley had urged Camden to write a biography of Elizabeth, and had given him records to help, but it was James' interest that got him to do it in this less risky way.

---

42 Malcolm Smuts, "Varieties of Tacitism," forthcoming in Paulina Kewes, ed. *Ancient Rome and Early Modern England: History, Literature, and Political Imagination*. My thanks to Prof. Smuts for allowing me to see this pre-publication.

43 Paulina Kewes, "Roman History, Essex, and Late Elizabethan Political Culture," in R. Malcolm Smuts, ed. *The Oxford Handbook of The Age of Shakespeare* (Oxford: Oxford University Press, 2016), 262–8.

44 Allan I. McInnes, "The Multiple Kingdoms of Britain and Ireland: The 'British Problem'" in Barry Coward, ed. *A Companion to Stuart Britain* (Oxford: Wiley-Blackwell, 2003), vol. 5, 3–25.

His annals of England and Scotland in the reign of Elizabeth appeared in 1615, just as nostalgia for the old queen was on the rise.[45]

When he died in 1623, Camden left his library to Sir Robert Cotton. An avid collector of manuscripts, Cotton, who organized his books according to the busts of Roman emperors that stood in his library's bays, was a facilitator of research. As Camden's student, he had been an early member of the Society of Antiquaries in the late 1580's. In the late 1590's, he helped organize a drive for the licensing of a royal historical academy under Elizabeth's patronage, but it was not created. A member of parliament from 1601, he supplied his fellow MPs with evidence for their arguments, based on historical precedents, that helped them in their disputes with the Crown. Though he published little himself, he was favored by James I, who knighted him in 1603 (he was of Scots descent), and he supported the Stuart claim to the throne. With his connections at Court, Cotton acquired a wide range of manuscripts that provided grist for historians of Tudor England, then and now.

John Selden was one of those Cotton helped. As a young lawyer, he began researching the history of English institutions, drawing conclusions with constitutional implications. His 1610 book on the history of trial by combat as a means of judicial proof presented some of his research, but he had done much more.[46]

That same year, his *Jani Anglorum facies altera* was printed. A study of the ancient laws of England, it systematically explained the governing structures of ancient Britons and of Anglo-Saxons (hence, "*Both Faces of the English Janus*"). He demonstrated how they shared sovereignty among the monarchs, nobles, clergy, and freemen. They had, he proved, used assemblies for lawmaking and legal interpretation. Their kings called together their "senators" for counsel, as when King Arthur's assembled nobles ratified his (mythical) grant to Cambridge University. Anglo-Saxons, like the Germans cited by Tacitus, governed through parliaments consisting of kings, nobles, and commoners. All England (*pananglium*) was represented in the making of laws. Eventually, these assemblies came to be called "parliaments" by the Norman French, but they were a continuation of an ancient mixed monarchy of the best Aristotelean kind. This sort of history, of course, was a negative commentary on the political behavior of Stuart kings.[47]

Selden went on publishing historical studies of English institutions, including his history of tithes, which asserted that the church could not collect tithes

---

45 Daniel Woolf, *The Idea of History in Early Stuart England. Erudition, Ideology, and 'The Light of Truth' from the Accession of James I to the Civil War* (Toronto: University of Toronto Press, 1990), 116–19.
46 John Selden, *The duello or single combat from antiquitie deriued into this kingdome of England...* (1610). STC (2nd ed.)/22171.
47 John Selden, *Iani Anglorum facies...* (1610). STC (2nd ed.)/22174.

without the permission and support of the monarchy. Ergo, the church was a creature of the state. Tithe collectors were not "gospel officers." Selden was feeding the arguments made against the claims of the King for absolute authority with history, just as his colleagues were deploying Tacitean similes to complain about tyranny and corruption at Court.

The way Selden was critiquing the King was striking. He was making a claim for historical truth that stood apart from received truth. As he told Robert Cotton in his dedication, "Historical Truth" was to be found through diligent search in the records, not in "sterile antiquities." The purpose of this research was "to give necessary light to the present in matter of state, law, history, and the understanding of good authors." Rather than collecting Roman coins, he was looking at documents. And he was sorting them critically, skeptical of received traditions. He sought only "Truth," and he would not argue anything he could not prove. If his study led him to conclusions that were not popular, it was because examination of the evidence forced him to them.

He declared his creed:

> For the old skeptics that never would profess that they had found a truth, showed yet the best way to search for any, when they doubted as well of what those of the dogmatical sects too credulously received for infallible principles, as they did of the newest conclusions … [One who] takes to himself their liberty of inquiry, is in the only way that in all kind of studies leads and lies open even to the sanctuary of Truth, while others, that are servile to common opinion and vulgar suppositions, can rarely hope to be admitted of her Temple which too speciously often counterfeits her inmost sanctuaries; and to this purpose also is that of Quintilian, most worthy of memory, *Optimus est in discendo, patronus incredulous* ["The best lawyer is incredulous."][48]

All this historical study could be dangerous. It created tensions between the King and the magistracy, his government and his church. Dr. John Cowell, Regius Professor of Civil Law and Master of Trinity Hall in Cambridge, learned this to his detriment. As a civil lawyer, he saw the need to find ways to blend Scottish law, which used Roman law as its basis, with English common law. Of course, Roman law was also the basis of the Roman Church's canon law, so he was also squaring the Pope's law with common law. Cowell believed all laws derived from God's natural law and that, though English common law seemed mutable by judges, it was, at base, still derived from the same place. For him, this was an issue of translation: matching terms in Latin from civil law with

---

48 John Selden, *The historie of tithes …* (1618), Dedicatory Epistle; xii–xiii. STC (2nd ed.)/22172.7.

terms in the Anglo-French of the common law. If he could display their common roots and purposes, a blending was possible. Remembering the form of the *Institutes* of Justinian, with its short statements of principles of Roman law for first-year law students, Cowell digested the laws of England and other polities.[49]

In 1607, Cowell produced *The Interpreter*, taking the word list further. Though it seems to only be about legal terms, Cowell had, in fact, included all sorts of things that one needed to know to understand the historical context of the laws. Plants, places, titles, and customs joined the technical terms. Deeply read, he defined words through historical usage.[50]

But Cowell committed an unforgiveable sin. He treated England's common law as if it were just another historical legal system. Cowell's opinion on royal power was clear: "I have heard some to be of opinion, that the laws be above the king," but he denied this on legal grounds, citing ancient writs. The King, he said, was a law unto himself: "He may alter or suspend any particular law."[51]

This deeply offended members of parliament, who embraced Bracton's famous dictum that the King was under God and the law as a matter of faith. Sir Edward Coke, the Chief Justice of the Common Pleas, even charged Cowell with sedition. Finally, the King intervened. He imprisoned Cowell, ordering his book destroyed. Ironically, James used his absolutist power to silence a scholar whose argument supported his own beliefs about kingship. One outcome was that James declared his hostility to dangerous researches into the pasts of kingly secrets.[52] Such scholarship meddled where it should not.[53] This condemnation temporarily cooled the public discussion of English national institutions and history—but only temporarily.

In 1622, when William Camden founded the first chair in history at Oxford, he carefully separated "useful" history from church history. The professor, he wrote, "should read a civil history, and therein make such observations, as might be most useful and profitable for the younger students of the University, to direct and instruct them in the knowledge and use of history, antiquity, and times past." The Camden Professor of History was forbidden to intermeddle

---

49 John Cowell, *Institutiones iuris Anglicani ad methodum et seriem institutionum imperialium compositae & digestae...* (1605), 6. STC (2nd ed.)/5899.

50 John Cowell, *The interpreter: or Booke containing the signification of vvords...* (1607), STC (2nd ed.)/5900.

51 Ibid., sub "King," Sig. Q.q.1.

52 Brian P. Levack, "Cowell, John (1554–1611)," in *Oxford Dictionary of National Biography* (Oxford: Oxford University Press, 2004). http://www.oxforddnb.com/view/article/6490 [Accessed November 29, 2018]. Debora Shuger, *Censorship and Cultural Sensibility. The Regulation of Language in Tudor-Stuart England* (Philadelphia: University of Pennsylvania Press, 2006), 244–50.

53 James F. Larkin, c.s.v. and Paul L. Hughes, eds. *Stuart Royal Proclamations, Vol. 1: Royal Proclamations of King James I 1603–1625* (Oxford: Oxford University Press, 1973), no. 110.

"with the history of the church or controversies farther than shall give light into those times, which he shall then unfold, or that author, which he then shall read, and that very briefly."[54] There was now a civil history, useful to the magisterial classes, that was not about religious truth.

Thanks to the historical debates about religion and the models provided by ancient historians, Elizabethans became interested in the history of their own institutions. Maybe it was because ancient history created a comparative platform, or maybe it was because national debates over succession, religious separatism, and the location of authority in church and state led to new questions about monarchy and institutional history. All came in a package that encouraged collecting and publishing the ancient laws and constitutions of the British Isles. They learned new narrative models from the Romans, especially Tacitus, as ways of thinking and talking about the individual's relation to the monarch, duty to commonwealth, and the nature of tyranny.

By the end of the Elizabethan era, history had acquired a new, powerful role in the self-conception of the communities of the realm. Through the mirror of history, people could see themselves as the Christian martyrs, as embodiments of the Briton and "Gothic" founders of their nation, or garbed in the togas of Roman senators. Each of these histories gave them new perspectives on their contemporary roles and duties.

This discovery of the distinctive histories of the English faith and nation contributed to the emerging national narrative of community identity. If John Aylmer could assert in 1559 that God was English, fighting on England's side, then later Elizabethans could explain in detail England's unique relationship to God's church through time, even if they had varying interpretations of that history. Thanks to historians like John Foxe and scholars like the translators of the King James Bible, history was used to tell a new story about English people and their God.

The same tools created secular narratives of national identity. History could be used to assert English distinctness in reaction to Scottish kings, just as it could in response to popes. A new institutional history was emerging that cherished English institutions, celebrated them, and proved their goodness. At the same time, the narrative of national history—the victories of Henry V, the violence against Richard II, and the rest—became popular entertainment cementing English pride. History was giving the English a national identity that went beyond dynastic politics.

---

54 H. Stuart Jones, "The Foundation and History of the Camden Chair. By the late H. STUART JONES Camden Professor, 1920–1927." *Oxoniensia* 1943–44; 175. http://oxoniensia.org/volumes/1943-4/jones.pdf [Accessed November 29, 2018].

7

Living Under Divine Providence

Elizabethans knew that a loving, fatherly God used plagues, wars, tragedies, and other messengers to reprove them when they failed Him. But, though everyone agreed the world was ruled by Divine Providence acting in history, they were confused about the providential messages they were receiving. Unsure about the right responses to social problems, uncertain how to judge the "good," unclear about whether their greater duty was to themselves or their community, Elizabethans still believed that God was in His Heaven and all would be right with the world if they obeyed His will. Obedience took varying forms, but it was assumed that there was one right way, if it could be found, and that those who did not conform to God's will would provoke monitory divine punishment.

This led to deep disagreements about what obedience required. In politics, economics, social mores, and many other areas, people loudly and angrily strove to do what they considered appropriate, and to force those who disagreed into conformity with what they knew God expected, lest they all be punished. Conformity to God's will guaranteed a happy commonwealth; disobedience was the source of misery, individually and communally.

God ordered the world, frequently intervening to guide the lives of erring humans, because He loved them. But it was not a coddling love; it was a stern love. As St. Paul's Epistle to the Hebrews put it:

[6] For whom the Lord loveth he chasteneth, and scourgeth every son whom he receiveth.
[7] If ye endure chastening, God dealeth with you as with sons; for what son is he whom the father chasteneth not?
[8] But if ye be without chastisement, whereof all are partakers, then are ye bastards, and not sons.[1]

---

1 Hebrews 12:6–8. King James Version (KJV).

Being Elizabethan: Understanding Shakespeare's Neighbors, First Edition. Norman Jones.
© 2020 John Wiley & Sons, Inc. Published 2020 by John Wiley & Sons, Inc.

Difficult—even terrible—things might happen to people, but they could take comfort in the message God was sending. He loved them as a stern father, and they should show him the love and fearful respect due to a father who punished them to improve them. God was the adult in their relationship, and knew better than they what was good for them. His providential messages had to be heeded.

God's providence was nothing else "but a wise guiding of things to their end," and God, the "workmaster of all things," had created the world for His own ends and His own glory. Therefore, He directed the world toward outcomes that suited Him. It was certain that He had created people for a purpose, and that He would herd them appropriately.[2] "What else is Providence, than the will of God uttered forth with reason, and orderly disposed by understanding?"[3] But how could you understand God's providential interferences? Providential chastisements and rewards were allocated as needed or deserved, but it was very hard for people to understand why. What was He trying to tell them?

When catastrophes struck, opinions varied regarding what caused them. In June 1561, God hurled a lightning bolt at St. Paul's Cathedral in London, burning off the steeple and roof. God "sore chastised us, and let us well know that he which hath not spared his own house will not spare ours, except we repent our former wicked life," opined John Stow.[4] Others, especially Catholics, blamed the fire on God's anger over the return of Protestant worship. Someone wrote a tract blaming the Protestants and dropped copies in the streets of West Chester. It concluded that if the nation did not turn back to the faith taught by Christ's church, "God's vengeance hangs over your heads, ready suddenly to fall upon you ... let this burning of Paul's be an example and token of a greater plague to follow, except ye amend."[5] This provoked Bishop James Pilkington of Durham to rush into print a long, learned refutation. Using the entire history of the church in England for evidence, he concluded that God's message was a general warning to the sinful nation, just like the Viking invasions and the Norman Conquest had been: "except ye repent, ye shall all likewise perish."[6]

Some said sorcerers and conjurors had called down the fire, but they were dismissed with the argument that God had to give permission to the Devil to

---

2 Philippe de Mornay, seigneur du Plessis-Marly, *A woorke concerning the trewnesse of the Christian religion, written in French: against atheists, Epicures, Paynims, Iewes, Mahumetists, and other infidels*. Philip Sidney and Arthur Golding, trans. (1587), 174–5. STC (2nd ed.)/18149.
3 Ibid., 151.
4 James Gardiner, ed. *Three Fifteenth-century Chronicles, with Historical Memoranda by John Stowe* (London: Camden Society n.s., 28, 1880), 116.
5 "A Confutacion of an Addition, with an Appologye Written and Cast in the Streets of West Chester, Against the Causes of Burnying Paule's Church in London...," in James Pilkington, *The Works of James Pilkington, B.D.*, James Scholfield, ed. (Cambridge: Parker Society, 1842), 486.
6 Pilkington, *Works*, 487–616.

use sorcerers, so it was still God's doing. A small minority blamed workers who were melting lead to repair the roof.[7]

On the evening of April 6, 1580 an earthquake struck London. God, tokening his wrath and fatherly admonition, was sending a message interpreted by the Privy Council as a demand for the nation to turn from its sins. He had been gentler with London than He might have been, since there were only two children killed and some buildings damaged, but it was proof "That heaven and earth will shake, but the Lord will be the hope of His people [Joel 3:16]."[8]

In the summer of 1585, God decided to drown the crops and destroy the harvest because, though He loved England, He was tired of its ingratitude. He had blessed it with bounty and "no noise or terror of war, but deep peace within the walls of England." But the cry "of our sins so many and so monstrous" had forced Him reluctantly to send a warning through bad weather. National prayers were ordered to appease Him, but clearly He was not mollified, for in the spring of 1586, England began praying for relief from the dearth following the drowned harvest of 1585. Official prayers were distributed, recognizing that "there is great hope that he will withdraw his heavy hand and send a plentiful harvest" if people turned to Him in repentance. The rich were to moderate their consumption and help the poor; the poor were to "bear patiently" the hunger, seeing it proceeded from God's visitation.[9]

In 1603, 13 436 Londoners died of the plague, mostly in the densely populated, poorer areas of East London, where refugees crowded around the rat-infested grain warehouses. The cause, said the Reverend Henry Clapham, was God. Those who died, died through lack of faith. Those who trusted God, were protected by God. The Reverend Lancelot Andrewes rejected the most absolute part of Clapham's interpretation, insisting that quarantines and flight were permissible to Christians, but "there is no mortality, but by and from a supernatural source."[10]

The list of God-given horrors goes on and on. Elizabethans lived in a world filled with suffering, violence, and evil. Children died in great numbers. Plagues and famines killed thousands at a time. Women frequently died in childbirth. Public executions, intentionally horrifying, were common. In warfare, indiscriminate killing, sexual violation, and pillage were normal. Poverty was treated as a crime unless it was caused by physical deformities, old age, or orphanhood.

---

7 Norman Jones, *The Birth of the Elizabethan Age. England in the 1560's* (Oxford: Blackwell, 1993), 44.

8 Natalie Mears, Alasdair Raffe, Stephen Taylor, and Philip Williamson (with Lucy Bates), eds. *National Prayers. Special Worship Since the Reformation. Volume 1. Special Prayers, Fasts and Thanksgivings in the British Isles 1533–1688*, vol. 20 (London: Church of England Record Society, 2013), 140–152.

9 Ibid., 156–63.

10 Paul Slack, *The Impact of Plague in Tudor and Stuart England* (Oxford: Clarendon Press, 1990), 158, 233–5.

All people, stained with original sin, were wicked, greedy, oppressive, and self-obsessed, committing evil individually and in groups. They sinned in what they did, and in what they left undone. They broke God's laws and they refused to act on God's commands. They did not fear God enough to obey Him.

Human disobedience that provoked divine correction explained why bad things happened. An active, loving God, paying close attention to the actions of people and communities, corrected them with national and personal disasters if they failed to obey His laws.

The necessary fear of God was taught assiduously. Musicians, poets, and preachers in England and abroad dwelt on it. The *Lamentations of Jeremiah*, sad Hebrew poems about the fall of Jerusalem, were frequently taken as instructive texts. Portraying the city as a widow overcome with misery, mourning the desolation wrought by God as punishment for its sins, Jeremiah demanded that Jerusalem repent. Leading composers such as Thomas Tallis and William Byrd set the laments to music for the Queen's chapel, as did anonymous composers, while poets translated them into English.[11] A 1587 songbook hymned the moral of Jerusalem's lament:

> Shall we forever be forgot?
> Wilt thou no mercy take?
> Oh why doest thou O Lord so long,
> Thy children dear forsake?
> Turn thou to us, O Lord, and we
> To thee shall turned be:
> Renew our days as heretofore
> That we may worship thee.[12]

Being reminded to worship God properly was a key lesson of providential tribulations. Dr. Edward Craddock, Reader in Divinity, was in Oxford when plague broke out. His neighbor "through the wall" fell ill, followed by his washerwoman, and so he fled Oxford into a self-imposed exile, in keeping with the plague maxim, "flee far, stay long, return slowly." But he was not worried. Recalling God's providence, his mind was not "brought out of quietness." The fact that he was healthy meant God was saving him for a purpose, which he divined to be the writing of a book showing God's providential government of the world. It was his task to encourage a comforting fear of God.[13]

---

11 Hilaire Kallendorf, "Tears in the Desert: Baroque Adaptations of the Book of Lamentations by John Donne and Francisco de Quevedo." *Journal of Medieval and Early Modern Studies* 2009; 39.1(31), 40 n. 4, 42.

12 Anon. *The Lamentations of Jeremie in Meeter. With apt notes to sing them withal* (1587), 82. STC/2108:10.

13 Edward Craddock, *The shippe of assured safetie wherein wee may sayle without danger towards the land of the liuing...* (1572), "To the Christian Reader." STC (2nd ed.)/5952.

Providence, he declared, means that God attends to the world, while allowing free will to perform actions that conform or depart from His will. God's providence holds creation together, working in all creatures according to their natural callings, from flies and gnats to men and angels.[14] By those natures, we are governed; therefore, we must know our nature and live by it. A part of knowing our human nature is unquestioningly accepting God's mysterious wisdom displayed in His providence. The more we try to know God's providence, says Craddock, the more we are beset with "darkness and misty clouds," since our nature is not God's nature.[15]

After nearly 500 pages, Craddock concludes that we must build on the rock of God's providence, shaking off sluggishness in God's service "as the chief root and occasion of all evil" and lifting our hearts to God. He concludes with a fine prayer asking God to keep our souls from being snatched by Satan, who, "like a wily kite," is ready to pounce.[16]

Most people tried other remedies against their fears of disease, suffering, and loss, too. Prayer was a fine defense, but what else should one do for oneself? Was it permissible to take up arms against your sea of troubles? Just as Craddock fled the plague rather than blissfully remaining in Oxford, secure in his faith that God would not take him, so everyone needed to respond to divinely sent tribulation as reason and opportunity dictated. That is what God wanted, even though those who got it wrong were still liable to His chastisement. God may have had other plans. God often sent troubles to individuals who, though they tried, did not understand His desires correctly.

In the spring of 1604, John Dowland dedicated a "sad" book of music to his new queen, Anne of Denmark, the wife of James I. Stuck at home in London, waiting for fair winds so that he could sail to Denmark, where he worked for Anne's brother, King Christian IV, Dowland produced a part book of consort music entitled *Septem Lachrimae* (*Seven Tears*). Though he insisted that tears could be joyful as well as sad, these slow pavans had striking titles: "Semper Dowland, Semper Dolens" ("Always Dowland, Always Grieving") and "Sir Henry Unton's Funeral" exemplify their melancholy tone.

The title page proclaimed the problem: "*Aut furit, aut lachrimat, quem non Fortuna beavit*" ("*He that Fortune has Not Blessed Must Either Rage or Weep*"). To drive home the point, a woodcut in the center of the page bears the motto, paraphrasing Genesis 3:19, "Thou shalt Labor For," with doves unfurling banners reading "peace" and "plenty" and God's hands delivering the Bible and a bundle of chastising rods to a standing figure.[17]

---

14 Ibid., 357–63.
15 Ibid., 376–7.
16 Ibid., 498–9.
17 John Dowland, *Lachrimae, or Seauen teares figured in seauen passionate pauans...* (1604). STC (2nd ed.)/7097.

Dowland, though famous to contemporaries as a lutenist and composer, had suffered exile and religious persecution because God's hand was upon him. By his own account, he converted to Catholicism about 1580 while serving Sir Henry Cobham, the ambassador to France. "I fell acquainted," he told Sir Robert Cecil, with several men who "thrust many idle toys into my head of religion, saying that the Papists' was the truth and ours in England all false." His Catholicism prevented him from getting a job as one of the Queen's musicians, and forced him to work on the Continent, where he met wicked priests and Jesuits. Hearing their plotting, he gave up his Catholicism, and, though he turned informer, his attempts to get work in England were frustrated, forcing him to make his living abroad once again.[18]

Unable to get the rewards he sought, he referred to himself as the "*infoelice Inglese*" ("*unhappy Englishman*") and put a Latin quote from Ovid's *Metamorphoses* on his first book of songs, declaring "The arts don't help the master of the arts which help everyone else." He was, said Henry Peacham, a contemporary, a man who "slipt many opportunities for advancing his fortune."[19] Dowland was always doleful about how hard he had to work, recognizing that God laid His heavy fatherly hand on him for his disobedience and stubbornness. Dowland's life was a warning to others about the wages of sin. Do what he could, he still suffered by God's will—but he had to keep striving, hoping God might vouchsafe him something better.

Good fortune was also God's to grant. Sir Robert Carey was deeply aware of his blessings. A cousin of Queen Elizabeth, he was the Warden of the Middle Marches and a member of the Council of the North in her reign. When Elizabeth died, he carried the news to King James, hoping to secure work, since he was no longer needed to guard the northern border. "Now was to begin a new world," he wrote. "I relied on God and the King. The one never left me, the other shortly after his coming to London deceived my expectation." God, his ready help, "put it into my mind" to go to Dunfermline to visit little Prince Charles, a weak child whom no one expected to live. He and his wife were made Charles' keepers, and "my gracious God left me not, but out of weakness he showed his strength, and so blessed the Duke [Charles]" that he became strong and healthy. Eventually, after many Court intrigues, "God so blessed me," that he became Master of the Robes for Charles. He died Earl of Monmouth. Carey's sense of God's providence is palpable.[20]

Carey knew that God had make Prince Charles into a strong boy, despite misguided medical attempts to cure him, for health, like illness, came from

---

18 CP 172/91.
19 Quoted in Diana Poulton, *The Life of John Dowland*, 2nd ed. (Berkeley: University of California Press, 1982), 78, 44. Ovid, *Metamorphoses*, I, 525.
20 Robert Carey, *The Memoirs of Robert Carey*, F.H. Markes, ed. (Oxford: Clarendon Press, 1972), 66–8, 72.

God. Elizabeth Carey argued the King out of radical cures, like making young Charles wear iron boots, in favor of allowing nature to take its course.

She recognized that providence might be persuaded to work in your favor if you lived according to God's law and your natural body. Paying attention to your body, of course, created an opening for medicine, since physicians could help regulate the body according to its humors. Because God had made all things for man's benefit, all things could be used to that end if one knew their properties, correspondences, and intended purposes. Bestselling books like William Bullein's *The government of health: a treatise … for the especial good and healthful preservation of man's body from all noisome diseases, proceeding by the excesses of evil diet, and other infirmities of nature: full of excellent medicines, and wise counsels, for conservation of health, in men, women, and children* expounded this belief.[21] Health, Bullein taught, always began with repentance and obedience, but was also a matter of diet and air, and hot and cold humors. His book was in print during almost all of Elizabeth's reign, its advice always useful.

Human actions against God's chosen punishments seem contradictory. If God was the cause, should not people be fatalistic? If a person was ill with a frightening disease like the plague, should not a Christian exercise love and charity by visiting, feeding, and caring for them, since the life of the Samaritan was in God's hands?[22] This irony was most obvious when plague and other infectious diseases struck whole communities. The use of quarantine as a way of preventing the spread of the disease, locking the sick and their housemates into their homes and stopping all direct social interaction, made it very hard to practice Christian charity. People feared God, but they feared their sick neighbors more, and, though governors used prayers to combat diseases, they also exerted official control to do what they could to protect themselves and their communities. The rich moved to the country; the middling sorts and the poor were left to care for one another under the unhelpful eye of the local government.

But was God sending punishments or tests? Did He license Satan to tempt the sufferers to strengthen their faith, or to warn them to repent? Given that God's providence ruled all, where did temptations come from? Was God teaching us our absolute dependence on him by blessing us with misery and despair? For most Elizabethans, the most delectable of religious experience was despair, leading to surrender to God's disinterested love.

Thomas Beard portrayed this in his very popular anthology, *The Theater of God's Judgements*, first translated from the French in 1597, and later amended

---

21 William Bullein, *The gouernment of health…* (1595), 3. STC (2nd ed.)/4042.
22 Kira L. S. Newman, "Shutt Up: Bubonic Plague and Quarantine in Early Modern England." *Journal of Social History* 2012; 45(3), 824–6.

and expanded as further editions went to press. In his introduction, he explained that God's judgments are past reasonable understanding, for "if we turn over every leaf of God's creatures from the tenth sphere to the center of the earth," we will find Him "sitting at the stern of the world." God has two arms, one of justice and the other of mercy, each of the same length. People should admire and revere His mercy, but they should not rely on it. They must think about His justice. More people are damned by presumption of God's love than for despairing of it. Therefore, Beard's book showed "justice manifested in the world upon sinners and reprobates, to the end that drowsy consciences" should be awakened. They shall see, he said, how vengeance pursues malefactors to their shame and confusion in this life and eternally.[23]

The hundreds of examples that followed showed how God punishes a long, long list of things that irritate Him, from blaspheming, to Sabbath breaking, to incest, to princes who do not execute justice. In conclusion, Beard cheerfully explained how the godly innocents who suffer collateral damage from divine punishments of the wicked should not take it personally, since they are assured of their salvation. As for the wicked:

> God's fierce wrath is clearly revealed from heaven upon all impiety and injustice of men, to consume all that rebel against him. Think upon this you inhabitants of the earth, small and great, of what quality or condition soever you be ... If you be mighty ... know that the Lord is greater than you; for he is almighty, all-terrible, and all-fearful; in what place soever you are, he is always above you, ready to hurl you down and overturn you, to break, quash, and crush you in pieces as pots of earth; he is armed with thunder, fire, and a bloody sword to destroy, consume, and cut you in pieces: Heaven threatenteth from above, and the earth ... being ready to spew you out from her face, or swallow you up in her bowels; in brief, all the elements and creatures of God look askance at you in disdain, and set themselves against you in hatred, if you fear not your Creator ... Forsake therefore ... the evil and corrupt fashions of the world, and submit yourselves ... fearing the just retribution of vengeance upon all them that do the contrary; for it is a horrible thing to fall into the hands of the Lord.[24]

Beard was suggesting that whatever trouble occurs, even if it appears to be natural, it is God's punishment on those who do not fear Him. Conversely, proper fear of the Lord, repentance, and prayer may—God willing—change the outcomes. If terrors are sent by God to warn and chastise, God may take them

23 Thomas Beard, *The theatre of Gods iudgements...* (London: 1597), Sig. A2–3v. STC (2nd ed.)/1659.
24 Ibid., 470–2.

away if He thinks the message has been received. We can see this assumption in action in churches across England.

In August of 1563, during the worst outbreak of plague in the century, Elizabeth issued an order to the archbishops of Canterbury and York for special prayers and fasting. It was intended to move God to end the plague. The prayer was meditative:

> We be taught by many and sundry examples of holy Scriptures, that upon occasion of particular punishments, affliction, and perils, which God of his most just judgement has sometimes sent among his people to show his wrath against sin, and to call his people to repentance, and to redress of their lives: the godly have been provoked and stirred up to more fervency and diligence in prayer, fasting, and alms deeds, to a more deep consideration of their consciences, to ponder their unthankfulness and forgetfulness of God's merciful benefits towards them, with craving of pardon for the time past, and to ask his assistance for the time to come to live more godly, and so to be defended and delivered from all further perils and dangers

Therefore, Elizabeth demanded her realm to pray to God, asking Him to turn away His "deserved wrath from us" and restore the health of their bodies and the wholesomeness of the air (bad air—*malaria*—was thought to cause the plague).[25]

To prove their repentance, every Wednesday was declared a day of general fasting, when all the English, between 16 and 60, would eat only one small meal. The money they saved on food was to be given to the poor and the sick. All those who could be spared from work were to spend the day in prayer, Bible reading, and godly exercises. Plays, pastimes "or idleness, much less ... lewd, wicked, or wanton behavior" were banned.[26]

When the plague disappeared in the winter of 1563/4, prayers of thanksgiving were ordered. Approved by Principal Secretary Cecil, these prayers repeated the assumptions of the penitential prayers and fasts. They thanked God for abating His anger against those who traduced His will. Like a loving father who must beat his disobedient child, God had sent the plague. Now, though the people were still undeserving, He, in His love, had taken it away. And, most importantly, He had seen fit to spare the Queen during the illness.[27]

This same response was used in other times of national political crisis and when international events threatened Christendom, or Protestantism. There

25 Mears et al., *National Prayers*, 59–61.
26 Ibid., 69.
27 Ibid., 83.

was a hierarchy of threat, with a matching hierarchy of prayer. National prayers of repentance and thanksgiving during national crises were most common, but attacks on the reformed religion and threats to the whole of Christendom prompted them, too.

Thus, in January of 1570, God was praised in every parish for having vanquished the Queen's multitudinous enemies in the form of rebellious northern earls. They had marched under the banner of the five wounds of Christ, intending to put a Catholic on the throne. God chose otherwise and defended Elizabeth and the truth of the Gospel. It was made clear, through a new addition to the *Book of Homilies*, that blaspheming of God's name and attacks on the Queen were the reasons the rebels were "most dreadfully … scourged … with terrible executions, justly inflicted." The prayers and homily taught repentance and obedience.[28]

This national thanksgiving was followed the next year with a celebration of Pope Pius V and Philipp II's victory over the Ottoman navy at the Battle of Lepanto. Western Europe had been saved, with God's help, from the invading Muslims, to the "universal benefit of Christendom." Bells rang, bonfires were lit, and prayers were said against the tyranny of the Turks, celebrating their overthrow.[29]

This victory of the Spanish and the Pope, however, worried Elizabeth's Privy Council. Sir Francis Walsingham expressed his concern that it would encourage Catherine de Medici and Charles IX to follow Spain's course and turn against the French Protestants.[30] Walsingham was right.

Common Christian unity disappeared even before the Turks rebuilt their fleet. English prayers had to be turned against the Catholic menace in 1572, after the St. Bartholomew's Day Massacre in Paris. The attempt of Charles IX to cleanse his nation of Protestants led to massacres of Huguenots throughout France, which so pleased Pope Gregory XIII that he had a special medal struck in honor of the genocide. Protestants everywhere turned in repentance to God for protection. In England, all parsons and curates were to exhort their parishioners to

> Endeavor themselves to come to the church, with as many of their family as may be spared from their necessary business; and they to resort thither, not only upon Sundays and holy days, but also upon Wednesdays and Fridays, specially in cities and great towns, during this dangerous and perilous time of troubles in Christendom, exhorting them there to reverently and godly to behave themselves, and with penitent minds, kneeling on their knees, to lift up their hearts, and pray to the merciful

---

28 Ibid., 127–9.
29 Ibid., 129–31.
30 TNA SP 70/121, fos. 4–4v.

God, to turn from us in this Realm, and all the rest of Christendom, those plagues and punishments, which we and others through our unthankfulness and sinful lives have deserved.[31]

The prayers used at these services included pointed biblical passages such as Psalms 95:6, "O come, let us humble ourselves, and fall down before the Lord our maker with reverence and fear," and Psalms 51:3, changed from the Bible's singular pronoun into the community plural for the purpose: "we acknowledge our faults, O Lord: and our sins are ever before our sight."

English fear of the Catholic menace and the Spanish military increased until open war broke out with Spain. By then, the English had developed a robust vocabulary for talking about God's providential treatment of England, embodied by their queen. Her Accession Day, November 17, had become a national holiday celebrating God's care for the nation.

When the Spanish Armada was sighted on July 21, 1588, the Privy Council sent out a flurry of letters. They summoned the nobility to bring their troops for defense of the Queen; they ordered the movements of militias and ships; and they asked the Archbishop of Canterbury to order public prayers to Almighty God, giver of victories, for defense against the malice of the Spanish and the Antichrist (the Pope).

It was a given that the nation needed to repent and ask God's forgiveness if it was to be successful in battle. "O Lord our God, Thou bringest the counsel of the heathen to naught, and makest the devises of the people to be of none effect," said one prayer. "There is no king that can be saved by the multitude of an host, neither is any mighty man delivered by much strength. A horse is but a vain thing to save a man, therefore we pray unto thee, O Lord, thou art our help and our shield." They asked He "show some token continually for our good, that they which hate us may see it and be confounded" as they fought enemies of His Gospel.[32]

Preachers echoed and elaborated on these themes. Oliver Pigge suggested that sins, including filthy stage plays, murder, whoredom, excess apparel, and Sabbath breaking—sufficient reasons for godly punishment—were compounded by the failure of the superiors in the commonwealth to do their duty to their inferiors. Those inferiors, however, were undutiful to their prince. In short, everyone was disobedient to God and deserving of Spanish chastisement. Repent, he told his auditors, asking God to "suppress the slights of Antichrist," the power of foreign enemies, and "papistical practices."[33]

---

31 Mears et al., *National Prayers*, I, 132.
32 *A Fourme of Prayer, necessary* for *the present time* (1588). STC/2010:07.
33 Bertrand T. Whitehead, *Brags and Boasts. Propaganda in the Year of the Armada*. (Stroud: Allan Sutton Publishing, 1994), 94–5.

In East Anglia, the Rev. Richard Rogers was disturbed when his neighbors in the militia, "gone to training," were suddenly ordered to the coast, without the chance to see their wives or order their affairs. He organized forty parishioners to fast in support of the defense of the realm, reflecting that they were in peril from the Spanish and "home papists," and expecting God to visit them with calamity. It moved him to "prepare better for affliction."[34]

God saw their repentance and saved them from the Spanish. Bad weather prevented the Spanish fleet from ferrying troops from Belgium to England, blowing it into the North Sea and wrecking many of its ships on Scottish and Irish rocks. As the medal struck by the English mint to commemorate the victory put it, *Flavit Jehovah et Dissipati Sunt*—God blew, and they were scattered. By 1589, philosophers at Oxford were asking their students to prove God's intervention with an exam question: "Were the English victorious over the Spanish through the influence of Heaven?"[35]

This clear sign of God's providential care for England required great thanksgiving, and Elizabeth, breaking with her usual protocol, personally attended a thanksgiving service on November 24 at St. Paul's, participating in a national day of worship. She processed to the cathedral from Westminster, to be greeted by the Lord Mayor and the aldermen at Temple Bar.

> Therefore to lovely London fair
> Our noble queen would go
> And at Paul's Cross before her God
> Her thankful heart to show
> Where princes and people did consent
> With joyful minds to meet
> To glorify the God of Heaven
> With psalms and voices sweet.[36]

Clothed in silver cloth, she rode in a chariot decked in silver cloth, pulled by milk white horses. Before her marched the men of the Court, the judges, the archbishops, the ambassadors, the nobility, the Lord Mayor of London with his scepter, the Earl Marshal and the Lord Great Chamberlain, and the gentlemen pensioners. Behind her came the ladies of honor, according to their degrees.[37]

---

34 M.M. Knappen, ed. *Two Elizabethan Puritan Diaries by Richard Rogers and Samuel Ward* (Chicago: American Society of Church History, 1933), 79–80.

35 Charles B. Schmitt, *John Case and Aristotelianism in Renaissance England* (Kingston, Montreal: McGill-Queen's University Press, 1983), 135.

36 "A Joyfull newe ballad of the Royall entracnce of Quene E[lizabeth] in the Cetye of London the 24 of November in the 3i yere of hyr majesties Reigne to gyve god praise for the overhtrowe of the spanyardes," in Steven W. May and Arthur F. Marotti, *Ink, Stink Bait, Revenge, and Queen Elizabeth. A Yorkshire Yeoman's Household Book* (Ithaca: Cornell University Press, 2014), 135–6.

37 HEH FBL 19, fos. 17–18.

At the door of St. Paul's, she knelt in prayer before processing down the nave to her private room. The Queen wanted God to be aware of how thankful she was for His actions.[38] God, says the poet,

> Have given us all just cause to say
> The Lord is good and kind.
> And that we might not thankless be
> Unto our gracious God
> That hath in mercy cast away
> His grievous scourging rod
> And for the blessings manifold
> Bestowed upon this land
> The state whereof makes all the world
> Amazed for to stand.[39]

Of course, the victory came as a great national relief, and produced lots of ungodly self-righteousness in England. One broadside publication, in the form of a "salutation" to the Spanish, warned them against their evil plans:

> And cannot repent,
> But keepeth intent,
> Come six or seven,
> Come Hell or Heaven,
> To undertake,
> With all he can make,
> A new invasion,
> At the Pope's persuasion,
> But Spaniard proud,
> The Lord hath vowed
> He will defend,
> Unto the end,
> His Church and sheep,
> That his law keep,

The poet even declared it was good for Protestant English people to eat fish that had dined on the drowned bodies of Spaniards.[40]

Naturally, these sorts of services shaped public understanding, and they were used as a tool of the royal government to inform, instruct, and propagandize

---

38 Mears et al., *National Prayers*, 183.
39 "A Joyfull new ballad," in May and Marotti, *Ink, Stink Bait, Revenge*, 134.
40 *A Skeltonicall salutation … and iust vexation of the Spanish nation that in a bravado, spent many a crusado, in setting forth an armado England to invado* (1589). STC (2nd ed.)/22620.

against the papists. Fasting fell out of fashion in England—though not in Scotland—but special prayers continued to be required in times of political and natural crisis and thanksgiving. God was presumed to be in charge, and His chastisements and rewards continued to rain down.

Protestantism, by removing the intercessory saints used by Catholics, increased the emphasis on God's providence as a bulwark against the Devil and other evils. The celebration of England's special place in God's plan to restore order in the world had become a standard trope in sermons, ballads, broadsides, and other popular literature.[41]

By the middle of the reign, Protestant thinkers had cataloged the enemies of the Gospel of Christ. According to medieval tradition, Muhammed was the Antichrist foretold in Scripture, but Elizabethans had to make room for the new Antichrist, the Pope, by reworking what he was and how his signs were recognized. The Devil, they knew, was behind all perversions of Christian truth, and so Muslims and Catholics must be the same thing on some level: all minions of the Devil. The Antichrist, foretold in the Gospels, was a false prophet who destroyed kingdoms and princes. Therefore, Protestants could accept that the papacy was another embodiment of the Devil, as Muhammed had been in his time.[42] Conversely, Catholics like William Gifford, a Jesuit, claimed that Calvin was the embodiment of Muhammed. Responding, Matthew Sutcliffe, in a 1599 book dedicated to Archbishop Whitgift, elided Muhammed and the papacy by arguing that they both taught false doctrine, undermining monarchies and promoting moral turpitude. As Muhammed was salacious and bloodthirsty, so were the popes. Gifford, on the Catholic side, insisted that the metrical psalms sung in the English church were just like the chants of the Muslims. Sutcliffe countered this by arguing that Muslims chanted from false, blasphemous, lying writings, just like the fables honoring popes and saints.[43]

These conflicting definitions of God's enemies forced Elizabethan Protestants to remap the place of the Devil in His creation. The Devil of the medieval church had a physical presence, presenting more of a Manichean alternative to a loving God. After all, if God is love, where does evil come

---

41 Alexandra Walsham, *Providence in Early Modern England* (Oxford: Oxford University Press, 2001), 245–7.
42 Matthew Sutcliffe, *De pontifice Romano, eiusque iniustissima in Ecclesia dominatione, aduersùs Robertum Bellarminum, & vniuersum Iebusitarum sodalitium, libri quinque* (1599), 549. Jones, "Adaptation of Tradition," 161–75.
43 Matthew Sutcliffe, *De Turcopapismo...* (1599), 17–18, 124. STC (2nd ed.)/23460 does a point-by-point comparison of the two religions, proving Islam is derived from the Roman Antichrist. He is responding to William Gifford's edition of William Reynolds' *Calvino-Turcismus id est, Calvinisticae perfidiae cum Mahumetana collatio...* (Antwerp: 1597). USTC 402394, which proves Protestantism is really Islam.

from? But the internalization of Protestant concepts of salvation elevated Satan into the psyche and out of the street, just as Purgatory disappeared from the map of creation. Celebrating God's absolute providence, the Protestants had to include Satan as one of His tools. Now, the sovereignty of God meant that Satan always acted as a tool of divine justice. He was permitted to do evil only when God chose. This followed from the doctrine of providence that Craddock laid out.

The Elizabethan Satan did not appear physically. He was the master of crafty persuasions and false illusions, using people's own weaknesses to undermine their belief. After all, if you were saved by faith, which is internal, you could be damned if you were tricked into losing it. Thomas Egerton, making notes on his reading on the fly leaves of a law book, learned this from Jacob Aconcio's *Stratagematum Satanae*. Dedicated to Elizabeth in 1565, *Stratagematum Satanae* is about the need to understand and internalize the Gospels, lest you be tricked by false reasoning. A naturalized Englishman with a pension from Elizabeth, Aconcio was also an engineer, brought from Italy to advise on fortification. His fame, however, rests on his argument that religious persecution does not work, and is in fact a strategy of Satan. Human reason, because it is fallible, can easily become the tool of Satan. Egerton summed up his argument by observing that opinions based on bad science are dangerous to the soul. It is these "infirm" reasons that Satan uses to mislead those who are too weak or too lazy to learn and internalize God's law.[44]

According to Aconcio, there is no hope of salvation for those who "rely on their own prudence and sagacity" or who are negligent and listless. There is only hope for those who know the perils of Satan's tricks and arm themselves with the breastplate of righteousness: a good conscience, doing everything for the glory of God rather than for one's own advantage.[45] Ironically, this argument was taken to be diabolical by Bishop Grindal of London, who excommunicated Aconcio. Grindal deeply distrusted the Italian's arguments for a tolerant broad-church policy. However, Elizabeth's church came to be much closer in attitude to Aconcio than to Grindal.[46]

There was a special Elizabethan spin to this Devil, too. The Catholic Church was seen as the Devil's masterpiece: the mystical body of the Antichrist.[47] Attempts early in Elizabeth's reign to assassinate her by sorcery had led to the

---

44 Egerton's note is on the back fly leaf of the Huntington Library's copy of Anthony Fitzherbert, *La Nouvelle Natura Brevium...* (1560). STC 10960. The Huntington Library call number is 379985. Egerton was reading Jacobo Acontio, *Stratagematum Satanae Libri Octo* (Basil, 1565), citing Aconcio's (the name is spelled "Aconcio" in library catalogs, but is "Acontio" on the title page) argument as being in Book 1, page 54. There is no direct quote matching Egerton's note, but it does catch the sense of the argument at the end of Book 1.
45 Acontio, *Stratagematum Satanae*, 403–4.
46 Collinson, *Grindal*, 151–2.
47 Darren Oldridge, "Witchcraft and the Devil," in Doran and Jones, *Elizabethan World*, 484–5.

enactment of new laws against treason and the revival of the crime of witch-craft, explicitly linking Catholic priests with diabolical magic.[48]

That is why Old Mother Waterhouse was convicted and hanged as a witch. How did they know she was a witch? In part because she admitted her cat, "Satan," insisted that she say her prayers in Latin. She told the Chelmsford assize in 1566 that whenever she wanted her black cat to kill a neighbor, murder her husband, spoil beer, or drown a cow, she would "say her *Pater Noster* [Lord's Prayer] in Latin." The judges pressed her further about her habits of prayer, exploring whether she attended divine service and in what language she prayed when she was there. When she admitted to praying in Latin, they asked why, "seeing that it was set out by public authority and according to God's word that all men should pray in the English and mother tongue that they best understand." She replied that "Satan would at no time suffer her to say it in English, but at all times in Latin."[49] Latin, the tongue of the Roman Church and all learned men, was now the religious language of Satan's Church when in the mouths of ignorant old women.

This was a new understanding of how Satan acted, since he now had a whole branch of Christendom at his disposal. But it also meant Elizabethans were increasingly seeing good and evil as matters of intention rather than action; conscience rather than temptation. We can see this in the advice handed out by Richard Greenham, the famous rector of Dry Drayton in Cambridgeshire. People seeking his advice recorded his answers, giving us a general idea of how the Devil worked with Elizabethans, and what they did about satanic influences.

As far as Greenham was concerned, all Christians could expect a life of challenges and pain. Their trials and sufferings were part of the battle between God and Satan, as they endured God's loving attempts to correct them and the Devil's hateful attempts to delude them into disbelief. The job of the minister was to help people distinguish between the poles of divine love and satanic despair, resisting the Devil.

Satan had various tricks. One of his best was using a person's desire for godliness to induce religious despair or crazed zealotry. Greenham told the story of a man who, having a "great pain in his leg … remembered that it was said in the scriptures, If thy foot offend thee cut it off." Laying his foot on a block, the man took a hatchet and struck it off. As he bled to death, he repented. Greenham

48 Norman Jones, "Choosing Superstitions: Catholic Sorcery and the Witchcraft Act of 1563," in Charles Carlton, ed. *State, Sovereigns and Society; Essays in Early Modern English History in Honor of A.J. Slavin* (London: Sutton Publishing, 1998), 187–203.
49 *The Examination and Confession of certaine Wytches at Chensford.* Reproduced in C. L'Estrange Ewen, ed. *Witch Hunting and Witch Trials. The Indictment of Witchcraft from the Records of 1373 Assizes held for the Home Circuit A.D. 1559–1736* (London, Routledge, 1929), 320, 322.

drew the moral that the man's Satan-afflicted mind had led him to misunderstand Scripture.[50]

A member of the Middle Temple named Brigges left us a detailed conversation with Satan that shows, in its madness, the way human relations with the Devil were scripted. In this conversation, which reminds us of the one Katherine Stubbes had on her deathbed, we see Satan trying all his tricks to get Brigges to abandon God and murder Lord Burghley. It was a lawyerly dispute over whether Brigges had sold Satan his soul for money, fine clothes, and silver plates. The Evil One tried to make Brigges believe God hated him, and that Scripture was not true. Then he tried to convince him that, since he was predestined by God, God did not care what he did. Naturally, he also tried to turn Brigges into a papist, but Brigges refused to betray his countrymen.[51] At the time, it was understood Brigges was mad, but he related just the sort of things Satan was expected to say.

Rev. Greenham's parishioners learned that God would never send suffering they could not overcome, but that Satan was God's instrument for testing and strengthening them. And so people had to love God and accept that His providential acts were for the best, while looking out for Satan.

How one provoked and deserved God's providential acts raised difficult questions. Commanded to use no worship contrary to the written word of God, and to obey the Ten Commandments, it was unclear whether people were still earning their salvation, as in the works-oriented soteriology of the Catholics, or confirming their election to salvation by God's grace, as taught by Calvinists. Contrarily, were English Protestants required to perfect the grace God had granted? In practice, these soteriologies were hard to tell apart. Did you visit the sick, relieve the needy, help prisoners, comfort the miserable, and reconcile quarrelling neighbors out of love of God or fear of God? Were you preordained to your eternal reward, or must you show your love of God in actions that influenced the outcome? If you were forbidden to do things not approved by Scripture, but Scripture was unclear, what should you do? Could you choose your own damnation, or were salvation and damnation already immutably determined by God? These were hard puzzles, and led to heated disagreements that shaped Elizabethan society.

Nicholas Byfield, a devoted Calvinist and Sabbatarian, wrote a catalog of sin explaining how a Christian, justified by Christ, would nonetheless be expected to follow God's will. Anyone who read the Bible knew that people were full of sin, said Byfield, and a good Christian wanted to know "What he should do to be rid of those many sins he hath been, and is guilty of: rid (I say) from the guilt & danger of them, and from the power and dominion of them. For the

---

50 Parker and Carlson, eds. *Practical Divinity*, 88–9.
51 BL, Lansd. 101, fos. 165–176v.

satisfaction of thy Conscience in this most needful question."[52] Freed from the dominion of sin, they would not be ruled by Satan. God had provided sure directions for the avoidance of sin, if people were not slothful procrastinators, but they needed to be "infallibly assured, concerning Gods favor, and [their] own salvation." He therefore laid out "As in a small map ... the sorts of sin, and so may get knowledge quickly, what evils to avoid, which hitherto he hath not taken notice of."[53] He illustrated the signs of election, using the biographies of seven truly wicked men and seven who were certainly saved.

Assured by these signs, the elect, heaven-bound, having "found out the gain of godliness, would ask ... 'What he should do in the whole course of his life to glorify God,' who hath thus loved him, and given his Son to die for him, and purchased such a glorious Inheritance for him?" Byfield therefore provided "*the rules of Life*, which will shew him distinctly, how he should carry himself both *towards God*, and *towards men* in all parts of his life; how he should behave himself at home and abroad, in company, and out of company."[54] Byfield's point was that there were innumerable sins of omission and commission, known and unknown, and the elect could be reassured of their salvation despite their inability to avoid all of them. However, the best way to find assurance of salvation was to live according to the laws of God. The good works thus performed were the *evidence* of the certainty of salvation, not the *cause* of salvation.

But Byfield's system did not answer the hard question of whether deliberate sins, which everyone admitted were done by the good and the bad alike, might lose a person eternal life in Heaven. Common sense urged that bad people should be damned by their behavior and the good saved by theirs.

The theological problems presented by predestination and salvation by faith were so complex that some minsters thought it was best not to talk about them. A group of ministers gave Elizabeth a declaration of doctrine when they returned from exile in 1559 that made it clear that though predestination was true, it was too hard a truth to explain to their congregations. Though predestination and the concomitant election of some people to heaven and some people to hell were scriptural, how God chose them was a "deep mystery" that had to be handled very carefully "or not at all in this carnal age: it were best that such articles be passed over in silence (indeed we do think discreet ministers will speak sparingly and circumspectly of them)."[55]

In 1604, King James, discoursing with the clergy at the Hampton Court Conference, said he wished the doctrine of predestination would be "very

---

52 Nicholas Byfield, *The beginning of the doctrine of Christ. Or A catalogue of sinnes...* (1619), 5. STC (2nd ed.)/4209.5.
53 Ibid., 56.
54 Ibid., 9.
55 CCCC, 121, pp. 146–8.

tenderly handled, and with great discretion, left on the one side."[56] But, by 1604, that was not possible, as James sadly recognized. The careful skirting of predestination in 1559 had collapsed by the middle of Elizabeth's reign as conflicting ideas about salvation and behavior came to a head. Open theological warfare over predestination and justification began in the 1580's.

Richard Hooker, whose *Laws of Ecclesiastical Polity* eventually defined Anglicanism, preached a sermon on justification in 1584 that made room for some human agency and context. He asserted that Roman Catholics who came before the Reformation might be saved, despite their erroneous belief, since they acted in good faith: "I doubt not but God was merciful to save thousands of our fathers." After all, they sincerely believed in Christ.

Newly appointed Master of the Temple Church, Hooker gave the sermon in the morning.[57] That same afternoon, the assistant pastor there, Walter Travers, preached denouncing Hooker's position. As Travers summed it up, Hooker had said "Our fathers are no precedent for us to follow in error. God I doubt not was merciful to save thousands of them, though they lived in popish superstition, in as much as they sinned ignorantly." Travers angrily responded that salvation belonged only to the Church of Christ. Those who did not "go out of Babylon" did not profit from Christ's death. Worse, in Travers' eyes, was Hooker's belief that works were important, and that sinners who earnestly prayed to God for forgiveness would be heard. Travers was contemptuous: "To hold that we are not saved by Christ alone without works is ... directly to overthrow the foundation of Christian faith."[58] The two continued their sermon duel for some time, and Travers was forbidden by the Bishop of London to preach. He appealed to the Privy Council for reinstatement, detailing his side of the debate. Hooker answered in a letter to Archbishop Whitgift, who supported him and continued Travers' suspension.[59]

As a consequence of his debates with Travers, Hooker eventually retired from the Temple to begin writing an answer to Puritan attacks on the form and worship of the Elizabethan state church. He would spend the rest of his life working on *The Laws of Ecclesiastical Polity*. Described as the first major work in the fields of theology, philosophy, and political thought to be written in

---

56 William Barlow, *The summe and substance of the conference, which it pleased His Excellent Majestie to have with the lords bishops, and others of his clergie (at which the most of the lords of the councill were present) in His Majesties privie-chamber, at Hampton Court, Jan. 14. 1603* (1804), 23.

57 Richard Hooker, "A Learned Discourse on Justification," in W. Speed Hill, ed. *Folger Library Edition of the Works of Richard Hooker, Vol. 5: Tractates and Sermons* (Cambridge, MA: Belknap Press of Harvard University Press, 1990), 105–70.

58 BL Lansd. 50, fos. 171–172v.

59 Walter Travers, "A Supplication made to the Privy Counsel," in Hill, *Works of Richard Hooker, Vol. 5*, 189–210.

English, it was a response to those who would not abide by the religious settlement of 1559. Hooker was addressing the pastoral problem of obedience to the state, even when it and its church are not always consistent with God's perceived will. He was answering the accusation that clergy who "maintain things that are established ... serve the time, and speak in favour of the present state, because thereby we either hold or seek preferment."[60] He emphatically rejected this criticism, making a case for obedience.

Hooker had many supporters, laying the groundwork for a distinctive Anglican approach to religion. He was also in line with many continental reformers of a Lutheran inclination.

Peter Baro, a French Huguenot refugee from the St. Bartholomew Massacre, was elected Lady Margaret Professor of Divinity at Cambridge, thanks to Lord Burghley, in 1574. As Cambridge became more and under the sway of Calvinist theologians, Baro felt called to defend the idea that people had some free will even though predestination was real. Preaching in the University church, he got into serious trouble with his colleagues in Cambridge for suggesting that people might have some small influence on their own salvation.

In a letter of complaint about Baro, written in 1596, it was alleged that for "fourteen or fifteen years" he had been undermining the Elizabethan church, broaching "new and strange questions in religion." If he was permitted to continue, said the complaint, signed by heads of Cambridge colleges, the "whole body of popery should by little and little break in upon us."[61] He was, in the shorthand of the day, a "Pelagian"—one who, like St. Augustine's enemy in the fourth century, thought a person could choose to be good enough to merit eternal salvation. All Catholics, they believed, were Pelagians, and so were Baro and people like him, including Hooker.

What Baro argued was:

> *That the liberty of mans will is not taken away by the purpose and decree of God,* least any man should think God's purpose and decree to be such a thing, as whereby men might be forcibly carried, as the dust of the wind: or by whose force and power alone, and not by their own, they may speak, like *Balaams* Ass, and do whatsoever they do. For he that thus thinketh, is in a very great error. Neither again do we attribute that liberty to man, whereby he may do everything (for so should be taken away not only Gods purpose and decree, but mortal man should be

---

60 A.S. McGrade, "Hooker, Richard (1554–1600)," in *Oxford Dictionary of National Biography* (Oxford: Oxford University Press, 2004). http://www.oxforddnb.com/view/article/13696 [Accessed November 29, 2018].

61 Trinity College Ms. B.14/9, pp. 184–5, quoted in H.C. Porter, *Reformation and Reaction in Tudor Cambridge* (Hamden: Archon Books, 1972), 376.

taken for a God) but whereby he may work and deal at liberty under the decree and determination of God, which is the property of that nature, that God hath made free and capable of power and life eternal.[62]

God had, he believed, predestined all people to salvation who chose to accept His free offer of grace. But they did not have to accept it. They were free to reject it and damn themselves. If they damned themselves, it was not God's fault. God was not the author of evil.

The Cambridge Calvinists were in an uproar. Already fighting about pre- and post-lapsarian election (did God choose people to be damned or saved before Adam and Eve fell from grace, or only because of their fall?), they agreed that Baro's teaching that people had some free will had to be anathematized. William Barret, Baro's student, was expelled from Cambridge, and Baro himself lost his Chair, retiring to London. Not even Baro's patron, Lord Burghley, could keep him in Cambridge. Baro sent Burghley, "not without great sadness of soul," a crystalline defense of his position, and asked for his help.[63] Though Burghley read it with care and did not believe removing Baro was just, the university's processes ground on. The Calvinists were victorious in Cambridge, but the position Baro espoused did not die.

The argument that people could participate in their own election was eventually fathered on James Arminius, a Dutch theologian who defended the same views, so that "Arminianism" became the shorthand used to tar English theologians who, in the eyes of their Calvinist brethren, were not absolutist enough in insisting that people can do nothing to influence their own salvation. On one end of the scale were the "Pelagianians," presumed to be Roman Catholics. In the middle were the Arminians, who thought that, though predestined to eternal life by God's immutable will, mutable people were given the power to choose, so they could damn themselves as a necessary consequence of their refusal of God's grace.[64] At the other end were the ardent Calvinist Predestinarians, who agreed there was no appealing or influencing God's eternal decree of election.

All believed the catechistical assertion that Christians must avoid Satan, evil inventions, and human imaginings that went against the word of God, but who had the authority to know good from bad, divine from satanic? How much power did individuals have over their eternal destinies? It was an irresoluble problem. Conflicting claims led to differing definitions of sin and obedience,

---

62 Peter Baro, "Two Theames or Questions, handled and disputed openly in the Schooles at Cambridge, in the Latin tung, by P. Baro, Doctor of Diuinitye and Englished by I. L.," in Andreas Hyperius, *A speciall treatise of Gods prouidence …* (1588), 517–18. STC (2nd ed.)/11760.
63 BL Lansd. 80, fos. 172–172v.
64 Peter Baro, "Summary of Three Opinions Concerning Predestination," in James Nichols, ed. and trans. *The Works of James Arminius*, 3 vols. (London: 1825), I, 98.

leading to differing lifestyles and values based upon disagreement over what God expected of His people. Their fear of God led them to conflicting conclusions about godly behavior for the same reason. Their heroic efforts and their guilt proved their righteousness, but they did not always make them comfortable neighbors.

These debates over how to live properly under God's law created new, exclusive communities within the older, inclusive parishes. These were built semi-voluntarily around religious values. Catholics might shelter close to powerful Catholic families, such as at the Petre family home, Ingatestone Hall, in Essex. The Calvinist reformed tried building their preferred religious world around places like Banbury, where their world view was tolerated. Separatist congregations even abandoned England for Holland and New England, searching for a place that would tolerate their vision of a godly society. These dissenters lived in tension with their neighbors, placing their allegiances outside of the traditional structures of parish, diocese, and county, but they remained a part of England. Even those who emigrated to America carried with them the legal structures and values of their other communities, while rejecting royal ecclesiology.

Later Elizabethans were very aware of these deviant communities in their midst, and found them troubling and exciting. They embodied growing tensions over how to obey God, and they encouraged the breakdown of community fellowship. At the same time, they represented the possibility of obeying one's conscience, no matter where it led. The dangers they represented were met by prosecutions (seen as persecutions by their victims), which helped reinforce alternative religious identities. They also spawned a lively, vitriolic debate within communities. At the heart of arguments over how to live under divine providence, avoiding God's righteous anger, was the question of how one should live. What sort of virtuous daily life pleased God?

8

Personal Virtue

If one was godly and well versed in Scripture, one lived a virtuous life in fear of the Lord. And one liked doing it. Henry Airay, lecturing at Queen's College, Oxford, took as his text Philippians 4.4, "Rejoice in the Lord always, and again, I say, rejoice." He argued:

> Hence then we may observe what and wherein the Christian man's joy and rejoicing ought to be: his joy and rejoicing ought to be in the Lord. To be glad, and to be merry, and to rejoice, is a thing which the heart of man very much even naturally desireth, so that there needeth no precept or exhortation at all that we should rejoice: but what and wherein our rejoicing should be, is a matter very well worth our due and diligent consideration.[1]

Delivering those words, he was touching an irony in Elizabethan society. He was not talking about the pursuit of secular happiness. His rejoicing was not that of "Renaissance Faire" Elizabethans, quaffing ale, Morris dancing, theater going, and carrying on like Shakespeare's drunken knight Falstaff. He juxtaposed "worldly rejoicing," where people took pleasure from the vanities of life and the pleasures of sin, with prayerful, "sad" rejoicing, where people dedicated themselves to doing their duty to God, rejoicing in their heavenly future.[2] Airay knew, as Sir Francis Hastings put it in a letter of condolence to his brother, that "It is written in the Evangelist, for our instruction and comfort, he that soweth in tears shall reap in joy."[3] Anne Locke wrote, "Let us be contented to be dead in this world, and to have life hid with Christ in God"; one could enjoy suffering, sure in the knowledge that nothing could "separate us from the love of GOD."[4]

---

1 Henry Airay, *Lectures upon the whole Epistle of St. Paul to the Philippians, delivered in St. Peter's Church in Oxford...* (1618), 572. STC (2nd ed.)/245.
2 Ibid., 756–7.
3 HEH, HA 5098.
4 Susan M. Flech, ed. *The Collected Works of Anne Vaughan Lock* (Tempe: Arizona Center for Medieval and Renaissance Studies in conjunction with Renaissance English Text Society, 1999), 144.

Being Elizabethan: Understanding Shakespeare's Neighbors, First Edition. Norman Jones.
© 2020 John Wiley & Sons, Inc. Published 2020 by John Wiley & Sons, Inc.

Obviously, there were many Elizabethans who happily enjoyed vanities and pleasures, but there were also those who, with cast-down eyes, sought vigorously to avoid them. For some, their love of the world was more powerful than their love of God; for others, the poles were reversed. There were many Elizabethans who might qualify as "religious fanatics," if we mean people who are willing to abandon the pleasures of life and suffer, even die, out of allegiance to God. Certainly, by the early decades of the seventeenth century, England was deeply torn by debates over proper behavior, as some rejected the values of sociability and community, asserting individual righteousness and holy self-control as more important than worldly values.

The struggle between personal conscience and community went back at least as far as the reign of Edward VI. The first generation of Elizabethan leaders—like Archbishop Parker and Lord Burghley—were intent on defeating Catholicism. The key to that was the enforcement of the uniform order of worship on the nation. When Archbishop Cranmer wrote the prayer book, he was of the belief that enforced worship would slowly convert the English nation as the older traditionalist died. He was right, in that by the 1570's there were few left who remembered fully functioning late medieval Catholicism. However, official attempts to reform public behavior failed, for—unlike many Protestant communities—the English church was never permitted to enact a new book of discipline that redefined Christian behavior. Ideas of proper behavior were inherited, and not officially reformed. Consequently, English people were torn between older ideas of propriety and sociability and the emerging concepts of conscientious purity.

The population explosion of the later sixteenth century added to this rapid mixing of old and new ideas of propriety. The younger generation, born in the 1550's, 60's, and 70's, knew little directly of publically lived Catholicism. For them, it was the "traditional" enemy associated with rebels and Spaniards. Brought up with the Protestant emphasis on the Word of God read and preached, they had a very different idea of religious behavior. They were being taught that every person must weigh the teachings of the Bible and obey them in so far as was possible, even if their neighbors did not. There should be no temporizing with the Devil/Pope, and every conscience should respond as God called it. There was no human power that could override conscience.

Dr. George Downame, a leading Cambridge Calvinist, preaching at Paul's Cross in 1608, declared that the conscience of a Christian is exempted from human power, and cannot be bound. Superior to the ecclesiastical and civil laws, personal conscience does not owe human laws absolute obedience; "neither can they make an particular, which is indifferent ... to be simply necessary."[5] His position may have derived from his conviction that the Pope was the

---

5 George Downame, *A treatise vpon John 8. 36 concerning Christian...* (1609), 67. STC (2nd ed.)/7124.

Antichrist, so no Catholic law could bind a Christian conscience, but it made conscience the arbiter over human authorities.[6]

Elizabethan Catholics, shepherded by priests trained in post-Tridentine seminaries on the Continent, shared this emphasis on conscience over communal obedience. Ironically, Jesuitical casuistry—the willingness to deny one was a priest in order to preach again another day—had its roots in the same certainty in conscience.[7] Called by a higher power, people of conscience demanded regime changes in God's favor, refusing on principle to obey Elizabeth in matters of religion.

Among those who rejected worldly lives, the amorphous lump of "Puritans" are the best known. The term came into use in the late 1560's to describe people in the established English church who wished to see the Elizabethan Settlement of Religion purified of all "popish rags." Originally a term of abuse, the definition of Puritanism was left to the pens of those who did not like these "precise" folks. It included some who disliked the way the church was governed—especially Presbyterians and Separatists—and some who demanded better ecclesiastical discipline that enforced God's expectations on sinners. These groups overlapped in confusing ways, but they all critiqued the establishment. John Jewel, who became Elizabeth's Bishop of Salisbury in 1559 and wrote the *Apology for the Church of England,* summed up the purifiers' disgust over the half-hearted reform in the new religious settlement: "The scenic apparatus of divine worship is now under agitation … [and is] now seriously and solemnly entertained [as if] … the Christian religion could not exist without some tawdry … Others are seeking after a *golden,* or as it rather seems to me, a *leaden* mediocrity; and are crying out that the half is better than the whole."[8] However they construed their theology, Puritans agreed that Elizabeth's church needed to be improved to please God.

A properly reformed church led inexorably to properly behaved people. The whole point of reformation was for people to be taught to lead biblically pure lives that pleased God. This required social reform. Sometimes referred to as the "reformation of manners," the reforms were to ensure that society abided by God's laws. It is this emphasis on godly behavior, which included suppression of many sources of pleasure and leisure, including the theater and Sunday football, that gives us the pejorative meaning of the word "Puritan."

The arch-foes of the Puritans were the Catholics, whose religious practices all right-thinking Protestants rejected. Believing that all Catholic behaviors

---

6 Kenneth Gibson, "Downham, George (*d.* 1634)," in *Oxford Dictionary of National Biography* (Oxford: Oxford University Press, 2004). http://www.oxforddnb.com/view/article/7977 [Accessed November 29, 2018].

7 Elliot Rose, *Cases of Conscience. Alternatives Open to Recusants and Puritans Under Elizabeth I and James I* (Cambridge: Cambridge University Press, 1975), 71–102.

8 Hastings Robinson, ed. *The Zurich Letters,* 2 vols. (Cambridge: Parker Society, 1842–45), I, 23.

had to be purged, English churchmen who dressed like Catholic priests, ecclesiastical decorations like the candles and the cross kept on the altar in Elizabeth's chapel early in the reign, liturgical behaviors such as kneeling, graven images, and many other "papistical" things were targeted for abolition. Occasions of sin were also targeted, such as church ales, Maying, and other events where bawdy behavior was licensed. The Puritans criticized Elizabeth for failing to enforce God's laws on her sinful subjects.

Real "popish" Catholics were dangerous to the state because they believed that God expected them to resist Elizabeth, accepting martyrdom in the name of the True Faith. Though in daily life English people generally tolerated many whose beliefs and practices were residually Catholic, or who were carefully hiding their true beliefs, there were those who were willing to die for their conviction that the Pope and his church were true. In the 1560's, Elizabeth was careful not to force Catholics into opposition, but after the 1569 rebellion and her excommunication by the Pope in 1570, they were defined as enemies of her state. As missionary priests began to arrive from the Continent, they became the willing targets of legal terror, sometimes achieving the martyrdom that marked their apotheosis into near saints. They embraced persecution as a sign of their holiness. Their deaths were described in glowing terms as they achieved "glorious martyrdom," "gave up their blessed souls," "made perfect their good confessions," and shed their blood with "utmost cheerfulness and gentleness."[9]

Catholic martyrs and the Protestant puritanical, some of whom separated from the state church to live their theologies, were on the fringes of Elizabethan life, loud but few. For the majority, the prayer book taught them they were a community of Christians united by a regimen of worship and communal good works. They thought they needed to praise God endlessly, while displaying their loyalty to Him in lives lived according to His law. For those whose consciences were scrupulously guided by their religious convictions, living purely was a necessity, even if they disagreed violently over what pure living looked like.

The tensions over behaviors and beliefs were often intergenerational. In the earlier part of the era, people raised in the older Catholic and evangelical ways of understanding behavior tended to link God's providential actions to the actions of individuals and the kingdom. *Quid pro quo*, sin was chastised and repentance was rewarded. That conformist state of mind was challenged by concepts of predestination that became increasingly popular as the reign progressed. By 1600, it was widely agreed that a person must believe the right things about God and Christ in addition to living a godly life. In the subtle distinctions of belief lurked vicious internecine violence.

---

9 Nicholas Sanders, *The Rise and Growth of the Anglican Schism*, David Lewis, ed. (London: Burns and Oates, 1877), 314–17.

As the Babbington conspirators were being executed in September 1586 for plotting to kill Elizabeth and put Mary Queen of Scots on the throne, they argued with their executioners about the subtleties of their Christian faiths. They claimed their Christian and Catholic faith was distinct from the Christian and catholic faith of their executioners. As each condemned man was led to the scaffold to be hanged, drawn, and quartered as a traitor, he was permitted to pray and speak. Around him on the scaffold stood royal officials: Sir Francis Knolles and Sir Dru Drury, as well as the Rev. Dr. White, there to provide spiritual counsel. When John Charnock was led to the ladder under the noose, a discussion ensued:

> CHARNOCK: When he came up on the ladder, he began and said;— "ave maria, gratiæ plena," etc.
> THEN SIR DRU DRURY ANSWERED: "What can mary do? she cannot hear thee."
> DR. WHITE SAID: "Charnock, pray when marie was alive this was but a salutation, and now when she is dead, when she cannot hear thee, what can it be now?"
> THEN CHARNOCK SAID: "I beseech all catholics to pray for me."
> THEN DR. WHYTE ANSWERED, CHARNOCK: "We be all true catholics." "then i beseech you all to pray for me":—and then said—"pater noster"— in latin: and then said,—"ave maria gratiæ plena," etc.—again...

> Then DR. WHYTE moving him to believe in Jesus Christ alone, HE [CHARNOCK] said:"I believe in Jesus Christ, and I trust he will save me."—And then crying he said,—"O Jesu c[hri]sto mihi Jesus, O Jesu esto mihi Jesus":—and so was thrown off the ladder, and hanged till he was dead: and afterward used as the others; and so died fearfully and obstinately in his religion.[10]

Each time the condemned asserted that they were Catholic, Dr. White insisted that everyone was a catholic. Clearly, those about to die were papist Roman Catholics, but the exchanges point to the things the papists had in common with their executioners: their faith in Jesus and his saving grace. They could be executed as traitors, but they could not be executed as heretics, thanks to English law. The willingness of people on both sides to kill and die cannot be doubted, even though they were all doing it in the name of Jesus. As they saw it, the love that God extended through Jesus required obedience to Him and His church. They disagreed on what that meant in practice.

---

10 BL, Harley 290, fo. 173.

This distinction between "right" and "wrong" belief was a sore one, impinging on family and community, since many Elizabethans had been or were, or knew people who had been or were, Catholics in faith. Must they all, including beloved family members, be sent to hell, and must all of them be unredeemable? And what about Protestants who disagreed with a particular theological interpretation? Was a Lutheran to be damned but not a Calvinist? How tolerant was God of people who did not worship correctly? Could you love your neighbor as yourself if your neighbor believed the wrong thing?

The tensions these questions created are exemplified in the previously discussed controversy between Richard Hooker and Walter Travers, which began not long before the Catholic Babington Plot to kill Elizabeth was discovered. Hooker was the newly appointed Master of the Temple Church in the Middle and Inner Temple. Travers had been the interim pastor there during the last illness of Hooker's predecessor, and he had expected to get the job. Rivals in business, the two pastors were theologically separate as well. Hooker took a more liberal position on who might be saved than did Travers. Hooker became the apologist for Anglican mediocrity; Travers was a Presbyterian of the most ardent sort.

The Reverend Walter Travers was not ordained a minister by an English bishop. After a difficult career in Oxford, he had moved to Holland, where he had been ordained in the reformed manner. Certain in conscience that God was calling him to ministry, he was examined, approved, and elected by the presbyters of the church, who ordained him through prayer and the laying on of hands.[11] In the mid 1570's, he introduced a form of worship among the English merchants living there that did not follow the *Book of Common Prayer*, forcing the Governor of the Merchants Adventurers in Holland to order a stop to his activities. But he did not stop; he "removed to a private space" and continued to preach. In a letter in 1578, Travers made it clear that he opposed keeping the religious peace, if peace required tolerating Catholics, Anabaptists, or Arians (non-Trinitarians). Allowing any freedom to error and superstition would overthrow true religion. Citing the example of the town of Libnah in Judah that revolted against King Jehoram because it had abandoned the God of its fathers, he told William Davison, his supporter and Elizabeth's representative with William of Orange, "your task may be not in healing the wounds of that beast from the sea, of whom John writes in the Apocalypse [Catholics], but in probing and irritating them."[12]

---

11 Walter Travers, *A ful and plaine declaration of ecclesiastical discipline out of the Word of God, and of the declining of the Church of England from the same* (1588), 17–22. STC (2nd ed.)/24185. This is the English edition of the 1580 book, translated by Thomas Cartwright.
12 TNA SP 83/10, fos. 26–26v.

In 1584, Travers and his compatriots were pressing parliament to enact a Presbyterian book of discipline for England, arguing that "this whole society and company and Christian common wealth, cannot well be kept, under their prince and king Jesus Christ" unless it followed the one true model for Christ's church. Published in Latin in Geneva in 1580, Traver's book declared, "by the testimony" of his conscience, that England must truly worship God and observe His discipline.[13]

With parliament still in session, on March 20, 1585, Richard Hooker preached his sermon on justification in the Temple Church—the first he had delivered in his new post. In it, he held that "God was merciful to save thousands of our fathers living in popish superstitions, in as much as they sinned ignorantly."[14] Walter Travers was horrified, preaching against Hooker's laxity that very afternoon. He and his fellows felt that Hooker was making room for the toleration of Catholics, suggesting the Church of Rome might be considered a part of Christ's church, its adherents worthy of salvation. Worse, Hooker's argument suggested that ecclesiastical forms were appropriate to times and places, undermining the ideas of predestination and the eternal purity of scriptural revelation. He was defending an establishment that made the *Book of Common Prayer* an acceptable compromise. Travers' response was so extreme—including an appeal to the Privy Council—that he was eventually silenced by Archbishop Whitgift in 1586, prompting him to seek help from his patron, Lord Burghley. His letter to Burghley snidely suggested that it would not be the first time that the power of the state had been used to persecute God's true church.[15]

Travers and his ilk were especially allergic to any argument that suggested that the Queen's church was good enough, or that people who refused godly discipline might still be saved, but the Supreme Governor of the Church of England did not agree. Twelve days after Hooker's sermon, Elizabeth closed parliament with a message reminding them that she herself was deeply learned in religion: "I suppose few (that be no professors) have read more". They wronged her, she said, when they accused her of being cold in religion. The matter of religion "touched her so near" she had to talk about it, for it was the "ground on which all other matters ought to take root." If, she said, "I were not persuaded that mine were the true way of God's will, God forbid that I should live to prescribe it to you." She did not, she said, wish to "animate the Romanists ... nor tolerate newfangledness," for they were both dangerous.

Elizabeth was especially troubled by the dangers to her royal authority presented by "every man having his own censure to make a doom of the validity and privity of his prince's government, with a common veil and cover of God's word."[16]

---

13 Travers, *Ecclesiastical Discipline*, 9, 201–2.
14 Hill, *Works of Hooker, Vol. 5*, 165.
15 BL, Lansd. 50, fo. 169.
16 Hartley, *Proceedings*, II, 32.

In this, she was speaking directly to Walter Travers, John Field, and others of the Presbyterian movement, as well as to the Jesuits and other Catholics who believed God demanded their disobedience to her.

Learned as she was, Elizabeth certainly understood the problem presented by people who put their own religious certainties before those of the community. She was ruling a kingdom in which there were different classifications of religious virtue, with conflicting ideas of what God expected of the individual and of the state. Peter Kaufman once divided Elizabethans into the "godly, godlier and godliest."[17] For each category, there were positions on state/church polity that created differing ideas of the required relationship of the individual to God and the community. Reconciling those differences was not easy.

One party took the position that the individual's fear of God required obedience to Him, even if it meant disobedience to the state. In their most extreme forms, these "godliest" people might become recusants, refusing to participate in the legally required worship of the English church. They might be "papists," and especially Jesuits, who accepted the Pope's order to separate from Elizabeth's schismatic church and were even willing to lie about and die for what they believed. Or they might be radical Protestants, whose consciences required them to refuse the pubic forms of worship required by the law because they were not close enough to the forms of the Primitive Church.

On the other extreme stood those who believed that obedience to God meant obedience to God's divinely appointed magistrates. Archbishop Whitgift and Elizabeth saw it that way, citing Romans 19, with its injunction that rulers were to be obeyed. They might have disagreed over who was the most important—bishops or Queen—but Whitgift never dared say what his predecessor, Archbishop Grindal, had told Elizabeth. Grindal tried to explain to her that she was a daughter of the church and must obey it. She responded by suspending him and placing him under house arrest, believing that she had authority over bishops.

Somewhere between those who individually chose to refuse and those who insisted that the state church was always correct were those who plumped for expediency over conflict.

A fine example of the examined conscience that led a person to defy authority is William Alabaster, who, as Aconcio warned against, relied on his "own prudence and sagacity," reading his way into a conversion to Catholicism. Alabaster was born in 1567. A member of the Puritan Winthrop family that would settle Massachusetts, he was a leading literary figure at Cambridge and the Court. Serving as chaplain to the Earl of Essex on his Cadiz expedition, he saw his first Catholics in Spain and was impressed by them. But it was his debates with Catholic recusant prisoners that converted him. After one of their

17 Peter Iver Kaufman, "The Godly, Godlier and Godliest," in Doran and Jones, *Elizabethan World*, 238–53.

disputes, Father Thomas Wright loaned him William Reynold's story of his own conversion from ardent Protestantism to Catholicism. Sitting on the edge of his bed, Alabaster took it up and read it, experiencing a conversion much like St. Augustine's.[18] Shortly thereafter, Alabaster's uncle, John Winthrop, noted in his diary that his nephew *"fatebatur se esse papistam"* ("fancies himself to be a papist")—a phrase that catches the way self-conversion worked when a person chose to change religions.[19]

Being a great poet in Latin (though not in English), Alabaster wrote sonnets about his conversion. Having written one chiding Luther for forsaking Christ's church and destroying its community, he declared the loyalty that he had willed, despite all obstacles:

> Though all forsake thee, Lord, yet I will die,
> For I have chained so my will to thine,
> That I have no will left my will to untwine,
> But will abide with thee most willingly.
> Though all forsake thee lord, yet cannot I,
> For love hath wrought in me thy form divine
> That thou art more my heart than heart is mine:
> How can I then from myself, thyself, fly?

But Alabaster recognized the irony in having a mutable will when it came to religious certainty. The poem continues:

> Thus thought St. Peter and thus thinking fell
> And by his fall did warn us not to swell,
> Yet still in love I say I would not fall,
> And say in hope I trust I never shall,
> But cannot say in faith what might I do
> To learn to say it, by hearing Christ say so![20]

William Alabaster's sense of mutability was accurate, in that his conversion did not last. In 1597, he was imprisoned for writing a "tragedy against the Church of England" and "perverting" his father, mother, and sister toward Catholicism.[21] He was subjected to "consultations" with leading Protestant divines, but they

---

18 Dana F. Sutton, ed. *Unpublished Works by William Alabaster (1568–1640)*. University of Salzburg Studies in English Literature Elizabethan and Renaissance Studies, 126 (Salzburg: University of Salzburg, 1997), 118. Molly Murray, The Poetics of Conversion in Early Modern English Literature. Verse and Change from Donne to Dryden (Cambridge: Cambridge University Press, 2009), 47–51.
19 J.J. Muskett, ed. "The Diary of Adam Winthrop," in *The Winthrop Papers Vol. I 1498–1628* (Boston: Massachusetts Historical Society, 1929), 71. BL Add. 37419, fo. 22.
20 Quoted in and interpreted by Murray, *Poetics of Conversion*, 55–6.
21 CP 55/49.

failed to change his mind. Imprisoned for several years, he escaped to the Continent and eventually reached the English College at Rome. There, he denounced its leader, Robert Parsons, to the Inquisition in 1610. Ironically, the inquisitors arrested Alabaster instead. He fled back to England in 1611, was received by James I, reconverted, took his doctorate at Cambridge, and became a minister in the Church of England until his death in 1640.

If Alabaster depended on his personal perspicacity and the motions of the Holy Spirit to determine the true church, he was not alone. Father Robert Southwell, condemned to death under the 1585 statute against Jesuits, wrote Sir Robert Cecil a letter from his imprisonment in the Tower of London. Southwell, who was repeatedly tortured by Richard Topcliff, his jailer, admitted he was a Jesuit priest and guilty as charged. He was true to the advice he had given others imprisoned for their faith. He said, "that which you conceive as a capital crime … I esteem a reasonable excuse … I will disanchor my thoughts from the joys of life … till God, the father of orphans and patron of the comfortless, shall land my poor soul at the haven of my desires."[22]

The Catholic recusants were convinced of their righteousness. They made problematic citizens because they placed divine order over royal authority, recognizing a power greater than Elizabeth's.

Edward Dering's choices demonstrate a Protestant extreme of conscience. A Cambridge don and eloquent preacher, he spoke truth to power, believing, as he said, "I am a minister of Christ, and I have sworn to speak the truth. And marvel not that I speak contrary to so many doctors and yet so boldly say, I speak the truth." The opinions of men are "no warrant of the truth. If it were, Christ had been crucified for his evil doing." This commitment to truth required brutal honesty, he thought. To Sir William Cecil, Principal Secretary of the Privy Council and Chancellor of Cambridge University, he wrote, in one of his many letters about abuses at the university, "I am sorry, Sir William Cecil, that you cannot see. The lord send you clear eyes, that you once delight in the beauty of this temple. If you believe not such men sparingly, you will in the end be deceived greatly."[23] If Burghley had clear eyes, he would fire all the heads of Cambridge colleges who stood in the way of Dering and all godly ministers.

Preaching before the Queen at Lent in 1570, Dering warned her of God's expectations for magistrates, and the divine retribution that was about to fall on her if she did not dismiss abusive patrons of ecclesiastical livings, as well as ministers who were ruffians, hawkers, hunters, dicers, carders, blind guides, and dumb dogs that would not bark. She, he told her, sat still while these

---

22 Robert Southwell, "Letter to Sir Robert Cecil," in Nancy Pollard Brown, ed. *Robert Southwell, S.J. Two Letters and Short Rules of a Good Life* (Charlottesville: University of Virginia Press for the Folger Shakespeare Library, 1973), 83, 85.
23 BL Lansd. 12, fos. 190–190v.

Babylonian whoredoms were committed. He attacked her bishops, too, with apocalyptical threatening. And he seemed surprised when she was angry![24]

The nastiness of the attack was understood by the biblically literate people in the audience, since he was suggesting that Elizabeth had sold out to the Devil and was enacting the role of the Whore of Babylon foretold by the Prophet Daniel. They also knew, if they had been going to Court sermons very often, that it was irrefutable that the Whore of Babylon was the Pope. She was Rome and the Church of Rome, usually associated with the seven-headed beast in the Book of Revelation.

A popular sermon by William Fulke in November 1570, often reprinted, made it clear that the Whore of Babylon was Rome, as proved by the Fathers and the Scriptures.[25] Thus, for Dering to associate his Queen with Babylon was deeply affronting, linking her to the Antichrist, the Pope, fornication, and drunkenness.

Dering knew England deserved chastening because most of its inhabitants, he believed, had no scruples in conscience about their light, lewd behavior. For every person willing to suffer denial and death for their religious beliefs, there were hundreds who got on with living, snatching their joys where they could find them. Naturally, this irritated the self-righteousness of the moral reformers.

To get a feeling for the differences between attitudes, meet Sir Thomas Posthumous Hoby. Sir Thomas, born after his father's death in 1566, was the son of Elizabeth Cooke. The Cooke sisters were forceful women, and a fierce strain of Protestantism ran in them. It is not surprising that Sir Thomas grew into a devout, if diminutive, man. By all accounts, he irritated his Yorkshire neighbors with his holiness, and, since he was a justice of the peace, he could impress his values on those around him.

Loutishly, his neighbor Sir William Eure, Eure's son, and some of his men, mocked Sir Thomas for his piety. In late August 1600, they had been out hunting and asked his hospitality for the night. What followed outraged their pious host. First, they began playing cards, to which Sir Thomas objected. Then, at supper, they talked of hunting and dogs, "sports whereunto Sir Thomas never applied himself," and lascivious subjects, every sentence beginning and ending with great oaths. They drank frequent healths, "abuses never practiced by Sir Thomas."

After dinner, Sir Thomas's household met for prayers, but his guests preferred to throw dice. Worse, when Sir Thomas and his household began to sing

---

24 Edward Dering, "A Sermon Preached before the Queenes Maiestie, the 25 day of februarie, by Maister Eward Dering. 1569," in *Maister Derings workes* (1590). STC (2nd ed.)/6675(a).

25 William Fulke, *A sermon preached at Hampton Court on Son[day] being the. 12. day of Nouember, in the yeare of our Lord. 1570. VVherin is plain[ly] proued Babylon to be Rome, both by Scriptures and doctors...* (1570). STC (2nd ed.)/11449.5.

a psalm, the gamblers answered with a "black saint," pounding their feet on the floor. Some even stood on the stairs and laughed all through the worship. When they began calling for more wine at breakfast, Sir Thomas locked his cellar and told them they could have none. He also told them he would appreciate it if they would "leave disquieting him with carding, dicing, and excessive drinking."[26]

Sir Thomas was so offended he complained to the Court of Star Chamber about their behavior. He also wrote his cousin, Sir Robert Cecil, the Queen's Principal Secretary. To his horror, he later heard that Sir Robert had laughed about his cousin's religious propensities with one of the offenders, and had said that "your Honor did make his son imitate my preacher, by using such gestures as my preacher did use in his evening exercises, and that your Honor did laugh very heartily at it."[27]

This story, probably known by Shakespeare and used to inspire the character Malvolio in *Twelfth Night*, puts flesh on the bones of the disputes between lifestyles. Sir William Eure did need a reformation of his manners, and Sir Thomas Hoby must have come across as an uptight prig. Ministers loved denouncing the Eures of their world.

One of the best-known denunciations of the terrestrial joys of the English was published by Philip Stubbes, a professional writer born in Cheshire about 1555. Called *The Anatomy of Abuses* (1583), it catalogs the "manifold sinful pride" of the English. Emphasizing the sins of the ego that lead to contempt for God, Stubbes was playing off well-established tropes and the rules of the church. Elizabeth herself expected people to honor the Sabbath and keep it holy. She expected people to live by the Ten Commandments. It is not surprising that some of her godliest subjects, seeing the biblical roots of her orders, thought they should be enforced.[28]

Stubbes knew that people who put themselves before God did not love their neighbors as themselves, as commanded, and spent their time massaging their own egos. That explains his obsession with how people dressed. Twenty-two chapters of his *Anatomy* are devoted to lascivious and excessive clothing. Besides costly shirts, great ruffs, expensive stockings, corked shoes, French hoods, and scarves, Stubbes ranted against the "palpable odors, fumes, vapors and smells of musks, civets, pomanders, perfumes, and balms" that were flags of pride and provocations to vice.[29]

---

26 CP 88/19. CP 90/80.
27 CP 251/39.
28 Kenneth L. Parker, *The English Sabbath. A Study of Doctrine and Discipline from the Reformation to the Civil War* (Cambridge: Cambridge University Press, 1988), 41–64.
29 Philip Stubbes, *The Anatomie of Abuses*, Margaret Jane Kidnie, ed. (Tempe: Renaissance English Text Society, 2002), 124–125.

Stubbes went on to denounce whoredom ("all mutual copulation, except marriage"), gluttony, drunkenness, covetousness, usury, swearing, Sabbath breaking, stage plays, May games, church ales, wakes and feasts, dancing, music, cards, dice, tennis, bowls, and wicked books. On the Sabbath, he pronounced, the English should be prevented from indulging in bear baiting, cockfighting, hawking, hunting, football, markets, fairs, and courts. He denounced theater going twice. In short, he found his countrymen enthusiastically committing the deadly sins and breaking the Ten Commandments. His dislike of their sinful behavior was so extreme that the book might be read as a satire, but he meant it to be serious. Punishment, in his estimation, should be biblical. Adulterers should be stoned to death, as the Law of God requires, or, lacking that deadly "drink from Moses' cup," they should at least be branded on the face.[30]

In another book, Stubbes, whose works sold very well, set out to describe the people of England. Having made, he said, a tour of the entire country, "partly for my private pleasure ... partly for the avoidance of the plague," he reported on the decay of public monuments and works, blaming his fellow subjects. He found the English "dissolute, proud, envious, malicious, disdainful, covetous, ambitious, careless of good works, and almost altogether irreligious."[31]

He wondered how, if Christians loved the poor, they could spend so much on frippery. If usury impoverished and imprisoned the borrowers, how could a Christian society tolerate it? Shouldn't Christians, obeying their loving God, cheerfully do good for their communities? True Christians, he argued, did good works that, unlike the good works of the papists, were good for their neighbors and communities. It was not enough to give up being Catholic; you had to reform your lifestyle and live a Christ-like life. "The badge ... of the children of God, whereby they are known and discerned from the children of the Devil, is love, as our savior Christ saith himself. By this shall all men know you are my disciples, if you love one another." Part of that love, he said, is intolerance of evil in others.[32] Put another way, Stubbes agreed with St. Augustine that the role of the state was to make the world safe for Christians, encouraging godly behavior while repressing opportunities for sin. The pleasures of the sinner tempted good Christians and brought God's wrath down on the community. So, why tolerate sinful enjoyments?

What were these evils that Stubbes found so intolerable? His neighbors would have told us that he was attacking rank, station, and sociability in the name of a theology that was tone deaf to these essential facets of community life. Stubbes called it fear of God and obedience to Scripture.

---

30 Ibid., 150.
31 Phillip Stubbes, *A motiue to good workes Or rather, to true Christianite indeede...* (1593), Epistle Dedicatory. STC (2nd ed.)/23397.
32 Ibid., 181.

Stubbes' horror at the way people dressed touched upon a constant worry in Elizabethan society. It was widely accepted that dress had to be regulated or God would be irritated, but the reason for regulating it was that it was the marker of social station. You should dress in a manner appropriate to your place. As Stubbes said, "By wearing of apparel more gorgeous, sumptuous, and precious then our state, calling, or condition of life requireth," people are "puffed up with pride, and induced to think of ourselves, more than we ought, being but vile earth and miserable sinners."[33]

Elizabeth's government agreed with Stubbe's concern, though for a different reason. While Stubbes wanted sinners controlled, the state wanted everyone kept in their place. Addressing the Justices of Assize in 1565, Lord Keeper Bacon made a detailed case for why the laws on apparel had to be enforced throughout the country. Sumptuary laws prevented four mischiefs: confusion of degrees, consumption of patrimonies, destruction of persons, and the universal impoverishment of the whole realm. Bacon jokingly asked, "who can now know a yeoman from a gentleman or a mean gentleman from a knight, or a knight from a baron? ... Yea, I am sure, you all think it is very hard many times to know a serving man from a noble man by his apparel and all for want of executing of this law."[34]

In 1564, commissions were issued to justices of the peace for a national investigation into women's forbidden fashions. Since clothing was taken as an index to personal wealth, the Privy Council tied what wives wore to how many horses their husbands could contribute to the defense of the realm. The justices accosted women wearing gowns of silk, French hoods or bonnets decorated with gold, pearls, or precious stone, or chains of gold around their necks, their partlets,[35] or anywhere else on their bodies. They also looked for those with velvet in the lining or other part of their gowns, other than in the cuffs and hems, or any velvet at all in their outer gowns, as well as for petticoats of silk.[36]

Reports came in from all over the nation, finding few men who needed to acquire horses, but creating an interesting picture of upper-class female fashion (see Figure 8.1).

In June 1566, the Lord Mayor of London ordered "sad and discrete persons" to watch at Bishopsgate from 7 a.m. until 6 p.m. for persons wearing "any great and monstrous hosen, silk, velvet or weapons restrained and prohibited." People detected wearing the forbidden fashions were to be arrested and brought to the Counter prison.[37]

---

33 Stubbes, *Anatomie of Abuses*, 66.
34 HEH HM 1340, fos, 27–27v.
35 Partlet: clothing worn over the neck and upper part of the chest, esp. by women to cover a low décolletage. OED.
36 TNA E178/469; E178/2004. Jones, *Governing*, 179–80.
37 London, Guildhall Library, MS 11588/1, fo. 150v

Figure 8.1 A bourgeoise English woman and a female merchant. Ghent, University of Ghent, MS D'Heere, Lucas, *Théâtre De Tous Les Peuples Et Nations De La Terre Avec Leurs Habits Et Ornemens Divers, Tant Anciens Que Modernes, Diligemment Depeints Au Naturel Par Luc Dheere Peintre Et Sculpteur Gantois.* Provided by Ghent University Library.

So, Stubbes' concern about "excess apparel" in England was commonly shared. It was a popular trope among magistrates and theologians. Bacon had described it as a civic problem of disorder and decay. Proclamations were issued regularly against excess of apparel from the reign of Henry VIII until that of James I, so it was continuously on people's minds. Theologians described it as evidence of the sin of pride, and apparel was sure to be mentioned whenever God's wrath fell on the nation. Parliament, too, feared the results of excess apparel, and there were various bills to address the problem.

One bill, probably from 1566, tried to both limit the excess and enforce appropriate costumes. It was high on Principal Secretary Cecil's list of things to be done in parliament that year.[38] One of the problems being addressed was new to the Elizabethans: what should bishops' wives wear? It was imperative that their clothes define their social station, earning them the deference due to their degree, but there had never, anywhere, been bishops' wives before. The bill set a ceiling on the costumes of bishops and ecclesiastical doctors: "their wives not to wear damask, satin or velvet but all other silks under that with one guard or welt of velvet without embroidery, on pain of £20 a garment a day, £5 of it to the surveyors and the rest to be estreated in the exchequer or to the sheriff by the justices of assize in the shire where they dwell."[39] This proposal would have made them visibly the equivalents in rank to the wives of knights.

The rules about how to dress were so complicated that Elizabeth had to remind people of what they could and could not wear through proclamations. These would repeat the old orders and add "necessary additions" to keep up with changing fashion. Thus, in 1580, long cloaks "being in common sight monstrous, as now of late are begun to be used." In general, fashions that were less than two years old were forbidden. Frustrated, she also banned "any new kind or form of apparel" that cost more than the things forbidden to each rank. Thankfully, the regulations were also occasionally relaxed, as when livery uniforms were finally exempted from the ban on silk buttons. In a world in which the trappings of your horse or mule indicated your status, the proclamations also regulated how horses could dress.[40]

The principle was that those who should wear fine clothes would be fined if they dressed down. Those who offended by wasteful dressing, which often required extra cloth, were also chastised. The monstrous breeches and "bull's head" hairstyles so fashionable in the 1560's were limited to men of the degree of baron and higher; otherwise, the wearer was to be fined the huge sum of £3 a day.[41]

Wearing "great hose" or breeches consumed lots of expensive cloth. The pumpkin-like short breeches were stuffed with rags, wool, tow, or hair to swell a man's waist and thighs. Just above the knees, they tied to fine stockings with expensive laces or points. They became so large that men could not easily sit down. In parliament, a scaffold was built around the walls that would allow the

---

38 TNA SP 12/40, fo. 149.
39 TNA SP 11/4, fo. 15v. Because of this discussion of clerical wives, this clearly belongs to Elizabeth's reign, not Mary's, where it was calendared.
40 H&L, II, 381–6, 454–62; III, 3–8.
41 TNA SP 11/4, fo. 14v.

members to rest their feet without fully sitting.[42] Accompanying them were extravagant codpieces. As a comedy of 1571 mocked:

> ... Merry here's trim gear ...
> These are no hose, but water buckets, I tell thee plain:
> Good for none, but such as have no buttocks.
> Did you ever see two such little Robin ruddockes,
> So laden with breeches?[43]

The female equivalent was the "bum roll," swelling the shape of a woman's behind in a way that allowed more yards of expensive fabric to hang down. Of course, a whole range of colors were available to enhance the display. "Goose turd green, pease-porridge tawny, popinjay blue, lusty gallant," and "devil-in-the-head" were cloth colors named by William Harrison.[44] Even the "sad" costumes of serious people were made from expensive cloths. Colors like rich black and bright white were especially hard to make, and therefore bespoke the wealth of the wearer.

A satirist summed up women's prideful costumes in a dialogue between various parts of the human body. Here, the Belly mocks the Back for its affectations in dress. Men's backsides, of course, are ridiculously clad in great hose, or hose like herrings, or baggy hose—but always wasteful hose. Women do the same:

> outward tricking and dainty trimming of their heads, the laying out of their hairs, the painting and washing of their faces, the opening of their breasts, and discovering them to their wastes, their bents of whale bone to bear out their bums, their great sleeves and bumbasted shoulders, squared in breadth to make their wastes small, their colored hose, their variable shoes, and all these are but outward shows.[45]

Obviously, many, many people understood the boundaries they transgressed in dressing above their station and spending more than necessary on their clothes. They wished to be more than they seemed for reasons of personal credit, pride, and attraction. Thomas Whythorne, musing about one of his courtships, recalled "I ... furnished myself with convenient apparel and jewels so well as I

---

42 Jones, *Birth*, 214–16.

43 Richard Edwards, *The excellent comedie of two the moste faithfullest freendes, Damon and Pithias...* (1571). STC (2nd ed.)/7514.

44 William Harrison, The Description of England, Georges Edelen, ed. (Ithaca: Folger Shakespeare Library, 1968), 148.

45 W. Averell, *A meruailous combat of contrarieties Malignantlie striuing in the me[m]bers of mans bodie ... With an earnest and vehement exhortation ... couragiously to be readie prepared against the enemie* (1588), Sig. Bi. STC (2nd ed.)/981.

could (with the glorious show of the which, among other things, a young maiden must be wooed)."[46] He knew what it took to look sexy.

Money was to be made from this demand for fancier clothing and accessories, so we must be careful about linking all of the concern about costume to morality. The legislation against certain kinds of dress was introduced to support particular industries. For instance, the Haberdashers of London secured a 1566 law making it illegal for anyone under the rank of a knight to wear a velvet hat and limiting the number of hatters in London. The Haberdashers and Cappers, fighting the fashion for tall wool felt hats imported from Spain, secured a 1571 law that required men, except peers of the realm, to wear knit woolen caps on Sunday, protecting the knitting industry from the felt hat competition.[47]

Clearly, the use and consumption of clothing was an important issue to Elizabethans, and they remained obsessed with its cost and its implications for social status. But Stubbes was worried about other things, too. Though he devoted a great deal of ink to apparel, he was just as disturbed by the "whoredom" and "gluttony" occurring around him.

Whoredom was "mutual coition betwixt a man and woman" outside of matrimony. Most people—"libertines"—saw it as a badge of love, a touch of lusty youth, a friendly dalliance, a restoration of love, and an ensign of good will. But for Stubbes, sex had only one divine purpose. When God said "multiply and be fruitful," He meant only within marriage. Unlike animals, humans were rational and had to live by God's law.

Naturally, all Elizabethans were interested in sex and marriage, and they spent a lot of time worrying about—and enjoying—lusts and temptations. Unlike on the Continent, young people in England could mix freely, which created opportunities for sexual temptations and "whoredom."

Alessandro Magno, an Italian merchant who visited England in 1562, was struck by this un-Italian freedom between the sexes. He reported that Englishwomen were free to go out without their menfolk and noticed that women served in shops. "Many of the young women gather outside Moorgate and play with the young lads, even though they do not know them. Often, during these games, the women are thrown to the ground by the young men who only allow them to get up after they have kissed them. They kiss each other a lot." He went on to say that, at banquets, the English slapped men on the shoulder, patted women on the belly, and cried "frolic!" At dances, this familiarity was even greater. The men "hold women in their arms and hug them very tightly, and for each dance they kiss them in a very lustful way."[48]

---

46 James M. Osborn, ed. *The Autobiography of Thomas Whythorne* (Oxford: Oxford University Press, 1961), 63.
47 8 Eliz. I, c. 11. 13 Eliz. I, c. 19.
48 Caroline Barron, Christopher Coleman, and Claire Gobbi, eds. "The London Journal of Alessandro Magno 1562." *The London Journal* 1983; 9(2), 144.

Nonetheless, people knew they were expected to resist lust. Adultery was forbidden by the Ten Commandments, and the Levitical laws were full of sexual behaviors abhorred by God. Salvation aside, honor and property turned around sexual chastity, especially for women. If they lost their sexual honor, they lost their value as property, and they lost their ability to marry well. Honor and salvation were at stake for men in different ways, since wives were the property of their husbands and could commit petty treason by having extramarital affairs. Cuckolded men were sometimes subjected to public ridicule. Sexually incontinent men and women might be punished in the present by their neighbors and the church courts, and in the future by God.

Stubbes' rant about sinful behavior suggests that the English were sinning lustily; the records of the church and secular courts, however, suggest that crimes of "whoredom" were occurring, but that they presented complex problems. "Whoredom" was the bailiwick of the spiritual courts, run by the church and charged with guarding the souls of the people. Secular courts, such as the Common Pleas, worried about defamation, trespass, and the welfare implications of lost reputations, broken marriage contracts, and bastardy.

It is hard to know much about the sexual morality of the common people, but in the Consistory Court of the Province of York, a majority of the business done between 1560 and 1640 concerned defamation "by words," and almost all defamation cases contained charges of sexual misconduct. Cases in that court detail charges against people who were said to be having or begetting bastards and to have engaged in adultery, fornication, cuckoldry, whoremongering, and being a whore. They show a rich vocabulary of sexual insult. One woman in 1597 accused another of being "Tinker whore, tinker's bitch, whore, queen, drab and scold, drunkard, drunken whore, drunken queen, drunken harlot, drunken drab, and drunken scold," adding she was a "naughty, an evil and a bad and lewd woman." The cases were brought almost entirely by people of the lower social orders, which proves that there was a great concern for maintaining a sexual good name and sexual honor.[49] It does not prove that the accused did the things they were imputed to be doing.

Sexual misconduct, then, was a sin again God, as was defamation of character, but when besmirching a person's sexual honor deprived them of an opportunity, it turned into an offense against the Queen's peace. In those circumstances, a remedy was available in the secular courts.

In 1600, the Court of Common Pleas took up the case of Mary Holwood against Roland Hopkins for having said to her servant, "Thy mistress is an errant whore and would have lain with me seven years ago. And I would not unless she would go to the hedge." The Common Pleas ruled that it had no

---

49 J.A. Sharpe, *Sexual Defamation and Sexual Slander in Early Modern England: The Church Courts at York*. Borthwick Papers No. 58 (York: Borthwick Institute of Historical Research, 1980), 9–10, 17, 22.

jurisdiction because this was a matter for the spiritual courts. But the next term, the plaintiff came back with a showing that because of this accusation, her marriage to a certain J.S. had been called off, and she had been deprived of her good name and of the marriage, to her financial harm. Losing a husband worth £200 a year was cause for damages, making it within the court's jurisdiction. This started an argument among the judges that went on for several terms. Under what conditions should the court accept defamation cases?

The justices researched the case law for hints, which gives us a look at the world of sexual insult. They found the Court of King's Bench held that if a slanderer claimed, "the plaintiff had had a child," it was actionable because it was provable. In the case of *Davis* v. *Gardiner*, it was actionable because the charge that she had borne a child was spoken to the prospective husband, who had then called off the wedding. In *Woolfe* v. *Snagge*, the plaintiff had been called "cuckold," but because his wife refused to testify, since it would have defamed her, there was no case. Citing cases of defamation all the way back to Henry IV, they argued the nature of sexual insult, and whether it was the same as if Ms. Holwood had been called a heretic. But, in a lawyerly fashion, they finally decided that there was no case because the defendant had said that she "would have lain" with him, rather than that she did lie with him. The mere slanderous words were referred to the church court.[50]

Though taught in their catechisms and their social codes to remain chaste, many failed. Presumably, many more tried very hard not to give in to the temptations of the flesh. God, said the *Book of Common Prayer* marriage service, created marriage to populate the earth, to control animal lust, and to ensure mutual care. Thanks to this divine remedy for lust, sexual impulses had a clear path to follow. Except that it was not easy to know when licit sex was possible.

Legally, marriage was a contract made between two people. It required the exchange of promises to live together as man and wife, the vesting of those promises through the exchange of gifts (usually rings), and sexual consummation. If a man and woman had privately performed the requisite three actions, they were married. They might, especially if there was a pregnancy, choose to have a church wedding to publicly confirm their clandestine contract, but none was required. Thus, you could hear a contradictory conversation between a man and a woman like this:

MAN: Be you not my wife? Why should you refuse me?
WOMAN: I am so … but what will folks say, because I am not married.[51]

---

50 R.H. Helmholz, ed. *Select Cases on Defamation to 1600* (London: Selden Society, 1985), 89–91.
51 Quoted in Ralph A. Houlbrooke, The English Family 1450–1700 (London: Routledge, 1988), 172–3.

These clandestine espousals created confusion, but the contractual nature of the relationship could not be broken if the couple had done the three requisite things. There was no divorce in Tudor England. The church might allow separation "from bed and board" for reasons of serious incompatibility, but the couple remained married until death did them part.

At the heart of this legal contract was the mutual promise. Both partners had to agree to the marriage. Because most marriages were arranged, this remained an important loophole for the intended. Before a father could give away his daughter at the west door of the church (they did not marry before the altar in the sixteenth century), she had to verbally consent to the marriage. This, however, did not prevent parents from arranging inappropriate marriages. As Phillip Stubbes says, "in England there is over great liberty permitted therein: for, little infants in swaddling clothes are often married by their ambitious parents and friends."[52]

He is exaggerating, of course, but not by much. The espousal of children did occur. One child recalled being "enticed with two apples" if he would say "I do."[53] In another case, a boy, aged three, and a girl, aged two, were carried to their wedding, where their "friends" spoke the words of acceptance on their behalf.[54] Since boys had to be fourteen and girls twelve to be of legal age, these espousals produced enough "divorces" to leave a record in the church courts. Technically, they were not divorces, since there was no consummation that completed marriage. But they were legal processes that dissolved what was otherwise an indissoluble marriage contract for lack of consent, even after childish voices had said "yes" and gifts had been exchanged.

"And besides" child marriages, says Stubbes, "you shall have a very saucy boy, of ten, fourteen, sixteen, or twenty catch up a woman and marry her."[55] Here again he is exaggerating—mostly. Apprentices, for instance, were forbidden to marry before the age of twenty-four—at least in theory. He may have been talking about forced marriages. It did occur that a girl was abducted, forced to undergo a wedding, and raped. This was a way to acquire her lands, and, until the introduction of a law against statutory rape in 1571, it was not illegal.

Rape itself was a well-known felony, punishable by hanging. Most sexual crime, however, only threatened the souls of the consenting "criminals," so it was dealt with by the church using shaming as a penance. Standing in church wearing a white sheet and a label declaring the crime might be an effective preventative in a small community, but in larger ones, shaming often consisted of "carting," "riding the skimmington," or a charavari, where the target of the

---

52 Stubbes, *Anatomie of Abuses*, 147.
53 Frederick J. Furnivall, ed. *Child-Marriages, Divorces and Ratifications … the Diocese of Chester, A.D. 1561–66* (Oxford: Early English Text Society, 1897), 45.
54 Ibid., 25–6.
55 Stubbes, *Anatomie of Abuses*, 147.

shame was carried physically or in image through the streets while being mocked. That these punishments were used is proved by records of towns like the Borough of Leicester; there, the records show payments for carting, whipping, and "papers to set upon the [market] cross of the punishment of whoredom."[56] Stubbes wanted all "whores" executed, which was more than the law was willing to do.[57]

Adultery and abuse strained marriages but did not annul them. Sometimes, the law, a couple's relatives, and even the Queen were willing to intervene in truly abusive marriages. But not usually. Spouses were bound together for better and for worse, and wives promised to obey. These promises yielded some very unhappy stories, like that of Sir Francis and Elizabeth Lady Willoughby.

Married by an arrangement brokered by the Earl of Leicester in 1565, they had twelve children together in sixteen years, and fought like cats and dogs until her death in 1594. Their families became involved, with Sir Francis' sister, Lady Arundel, attacking Elizabeth, and Elizabeth's father attempting to reconcile them. Screaming matches, angry letters, armed servants locking her from the house, and a ten-year separation led to an order from Queen Elizabeth that Sir Francis pay Elizabeth £200 a year in maintenance. At one point, Sir Francis ordered "That my wife shall have nothing to do with the children, but that they shall be ordered by such as I shall authorize."[58]

Sir Francis listened to those who claimed Elizabeth had been impregnated by someone else ("played the whore," as Stubbes would say), and his servants helped spread the rumor. She defended her reputation and her conscience. He, in return, defended his, commenting that because of her "forward" mind, "my softness hath rather deserved reprehension than commendation. The husband's leniency ought [not] to be such as to increase the wife's folly."[59] He nonetheless signed one of his letters in a way that recognized his husbandly duties: "By him that will serve you if you say yea. And will love you and serve you though you say nay."[60]

Sir Francis reminded his wife that "according to the ordinance of God, and the covenant of your marriage, you endeavor to subdue and submit your will to the pleasure of your head, in all honest and lawful things, seeking rather to win his good will with covering his faults and bearing with his infirmities, than to wrest him to your own, by revealing his shame and resisting his commandments." Her honor and reputation was based on obedience: "it is fully

---

56 Martin Ingram, *Carnal Knowledge: Regulating Sex in England, 1470–1600* (Cambridge: Cambridge University Press, 2017), 351.

57 Stubbes, *Anatomie of Abuses*, 151.

58 University of Nottingham Library, Mi LM 26 in Middleton Collection, MSS Division, fo. 93.

59 Alice T. Friedman, "Portrait of a Marriage: The Willoughby Letters of 1585–1586." *Signs* 1986; 11(3), 553.

60 BL, Lansd. 101, fo. 147.

warranted by the word of God which binds all women, of what birth or calling soever they be, to yield due benevolence and obedience to their husbands, the which if your Ladyship shall do, (as I doubt not but you will) besides that you shall bridle the ill tongues of your ill cholers, and give the world cause to witness on your side, you shall have the testimony of a good conscience at home."[61]

Reconciled with him in 1588, Lady Elizabeth took control of his show house, Wollaton Hall, near Nottingham. They were never happy in wedlock, but she agreed to resume her wifely duties. The Willoughbys had social obligations to maintain, alongside their marital stations. One of those obligations was hospitality, and it is probable that, as Stubbes feared, they failed at that just as they failed at marriage.

Stubbes defined hospitality as giving liberally to the poor who needed food and lodging. Hospitality was a part of your station, and your liberality had to match your social standing. Stubbes' condemnation of the Elizabethan diet could have been written by a twenty-first century health fanatic. He described their unbiblical gluttony: too much meat, too much wine, too much sugar, too many sauces, too much spice, "prodigality ... vanity ... excess, riot and superfluity." In the days of their forefathers, he proponed, people fed on grains, roots, pulses, herbs, weeds, and "such baggage," and yet lived longer, healthier lives with better complexions and greater strength. The diet of the 1580's, he said, caused disease and shortened lives. Worse, too much meat and drink provoked lust, lust brought forth sin, and sin brought forth eternal death.[62]

Stubbes, and his Jesus, would not have approved of the diet provided for members of the Star Chamber when they were at Hertford Castle, eating as men of their station were expected to eat. Four men, at one table, were supplied with "two good messes of meat always according to the days, and always on the fish days two dishes of fish." The leftovers went to their gentlemen and servants, who were also supplied with beef and mutton. Red and white wine, beer, and ale were served, and several kinds of salt fish were available from the Queen's stores. The poultry was "brought daily by Robert Jorden of London; the fish as pikes, carpes, tenches, eels, &c., weekly from Cambridge by Wm. Raven of London, pikemonger."[63] There is no mention of the grains, roots, pulses, weeds, and other things urged by Stubbes.

Gluttony, as Stubbes defined it, was practiced intentionally as a badge of status. He also complained against drunkenness—which leads to blaspheming, which leads to damnation—telling warning stories of Dutch drunkards who came to bad ends. Certainly, English people drank alcohol at every meal (though breakfast beer was "small beer," so it was very weak) and on almost all occassions.

---

61 BL, Lansd. 101, fo. 151.
62 Stubbes, *Anatomie of Abuses*, 152–4.
63 CP 162/73.

Figure 8.2 St. George's Kermis and Maypole. Peter Breughel the Younger, ca. 1616. The Picture Art Collection / Alamy Stock Photo.

Philip Stubbes and his godly fellows were disgusted by the parish social customs of "church ales" and other festivities in which communities celebrated and raised money. Opportunities for drunkenness, lust, blaspheming, whoredom, and ungodliness, they were denounced by the reformers, who also insisted that the taverns be closed during worship so that there was no competition with the Word of God. They knew that the Word, rightly taught, would change peoples' hearts, but first you had to get their attention. All this drinking and carousing lured them away from serious obedience to God.

Ironically, Stubbes' *Anatomy of Abuses* catalogs the folk culture that he was hoping to kill, just as it was dying.[64] If Stubbes had not written, we would know much less of church ales, wakes, May poles, plough Mondays, and other jollities that supported the expenses of parish churches and marked the agricultural and liturgical year (see Figure 8.2). These festivals were, across Elizabeth's reign, slowly dying, being pushed out by strict Sabbath keeping, attacks on stage plays, and new ways of paying for parish expenses, such as pew rents. As parishes became more dominated by bureaucratized "select" vestries of the "better sort," these moments of misrule were tamped down and sometimes extinguished or

---

64 Ingram, *Carnal Knowledge*, 425–6.

replaced with new holidays, like the celebration of the accession of Queen Elizabeth on November 17.[65]

To be fair to Stubbes, many of these festivals were what he said they were: opportunities to drink too much and to indulge in lusty hijinks. The traditions of the May pole and "going a-Maying" were connected to the celebration of spring and were probably pre-Christian. But like all good pagan holidays, they had been baptized, falling on the seventh Sunday after Easter, Whitsunday, in late May or early June. It was the time when the hawthorn hedges of England, known colloquially as "May," were in full white blossom—associated with baptismal white. As the daylight lengthened and the weather warmed, people went into the woods and spent the short night in "pleasant pastime," bringing home a May pole. Drawn by oxen wearing nosegays of flowers in their horns, the pole was decorated with handkerchiefs and flags and erected on a green. Feasting and dancing around the pole, like "heathen people did, at the dedication of their idols," they engaged in drunkenness and revelry.

It was common for young people to spend the night in the woods picking flowers for the May games. Edmund Spenser, writing in his deliberately antique style, had the Catholic shepherd (in the sense of a religious pastor) Palinodes, speaking in dialect, portray the Maying thus:

> IS not thilke the mery moneth of May,
> When love lads masken in fresh aray?
> How falles it then, we no merrier bene,
> Ylike as others, girt in gawdy greene?
> Our bloncket liveries bene all to sadde,
> For thilke same season, when all is ycladd
> With pleasaunce: the grownd with grasse, the Wods
> With greene leaues, the bushes with bloosming Buds.
> Yougthes folke now flocken in euery where,
> To gather may buskets and smelling brere:
> And home they hasten the postes to dight,
> And all the Kirke pillours eare day light,
> With Hawthorne buds, and swete Eglantine,
> And girlonds of roses and Sopps in wine.
> Such merimake holy Saints doth queme,
> But we here sytten as drownd in a dreme.[66]

65 Ronald Hutton, *The Rise and Fall of Merry England. The Ritual Year 1400–1700* (Oxford: Oxford University Press, 1996), 162–4.
66 Edmund Spenser, "The Shepherds Calendar," in William A. Oram, Einar Bjorvand, Ronald Bond, Thomas H. Cain, Alexander Dunlop, and Richard Schell, eds. *The Yale Edition of the Shorter Poems of Edmund Spenser*, (New Haven: Yale University Press, 1989), 88–9.

Spenser's Palinodes is arguing from a Catholic position in the eclogue. Piers the Protestant "shepherd" responds by grousing about letting the sheep run abroad in "lustihede and wanton maryment."[67] Piers may have read Stubbes: "I have heard it credibly reported that of forty, threescore, or a hundred maids, going to the wood overnight, there have scarcely the third part of them return home again undefiled."[68] Clearly, it was a festival made for the Devil, promoting whoredom.

Thomas Morely's famous madrigal, "Now is the Merry Month of May," published in 1595, set the lusty spring festival to music, while Thomas Dekker wrote a song about Maying for his play the *The Shoemaker's Holiday* in 1599. The behavior portrayed in both would have appalled Stubbes and his like.

These festivals were occasions for lewd behavior that the puritanical found disgusting. In Beaumont and Fletcher's early seventeenth-century comedy, *The Womans Prize, or The Tamer Tam'd*—an alternative version of Shakespeare's *The Taming of the Shrew*—the shrewish townswomen attacking Petruchio are described thus:

> There's ne'r a one of these, the worst and weakest,
> (Chuse where you will,) but dare attempt the raising,
> Against the sovereign peace of Puritans,
> A May-pole and a Morris, maugre mainly
> Their zeal, and Dudgeon-daggers: and yet more,
> Dares plant a stand of batt'ring Ale against 'em,
> And drink 'em out of the parish.[69]

Communities were being split over these festivals. To many—and especially to church ales—the churchwardens of the parishes brought malt for brewing. In King James I's reign, old people in Minehead, Somerset fondly remembered how the churchwardens lopped and topped the trees in the churchyard to fire the brewing of the church ale, needing no permission from anyone.[70] Having made many barrels, they held a parish party and sold it to the parishioners. As Stubbes put it, people who drank the most considered they were the most meritorious, doing good service to God until they were "drunk as swine, and as mad as March Hares."[71] These revelries were defended as necessary for covering the operating expenses of parishes and paying for service books, communion cups, and roof repairs. As the Sheriff of Banbury reported in 1589, when

---

67 Ibid., 89.
68 Stubbes, *Anatomie of Abuses*, 210.
69 *The Womans Prize*, in A.R. Waller, ed. *Beaumont and Fletcher* (New York: Octagon, 1969), 33.
70 Andy Wood, *The Memory of the People. Custom and Popular Senses of the Past in Early Modern England* (Cambridge: Cambridge University Press, 2013), 85.
71 Ibid., 211.

"pastimes used in the country, as may poles, morris dances, Whitsun ales, and others" were abolished, folk "find themselves grieved to be restrained of their honest liberty for their maintaining of their charges [parish expenses], which are the better done by some of these means and especially not knowing any law made to the contrary."[72] Godly citizens, could, however, help end these devilish activities by providing alternative funding to the parishes. Henry Hastings, Third Earl of Huntingdon, specified in his will that several Somerset parishes would receive bequests from him on the strict condition that they never again have church ales, "to the profaning of the Lord's Sabbath, the abusing of his creatures in drunkenness and riot and the corrupting of their youth by training them up in gaming and lascivious wantonness."[73]

The troubles over these customs in Banbury were a foretaste of the tensions to come between the moral reformers and their less scrupulous neighbors, catching the magistrates in the middle as they fought over Sabbath keeping and parish traditions. Banbury was the seat of Anthony Cope, a leading member of the Presbyterians in parliament, remembered for introducing Cope's Bill and Book in 1586. This was another proposal to get rid of the *Book of Common Prayer* and reform the church government along Presbyterian lines. He was arrested and imprisoned in the Tower for introducing religious legislation without permission of the Queen.

Afterward, Cope went home and set about turning his parish at Banbury into a properly reformed congregation, aided by the minister, Henry Brasbridge. Certain that Catholicism could not be defeated until all popish practices were repressed, Cope and Brasbridge attacked the ales and May festivities with frequent sermons. On May 20, 1589, Richard Wheatlye, Constable of the Hundred of Banbury, ordered that all May poles should be taken down, all Whitsun ales, May games, and Morris Dances stopped, and all wakes and fairs forbidden on the Sabbath.[74]

Two days later, John Danvers, Sheriff of Oxford, wrote to the justices of the peace of the shire, informing them about what Wheatlye had done, contrary to Her Majesty's good order, "causing peace to be disturbed and broken, and great and dangerous assemblies made." He blamed it on Anthony Cope, who, he said, was housing banned ministers and their wives, stirring up trouble under the pretense of good religion.[75]

On May 24, the Privy Council sent a letter to Lord Norris, Lord Lieutenant of Oxfordshire, with a clear set of instructions: "We see no cause that these

---

72 TNA SP 12/224, fo. 86.
73 Clair Cross, The Puritan Earl. *The Life of Henry Hastings Third Earl of Huntingdon 1536–1595* (London: Macmillan, 1966), 52. Citing HEH "HA Family Papers. Unindexed wills of Francis Hastings of Bosworth [c. 1580] and Francis Hastings of North Cadbury [before 1596]."
74 TNA SP 12/224, fo. 82.
75 Ibid., fo. 86.

pastimes of recreation, being not used at unlawful times, as on the Sabbath [or] any time of divine service, and in disordered and riotous sort should be forbidden the people." If, the letter said, any refused their orders to allow these recreations, Norris was to send them to the Privy Council to explain themselves. "So on the other side we think it meet that under color of setting up of May poles and likes pastimes there be no liberty sought to make unlawful assemblies or to counsel any disorders riots and unlawful acts whereof further mischief may ensue." Norris was told that the people were not to be forbidden lawful, peaceful recreation.[76]

This 1589 attempt to prevent contention between the pro-May traditionalists and the people who wanted to reform their manners presaged many more conflicts all over England. "Merry England" was in decline as the nation's religious structures and values changed, and the stresses of the late sixteenth century took their toll.[77]

In Chester, the traditional midsummer festivities were ended by Mayor Henry Hardware in 1600. Hardware seems to have been a godly man, and when he caused the giants in the Midsummer Show to be broken, the Devil in his feathers to be put away, and the dragon and the naked boys to be removed, his Puritan opinions were blamed. But Hardware was acting in a national context of bad harvest and political disturbances, as well as under local stresses caused by the war in Ireland. The unruly soldiers in the city, passing to and from the Irish war, had caused him to create a localized form of martial law, erecting a gibbet and nailing drunkards and ale sellers through their ears. Thus, his hard-nosed actions were popular in many quarters. And, of course, he had a religious ideology that suggested that his city could not thrive if it tolerated abuses God did not like.[78]

In 1613, the town of Dorchester burned. More than half the city was destroyed, and in the fire's aftermath, it became the most reformed city in England. Its minister, John White, interpreted the fire as the equivalent to the fiery judgment that destroyed Sodom and Gomorrah, a sign and a warning requiring repentance. He had been battling with the town's steward, Matthew Chubb, for its souls. Chubb thought the old ways of community solidarity and mutual obligation were necessary, rather than the reform of manners White sought. But the fire turned things in White's direction, and, for a while, Dorchester tried to be as godly as God wanted it to be. Not everyone liked it.[79]

---

76 Ibid., fo. 90.

77 Hutton, *The Rise and Fall of Merry England*, passim.

78 Robert Tittler, *Townspeople and Nation. English Urban Experiences 1540–1640* (Stanford: Stanford University Press, 2001), 140–55.

79 David Underdown, *Fire from Heaven Life in an English Town in the Seventeenth Century* (New Haven: Yale University Press, 1994).

Tensions over obedience to God and communal governance that began in Elizabeth's reign continued and worsened under James I and Charles I. James I's issuance of the so-called "Book of Sports" in 1617 demonstrates the increasing angst. The justices of the peace for Lancashire, attempting to ensure that recusants had no excuses for avoiding church, tried to ban all Sunday pastimes. Piping, dancing, bull baiting, and other things were forbidden. Everyone was to be in church, or be clearly known to be avoiding church. Appealing to the King as he passed through Lancashire, protesting local people demanded what the people of Banbury had been assured by the Privy Council back in 1586: liberty to enjoy harmless pastimes on Sunday.

These arguments between those who wanted people's ungodly behavior repressed in favor of God's law and those whose idea of a good life included many of the things condemned by their opponents continued into the Civil War. God's anger at personal misbehavior was seen to be so great that the English Civil War itself was blamed on excess of apparel, drunkenness (especially among women), swearing, lying, and Sabbath breaking. Too much human pride finally had serious consequences.[80]

The moral tensions springing from Elizabethan confusion over conscience and obedience became worse and worse. As the individual soul became the unit of measure, individual piety started to part from communal duty. Individuals following their inner convictions made choices that conflicted with political conformity. Conscience became the measure of piety.

Consciences were unseen by any but God, who knew the secrets of the heart. Therefore, individual virtue could only be determined internally, unless a person's actions resulted in things that damaged their neighbors. Though there was broad agreement on sinful actions, the emphasis on intention left many former sins open for interpretation. This created the need for treaties of private toleration as individuals found themselves living in families and communities that did not agree on religion, but that needed to cooperate for the common good. We can see this contention in the way in which business was done.

Stubbes spent a portion of his *Anatomy of Abuses* on the sinful, insatiable desire for money in England. As he denounced covetousness, he touched another raw nerve in Elizabeth's world, where economic behaviors and philosophies were evolving rapidly in response to globalizing opportunities. The changing economy was creating more choice, more opportunity, more wealth, and more poverty, all making it harder than ever to live in a morally simple universe. There was more and more joy in consumption, and that bothered many.

---

80 Nicolas Proffet, *Englands impenitencie under smiting, causing anger to continue, and the destroying hand of God to be stretched forth...* (1645). Wing/P3647. https://www. westminsterassembly.org/primary-source/englands-impenitencie-under-smiting/ [Accessed November 29, 2018].

9

Moral Economies

When Philip Stubbes declared that the "pouch of the greedy is the mouth of the Devil," he was echoing an ancient Christian belief. Covetous people were presumed to have insatiable desires for more and more wealth. The greedy were always gaping for more, drowning in the devilish "quagmire of avarice, and plunged in the plash of ambition."[1] The desire for profits, the incentive of modern capitalism, was to Elizabethans the obvious sign of a hellbound soul, but determining what economic behavior was allowable opened debates about wealth, poverty, and human nature. How did God want people to live in economic relationships? What was the right way to think about *Homo economicus*?

Elizabethans knew Christ loved the poor, declaring that the rich "shall hardly enter into the kingdom of Heaven," for it is "easier for a camel to go through the eye of a needle, than for a rich man to enter into the Kingdom of God." The rich young man who wished to follow Christ was told: "If thou wilt be perfect go, sell that thou hast, and give it to the poor, and thou shalt have treasure in heaven, and come and follow me." With precedents like that, it is not surprising that godly Elizabethans were morally troubled by spectacles of wealth and the new economic opportunities occurring around them. Giving up greed was hard. As the Geneva Bible glosses this passage in Matthew, "who can frame men's hearts, so that they shall not set their minds on their riches?"[2]

Those following this Christian teaching believed the interest of the poor had to be looked after by their wealthier neighbors, and that God wanted the covetous to be prevented from excessive greed that hurt their communities. This traditional view meant that everything from the price of bread and ale to the wages of workers were regulated for the community's greater good.

But other godly Elizabethans were not so sure. When they read the Gospel of Matthew, they noticed the "similitude" or parable of the talents and thought about how each was called by God to work hard in their calling. "For to every

---

1 Stubbes, *Abuses*, 167.
2 Matthew 19:20–25. Geneva Bible.

Being Elizabethan: Understanding Shakespeare's Neighbors, First Edition. Norman Jones.
© 2020 John Wiley & Sons, Inc. Published 2020 by John Wiley & Sons, Inc.

man that hath, it shall be given, and he shall have abundance, and from him that hath not, even that he hath, shalbe taken away."[3] Interference in the markets was not, for them, a moral requirement. Instead, people should be left free to follow their callings, fulfill their God-given potential, and increase their abundance, unless they harmed their neighbors. As Sir Walter Raleigh asserted in parliament, "I think the best course is to set it [the market] at liberty, and leave every man free, which is the desire of the true English man."[4] The Christian ethics of economic exchange were being debated, to the discomfort of many.

Among those who believed that greed had to be limited by sharp laws were many whose theology did not agree with Stubbes' Calvinism, but who did demand economic regulation in their Christian community. Thomas Nashe, who satirized Stubbes with comments about "those who anatomize abuses and stubbe up sin by the roots," nonetheless thought he was right about the social effects of money.[5] Nashe translated "*bursa avari os est Diaboli*" as "the usurer's purse is hell mouth," while Stubbes translated it as the "pouch of the greedy is the mouth of the Devil," but they agreed on what it implied. Taking his cue from St. Augustine, who taught that greed was a dropsy that caused the rich to swell and swell, Nashe lashed out at those who compounded their incomes, gave credit, and generally oppressed those who relied on their lands and goods. He called them usurers, but he, like Stubbes, was using the term generically, not legally. Nashe wrote of the greedy who trade in money:

> In the country the gentleman takes in the commons, racketh his tenants, undoeth the farmer. In London the usurer snatcheth up the gentleman, gives rattles and babies [*sic*] for his over racked rent, and the commons he took in he makes him take out in commodities. None but the usurer is ordained for a scourge to pride and ambition. Therefore it is that bees hate sheep more than anything, for that when they are once in their wool, they are so entangled that they can never get out. Therefore it is that courtiers hate merchants more than any men, for that being once in their books, they can never get out. Many of them carry the countenances of sheep, look simple, go plain, wear their hair short; but they are no sheep but sheep biters: their wool or their wealth they make no other use of but to snarl and enwrap men with.

Nashe mocked the lenders' unctuous speech and their pious phrases: "God be praised"; "Much good do it you"; "We are nought"; "God amend us"; "Sir, I

---
3 Matthew 25:14–29. Geneva Bible.
4 Hartley, *Proceedings*, III, 451.
5 Thomas Nashe, *Christ's Tears over Jerusalem*, in Ronald B. McKerrow, ed. *The Works of Thomas Nashe*. 5 vols. (London: Sidgwick & Jackson, 1910), I, 20.

drink your health." But he, like Stubbes, warned them that God would stop their mouths and scatter their treasure.[6]

Francis Hastings, reflecting on the debts of his recently deceased brother Henry, the Third Earl of Huntingdon, explained that merchants and moneyed men undermined the natural order. The earl, he said, was "injuriously dealt withal by some of that usuring sort, whose humor it is to insult both honorable and others their betters far, and to tyrannize over their equals and inferiors, and yet will they not be satisfied without use upon use: a most viperous generation, from whose clutches God deliver all noblemen, gentlemen and all other honest men of the meanest sort."[7]

The established way of reining in these "usuring sorts" whose profits oppressed their neighbors was through market regulation. The Tudor state had elaborate methods of controlling markets, beginning with the medieval licensing systems that restricted trade through guilds for manufacturing and sale of goods and services, and including laws against lending money at interest. Much local business in English cities was in the hands of self-governing monopolies, such as the Merchant Adventurers of London or of Bristol, which controlled cloth exports, overseeing both quality and price. Food and other staples were marketed under controlled circumstances, too, since fair prices and adequate supplies were essential to safety and security. Greedy sinners who hoarded produce, drove up prices, or sold substandard goods were subject to prosecution and shaming. Detected by informers, they were publicly punished as enemies of the community. Fair prices were more important than open markets. Better that the ambition for riches be constrained than the poor suffer.

In the reign of Edward VI, a vein of theological social criticism had emerged in a group that historians refer to as the "Commonwealth Men." Typified by Bishop Hugh Latimer, they talked of economics in the language of communal duty. Their ideal society was static, with everyone living in their established place, acting out of love for their fellows according to their stations in life. Disorder was the result of human sin, so if sin could be prevented, divine order would prevail. Raised in the early English humanist tradition, they optimistically believed that if people truly learned what God taught, they would repent and reform, curing the economic distresses of the commonwealth.

In this, the theology met a matching legal assumption. The common law assumed that commercial life was made up of masters and servants, of classes of people with distinct places in the social order with fixed relationships, rather than of individual enterprises and contracts. Consequently, legal attempts at economic justice were frequently about forcing people to accept their place

6 Ibid., II, 98, 101.
7 HEH HA 5099.

and the communal role it thrust upon them. Statutes tended to have a blind disregard for what moderns would think of as the facts of economic life.[8]

Calls for economic reform were given concrete form in Edward VI's time, when statutes talked of teaching God's lessons. For instance, an Act of 1549 denounced ungodly "conspiracies" among food sellers, craftsmen, and laborers. They, "not contented with moderate and reasonable gain," had conspired to sell food for unreasonable prices, to drive up the prices of their manufactures, and to refuse to work for less money. This was willful on their part, and therefore sinful. The King had an interest in ensuring they charged only the natural costs of things.[9]

This kind of thinking was carried into Elizabeth's reign. She and her councilors, some of whom were authors of Edwardian Commonwealth ideology, passed more laws against greed and market manipulation—engrossing, regrating, and forestalling. These were all offenses that had to do with hoarding: creating artificial scarcity to inflate prices. At the same time, the laws were used to regulate the flow of goods in and out of the realm, to keep people working and merchants prosperous. They wished to ensure fair trade, not free trade.

The traditional way of dealing with people who offended in the markets was shaming, as Henry Machyn described in 1559, when a carter tried to cheat his customers by shorting his load of wood:

> there was a carman that carried wood unto certain men, and he sold some by the way, and when that he came to tell [count] the billets he told them that he would a saved the number of the billets, but he was spied, and so the billets was told over again, and so he was carried to the Counter [jail] till Friday the market day, and then he was fetched out and set on horseback, his face to the horse's tail, with 2 billets afore him and 2 behind his (back) round about London (to) his dwelling.[10]

These assumptions about the ethical necessity of a regulated economy were threaded through Elizabethan society. In 1598, a plasterer in London named Hugh Alley created a delightful little picture book entitled *The Forewarning of Offenses, Against Penal Laws*. Depicting every London market, he described the "imperfections" in them. Alley was concerned about things that impoverished the citizens in the hungry times of the late 1590's, such as "forestalling, regrating and engrossing," which drove up prices. But he was also opposed to the "hagglers, hawkers, hucksters, and wanderers"—middle men—who bought

---

8 William Jones, "The Foundations of English Bankruptcy: Statutes and Commissions in the Early Modern Period." *Transactions of the American Philosophical Society* 1979; 69(3), 11.

9 2&3 Edward VI, c. 15.

10 "Diary: 1559 (July–Dec)," in Nichols, *The Diary of Henry Machyn*, 202–21. http://www.british-history.ac.uk/camden-record-soc/vol42/pp202-221 [Accessed November 29, 2018].

Figure 9.1 Eastcheap Market, London, 1598. Notice the pillory labeled "Engrossers" on the left end. From Hugh Alley, *A Caveatt for the Citty of London, Or A forewarning of offences against penall Lawes.* Folger Shakespeare Library, V.a.318. Used by permission of the Folger Shakespeare Library.

food in the markets and then sold it on the streets, "for their own lucre, and private gain," breeding dearth. He wanted them all punished by officials, and prominent in his illustrations are the pillars in the markets where regrators, forestallers, and cheaters were pilloried (Figure 9.1).[11]

Alley's warning came during a famine in England, when successive lord mayors were trying to re-impose controls on food prices. During the dearth in the mid-1590's, riots broke out in London, when crowds of unruly apprentices forced market people to sell their goods at the official prices rather than at the higher market prices. They drove butter down from 5d to 3d a pound; in Billingsgate, they seized fish from the fishwives and sold them at the lower price declared by the Lord Mayor.[12]

A population explosion was doubling the size of the nation in Elizabeth's reign, creating shortages of land and work, as well as of food. Wars in Ireland and on the Continent were making things worse, too. These changes produced and exacerbated arguments over the proper regulation of markets and the need

---

11 Ian Archer, Caroline Barron, and Vanessa Harding, eds. *Hugh Alley's Caveat. The Markets of London in 1598: Folger Ms. V.a.318.* (London: London Topographical Society, 1988), 35.
12 Ibid., 25.

for a reformation of manners. We can see this in battles like that over the ethics of land enclosure.

In the countryside, there was a perennial complaint against enclosing, the process whereby land owners turned intensively farmed land and commons into private pastures, displacing the peasants and villagers who depended on them for a living. Since the reign of Henry VIII, statutes forbidding and controlling enclosure had piled up, trying to keep arable land tilled to ensure the food supply and keep the population from moving. Protection of tillage, however, was not in the interest of landowners, who could produce valuable wool with less labor, or improve farming practices by reengineering their fields to create water meadows. Either way, enclosures displaced the people who lived and worked on the land and exacerbated food shortages.

To protect the food supply, regulations controlled land use, the markets, and the labor supply. Lord Keeper Bacon was eloquent on these issues before the judges. The agricultural labor supply, he told them, was so important that they should "never suffer him that ought by the laws to lay his hands to husbandry to meddle with manual [manufacturing] occupation."[13]

The brokers of commodities had to be controlled, too. The cause of high food prices was not absolute shortages, since in some places there were surpluses, but the distribution: "the ill disposition of the people by engrossing and regrating and false bruits [rumors] raising for greedy gain's sake hath been the chief and principal cause of this dearth and not scarcity alone."[14]

He did not forgive the farmers who enclosed their fields, either. They had to be forced by law to keep their land in traditional production, employing the people who were being forced to stay on it. Bacon was caught between the need for production and the goal of controlling the burgeoning population.

Incentives were sought to increase tillage and put laborers to work by land reclamation, which mainly took the form of draining marshes. Legislation to drain Plumstead and Erith Marshes around Greenwich was passed in 1563.[15] Parliamentary permission for drainage projects and Privy Council licenses were sought in Lincolnshire, Norfolk, Cambridgeshire, and Huntingdonshire, with varying levels of political and engineering success, over the next hundred years. Requiring high levels of capital, the draining of marshes could only be undertaken by wealthy syndicates supported by law. Naturally, the marsh dwellers across the country fought "improvers," especially in the fen country of East Anglia.[16] Slowly, hundreds of thousands of acres of marsh land were

---

13 HEH, EL 2579, fos. 14–14v.
14 HEH HM 1340, fo. 28v.
15 5 Eliz. I, c. 7.
16 David Dean, *Law Making and Society in Late Elizabethan England* (Cambridge: Cambridge University Press, 1996), 159–60.

drained, surveyed, and turned into arable farms and pasture lands, remaking huge parts of the countryside.

Drainage was a special kind of enclosure. The more common kind occurred when fields were ditched and hedged to keep animals in (and out). For instance, in 1569, Geoffrey Bradshaw began to hedge and ditch Mayston Field, a common pasture, near Chinley in Derbyshire. The villagers of Chinley filled the ditch and tore down the hedges, refusing to lose their grazing. When confronted by an order from the Chancellor of the Duchy of Lancaster to permit the enclosure, they took up arms, threatening to burn Bradshaw's house.[17] The people of Chinley knew what Lord Keeper Bacon was talking about when he warned that if enclosures were allowed, "villages should be decayed."[18]

In the 1570's, Sir Francis Hastings, inspecting his family's lands in Devon and Cornwall, found local farmers converting the Earl of Huntingdon's arable farms into pastures. On the reputed site of King Arthur's Camelot, he found 280 sheep grazing in what had been the village of Hardington. Totally enclosed, the village was gone except the farmer's own house. Even the church had been torn down, and its glebe turned to grass. Having converted the whole place to stock raising, the farmer was no longer paying anything to the earl but his common fine—there were no crops to tax.[19]

All these attempts to ensure the food supply and keep people working rested on a belief in a golden age when there had been enough work, enough food, and fair prices; when there were no vagrants, no famines, no oppressive landlords. This halcyon time in Merry England had been destroyed by sinful greed, so the law sought to turn back the clock. But despite parliament's best efforts, freezing the agricultural economy in place did not work. By late in Elizabeth's reign, people were rethinking how to achieve food security.

In 1593, parliament repealed the laws concerning enclosure and tillage, freeing landlords to use their property as they saw fit. Almost as if the statutes against enclosure had worked, there were immediate food shortages, with harvests failing in 1594. Many faced famine, and a tiny rebellion broke out in Oxfordshire in November 1596. Calling for an end to enclosure, the rebels failed to attract an army and were easily arrested. But, in 1597, parliament put the laws against enclosure back into force.

Sir Francis Bacon explained to the Commons that, though "it may be thought ... very prejudicial to lords that have enclosed great grounds ... and converted them to sheep pastures," tough measures enforcing the re-conversion of pasture to arable were essential "considering the increase of people and the benefit of the common wealth."[20]

17 Jones, *Birth*, 239–41.
18 HEH HM 1340, fo. 29.
19 HEH HAP Box 12 (9).
20 Hartley, *Proceedings*, III, 230–1.

Bacon's argument, agreeing with social critics like Stubbes, Hastings, Nashe, and his father the Lord Keeper, represented those who thought profit gained at the expense of others was sinful. They were supporters of the traditional values of fairness and equity, which demanded governmental interference in markets, lest sinful profiteers oppress the weak. They recognized that the people who worked the land had some right to use it and urged everyone's divine entitlement to a decent living according to their station. Their opponents stressed that God had called each person individually to a vocation, and it was that person's duty to individually perform that calling. Anyone attempting to prevent fulfillment of a person's vocation was wrong, so landlords should use their property according to their own interests, not their tenants' preferences. Moreover, God had distributed the callings across all sorts of people and economic activities, so all had to work efficiently together in accord with the divine invisible hand. England's first economists, writing in the early seventeenth century, were men who thought about simple economic cause and effect, dismissing morality of outcomes as outside their purview.

We can see, in the parliamentary debates about enclosure and famine, that the moral ideas that inspired resistance to enclosure were losing their force. Some no longer thought they could return to the golden age of balanced markets and fair trade. It was being argued by MPs like Sir Walter Raleigh that, though there was dearth in some places, there was surplus in others, and it was easier to buy the surplus and move it than to attempt a return to the presumed *status quo ante*. In 1601, when Sir Francis Bacon praised a law creating a floor for the price of grain to ensure the livings of ploughmen, Raleigh responded by urging its repeal. It was, he said, cheaper to buy food abroad, even from "barbarians," than to maintain artificially high prices in England.[21] If everyone was left to follow their vocation, it would, with a divine invisible hand, produce the economy God had called them to create.

People like Raleigh were making a claim rooted in the belief that individual consciences had to be free to find and fulfill their God-given potentials. Taught as good doctrine in a 1380's sermon by Thomas Wimbledon that was supposedly "found in a wall," the concept had wide Elizabethan circulation. Wimbledon's sermon, preached at Paul's Cross during the Wycliffite crisis and the Peasants' Revolt, was entitled "Look to Your Bailiwick" and demanded that all people perform their God-given roles. He was especially critical of the clergy, which is probably why his sermon was reprinted three times between 1541 and 1550. Revived as part of the Protestant assertion that the truth had been hidden but never extinguished in the time of popery, John Foxe printed it in the *Acts and Monuments*, and it went through many individual editions in Elizabeth's reign and on into the early eighteenth century.[22]

---

21 Ibid., III, 451.
22 Alexandra Walsham, "Inventing the Lollard Past: The Afterlife of a Medieval Sermon in Early Modern England." *Journal of Ecclesiastical History* 2007; 58(4), 628–55.

Wimbledon's sermon may not have been the Lollard artifact John Foxe thought it was, but it was popular because of its emphasis on the moral autonomy of individuals in pursuit of the common good. It cited the Biblical parable of the workers in the vineyard, in which the master pays his workers the same amount no matter how long they work, answering their complaints, "Is it not lawful for me to do as I will with mine own? Is thine eye evil because I am good? ... So the last shall be first and the first last: for many be called, but few chosen."[23] From this, Elizabethans might conclude, as the gloss of this passage in the Geneva Bible taught them, that "every man in his vocation as he is called first, ought to go forward and encourage others, seeing the hire [wage] is indifferent [the same] for all."[24] In a vineyard, as in life, many people must work together to make society productive. Moreover, each person must exchange with others to live. Unlike the beasts of the field, people have nothing they can eat without preparation. Citing 1 Corinthians, Wimbledon reminded his readers that "In laboring on the earth, as in divers crafts, which pertain to the laborers, when the day of reckoning shall come, that is the end of this life, right as he lived here without labor or travail, so shall he want there the reward of the penny, that is the endless joys of heaven." They must each follow the calling God gave them if they wanted heavenly reward, each contributing according to his or her talents, and all rewarded with the same wage: salvation.[25]

This doctrine of calling, read by Elizabethans living in a more urban and integrated trading economy, became a theory of the division of labor wherein the free practice of calling took on a moral significance. Regulation should not prevent natural competition, making many hostile to the patents of monopoly that engrossed opportunities.[26]

The known cause of economic pain was the sinful nature of stiff-necked, hard-hearted men who perverted natural markets and made unfair profits. But there was another problem: the terrible inflation wracking Europe in the sixteenth century. For this, there was a monetarist explanation, often improperly fathered on Sir Thomas Gresham, the great early Elizabethan financier and founder of Gresham College. "Gresham's Law" states that "bad money drives out good." According to this explanation, most associated with *The Discourse of the Commonwealth*, attributed to Sir Thomas Smith (written in the late 1540's but not published until 1581), debased coinage was inflating prices.

---

23 Matthew 20:1–16. Geneva Bible.
24 Ibid., gloss d at verse 16.
25 Thomas Wimbledon, *A godly sermon no les fruitfull the[n] famous made in the yeare of our Lord God M.CCC.lxxxviij. and found out beyng hyd in a wall...* (1575), [Sig. Avi]. STC (2nd ed.)/25827.5.
26 David Harris Sacks, "Commonwealth Discourse and Economic Thought. The Morality of Exchange," in Doran and Jones, *Elizabethan World*, 389–410.

If the silver or gold content of coins was reduced, canny people understood that the price of goods had to increase to stay the same in real bullion terms.[27]

Whether the cause of inflation was greed, debased money, or both, no one knew, because there were no easy ways to track prices or profits. But that was changing with new bookkeeping practices. In 1553, James Peele published a book called *The Manner and Form how to Keep a Perfect Reckoning after the Order of the Most Worthy and Notable Account of Debtor and Creditor*.[28] He was introducing the new idea, just published by a German in France, of arranging accounts in double-entry form so income and expense could be compared.

When it was reprinted posthumously in 1569, the new edition of Peele's book was called *The Path Way to Perfectness, in the Accounts of Debtor, and Creditor ... Very Pleasant and Profitable for Merchants and All Other that Mind to Frequent the Same...* Much expanded, it provided examples of the practice of double-entry bookkeeping, reproducing the ledgers of Francis Twyford, a London cloth merchant trading into Spain and the north of England.[29]

Understanding that accounting textbooks can cause the eyes to glaze, Peele wrote little poems to explain the method and purpose of his double-entry system:

All yet that your accounts by debt and credit use,
Each journal parcel when you write: in no wise do refuse
To make each thing received, or the receiver,
Owe to each thing delivered, or the deliverer.
And each in places train, of ledger look yet set,
Each parcel that in journal stands. The first must be the debt.
Which debt shall answered be, in creditor alone,
(Reparations only except, where many springs from one.)
And or he write receive, but write before you pay:
So shall no part of your account in any wise decay.
And reckon justly oft all variance for to cease,
For reckonings even make friendship long, and daily to increase.
If you these rules observe as guides to your account,
Your work shall then be perfected sure, no doubts shall truth surmount.[30]

---

27 Mary Dewar, ed. *A Discourse of the Commonweal of this Realm of England. Attributed to Sir Thomas Smith* (Charlottesville: University Press of Virginia, 1969).
28 James Peele, *The maner and fourme how to kepe a perfecte reconyng after the order of the moste worthie and notable accompte, of debitour and creditour...* (1554). STC (2nd ed.)/19547.
29 James Peele, *The pathe waye to perfectnes, in th'accomptes of debitour, and creditour in manner of a dialogue...* (1569). STC (2nd ed.)/19548.
30 Ibid. This appears on the page after the title, "The Journal or daily book of letter 'A' for the accounts in traffic of merchandises."

The ultimate reason for care in accounting he explains in another set of verses:

Thus in thy calling if warily thou walk
Of promise be just confirming thy talk,
Weighing beforehand with whom thou doest deal
Let diligence seek all doubts to reveal:
For credit once cracked that maintains the state,
Then dame repentance will come very late.[31]

When Peele's book was reprinted in 1569, with his portrait on the frontispiece, it was dedicated, appropriately, to James Marsh, the Governor of the Company of Merchant Adventurers, and its twenty-four assistants. Holding a monopoly of cloth exports from England, this ancient company was England's most important commercial organization—and probably the most in need of double-entry bookkeeping.

The Merchant Adventurers were at the heart of the English export economy. They, along with the Merchants of the Staple, who had traded wool through the Staple at Calais, controlled England's primary exports. Unfortunately for Elizabeth, and even more for them, this medieval system of export control and customs taxation was badly upset at the opening of her reign. The loss of the city of Calais to the French in January 1558, followed by tensions with the Spanish government in the Spanish Low Countries, which disrupted the Antwerp market for woolen cloth in the mid-1560's, created hardships for workers, merchants, and Elizabeth alike. The Merchant Adventurers were the Queen's main source of ready money, often forced by the Crown to make loans and advances on the customs duties. In those disturbed times, it was easy to see the attraction of a more accurate system of accounting like that proposed by Peele. Knowing what was owed, to whom and by whom; what debts were outstanding; when the money should come in; what one's expenses were; what one's factors were spending and making; who was not paying debts on time; and all the other things that this system of ledgers promised made it possible for a merchant to maintain personal credit (see Figure 9.2).

Credit, in the Elizabethan world, rested on your "credibility," not your fiscal condition, and these new ways of accounting were as much about the rhetoric of equity as about the financial condition of a merchant.[32] Peele's model ledgers

---

31 Ibid., following the dedication.
32 Bruce G. Carruthers and Wendy Nelson Espeland, "Accounting for Rationality: Double-Entry Bookkeeping and the Rhetoric of Economic Rationality." *American Journal of Sociology* 1991; 97(1), 31–69. John Ryan, "Historical Note: Did Double-Entry Bookkeeping Contribute to Economic Development, Specifically the Introduction of Capitalism?" *Australasian Accounting Business and Finance Journal* 2014; 8(3), 85–97.

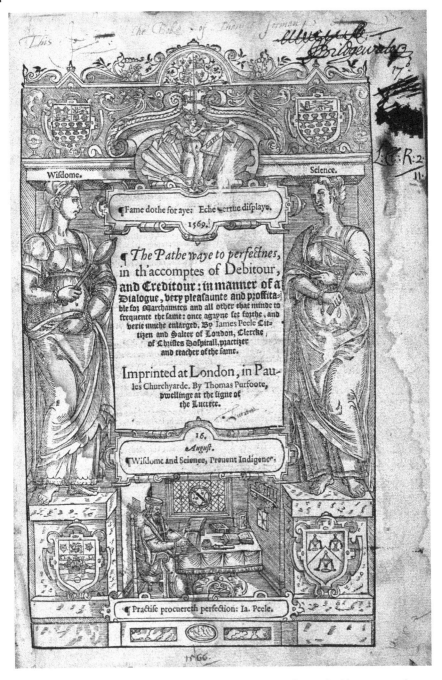

Figure 9.2 Frontispiece of James Peele *The pathe waye to perfectnes, in th'accomptes of debitour, and creditour in manner of a dialogue…* (1569). STC (2nd ed.) / 19548. Henry E. Huntington Library and Art Gallery.

contain remnants of the older world of credit, with entries like the one noting the a grocer, John Alford, owed Twyford £3/13s/4d to be "paid at the birth of his next son, or else at his or mine hour of death per his bill received as in his former account in creditor."[33] In the cold reckoning of double-entry bookkeeping, Alford's debt was neither fish nor fowl—real, but not fungible.

This accounting had the effect of bringing in a new way of talking about "good" business that permitted the concepts necessary to capitalism to take hold. Thomas Gresham, an early user of double-entry ledgers, began his 1546 one with: "In the name of God, Amen. This present book shall be the Journal called + appertaining to me Thomas Gresham of London mercer ... Pleaseth God to give me profit and prosperity to defend me from evil fortune loss and damage. Amen."[34]

But "good" outcomes on a double-entry ledger were about moral qualities as well as sharp management. The concept of "accounting for oneself" and being "called to account" took on new meaning in a world of explicit bookkeeping.

Knowing if God had given one profit and defended one from loss was the point of a good accounting system, but the English merchant community was far behind its colleagues in Antwerp and Italy in systematizing its accounts. The large international traders, like the Merchant Adventurers, had often apprenticed in Antwerp to learn its methods, but they were just beginning to keep proper ledgers when the great expansion of English international trade began in the 1550's. The development of the "principle/factor" system meant that they needed a way for the owner/financier to keep track of money given for long periods of time to factors who traded on his behalf. Joint trading— where more than one person owned the capital—and the use of international systems of credit made accounting more desirable, too.[35]

The developing sophistication in financial record keeping was stimulated by some spectacular business failures. The failure of the Johnson family firm in 1553 created such a confusion that the Lord Chancellor had to appoint a commission of seven merchants to try to figure out what they had, what they owed, and how to distribute their assets. (On the plus side, the Johnson correspondence ended up in the National Archives, giving us an intimate look at these Lutheran merchants.)[36]

---

33 Peele, *Pathe waye to perfectnes*, fo. 25, entry for March 9, 1567 in "Accounts for the Year Ensuing."
34 P. Ramsey, "Some Tudor Merchants' Accounts," in A.C. Liulelon and B.S. Yamey, eds. *Studies in the History of Accounting* (London: Sweet & Maxwell, 1956), 189.
35 G.D. Ramsay, ed. *John Isham Mercer and Merchant Adventurer. Two Account Books of a London Merchant in the Reign of Elizabeth I* (Northampton: Northamptonshire Record Society, 1962), lii–liii.
36 David Oldroyd, "John Johnson's Letters: The Accounting Role of Tudor Merchants' Correspondence." *Accounting Historians Journal* 1998; 25, 1.

Another enormous failure was that of Thomas Lodge, Lord Mayor of London in 1562, who had invested heavily in lead and iron. He also led coalitions of merchants who were expanding trade into new markets, such as Russia and Africa. He and his partners' 1562 voyage to Africa may have inaugurated slave trading by Englishmen.[37] His crisis of liquidity in 1563 severely disrupted the London economy. Lord Treasurer Winchester, suggesting that Lodge was "too big to fail," proposed that he be spared his customs and his shipping duties for six years as a way of getting him back on his feet, or that the Queen should lend him money.[38] But Lodge did fail, and was imprisoned in the Fleet for his debts. His collapse, the plague, and the trade embargo with the Spanish Netherlands in 1564 created a cascade of bankruptcies that led to the creation of a new bankruptcy law in 1571.[39]

The 1571 Act Touching Orders for Bankrupts was a renovation of a 1543 statute that was the first English attempt to curb bankruptcy. 13 Eliz. I, c. 7 was concerned with how to know if a person was a bankrupt. The sure signs were fleeing the realm or refusing to leave the house. Under those two conditions, no legal process could be served on the debtor, so the debt could not be collected. The bankrupt, always described in the statute as "him or her," could be complained against to the Lord Chancellor, who would set up a commission to investigate. The commissioners had the power to seize assets and to sort out creditors, assigning payments as justly as possible, and giving anything left over to the hospitals of London. It was the beginning of bankruptcy receivership as we know it.

As the commissioners were empowered to call in all "proof, ways and means" of knowing what was owed to whom, on both sides of the ledger, having systematic ways of accounting was more useful than ever.[40] It changed the nature of credibility.

The need to be accountable had a corollary in the system of patents and monopolies preferred by Lord Burghley and other Elizabethan managers. Burghley was trying to solve several problems at once. First, there was the need to encourage skilled manufacturing. Second, there was the need for a steady income for the Crown from taxes and duties. Third, there was the need to privatize enforcement, as the state's system of policing was very weak.

There may have been a golden age of agricultural production in England, but the same was not true of manufacturing. Most of the manufactured goods early Elizabethans consumed were produced abroad. This consumption created balance-of-trade issues that worried monetarists. To keep coins in the realm, and to ensure the supply of military goods, patents were used to create copyrights

37 TNA SP 12/26, fos. 87–95v.
38 BL, Lansd. 6, fos. 112–112v.
39 Ramsay, *Isham*, lvi–lvii.
40 13 Eliz. I, c. 7.

on new processes. When Jacob Aconcio was not writing about the stratagems of Satan, arguing for religious toleration, or designing fortresses, he was taking out patents for the making of machines for grinding, crushing, and wood cutting, all driven by wind power. He also patented a new, efficient wood furnace for the manufacture of ale and dyes. Others promised to make soap as good as that made in Seville, or "white salt," or greenhouses.[41] Military supplies received the same protections.[42]

The Queen's promotion of desirable industries led to interventions on behalf of manufacturers. Intent that the science of making sheet glass for use in glass houses (greenhouses) be promoted, Elizabeth patented Antony Beckewe, a Dutchman, to set up shop in Sussex. A dispute with his neighbors prompted the Privy Council to intervene to protect his work and the Queen's interests. Obviously, these patents had value—though in this case, years of arbitration failed to calm the disputes.[43]

Patents—grants by letters patent of the right to the sole use of a thing or process—may have introduced legal protection for desirable industries, but they had less benign uses, too. The most common form involved the licensing of a process or product to a patentee, who purchased (or was granted) the license from the Queen. This was a preferred method of regularizing royal income, since the patentee guaranteed an annual return to the Exchequer. In exchange, they got to keep any surplus.

Outsourcing the collection of fines and customs duties through patents was an effective way of increasing revenues. When two courtiers, Mackwilliams and Colshill, were given the patent on searching for and trying offenders against the usury law in 1571, accusations of usury rose—though not necessarily prosecutions. Rather than be tried in the Exchequer, the accused could "compound" with the patentees for a sum less than the possible fine, ending the suit. Half of the Queen's share of the composition, plus ten per cent, went to the patentees. The accused was spared further expense, the Crown got some cash, and the patentees made a profit.[44]

Of course, what really happened was that the informers used the threat of court action to extort bribes, rather than sharing their income with the queen. An investigation by the Exchequer in 1575 asked pointed questions like, "How many compositions did you make before you notified the court?" and "How many suits did you protract to bring the parties to composition?"[45] It found

---

41 *Calendar of Patent Rolls Preserved in the PRO, Philip and Mary, Elizabeth*, 9 vols. (1937–66), 1560–1563, 98; 1563–64, 119, 331; 1561–63, 213; 1564–66, 331.

42 Ibid., 1560–63, 98; 1563–64, 119; 1564–66, 330–1.

43 *More Molyneux Family of Loseley Park, Historical Correspondence*, vol. 8, 1564–1628, 6729/10/34. Surrey History Centre. http://www.nationalarchives.gov.uk/a2a/records. aspx?cat=176-6729&cid=-1#-1 [Accessed November 29, 2018].

44 *Calendar of Patent Rolls*, 1570–71, 279.

45 TNA, E 133/2/284.

Mackwilliams and Colshill were running broad networks of informers, threatening people with subpoenas and then settling out of court for a cash payment or services rendered. One informer, Thomas Bunning of Denton, Norfolk, allowed a Mr. Foxe to work off his bribe by turning in other usurers to the value of £60.[46]

In this case, Bunning was creating "promoters." Promoters were defined by Thomas Egerton in parliament in 1585 as "caterpillars and blood suckers of the common wealth."[47] Egerton's moral disgust recognized the irony that laws made to control the economy for moral reasons provided new opportunities for immoral, antisocial behavior.

Patents like those held by Mackwilliams and Colshill were unpopular, and they did little to prevent economic immorality, but the regime continued to use them, extending them over more and more taxable items. They promised to deliver a dependable income for the Crown, while making their owners very happy. They also could be sold to the highest bidder, or granted to a person you wished to please, or used to pay for services.

In a letter to Sir Nicholas Throckmorton, the new owner of the right to collect customs on wine imported into Devon, Edward Tremaine, the Deputy Butler of Devonshire, tried to estimate the patent's annual worth. Tremaine explained it was very profitable, even after the Exchequer was paid:

> Working after this sort, I made him [Anthony Throckmorton, previous owner of the patent] in money (above my £20 and pipe of wine yearly), the first year £120, when £30 might satisfy the Exchequer. The next year above £200, when £60 would have paid the Exchequer. The third year about £80, the Exchequer near about £30. These years past all has arisen upon sack, more claret having been brought in this year than in the three former ones.[48]

Throckmorton had a permit to collect customs duties for the Crown. Other patents of monopoly were legally sanctioned restrictions on manufacturing and trade. They were first used to encourage overseas trade beginning in the 1550's, when joint stock companies like the Company of Merchant Adventurers for the Discovery of Regions, Dominions, Islands, and Places Unknown and the Muscovy Company were chartered. Elizabeth extended the principal of trade monopolies with the Barbary Company, the Turkey Company, the Levant Company, and the Eastland Company (trading to the Baltic). Most famously, in 1600, she chartered the Company of Merchants of London. Trading into the

46 Ibid. Norman Jones, *God and the Moneylendes. Usury and Law in Early Modern England* (Oxford: Basil Blackwell, 1989), 93–8.
47 Hartley, *Proceedings*, II, 120.
48 TNA SP 15/12, fos. 132–132v.

East Indies. The charter gave its 250 members a monopoly on trade with all countries east of the Cape of Good Hope and west of the Straits of Magellan—all of South Asia. In 1606, King James licensed the Virginia Company and the Plymouth Company to promote settlement and trade in North America. These joint stock companies were "limited," choosing their own members and limiting membership, preventing non-members from trading from England into their licensed territories.

In the later years of Elizabeth's reign, grants of monopoly proliferated as the Crown's desperation for money increased. The war with Spain and the Irish rebellion were stressing the Exchequer, so Elizabeth sold and granted patents of monopoly and impositions (taxes) on all sorts of things. A list from 1594 to 1600 includes saltpeter, steel, linen rags (used for paper making), various woolen clothes, Irish yarn, beer for export, bullet and powder boxes, glasses, school books, the Psalms of David, the works of Tacitus, tin, old shoes, and sundry other things.

New taxes appeared, too, collected by people who owned the profitable right to do so. A tax on sea coals (coal gathered on the shore) was rented to a monopolist for £200 a year. A patentee was given the right to collect 12d on every bill filed in Chancery, and a license to trade in currants in the Levant was sold for £4000 a year.[49] It was not lost on Elizabethans that tax farmers were lumped together with sinners in the Gospels. "Publicans" (*publicani* = tax collectors) and sinners, says Luke, came to hear Jesus, and people were scandalized when he ate with them. As Jesus recognized in the parable of the Pharisee and the Publican, tax collectors were as immoral as extortioners and adulterers. This religious sensibility fed the righteous hatred of the patentees.[50]

Patents were issued under the Queen's prerogative, so attacks on monopolies were attacks on her. As a doggerel of the time put it:

> The Courtiers craved all
> The Queen granted all
> The parliament passed all
> The keeper sealed all
> ...
> The judges pardoned all
> Therefore unless your majesty speedily amend all
> Without the great mercy of God the Devil
> will have all.[51]

---

49 TNA SP 12/282, fos. 52–52v.
50 Luke 15:1; 18:9.
51 TNA SP 46/26, fo. 148.

Parliament raised the issue in 1597, and by 1601 the attack on patents and monopolies was so fierce that the Queen herself, treasuring her prerogative and unwilling to let parliament meddle with it, revoked some of the patents and spoke to about 140 members in the Council Chamber at Whitehall. It was her "Golden Speech," in which she laid out her conception of the duties of monarchy, though the members were more interested in her apology for the abuse of the patents. She claimed to have granted them for the good of the commonwealth. Everyone who sued for a patent, she said, had "pretended to me that all my subjects should have a public benefit and profit … This they pretended, and this I intended." But the "varlets" lied to her. Hearing the patents were being abused, she thanked the members of parliament for the knowledge, swearing to keep their love by remedying the situation.[52]

For the Queen, this was a constitutional problem, an attack on her authority by lawyers who claimed parliament should approve grants of patents. For many of her subjects, it was about their conception of the individual's place in the economy. Monopolies were considered to be unethical and contrary to the exercise of godly virtue, which required people to work hard, freely performing their divinely established role in the commonweal. Remembering the divisions of labor and the concept of calling taught by Jesus, people found anti-competitive monopolies repugnant because they interfered with callings and oppressive because they interrupted the natural price. Monopolists and patentees were distorting the economy in ways many people thought unfair.

Venal office holders, on the other hand, were not. Getting a position by purchasing it as property was perfectly acceptable. Nor did economic morality that opposed manipulated markets and unnatural prices take issue with the way offices holders maximized their incomes by accepting gifts and fees. An office was a peculiar sort of property, since the one who held it owned the right to extract profit from it, but at the same time had to perform a service. Very few people who performed government services were directly paid by the state. Instead, they owned their office as personal property, and the fees produced by that office supported them financially. Selling offices and revenues in exchange for service was a necessary tool of Crown management. Royal offices were distributed upon the assumption that the office holders would have an interest in collecting the money due, providing incentives. A variant on fee farming, it was a means of indirect taxation.[53]

Since these offices were granted or sold for life, oversight was poor, and it was very hard to reform lazy or immoral officials. To modern eyes, it seems a system open to corruption, but it is striking that there is little contemporary evidence that Elizabethans saw it that way. It was how business was done. It

---

52 Hartley, *Proceedings*, III, 289–90.
53 Douglas Allen, *The Institutional Revolution. Measurement and the Economic Emergence of the Modern World* (Chicago: University of Chicago Press, 2011), 12–13.

appears that most functions were performed, but if they were not, it was hard to make the owner responsible. A good example of this comes from the Mint.

In 1572, the Queen granted John Lonison, the Master Worker of the Mint, the farm of the institution. He and Lord Treasurer Burghley negotiated the terms of his "occupation," establishing how much he would pay the Queen on each step of the minting.[54] They reached a settlement, and a patent was issued for Lonison to farm the Mint on April 18, 1572.[55]

Shortly thereafter, trouble began. Lonison was accused by his colleagues of fraudulent practices. He was embezzling by lowering the quality of the gold and silver coins stamped at the Mint.[56] An investigation was launched, and a group of Privy Councilors examined the accounts. They did find that there were problems, and they concluded that Mr. Martin, the whistle-blower who brought Lonison's fraud to their attention, was not acting out of any interest but the Queen's. However, they faced a problem in what to do about Lonison. Their findings tell us how hard it was to manage men who owned their jobs.

Lonison claimed that as Master of the Mint, he owned the right to run it as he had. This, the Privy Council agreed, was true. However, Lonison had acted contrary to the Queen's interest, so his indenture was cancelled, depriving him of valuable property. Nonetheless, because he owned the mastership, he had to be compensated for its lost value. The investigating commissioners recommended "that he have a pension of three hundred pounds by the year, during his life to be paid out of the coinage or (that wanting) then out of her Majesty's receipt and one hundred pounds by the year after his decease, unto his wife during her life out the coinage."[57]

Despite these payouts, he had defrauded the Mint. Therefore, after he died, Lonison's estate was calculated to owe the Queen £1939/2/2/- "as in his time he impaired the monies of weight and fineness under their just standard."[58] So, Elizabeth had to buy out his patent and pay him a pension, and then sue his estate for what he had stolen.

It was normal for the owner of an office to stretch its duties to maximize his income. In a world that was closely attuned to social status, a man like Sir William Dethick, Garter King of Arms in the College of Arms, could make a good income confirming gentle social status for a price. From the time he was appointed in 1586, in succession of his father, Gilbert, until 1606, when he resigned, he was frequently accused of selling inappropriate coats of arms to people who did not deserve them. He also issued patents of arms even though

---

54 TNA SP 12/85, fos. 166, 168, 177, 178, 182.
55 BL Lansd. 14, fo. 15. TNA SP 12/86, fo. 37.
56 TNA SP 12/90, fo. 144.
57 HEH EL 2219.
58 BL Lansd. 26, fo. 29.

he was just a herald. A great antiquarian and historian, Dethwick was a violent and dangerous man, many times charged with assault, even at funerals he was overseeing. Once he nearly killed a colleague's wife by stomping her head into a fireplace and pouring hot ashes, alcohol, and the contents of her chamber pot over her head. But he kept his office until, in the end, James I bought out his patent to get him out of the College. To secure his resignation, James had to increase his annuity from £40 to £200 and exempt him from taxation.

By the time James was ruling the country, cries of corruption were more and more common. When the attempt to abolish patents for the collection of Crown revenues through the Great Contract failed in 1610, James went back on his promise, made in his *Book of Bounty* in 1608, to no longer grant individuals the right to profit from penal acts. In August 1609, Sir Stephen Procter was made "particular receiver and collector" of fines on penal statutes, a job that he did energetically.[59] Procter, who had convinced James and the Earl of Salisbury that sheriffs and justices of the peace were pocketing fines, was denouncing corruption in governing and offering to correct it. But, in naming the corruption, he ironically came to stand for it.

His nasty attacks on the magistracy provoked a parliamentary reaction, for, as a member of parliament said, "I will not speak against so poor a thing as Sir Stephen Procter, but to clear our House. His actions did so thunder in our House as we had thundered again upon him it might have fallen." The Lord Treasurer added, "I never knew any man make a fairer show of religion and honesty," but "I never knew him to deal honestly in any matter."[60] That thundering took the form of a bill against him, which, if it had passed, would have stripped him of all authority to collect the King's revenues. Worse, because he had "so basely and unworthily demeaned himself," the bill would strip him of his knighthood and his right to a coat of arms.[61] The corrupt anti-corrupter would have been declared corrupt by the law.

The anger against Procter displaced some of the frustration about real corruption. The Crown was increasing investigations into corrupt officials, and parliament saw fit to revive the procedure of impeachment to remove royal officers. In 1621, it charged Sir Francis Bacon, by then Viscount St. Alban and Lord Chancellor, with corruption, impeaching him. He himself admitted "that I am guilty of corruption" in the matter of patents and monopolies.

In that same parliament, legislation was written to curb patents and monopolies—decreasing corruption, it was hoped. It was not until 1624 that it was passed, forbidding the king to grant to anyone the sole right of buying and

---

59 TNA, C66/1820.
60 Elizabeth Read Foster, ed. *Proceedings in Parliament 1610*, 2 vols. (New Haven: Yale University Press, 1966), I, 162–3.
61 Ibid., II, 412–14.

selling things.[62] By then, the new ways of thinking about economic transactions were evident. The good of the commonwealth was the proper measure of government, and parliament did not believe that the personal preference of the King and his friends should take precedence.

The economic world of the Elizabethans was a complex place, especially since increasing specialization and consumption required capitalization. They had conflicting ideas about money, how it should be used, and who should have it. All this angst about money was distilled into the debates about usury. As Sir Francis Hastings said, the "usuring sort" were eating up the gentlemen and grinding down the poor. Parliamentary debates and legal actions give us a good picture of how money was understood and used in the Elizabethan world.

Usury had become a secular offense in England only in 1487, thanks to the Lord Chancellor, Cardinal Morton, who believed "every law should be consistent with the law of God." Since God forbade usury, he wanted the state to punish it. Already punishable by the church courts, the statute against usury was to put the usurer into double jeopardy. The church could excommunicate him, and the King could seize the principal of the loan.[63]

These courts were enforcing a conception of economic relations grounded on Thomas Aquinas' natural law interpretation of God's purpose for money. Lending money at interest is condemned in the Old Testament in several places, beginning with Exodus 22:25. Deuteronomy only allows interest to be taken from enemies. Leviticus forbids lending at interest to the poor. Psalms declares that the godly will help their neighbors and not lend money at interest. Jesus caps these condemnations with his order, "Lend freely hoping for nothing in return." Aquinas, looking at all this, applied his Aristotelian understanding of the natural uses of money to Scripture and derived an understanding of God's dislike of usury. It was unnatural, and therefore sinful, to expect money—which is barren—to yield an increase. A cow can have a calf; money cannot. A house can be rented for a time and returned; money cannot, since to be useful, it must be consumed. Money is like food. It does you no good unless you eat it, and, once eaten, it cannot be returned to its previous owner, so it cannot be rented.

Out of this came a doctrine that required shared risk. If the lender shared in the borrower's risk, God was happy. A merchant could borrow for a voyage. If the voyage was profitable, the person financing it might make a huge profit. Even a fifty per cent return on the money would be acceptable. But if the ship sank, the investor lost the entire investment, just like the merchant.

---

62 Linda Levy Peck, *Court Patronage and Corruption in Early Stuart England* (London: Routledge, 1993), 137–9. My thanks to David Chan Smith for clarifying corruption.
63 3 Hen. VII, c. 5; 11 Hen. VII, c. 8. I.S. Leadam, ed. *Select Cases in the Court of Requests 1497–1569* (London: Selden Society, 1898), lxxvii.

It was the guaranteed return that made a loan criminal, because it supported the sin of greed. According to this Aquinian definition, usury was, as Nicholas Sander wrote in 1568, "all manner of gains ... either bargained or hoped for by the force of the contract of giving loan, whether money be lent, or oil, corn, wine, or any like thing that is spent with the first natural and proper use thereof."[64]

By the fifteenth century, a contrary analysis had developed from nominalist scholastics, which said that usury was a crime of intent rather than of contract. Jean Gerson argued that acts not intended to be evil were not evil, even if they looked evil. If the lender and the borrower were both happy, why not agree to an interest charge? By the early sixteenth century, scholars of this school were arguing in support of merchant loans at as much as five per cent interest, if they were made in good faith. Only lenders who intentionally preyed upon the needy were usurers.

The debate over usury continued into the Reformation, and the Protestant theologians gave some new spin to it. Those who believed in justification by faith tended to side with the intent argument, since faith, like usurious intent, could not be judged externally. Then, too, their emphasis on Scripture prompted them to return to the original languages of the Bible and to reinterpret passages with new linguistic knowledge.

One school of Protestants was fundamentalist, insisting that what Scripture had forbidden was not subject to philosophical dilution. Luther took this position, against Eck's arguments, but Melanchthon was more adaptive. The Calvinists argued that money was only useful if it was used, and that prohibiting usury prevented its use. Jean Calvin added a linguistic turn to the argument, asking what God's intention was in the prohibition, and using Hebrew to provide the answer. In the original language of the Old Testament, the word translated as "usury" meant "biting," so the Prophets were forbidding harm, not legitimate increase. "We see," he wrote, "that the end for which the law was framed was, that men should not cruelly oppress the poor, who ought rather to receive sympathy and compassion."

By the mid-sixteenth century, there were two distinct positions on usury. The objectivists said usury was lending with a guaranteed return of more than the value of the loan. The subjectivists refused to accept external evidence as proof of the crime, insisting that it was evil intent that made lending at interest a sin.[65]

Both positions were well understood in England, and the history of laws against usury reflects the debates. The 1497 law forbidding usury was repealed in 1545, and lending at interest was legalized with a limit of ten per cent.

---

64 Nicholas Sander, *A briefe treatise of vsvrie* (1568), fos. 3–3v. STC (2nd ed.)/21691.
65 Jones, *God and the Moneylenders*, 6–24.

The new law not only legalized usury, it left out any mention of God's law. This scandalized the fundamentalists. In 1549, Robert Crowley told the members of parliament: "If you ... do glory in the knowledge of God's spirit, who hath spoken these words by the Prophet, how can you suffer this act to stand, which shalbe a witness against you in the latter day that you allow that which God's spirit forbids?"[66]

When the "godly imp" Edward VI came to power, his more literal-minded Protestant council rewrote the law, forbidding all usury once again in an Act that would have pleased Thomas Aquinas. "For as much as usury is by the word of God utterly prohibited, as vice most odious and detestable, as in divers places in holy scripture it is evident," as a thing that teaching and persuasion cannot "sink into the hearts of divers greedy uncharitable and covetous person," it must be outlawed so people will forsake their filthy gain and lucre. God's vengeance, says the statute, "justly hangs over this realm" for the usury practiced in it, making temporal punishment necessary to ward off God's providential justice.[67]

Attempts by lawmakers to please God reflected the tensions between different schools of theology, but when codified in law, they had real-world effects. By 1558, the realm was deeply in debt to moneylenders based in Antwerp. Worse, embargoes hindered trade with the Low Countries in the middle of the 1560's. It was clear that the health of the realm required the creation of some sort of legal English money market. Richard Clough, the factor for Thomas Gresham, was the man who brokered Elizabeth's debts in the Netherlands. His letters chronicle the developing civil war there. The cost of borrowing rose and rose, and then there was no more money to be had. In October of 1566, he wrote Gresham, urging him to put Secretary Cecil "in remembrance" for the parliament that was then meeting for a relaxation of the usury laws. Some "reasonable interest between man and man," he thought, would be "more commendable before God than as the matter is now used." Creating a legal form of interest would produce more money in London than in Antwerp, for whenever the Queen needed it.[68]

Such a bill had been introduced in 1563, and another was introduced in 1571. The 1571 bill would repeal the total prohibition of the 1552 law and legalize lending at ten per cent once more. We have a detailed account of the debate over this bill in the House of Commons, and we have a long analysis of the issues in Sir William Cecil's own hand. From these, we can see how the Elizabethan lawmakers were agonizing about applying God's law. Not surprisingly, given the times, they were not agonizing about the economic effects of

---

66 Robert Crowley, *The Select Works of Robert Crowley*, J.M. Cowper, ed. (London: Early English Text Society, 1872), 173.
67 5&6 Edw. VI, c. 20.
68 TNA SP 70/86, fo. 98v.

liberalizing the money market; they wanted to know if usury was *malum in se*, an evil "in itself" and therefore condemned by God, or *malum prohibita*—not inherently evil, but subject to regulation.

Traditionalists held that usury was an act of oppression and extortion, springing from greed arising from a lack of trust in God. They pointed out that the Fathers of the Church had condemned it, and that it was always wrong. Athenians, Spartans, and English law banned it; Plato said it was murder. Sir William Fleetwood, a leading London lawyer, summed up the argument when he said "by scripture he knew it was damnable, and therefore wither it were good or not good, it was no good question."[69] If the old law was not preventing usury, the right move would be to increase the penalty. Make it a felony and hang the usurers.

Those fighting for change claimed it was a matter of intent. "To take reasonable, or so that both parties might do good was not hateful" to God.[70] Those on this side could cite Roman law, which allowed twelve per cent, and the civil law on the continent, which made it a political matter to be decided by princes. They made the argument that the Bible, translated correctly, did not forbid it, except for Jews lending to Jews. God's denunciation of usury was not a prohibition; it was more of a guideline encouraging neighborliness. They also pointed out that people who need money to do business must get it from somewhere, and that people who have money should benefit from helping those who need it. The absolute prohibition of lending at interest hindered trade.

Believing that God would punish the secrets of the heart, those wishing to liberalize the law argued that it was not the function of government to punish sinners. The state was there to maintain equity and promote community. "We are not so straightened to the word of God that every transgression should be severely punished here: every vain word is forbidden of God, yet the temporal law doth not so utterly condemn it." If the law were to require people to commit usury, it would be ungodly; to permit them to choose if they wished to lend or borrow at interest was a different thing. Besides, a total prohibition of a sin was unenforceable.[71]

Serjeant Lovelace, a senior lawyer, suggested usury should be treated like drunkenness and other offenses. The law should recognize degrees of the crime, punishing it more sharply as it became more egregious.[72]

It was Lovelace's solution that broke the impasse. A Commons committee rewrote the bill, and when it returned, it decried usury as sin, always to be condemned, but made a distinction between petty usury, which included loans up to ten per cent, and grand usury, whose rates over that amount had serious

---

69 Hartley, *Proceedings*, I, 236.
70 Ibid., 231.
71 Ibid., 232.
72 Ibid. 234–5.

social consequences. Those usurers who charged less than ten per cent would risk forfeiting their principal. If they charged over ten per cent, they would forfeit triple the principal. After much more wrangling and committal in the Lords, it passed. Usury had not been legalized, but the new statute eased restrictions on lending without permitting sin.[73]

Though the new Act Against Usury asserted that it was forbidden by God's law, it effectively made ten per cent the legal ceiling for loans at interest. The Elizabethan commercial world began structuring its contracts to avoid the penalties in the law. Over time, the public accepted that usury was lending at more than ten per cent and assumed that loans at less than that were natural.[74] By the early seventeenth century, the moral issues had been internalized, and the social issues forced to the fore. As far as the Queen's law was concerned, the sin of usury had become a matter of individual conscience unless the usurer was so oppressive he threatened the peace of the community.

By late in Elizabeth's reign, the conversations about money and morality were heated, and ideas about who was responsible for economic morality were changing. External regulation for the good of the state was increasing as regulation in the interest of the individual soul was declining. Sins, such as swearing, that might bring down the wrath of God on the community had to be controlled, but the state was now less interested in internal equity of trade and more concerned about its social impacts.

The later Elizabethan era saw a continued debate between the moralists and the monetarists over the causes and effects of economic behavior. What is striking in these conversations is the emergence of a form of economic discourse that exempted the operations of economic behavior from the moral categories preferred by Stubbes and his godly colleagues. Though no one was giving up on God's law, they were willing to argue that money obeyed laws of its own.

William Perkins, with his theological emphasis on conscience, helped reorient the relations between secular and divine law. He wrote that men must always obey their internal moral compass, their conscience. Subjected to God and His Word, the true nature of the conscience is known to none but the individual and God. It follows, therefore, that no human law can, by itself, bind a person's conscience.[75] According to this standard, human laws had to be obeyed only "as far as they are agreeable with God's Word, serve for the

---

73 Jones, *God and the Moneylenders*, 47–65.
74 Ibid., 144.
75 William Perkins, *Cases of Conscience*, in William Perkins, *The first part of The cases of conscience Wherein specially, three maine questions concerning man, simply considered in himselfe, are propounded and resoluted, according to the word of God* (1604), 43. STC (2nd ed.)/19668, III, 11.

common good, stand with good orders, and hinder not the liberty of conscience."[76]

This made sins like usury subject to individual testing. Perkins said that in judicial law, because of the hardness of men's hearts, some sins cannot be totally abolished by the magistrates. Usury is among those evils for which God allows some toleration in order to restrain a temptation so strong that men cannot be forced to give it up. "In our land," he said, "the states of this kingdom, have out of their wisdom, provided a law for the toleration thereof after a sort, and that upon special cause. For if the magistrate should have enacted a law utterly to abolish it, it would before this (in likelihood) have grown to great extremity."[77] It followed that the state might permit something that one's conscience condemns, leaving it to the individual to choose whether to sin.

There were many who disagreed with Perkin's view of morality in conscience, but arguments like his carried the day. When the rate of legal interest was lowered to eight per cent in 1624, there was very little discussion of religion and usury, and a great deal of discussion of the impact of changed interest rates on markets. The legal rates were being forced down for the good of the realm; it had nothing to do with whether men should or should not, under God's law, lend at interest. The bishops in the House of Lords admitted as much when they added a provision to the Act that read: "That no words in this law contained shall be construed or expounded to allow the practice of usury in point of religion or conscience."[78]

This limited toleration of economic sins also extended to the conditions of the times and people's callings. Christians had to obey the magistrates, as God commanded, and it was not always possible to live as pure a life as Christ desired. Moreover, Christians only had choice and responsibility within the limits of their personal callings. As each conscience and calling was different, Christians had to respect the differences in them. There were new economic communities that depended on networks and reciprocities that went beyond membership in a guild or a town, and these required a rethinking of what it meant to be in an economic relationship. These new communities were separating duty to one's neighbors from the more abstract expectations of economic necessity.

These late Elizabethan confluences of theology and economic experience began to separate vocational calling from sin in ways we can see in the work of Gerard de Malynes. As Joyce Appleby once observed, thinkers like Malynes did not reject the moral discourse around economics, they prepared the ground

---

76 William Perkins, *A Discourse of Conscience*, in *Works*, I, 525.
77 William Perkins, *The whole treatise of the cases of conscience distinguished into three bookes...* (1614), 284. STC (2nd ed.)/19671.5.
78 21 Jas. I, c. 17. Jones, *God and the Moneylenders*, 175–98.

for its irrelevance by resorting to the calculation of individual decisions: "The faceless relations of algebra moved to the fore."[79]

Gerard de Malynes was the son of a Dutch mint worker who came to England during the re-coinage in the early 1560's, when Elizabeth returned her money to a high standard of purity. Born in Antwerp, he was very young when his family moved to London, where he became a successful merchant by the early 1580's. Mixing trade with spying on Spain for the English state, he made friends in high places, but he got into a great deal of financial trouble in the 1590's. He was imprisoned twice for debt, but received some sort of pardon thanks to Sir Robert Cecil.[80]

In 1600, he was appointed one of the commissioners to establish the true par of money exchange and began his career as an expert on money and trade in general. In 1622, Malynes published what amounts to a textbook for merchants, entitled *The Ancient Law-Merchant*, a summary of mercantile practice in the early seventeenth century: "And even as the roundness of the globe of the world is composed of the earth and waters: So is the body of *Lex Mercatorai* [Law Merchant], made and framed of the merchants' customs, and the sea-laws, which are involved together as the seas and earth."[81]

Malynes' treatment of usury was identical to Perkins' explanation of it. Calling it "usury politic," Malynes explained that "usury" had to be defined as "biting," "and the matter of conscience consisteth in the not getting of your debtor, and not in the taking of much or little interest." How much you made was not the issue; "for no man is bound by law ... to lend money unto those that have no need of it; and there is on the other side a conscience to be used, if a man have gotten well by another man's money, and doth pay the same gain without any interest or profit."[82]

Though Malynes made his obligatory bow toward God in talking about usury, he was much more concerned about the terrestrial effects of interest rates and the logic of the market place. Taking it as a given that people would lend at interest for business purposes, he concentrated on the issues of profit and loss, custom and law in an international context.

This debate between those who believed that profiting at the expense of others—"the trade of usury"—was a sin and those who measured that sin against the intention in conscience and the social impact of the loan demonstrates the later Elizabethan ways of thinking about economic relations. For

---

79 Joyce Appleby, *Economic Thought and Ideology in Seventeenth-Century England* (Princeton: Princeton University Press, 1978), 52–3.

80 CP 173/95.

81 Gerard Malynes, *Consuetudo, vel lex mercatoria, or The ancient law-merchant Diuided into three parts: according to the essentiall parts of trafficke...* (1622), "The Epistle." STC (2nd ed.)/17222

82 Ibid., 329–30.

Stubbes, Nashe, and their fellows, equity remained the issue. Poor people were being gulped into the Devil's purse by greedy, evil profiteers who broke God's law. Therefore, the law of the state should control prices and consumption for the good of all. For Perkins and his theological brethren, conscience was the guide to economic activity. It was not profit that was sinful, it was profiting at the expense of others. Sin was internal and invisible, unless the act was truly egregious. For Malynes and his colleagues, it was natural and good that people sought to profit, and their desires should be channeled by law and custom but not forbidden. God cared about your intentions in business, not your success. Greed could be a virtue.

On the stage, we see this same shifting attitude toward money. The stock character of the greedy usurer was being replaced by the comic figure of the social-climbing rich man. Oppression of your neighbor was no longer the major vice—it was the use of wealth to rise above your station that was ridiculed. Thomas Middleton, in his 1604 city comedy entitled *Michaelmas Term*, mocks a bevy of greedy buffoons, each trying to trick the other. At the heart of the complicated plot is Ephestian Quomodo, a cheating, evil moneylender who outwits himself by pretending to be dead long enough for his wife to marry another man. After she tricks him into signing back the lands he had gulled from Easy, an ignorant countryman, Quomodo complains, "Is this good dealing? Are there such consciences abroad?" unable to believe anyone could outdeceive him. "For craft once known, does teach fools wit, leaves the deceiver none." In closing, the Judge ties up all the ridiculous plots. He tells Quomodo, "Thou art thine own affliction." The nasty usurer has become a selfish object of ridiculous vanity.[83]

The Elizabethan tug-of-war between community good, personal greed, and conscience was not resolved, but the internalization of judgment made it more comfortable to change social status, and to get rich. One of the reasons Shakespeare's comedy *The Merchant of Venice* is an uncomfortable play is the confusion over religious duty, personal desire, and legal duty. When Shylock demands the pound of flesh to be granted to him should Antonio forfeit his penal bond—the instrument used for lending money without interest—the characters become embroiled in a complex debate over justice and mercy, summarized in Portia's declaration that the "quality of mercy is not strained." But she goes on: "Though justice be thy plea, consider this—That in the course of justice none of us should see salvation." The law, being blind, does not judge conscience. It is a dumb thing that deals only in rules—which, if God dealt that way, would damn all.[84]

---

83 Alexander Dyce, ed. *The Works of Thomas Middleton in Five Volumes* (London: 1840), I, 509–13.
84 Shakespeare, *The Merchant of Venice*, IV.1.196–200.

If God permitted you to become rich, did He expect you to use your wealth to help the poor? Philip Stubbes was very clear that English greed created English poverty. The covetousness was so bad that "every one that hath money, will not stick to take his neighbor's house over his head ... whereby many a poor man with his wife, children and whole family are forced to beg their bread."[85] Blaming the sinful covetousness of the wealthy for poverty implied that repentance would cure it. Stubbes did not spend much time thinking about alms for the poor, except to note that the greedy rich only gave beggars scraps. But he was opening the question of how and why people made money, and the proper use of riches. In the Protestant Christian commonwealth, what was the duty of the wealthy toward the poor? Whose duty was it to care for them? Stubbes knew the rich were damned for their greed, but, as the Clown in *All's Well That Ends Well* ironically comments, "'tis not so well that I am poor, though many of the rich are damned."[86]

Jesus had said that the poor are always with us, but, true as that is, the nature of poverty and responses to it were changed by the demographic crises of the sixteenth century and the theological reworking of the individual's relations with God and society. Before the Reformation, ecclesiastical institutions, such as monasteries, had been part of the system of poor relief. Gifts to the poor shortened the donor's time in purgatory, making giving almost obligatory. The destruction of these sorts of pious institutions had upset the system of poor relief and hospitality across the nation in the 1530's and 40's, so Elizabethans developed new ways of responding to poverty.

They understood their Christian duty to give alms, but the homily on alms deeds very carefully explained that generosity to the poor was a sign of the acceptance of divine grace, not a payment toward salvation.[87] St. Paul had told the Christians of Thessalonica, "if there were any, which would not work, that he should not eat. For we heard, that there are some which walk among you inordinately, and work not at all, but are busy bodies." The Geneva Bible glossed this to mean that, by the Word of God, "none ought to live idly, but ought to give himself to some vocation, to get his living by, and to do good to others."[88] The necessity of alms deeds and the rejection of idleness shaped the internally contradictory understanding of the poor and how to deal with them.

Despite pious calls to end greed, there were more and more poor people, undermining established ideas about social station and reciprocal responsibility. The under- and unemployed tended to be both masterless and mobile as they sought ways to support themselves. In a society that knew it had to love its neighbor as itself, this mobility—this not belonging—created a conundrum.

---

85 Stubbes, *Anatomy*, 172.
86 Shakespeare, *All's Well that Ends Well*, I.3.13–14.
87 "The Second Part of the Sermon of Alms-Deeds," in *Homilies*, 416–17.
88 2 Thessalonians 3:10–11 and gloss e in the Geneva Bible.

The established, stable people were puzzled, frightened, and irritated by the aggressive needs of poor misfortunes who were clearly not their neighbors.

It was accepted that there were poor people who deserved charity. The elderly, widows, orphans, cripples, and mad who were your neighbors in your parish deserved your alms. The able-bodied did not. Nor did those who were not of your parish family. Mid-Tudor people threatened the able poor with whippings and enslavement, but across Elizabeth's years their numbers grew. Elizabethans were forced by circumstances to slowly bureaucratize the relief of the poor.[89] This bureaucratization depended on defining social relationships in new ways. As the poor became a national problem, neighborliness slowly began to decline. The deserving poor, though neighbors, were increasingly treated as lesser parts of the community, to be managed by their betters.[90]

The poor became anonymous as burgeoning population growth, religious separation, economic specialization, enclosure, and geographical mobility broke apart communities. Seeking work, they traveled a good deal ("vagrant" means one who wanders aimlessly). So whose poor—whose neighbors—were they?

This was a personal test of faith. Christ taught Elizabethans, in his Sermon on the Mount, that feeding the hungry, clothing the naked, and visiting the imprisoned were necessary virtues. They outlined the personal side of dealing with poverty. Therefore, Elizabethans knew that when you met the poor face-to-face, they should be helped.

The accounts of William Bowyer's servant, for instance, record direct gifts to the poor made by his master on a regular basis in the 1560's. Mixed in with expenses for candles, wine, shoes for the children, and feed for the horses were regular spontaneous generosities like "Given to hunchback at the Rose at Charring Cross," 4d; "Given to a poor man at Mr. Seres his house," 2d; and "Given to a poor man in Knight Rider St.," 1d.[91]

Householders often made gifts of food to the poor (though Stubbes insisted they stingily gave only parings and leftovers). They might extend casual hospitality, too, allowing beggars to sleep in their barns, using straw piles for beds. But these sorts of "shifts" were disorganized. Haphazard charity did little to stem the floods of beggars that were creating national angst. Most of the indigent poor were assumed to be criminals, objects of suspicion. Having little personal relationship with them, householders feared them.

Thomas Harman, a justice of the peace in Kent, wrote a popular book entitled *A Caveat for Common Cursetors Vulgarly Called Vagabonds*. First published in 1567, and remaining in print into the 1590's, his warning against tramps and beggars was written, he said, to help justices and householders

---

89 Steve Hindle, "Poverty and the Poor Laws," in Doran and Jones, *Elizabethan World*, 301–15.
90 Keith Wrightson, "The 'Decline of Neighbourliness' Revisted," in Jones and Woolf, *Local Identities*, 19–49.
91 College of Arms, Ms. B 16, pp. [2]–3, 15–[16], 4 ff.

distinguish between these rogues and the deserving poor. Full of tales of his encounters with "Doxes," "Fraters," "Whiptackes," "Abraham Men," and other criminals, it lets us see them at work stealing drying clothes off hedges, pretending to be shipwrecked, faking collections for the poor, displaying self-inflicted sores, and engaging in other irritating crimes. But it also gives us a look at the lifestyle of these poor people. Interviewing a "Doxe," or street-walking prostitute, about her male protectors, he, having paid her for the information, wanted to know their names and descriptions so he could recognize them. She wittily replied that she could describe them, but it would not do him much good since they were mostly dead:

> Dead quoth I? how died they? for want of cherishing or of painful diseases?
> Then she sighed and said they were hanged.
> What all quoth I, and so many walk abroad as I daily see?
> By my truth quoth she I know not past six or seven by their names, and named the same to me.
> When were they hanged quoth I?
> Some seven years agone, some three years, and some with in this fortnight, and declared the place where they were executed, which I knew well to be true, by report of others.
> Why (quoth I) did not this sorrowful and fearful sight much grieve thee, and for thy time long and evil spent.
> I was sorry quod she, by the masse, for some of them were good loving men, for I lacked not when they had it, and they wanted not when I had it, and divers of them I never did forsake, until the Gallows departed us.
> O merciful God quoth I and began to bless me.
> Why bless ye quoth she? Alas good gentleman, everyone must have a living.[92]

Harman's surprise that she had not been convinced to change her lifestyle by the execution of her men went against the official position on how to treat the undeserving, idle poor. The frontispiece of the 1567 edition showed the cart at whose tail offenders where whipped, along with the various sorts of whips used.

Generally, Elizabethans agreed that poverty was a choice and that the poor could be convinced to work for a living by stern laws, sharply enforced. Lord Keeper Sir Nicholas Bacon defended strict corporal punishment as a preventive of begging and poverty:

> But here some perchance will say that it is a pitiful thing to see whipping … meet for dogs … imposed upon men. I for my part am very sorry to

---

92 Thomas Harman, *A caueat or warening, for common cursetors vulgarely called vagabones…* (1573), Sig Fiiij-Fiiijv. STC (2nd ed.)/12788.

see a man whipped but yet no more sorry to see a man hanged. Yea if by whipping hanging might be taken away then were it a great cruelty not to whip. Were it not much better, know you, to see a man whipped and thereby unhanged, then hanged because he was unwhipped ... If you saw as I do every half year the number of men that be within this realm put to death for robberies and other felonies whereof in my judgment the one half should be saved alive if these two laws of apparel and vagabonds were well executed ... you should also by this mean be better provided of all sorts of laborers then you now are. And those that you already have should be better ordered[93]

The Lord Keeper, however, knew that the increasing poverty was not just creating ungovernable vagabonds; the poverty of the "legitimate" objects of pious charity was getting worse, too, and parishes were failing in their duty to care for their own people.

His brother-in-law, Lord Burghley, was looking at a different way to tackle local poverty, creating a national policy for helping the deserving poor. He drafted orders to the bishops to survey their dioceses, ask their deacons and archdeacons to work with the leading citizens to identify poor households, and determine what money the parish could gather to help them. They would write it all down, collect it regularly, and send it to the bishop for distribution. Additionally, a "poor box" was to be installed in every church, to supplement the formal collection of money for poor relief.[94] The process he envisioned was turned into a series of Acts for the relief of the poor, beginning with "A Bill for Relief of the Poor, by weekly Alms in every Parish" in 1563.[95]

The law of 1563 gently demanded that people give money to the poor in the parish; by the end of the century, a full-blown system of poor relief had been created. In 1572, a new law that lumped relief of the poor together with the control of vagabonds recognized the community's legal duty to care for its own, and its desire to end vagrancy. It introduced compulsory assessment and collection of money for the poor. Justices were required to survey and assess a community's inhabitants, while overseers of the poor were appointed to "make a view of the aged, impotent and lame" in the parish, ensuring undeserving outsiders did not get any of the relief.[96] Like many Elizabethan statutes, it was vague about the processes, and its enforcement was haphazard, but it set the nation on the path toward more and more official oversight of the poor.[97]

---

93 HEH, HM 1340, fos. 27v–28.
94 CP 185/158.
95 5 Eliz., c. 3.
96 14 Eliz., c. 5, 14–15.
97 Steve Hindle, *On the Parish? The Micro-Politics of Poor Relief in Rural England c. 1550–1750* (Oxford: Clarendon Press, 2004), 11.

In 1597, it became the "Great" Poor Law, setting the tone for the next couple of centuries. Accompanied, as usual, by an act against vagabonds, the 1597 statute created a system of work houses in which the deserving poor could be housed, fed, and forced to work to support themselves. The able-bodied poor were to spin or do other work, which would help finance the care for the lame, old, and blind.[98]

The 1597 statute was updated and improved in 1601, when a new Act for the Relief of the Poor was introduced. New boards, made of churchwardens, elected substantial householders, and justices of the peace, were empowered to put the poor to work.

By the early seventeenth century, England had a coordinated national system of parish-based taxation. At its heart were the dole, a pension paid to persons recognized as deserving the aid of the parish, and the work house, both supplementing the casual charity of the kindly and the godly.

The parish dole was managed by the overseers of the poor, who determined who was deserving of charity. They also managed parish endowments, since it was increasingly fashionable to bequeath money and goods, including things like livestock, to aid one's poor neighbors. Recipients were the obvious people: the old, the lame, and families who had lost their means of livelihood. Generally, aid was denied to anyone whose life was dissolute. Drunkards, swearers, thieves, prostitutes, and others were not deemed worthy of their neighbors' charity.[99]

The children of poor families could be taken by the overseers and bound as apprentices until the boys were twenty-four and the girls twenty-one. People who resisted the overseers were to be sent to the common jail.[100]

Anyone who was physically able to work but who had no occupation presented a different sort of moral problem. They might need food and shelter, but they were not suitable objects of Christian charity. They had to work for their food. Parishes acquired a stock of raw manufacturing materials, as required by the Act of 1597, and the indigent were put to work making money to support themselves. Unpaid, the poor were expected to labor for their own support under the supervision of the overseers. Those who were considered "willing and tractable"—properly subservient to their betters and grateful for the help—were given supplies, like hemp or wool, to spin at home in return for support. The "willful," "negligent," and "fraudulent" poor were punished by being sent to a house of correction, where they, too, were forced to work for food.[101] If this sounds like the plot from *Oliver Twist*, it should. The poor law of 1601 was not changed until 1834.

---

98 39 Eliz. I, c. 3.
99 Hindle, *On the Parish?*, 96–170.
100 43 Eliz. I, c. 2.
101 Hindle, *On the Parish?*, 174–91.

The conundrum of poverty was another part of the changing economy that so irritated Christians like Philip Stubbes, who believed social ills were caused by sinful natures. Just as usury and greed led people to exceed their God-given stations, so the presence of poor people proved the sinfulness of a society in which greed was unchecked. The response was to create a new way of getting the disturbing beggars off the streets, forcing them to work as bound labor until they were reformed. As for the deserving poor, the Elizabethans proved generous in their ways. Occasional relief continued on a person-by-person basis, especially for the obviously deserving. The dangerous, runagate "strangers" and the able-bodied unemployed, who disturbed the parishes with their begging and their unsightly poverty, were now objects of regulation, punishment, and control.

The evolving treatment of the poor underscores changing ideas about moral regulation and individual conscience in the economy. As concepts of sin became internalized, the state moved away from conformity with God's law and toward a logic of social good. Individuals were given the right "in conscience" to follow their own vocations, even if these included economic behaviors traditionally condemned. The able-bodied poor, with that same right, were choosing unemployment out of lazy greed. Beggars were a social problem that had to be solved, and the assumption that beggary came from choice called for a social response designed to make them change their minds and become productive workers. The new moral economy no longer saw the poor as God's gift to the rich, the object of their charity. They had become a social problem, the object of social control. One of the ironies of the Elizabethan age was that as ideas of economic morality became less constrictive, social control increasingly targeted people who were defined as a bad influence in the community.

10

Creating the Godly State

Officially, God providentially made Elizabeth Queen of England on November 17, 1558. In fact, the Elizabethan history of the English Reformation was entirely providential. Henry VIII and Edward VI tried to lead the nation out of the blindness and ignorance of popery. The "Young Josiah," Edward, had toppled superstition and created a godly church. But England's stiff-necked sinners had failed to be as godly as was demanded, causing God to kill the teenaged Edward and put his Catholic half-sister Mary on the throne as a punishment. Chastising England, Mary returned the nation to superstition and tried the faith of the godly through persecution. When the English had learned their lesson, God killed Mary and gave England a second chance with Elizabeth. The moral was that obedience to Elizabeth in matters of religion was obedience to Him. She was the anointed Handmaiden of the Lord, His servant doing His will, just like the Virgin Mary.

Catholics were unhappy with Elizabeth's settlement of religion, which restored Protestant worship using the *Book of Common Prayer*, but they were confused about how to respond. Until Pope Pius V excommunicated Elizabeth in 1570, they were in a sort of limbo regarding whether and how to resist her church.

On the other hand, there were Protestants who, though pleased the Pope was expelled, knew that God required further reform, and complained Elizabeth had not gone far enough. They disliked the scripted worship in the prayer book and thought the church's discipline was too lax. At first, they thought Elizabeth would allow more change, but she did not, creating a crisis for them. They knew that God expected everyone to personally obey Him in conscience, so when Elizabeth did not create a truly godly state—as they defined it—they had to say something. Otherwise, they opened themselves and all England to another round of providential punishment.[1]

---

1 Jones, *Birth*, 17–65.

Being Elizabethan: Understanding Shakespeare's Neighbors, First Edition. Norman Jones.
© 2020 John Wiley & Sons, Inc. Published 2020 by John Wiley & Sons, Inc.

Thus, from the beginning there were people of all theologies who were critical of the Elizabethan church. It was heretical and schismatic to Catholics. It was good, but insufficiently pure, to many Protestants. The nature of its impurities, however, was disputed. Some disliked its governance, seeing bishops as Catholic leftovers who needed abolition. Some disliked its liturgical practices, objecting to the use of candles and crosses, as well as the Queen's expectation that ministers in her church would dress like priests. Yet others hated prayer book worship, with its scripted prayers, preferring learned sermons. Eventually, some of these Protestant complainers became separatists and recused themselves from worship in the Queen's church, just as some Catholics did.

All these groups had political expectations guided by their faith, and all of them created problems for the Supreme Governor of the Church in England. Managing these religious conflicts became a preoccupation of Elizabeth's government.[2]

The tension between God's anointed queen and those who knew her church needed greater change is a central narrative of early modern English history. The nature of late feudal English government gave Elizabeth's responses to these challenges an especially English flavor. It was assumed that God had created order in the world, and that order rested upon a hierarchy of authority. Certain people were, because of their birth and gender, given responsibility for others. The Elizabethan state was built on the belief that men born into the magisterial classes had a duty to serve, govern, and lead under God, the law, and the Queen.

Sir Thomas Smith, in his 1564 classic *De Republica Anglorum*, divided English society into four sorts of men. The fourth group, classified as proletariats (*proletarii*) or workers, he called the "sort of men which do not rule." The other three sorts—nobles, gentlemen, and burgesses—were governors. They were represented in parliament: the nobles and bishops sat in the House of Lords, the gentlemen and burgesses in the House of Commons. All served in the magistracy: "each of these hath his part and administration in judgments, corrections of defaults, in election of offices, in appointing tributes and subsidies, and in making laws."[3] The magisterial orders made and enforced the law because of their station in society, *noblesse oblige*. Tudor magistrates ruled because of and by God-given virtue.

Virtue meant two things. First, there was the virtue, or power, of God in Christ. This divine ordering of the world made it possible for grace to overcome sin. God's power ruled, and in ruling, gave power to those chosen by Him as rulers. As Thomas Norton's translation of Nowell's Catechism puts it,

---

2 Jones, *Governing*, 189–213.
3 Thomas Smith, *De Republica Anglorum*, Mary Dewar, ed. (Cambridge: Cambridge University Press, 1982), 76–7.

"All things would run to ruin, and fall to nothing, unless by his virtue, and as it were by his hand, they were upholden."[4]

Ergo, magistrates must strive for a virtuous life to please God. As it said in the Book of Kings, they were to take heed of the charge of the Lord God to walk in His ways and keep His statutes and commandments.[5] But knowing what this meant was difficult, and required even King Solomon to pray for an understanding heart to judge the people, discerning right from wrong, "for who is able to judge this thy mighty people?"[6] The magistracy's duty to God gave it the right to make and enforce law, to dispense justice and mercy in God's name, and the Queen's.

These magistrates, whose right to sit in parliament was tied to their larger responsibility as rulers of their own peculiar commonwealths at home, ultimately took their authority from God, who had ordered society and given them rule over it. The Almighty had expectations of those to whom He had given authority, for the sins of the people would be held against the magistrates, the masters, and the householders who bore authority over the lesser orders. As Archbishop Sandys announced at Paul's Cross early in the reign, God would require the blood of the magistrates if, through negligence, evil example, or want of correction, those in their charge were lost.[7] Francis Darby repeated this warning in 1601, declaring that if parliament did not curb drunkenness, the Almighty would "lay his heavy hand of wrath and indignation upon this land."[8] In Hardwick Hall, built in the early 1590's, the figure of Justice dominates one fireplace in the Long Gallery and her sister Mercy the other, representing the duties of the magisterial orders.

The duty of the magistracy to God was stressed whenever Elizabethans were involved in the legal system. Assize sermons emphasized and reemphasized it; members of parliament invoked it; jury charges summarized it. In Richard Crompton's 1584 reworking of Fitzherbert's book on the office and authority of the justices of the peace, a charge to the jury was printed that neatly listed the duties of those invited by the Queen to participate in ruling the nation. The exhortation was a complete cosmology, beginning with Creation and progressing through the Fall, the unruly life in a state of nature, and the Flood, until it arrived at the creation of the law by God in the Decalogue. After the law was made, God set kings over men, who must be obeyed as the ministers of God, protecting the righteous and taking vengeance on sinners. The justices of the peace and members of the jury shared in God's authority, owing their duty to

---

4 OED sub virtue.
5 1 Kings 2:3. Geneva Bible.
6 1 Kings 3:7. Geneva Bible.
7 Edwin Sandys, *The sermons of Edwin Sandys*, John Ayre, ed. (Cambridge: Parker Society, 1841), 265.
8 BL, Stowe Ms. 362, fos. 84v–85.

the Queen and to God—a sacred trust sealed with an oath on the Bible. The oath bound them, among other things, to enforce the "good laws and statutes, which we have received by the authority of the high Court of Parliament of this realm, for the common wealth of her Majesty's subjects."[9]

The plenipotentiary power of members of parliament to give consent for the entire realm was believed to descend on them by right of their birth and office, a natural result of their position in the social hierarchy. It was not granted by "the people"; it came from God through the monarch.[10] Therefore, consultation with a constituency was not required. Members of parliament could speak and vote on any issue freely, without reference to those they governed. Moreover, they did not have to live in—or even visit—their constituency. Their votes bound the entire nation, but the entire nation was not invited to their selection.

The House of Lords was unelected, with each peer speaking only for himself. Not even the bishops, dividing their time between parliament and ecclesiastical provincial convocations, consulted their clergy. In the Commons, the county members were returned by the electors of their shires. The electors were men who could meet the financial qualifications for the franchise, and deference bade many of these moderately wealthy individuals to consent to the choices of their betters. Their right to vote came from God, their social position, and, crudely, their power. As the Privy Council put it in 1597, "we doubt not much but the principal persons of that county will have good regard to make choice without partiality or affection."[11] Those "principal persons" were the leaders of a few dominant families, making their selection of members of parliament long before the electors were invited to ratify their choices.

This same group of men filled the ranks of the justices of the peace, the commissioners of sewers, trial juries, coroner's juries, militia officers, and other offices in the commonwealth. They were worthy of doing it because of who they were, not who they represented. Because magistrates were expected to walk in the ways of the Lord, people of their sort were taught the need for self-control and responsibility. Accepting God's calling, they should serve not for self-exaltation, but out of duty.

It was this self-control that was expressed in the second meaning of virtue. This virtue was manifested by a life lived in conformity with the principles of morality. The virtuous governor voluntary obeyed and enforced moral laws and abstained, on moral grounds, from vice. Thomas Elyot recognized this in

---

9 "An Exhortation to the Jurye," in Sir Anthony Fitzherbert and Richard Crompton, *L'Office et Aucthoritie de Justices de Peace 1584* (London: 1972), Sig. CCi ff.

10 Vernon F. Snow, ed. *Parliament in Elizabethan England, John Hooker's Order and Usage* (New Haven: 1971), 182. David Dean and I have argued this point before in *The Parliaments of Elizabethan England* (Oxford: Basil Blackwell, 1990), 2–4.

11 APC, 27, 361.

his *The Book Named the Governor,* noting that "virtue be an election annexed unto our nature, and consisting in a mean, which is determined by reason."[12]

The rational part of obedience demanded the recognition of the higher good of the community, as well as the higher power of God, and Tudor magistrates in search of an understanding of virtue, enforced by conscience, found their definitions in the law, the classics, and theology. Their virtue was a compound of feudal values, in which service to one's lord was enshrined; humanistic ideas of *virtu* imbibed from extended exposure to Roman authors; and the workings of English legal culture. It assumed the natural existence of a monarch, and it envisioned members of the governing classes as a part of the same authoritarian chain of being. Magistrates could quote Romans 13:1, "Let every soul be subject unto the higher powers: for there is no power but of God: and the powers that are, are ordained of God."[13]

Members of the magisterial community knew that this passage meant not only that they should obey their monarch, but also that they, in their positions as landlords, aldermen, justices, and other things, ought to be obeyed. According to their place in the hierarchy, everyone owed them obedience, "not because of wrath only, but also for conscience sake." Conscience required them to "Give all men therefore their duty, tribute, to whom you owe tribute: custom, to whom you owe custom; fear to whom fear: honor to whom you owe honor." Magistrates were the ministers of God, and they had to be obeyed for conscience's sake, even if they did evil. The duties of the magistrates were described by Paul as casting away the works of darkness and putting on the armor of light, governing in accordance with God's law of love and the second table of the Ten Commandments.[14] As William Cecil was wont to say, "seek first the Kingdom of Heaven," for honesty and religion "are the grounds and ends of good men's actions."[15] The magistrates might also have been able to quote Isaiah 49:23 when thinking of the Tudor dynasty: "And kings shalbe thy nursing fathers, and Queens shalbe thy nurses."

The magistrates' divine appointment was clear. As a preacher told Sir Francis Hastings, "the magistrate is the minister of God and must submit himself to his word ... the magistrate must command in the Lord. The subject must obey in the Lord." Obedience "is due unto the Lord only."[16]

This ideal of government was hierarchical and presumed that men of the right birth had authority to enforce God's will. In this, of course, they were assisted by the church, whose bishops were appointed by the Queen.

---

12 Elyot, *Book Named the Governor,* II, x.
13 Geneva Bible.
14 Romans 13:1–13. Geneva Bible.
15 Arthur Collins, ed. *The Life of the Great Statesman William Cecil, Lord Burghley* (London, 1732), 68–9.
16 HEH, HA Religious Box 1 (9).

These authorities imposed godly values on their communities as a part of the natural order. They knew better because God gave them their positions.

The worms in this theory of hierarchical authority were disobedient consciences, unwilling to fear God, and consciences that distinguished between duty to God and duty to the ruler. St. Paul insisted that evil rulers were owed obedience "for conscience sake," but for some, God trumped monarch when there was a conflict in conscience.

The rebellious, tender conscience was an important theme in Protestant theology from the time Luther wrote his "Address to the German Nobility." Calvin, as usual, sharpened the call for the "lesser magistrates" to resist ungodly rulers. His successor in Geneva, Theodore Beza, took it even further. In England, the idea came with Peter Martyr Vermigli to Oxford in Edward's reign and was nourished in the English exile community in Geneva in the later 1550's.

During the Marian years, when Protestant leaders were being burned for heresy, John Knox, writing in Geneva, used Calvin's arguments about the lesser magistrates to call for rebellion against Mary Tudor, Mary Queen of Scots, and Marie de Guise, Regent in Scotland. Female authority was, he said, unnatural. Because it was unnatural, it was against God's law, and the "lesser magistrates," the nobility and gentlemen, had a duty to God to overthrow their unnatural female governors. Speaking of female rule, he said magistrates "must refuse to be her officers … They must study to repress her inordinate pride." Abolishing female tyranny, the nobility and the estates of the realm must "remove from authority all such persons." Doing so, they would be acting out God's providence, for "the fire of God's word is already laid to those rotten props (I include the Pope's law with the rest) and presently they burn."[17] His attack on female rulers led Elizabeth to ban him from England.

Pope Pius V agreed with Knox that ungodly rulers must be overthrown, though from a very different theological angle. Pius excommunicated Elizabeth with his bull, *Regnans in Excelsis*, in February 1570. "Elizabeth, the pretended queen of England and the servant of crime" was a heretic who had abandoned the true faith and taken her country with her. Therefore, Pius pontificated, "the nobles, subjects and people of the said realm and all others who have in any way sworn oaths to her, [are] to be forever absolved from such an oath and from any duty arising from lordship, fealty and obedience." He informed "all and singular the nobles, subjects, peoples and others afore said that they do not dare obey her orders, mandates and laws. Those who shall act to the contrary we include in the like sentence of excommunication."[18]

Whether the magistrates thought the Pope, not Elizabeth, was the proper governor of the church, or if they sided with Presbyterians and rejected the

---

17 Knox, *First blast of the trumpet*, fos. 523v, 56v.
18 "Regnans in Excelsis: Excommunicating Elizabeth I of England. Pope Pius V—1570." http://www.papalencyclicals.net/Pius05/p5regnans.htm [Accessed November 29, 2018].

Queen's hierarchal church, they might see their duty to God superseding their duty to their monarch. These ideas threatened the Elizabethan church, undermining its core belief that it was established providentially under the hierarchical authority of Elizabeth, God's handmaiden.

We can see this problem beginning in the 1560's, when the new Protestant bishops began cataloging justices of the peace as favorers, "faint furtherers," or enemies of the Queen's established religion. In conscience, some resisted the Queen's law. And some must have thought their duty to their community required them to shelter people from yet another round of religious turmoil. Clearly, some justices were trying to prevent those in their care from being cast over the precipice of Protestantism, while others thought the Queen was not pushing them off the cliff fast enough.[19]

In 1569, the Privy Council tried to get Catholics off the commissions of the peace. Edmund Plowden, an eminent lawyer, was called upon to subscribe to the "book and statute" for the uniformity of common prayer. Attending a meeting of the commission, he was expected to subscribe on the spot. He demurred, saying he could not in conscience swear that he believed in *everything* the *Book of Common Prayer* said. He insisted that he remained a loyal subject of the Queen. He remained a justice of the peace, giving bond for his own good behavior.[20]

Protestant ministers had similar issues in conscience, and by the late 1560's, some were refusing to conform to the established church. The flash point for them was clerical costumes, with the "Vestiarian Controversy" in Cambridge and London centering on whether ministers had to dress like priests. Many refused, and condemned the bishops for trying to make them.

The bishops themselves were frustrated because Elizabeth refused to let them enact articles defining their faith, create a new church discipline, or pass legislation that would, they believed, complete the reform of the English church. It was not until 1571, in the aftermath of Elizabeth's excommunication by Pius V, that they got the 39 Articles defining their church's theology approved by parliament. Much of the rest of the bishops' agenda never was allowed.

The disputes with Protestants (all of whom appreciated Elizabeth's reestablishment of "true religion") began in earnest with the "Admonition Controversy," named after the "Admonition to Parliament" of 1572, a pamphlet and proposed legislation that would have "purified" the English church, making it "fully reformed." The publication, by the young London preachers John Field and Thomas Wilcox, attacked the Elizabethan church with such energy it was declared a seditious libel, and its authors imprisoned. The Privy Council well

19 Peter Iver Kaufman, *Thinking of the Laity in Later Tudor England* (South Bend: University of Notre Dame Press, 2004), 70–1.
20 TNA SP 12/60, fos. 130–130v, 135.

understood its purpose: "some persons of their natures unquietly disposed, desirous to change, and therefore ready to find fault with all well-established orders … were using of their own devices other rites and ceremonies" to make divisions, dissensions, and disputes against common order. Because they were attacking common prayer, the Queen banned all books that found fault with the "Church and commonwealth of England."[21]

This attempt to silence the critics did not work, though it did drive Thomas Cartwright, the Cambridge scholar whose arguments inspired it, to leave the country. The storm it caused continued to grow. Cartwright's old enemy at Cambridge, John Whitgift, took up the cudgel against it, and he and Cartwright exchanged blow after rhetorical blow. At the heart of the controversy was the role of Scripture. Was God's Word binding in all circumstances? Cartwright and his fellows insisted it was; Whitgift allowed some room for interpretation. Both disturbed the community.

A few months after the Admonition Controversy began in 1572, the Queen issued a proclamation ordering the destruction of seditious books. It recognized that Catholics, too, were attacking established order. These traitors, "conventing themselves together in routs and … conventicles" and "having a trade in penning infamous libels, not only in the English, but also in Latin and other strange languages," were commissioning "seditious books and libels to be compiled and printed in diverse languages, wherein their final intention appeareth to be blaspheme and as it were to accurse their native country."[22] This proclamation was caused by a book called *A Treatise of Treasons against Queen Elizabeth*, which accused Lord Burghley and Sir Nicholas Bacon of having duped Elizabeth into being a Protestant.

Meanwhile, Puritan-inclined clergy began gathering in informal groups like the so-called Dedham Classis. In October of 1582, thirteen of them formed a conference and chose three leaders. Like others established at Bury St. Edmunds and Norwich, their purpose was "prophesying." They would take turns preaching and discussing the meaning of the biblical texts being expounded. These were secret meetings, "Silence also to be kept as well of the meeting as of the matters there dealt in."[23] This secrecy was required because they were going around the bishops for self-education, inspired by Calvinist, Presbyterian assumptions about the nature of Christian ministry.

Elizabeth had ordered Archbishop Grindal to suppress the prophesyings in 1576. He refused, informing her that he would rather offend her than the heavenly majesty of God. "Remember Madam, you are a mortal creature," he wrote, insisting that she had no right to tell her spiritual leaders their business. In the "bowels of Christ," he begged her to put God's majesty before her own when

---

21 H&L, II, 375–6.
22 H&L, II, 377–8.
23 Patrick Collinson, *The Elizabethan Puritan Movement* (London: Jonathan Cape, 1967), 224.

dealing in spiritual matters.[24] Naturally, Elizabeth suspended him from office for this impertinence, though she never removed him. He was tolerating exercises that were associated with religious insubordination. Worse, as Archbishop of Canterbury, he seemed to be putting the church over the Queen, just like the Pope.[25]

Grindal died and was replaced as Archbishop of Canterbury by John Whitgift in 1584. Whitgift set about silencing the Protestant dissenters, making him the target of one of the English-speaking world's great satirical campaigns. Known collectively as the "Martin Marprelate Tracts," this series of pamphlets attacked the bishops, and especially Whitgift, anonymously and hilariously. The introductory epistle was addressed to "the right puissant and terrible Priests, my clergy masters of the Confocation House, Whether Fickers General, worshipful Paltripolitans," to "right poisoned, persecuting and terrible priests," and to "petty popes and petty antiChrists" who usurp the authority of pastors over their congregations. Calling the Archbishop John Whitgift of Canterbury "John of Cant," it declared that no bishop was to be tolerated in a Christian commonwealth. "They are petty popes and petty antichrists, whosoever usurp the authority of pastors over them, who by the ordinance of God are to be under no pastors."[26]

In all, "Martin" produced seven tracts, including the *Theses Martinianae*. This list of 110 propositions made clear the political implications of their certainty that no true Christian church should have bishops. Number 98 proposes "That our magistrates in maintaining both the doctrine of our church, and also the hierarchy of our bishops, maintain two contrary factions under the government which their wisdoms know to be dangerous." Given that those who defend the true church are not going to surrender to the bishops, and that the bishops are not going to surrender to their critics, Number 102 declares presciently, "the continuance of these contrary factions is likely in a while to become very dangerous unto our state, as their wisdoms who are magistrates do well know and perceive."[27]

The Marprelate Tracts touched a nerve, triggering an avalanche of responses from those who opposed them, and creating lots of opportunity for authors like Thomas Nashe to show their wit in writing scurrilous diatribes. But the danger inherent in them was real, and John Penry was hanged in 1593 for his part in publishing them. Though he denied being their author, he clearly had a role, and he certainly supported their anti-episcopal anger.[28]

---

24 William Nicholson, ed. *The Remains of Edmund Grindal* (Cambridge: Parker Society, 1843), 389.
25 Jones, *Governing*, 195–7
26 Joseph L. Black, ed. *The Martin Marprelate Tracts. A Modernized and Annotated Edition* (Cambridge: Cambridge University Press, 2008), 7–9.
27 Ibid., 156.
28 Ibid., xxxix–xli.

On the other side of the religious ledger, Catholic missionary priests were beginning work in England. Edmund Campion, born in 1540 and educated at the expense of the Grocers' Company of London, rose to be Proctor of Oxford University. He decided he must leave England in 1569, not long before Pope Pius V excommunicated Elizabeth in February 1570. Campion became a Jesuit in 1573, and in 1580 he returned to England in the first Jesuit mission. The Jesuits were highly trained members of an order sworn to serve the Pope. Well-educated, they specialized in combating Protestantism, making scholars like Campion ideal for missionary work.

Campion proclaimed he had come home to England "to cry alarm spiritual against foul vice and proud ignorance, wherewith many of my dear country-men are abused." Knowing he was running the risk of capture, Campion wrote a testament, known as "Campion's Brag," that invited England into a conference or debate over religion. He offered to prove to the Queen and her Council, the universities, and the lawyers that Protestantism was wrong.[29]

Campion declared that he was ready to die for this truth, and he did. Captured in July 1581, he was executed for treason the following October. Like the prophesying ministers of the Dedham Classis, Campion and his fellow mis-sionaries were challenging Elizabeth's authority and the structure of her church. In a prayer she wrote, she begged God to release her "from the enemies of religion as well as those who hate me—AntiChrists, Pope lovers, atheists, and all persons who fail to obey thee in me."[30]

These battles for consciences contributed to national security scares in the 1580's and 90's. As war with Catholic Spain in the Netherlands, English mili-tary interventions in France on behalf of the Huguenots, the plots of Mary Queen of Scots, and rebellions in Ireland unfolded, fervid debates about how to ensure "homeland security" broke out. Archbishop Whitgift preferred using the Church to repress dissent; Burghley preferred the law. In parliament, ardent members proposed that Catholics be subjected to more and more punitive regulations, while some launched attacks against episcopal government and the *Book of Common Prayer*.

Rumors of dangerous irreligion flew. There was report in the House of Commons that people in Wales were worshipping idols, "amongst bushes, where they abuse other men's wives." At this, Richard Topcliff got up and com-plained about the superstitious use of the spa at Buxton (formerly known as the Well of St. Anne, it was valued by Elizabethans for its curative powers) and how people were bringing their children there to be christened. He demanded that every man make note of the abuses in their countries, all caused by want of

---

29 Edmund Campion, *Ten Reasons Proposed to His Adversaries for Disputation...* (St. Louis: B. Herder, 1914), 8.
30 Leah S. Marcus, Janelle Mueller, and Mary Beth Rose, eds. *Elizabeth I. Collected Works* (Chicago: University of Chicago Press, 2000), 163.

learned ministers. Mr. Bainbrick summed it up: these abuses must be reformed "to divert God's plague from us."[31] Topcliff added to the paranoia by reporting that "weapons and all massing trumpery with books papistical were found in the very next house joining to the Cloth of Estate by the Parliament House."[32]

Richard Topcliff, a professional hunter of papists, was a man who willingly tortured suspected Roman Catholics in defense of God's establishment in England. Describing himself as a "diligent scout and watchman," Topcliff presented himself, McCarthy-like, as an expert on papists and their dangerous activities. A document, thought to be by him, argues that mass incarceration of Catholics is highly desirable, and urges that they not be held near their homes, where they can communicate with family and friends. "Patronesses of priests" should be locked up, too, since, as he rightly observed, female Catholics were important in maintaining priests.[33]

Topcliff did not get his concentration camps, but many Catholic men were arrested and examined. He was so enthusiastic about defeating the Catholic threat and protecting the true religion, he gained lasting infamy in his own lifetime. His nephew changed his name so he would not be associated with Topcliff's reputation. But for a while, in the early 1590's, his practice of torturing Catholics into confessions was so commonly known that a contemporary could refer to Sir Francis Bacon as one who, contrary to "our Topcliffian custom," won more with words than with the rack.[34]

Fear of God's plague combined with fear of Satan's Fifth Column, papists, and Puritans. Archbishop Whitgift, with the Queen's approval, promoted more radical defenses. Rigor against those who dared to disagree with Elizabeth, fearing God more than men, was aimed at ministers who did not swear to articles of faith set out by the Archbishop. He was attempting to rid his church of Presbyterians and would-be separatists. Sitting beside Topcliff's proposal for Catholic internment camps is a letter to Elizabeth from imprisoned "Puritan" ministers, complaining that they have been arrested under "secret information" and deprived of their livings by the Ecclesiastical High Commission, using the oath *ex officio mero*, contrary to proper legal proceedings. They denied they "impeached" the royal supremacy, were rebellious, abused excommunication, or held illegal conferences.[35]

Though the ministers may have a had a good legal argument, they, like the papists Topcliff hunted, were men bound by the Word of God to obey a power

31 Ibid., II, 390–1.
32 Hartley, *Proceedings*, II, 388.
33 BL, Lansd. 72, fos. 133–135v.
34 Thomas Birch, *Memoirs of the reign of Queen Elizabeth, from the year 1581 till her death...* (1754), I, 160. http://babel.hathitrust.org/cgi/pt?id=mdp.39015023127536;view=1up;seq=170 [Accessed November 29, 2018].
35 BL, Lansd. 72. fos. 136–8.

greater than the Queen's. Both groups found themselves the targets of investigations and prosecutions because of the threat their disobedient consciences created for the state. All believed that God would chastise the nation and themselves if they did not work for His kingdom on earth as well as in heaven. Elizabeth, Whitgift, and other supporters of the Elizabethan Settlement believed that God would chastise them in they did not repress these people whose consciences denied the legitimacy of the English church.

We can see these tensions in episodes of religious madness. In the summer of 1591, Jesus Christ returned to judge the world, embodied in William Hacket, a malt maker. Though he was illiterate, he was caught up in the Presbyterian enthusiasm so feared by Whitgift. Having received his divine commission in a dream, he declared himself King of the World and deposed Elizabeth for tolerating bishops. Well known to Presbyterian leaders like Walter Travers and Edward Dering, who thought him crazy, he represents a popular enthusiasm for radical reform crossed with folk beliefs. Quickly arrested, he was condemned to death for treason and his story became fodder for Whitgift's attacks on Presbyterianism. The Archbishop and his colleagues thought Hacket proved just how dangerous it was to tolerate Protestants who did not conform to the state church.[36]

In the middle of these contending godly consciences there was another position, one that held that the law of God's established state was a localized form of divine will, created to civilize and keep the peace. Therefore, a conscience rightly guided recognized that obeying an authority beyond Elizabeth, whether a pope or abstract theology, was wrong unless it was permitted by law. Lord Burghley found himself leading this argument. When Walter Travers had sneered at people who put expedience before God's word, care over conscience, he may have had Burghley in mind.

Attacking Whitgift's use of *ex officio mero* oaths in the Ecclesiastical High Commission, aimed at silencing Protestant dissent, Burghley said: "I desire the peace of the Church ... I desire concord and unity in the exercise of our religion. To favor no sensual and willful recusants. But I conclude that according to my simple judgment, this kind of proceedings is too much favoring of the Romish Inquisition: And is rather a device to seek for offenders, than to reform any. This is not the charitable instruction that was intended." It may be, he said, that the church lawyers could defend the procedure in canon law, "but though *Omnia licent* [all is permitted], yet *Omnia non expedient* [not all is profitable]."[37]

---

36 Alexandra Walsham, "'Frantick Hacket': Prophecy, Sorcery, Insanity, and the Elizabethan Puritan Movement." *The Historical Journal* 1998; 41(1), 27–66.
37 John Strype, *The Life and Acts of ... John Whitgift* (London, 1718) III, appendix, IX, 63–4. For a fuller discussion of these issues, see Jones, *Governing*, 206–11. Burghley is quoting 1 Corinthians 6:12: "Omnia mihi licent, sed non omnia expedient," but makes it pithier, and less personal.

Fearing that too sharp a prosecution of any of the groups who had fixed their eyes on God and ignored the Queen's law would push them into rebellion, Burghley argued that, in England, no one was punished for religion. They could believe what they wished, so long as they did not disturb the godly peace of Elizabeth's state. Burghley knew that obedience arose from a rational conscience, properly tested. His position encouraged dissenters to argue for toleration based on conscience.

In July of 1588, Lord Burghley received a letter from Francis Blount, a Catholic refugee in Paris, asking him to deliver a petition to Queen Elizabeth. Burghley's clerk summarized its contents on the back: "The humble petition of Mr Francis Blount ... for Liberty of his conscience." In his petition, Blount asked to be allowed to come home. He said he feared, "being a Catholic to approach near your dominions (much less your Court)." But "when I do search the secret corners of my conscience and find that none whom you have justly executed or now have in prison have, can or may" implicate him in their crimes, "I may therefore (your accustomed clemency extended to a number surmounting me in fault although in vocation my inferiors) be induced to hope for the like mercy." He was convinced Elizabeth would be kind to him, "seeing your merciful Majesty hath protested to hurt none for their conscience."[38]

Blount's pleading for toleration for his conscience was one thing. The exultation of individual conscience over the law was another. Henry Barrow, founder of the Barrowists, a radical Protestant separatist group that believed the English church was irremediably corrupt, was tried for sedition in 1593. At his trial, Chief Justice Wray insisted that the law made room for those who were open to having their minds changed, suggesting a way for Barrow to save himself. The Chief Justice affirmed, "men should incur no penalty for opinions which they held doubtingly. And whether a man may not without breach of law Divine or Human, for his further satisfaction make queries and doubts in special causes, shewing withal the reason of his doubting: affirming nothing peremptorily or positively, but submitting himself to sound resolution."[39]

Lord Burghley assured Barrow that the sword of the Queen was not yet drawn against him, and asked if he had been given a chance to discuss his belief with learned men. He was asking if anyone had tried to reason him out of his

---

38 BL Lansd. 58, fo. 24.
39 *A petition directed to Her Most Excellent Maiestie wherein is deliuered 1. A meane howe to compound the ciuill dissention in the Church of England, 2. A proofe that they who write for reformation, do not offend against the stat. of 23. Eliz. c.2. and therefore till matters be compounded, deserue more fauour ... : here vnto is annexed, some opinions of such as sue for reformation ... : also, certayne articles vvherein is discouered the negligence of the bishoppes ... : lastlie, certayne questions or interrogatories dravvn by a fauourer of reformation...* (1591), 74. STC (2nd ed.)/1522a.

error, to correct his conscience. Barrow replied that a Mr. Some had come to him, recalling Some

> never would enter disputation: he said he came not therefore but in rea-soning manner to know some what of my mind more clearly.
>
> Some was then by the Arch B. [Archbishop Whitgift] called and demanded whither we had conference or no? Some shewed how that at our last conference before Sr. A. G. [Attorney General Thomas Egerton] there arose a question betwixt us, whether the Prince might make a posi-tive law *de rebus mediis* of things indifferent:
>
> I denying it, he asked me whither she might make a statute for the reforming excess of apparel?
>
> I granted that she might.
>
> He then said it was a doctrine of Devils to forbid meat by a positive law: he shewed me then that the Prince's law did not bind the conscience and that there is a difference betwixt *forum civile* and *forum conscientiae*...
>
> Then I beseeched the Lords to grant a public conference, that it might appear to all men, what we held, and where we erred. The Arch B. in great choler said, we should have no public conference, we had pub-lished too much already, and therefore he now committed us close prisoners.[40]

Lord Burghley tried to prevent the hanging of Barrow and his confederates for publishing seditious, if Protestant, books.[41] The Lord Treasurer accepted their supplication, claiming that in a land where no papist was put to death for religion, theirs should not be the first Protestant blood spilled for supporting the national faith. It was said that Archbishop Whitgift preempted the appeal by having the executions carried out.[42] Parliament apparently agreed with Burghley, passing a law that would have exiled rather than executed them only a week after their hasty hangings.

These people all believed the catechistical assertion that Christians must avoid Satan, evil inventions, and human imaginings that went against the Word of God, but disagreed over the question of who had the authority to know good from bad, divine from satanic. It was an irresoluble problem. Conflicting claims over authority led to differing definitions of sin and obedience. Some were moved to Catholicism and active papism; a tiny few of those toward religious

---

40 *The examinations of Henry Barrowe Iohn Grenewood and Iohn Penrie, before the high commissioners, and Lordes of the Counsel. Penned by the prisoners themselues before their deaths* (1596?). STC (2nd ed.)/1519.
41 CP 167/102.
42 TNA SP 12/244, fo. 219.

terrorism in the 1605 Gunpowder Plot. It led some to biblical literalism and separatism, and a few into self-exile in Holland and New England. It led most people to a comfortable membership in God's episcopal Church of England, where there was room for dissent that did not challenge the authority of state and church. But even in that broad community, there was a great deal of disagreement over what God expected of His people. Their fear of God led them to differing actions, but for the same reasons.

Robert Southwell wrote what he called an "epistle of comfort" to other imprisoned Catholics. The twenty-six-year-old Jesuit explained why God, in His wisdom, was subjecting His faithful to tortures, imprisonment, and hideous executions. It was a meditation on divine providence. He hoped in "this foggy night of heresy, and the confusion of tongues, which it hath here in our island procured, this dim light, which I shall set forth before you, and these my Catholic, though broken speeches, which I shall use unto you will not be altogether unpleasant."[43] They should recall, he said, all the private terrors that face individuals, and the "general scourges of plagues, war, a thousand hazards and calamities … that in any respect are incident into this life, they are for the divers sins and offences of men, we shall find them so many, so terrible, and so intolerable, as the very imagination of them without the experience, were able to affright a right courageous, and stout heart." But these scourges come because God loves humanity, despite its heinous and continual sins. Punishing sinners as a warning, God chastises "far underneath the rate of our misdeeds."[44]

If his Catholic compatriots, therefore, were suffering for their faith, they would be rewarded for resisting Queen Elizabeth's heretical church, receiving eternal bliss after their short quarter hour of terror. Mixing biblical quotes with prose to build a powerful argument, he wrote:

> you most glorious Confessors remember … he measures the waters of your short miseries with his closed fist; heaven and his eternal rewards he will measure unto you with his open span. If here he hath made darkness his secret place: he will afterward shew himself unto you clothed with light as with a garment, and will make the comfortless desert wherin you now dwell as it were a place of delights: and the wilderness of your desolation as the garden of our Lord: In the meantime, you must be contented to say with Job, I have been a brother unto Dragons and a fellow of Ostriches[45]

---

43 Robert Southwell, *An epistle of comfort to the reuerend priestes, & to the honorable, worshipful, & other of the laye sort restrayned in durance for the Catholicke faith* (1587), fo. 3v. STC (2nd ed.)/22946.
44 Ibid., fos. 60–60v.
45 Ibid., fo. 210. Dragons and ostriches: Job 30:29; 39:13.

Southwell's promise that God's providence was looking after His faithful flock permitted a powerful critique of the state, one which could not be answered with prosecution. As Job knew, the ostriches hated their own children, just as the heretic Elizabeth hated her own people. In God's name, Catholics had to deny her the pleasure of victory—a victory that increased God's plagues upon England.

Southwell ended this epistle with thanks to God that the "martyrquellers now in authority" were going to make saints enough to furnish all the churches. Southwell himself often spoke of his desire for martyrdom, and his prayer was granted. He was arrested by Richard Topcliffe, tortured, imprisoned for three years, and hanged, drawn, and quartered in 1595.[46]

Philip Howard, Earl of Arundel, another martyr, explaining his recusancy to Elizabeth in 1585, shaped it as a matter of imperative conscience. "As such as ye think hate me most," he wrote, "whether, being of that religion that I profess … they would not have taken that course for the safety of their souls and the discharge of their conscience, which I did." Anyone who would not do as he did, he said, "acknowledge themselves to be mere Atheists."[47]

As Arundel suggested, their neighbors would agree that God's providence required the state to be godly, and the individual to follow God in conscience. But they could not agree on which form of church God expected His state to provide, so no matter which form the Queen demanded, there were some who would, in conscience, refuse to worship in her church.

Such people placed great value on a conscience informed by right reason: the assumption that good science—theology properly done—would lead people to change their minds and follow the true church. For instance, when young Henry Caesar, the brother of Sir Julius Caesar, Judge of the Admiralty, turned himself in for being ordained a Catholic priest while he was in Paris, he was sent to the Tower of London by the Privy Council. The Keeper was instructed that "because we are informed that he [Henry] hath been misled by some that have infected him with lewd persuasions and that there is good hope he may be reclaimed with good counsel, and better instruction by some learned preachers," he was to be given conference with preachers and kept away from other Catholic prisoners. It worked. He was released because the Council was informed "that through conference of learned preachers he hath conformed himself in religion, and doth profess that he is resolved indeed in his conscience according to the truth." Disabused of papist error, he was "set at liberty to be at the disposition of Mr. Doctor Caesar his brother, who as he hath given us to understand doth mean to place him in the university for his better instruction

46 Nancy Pollard Brown, "Southwell, Robert [St Robert Southwell] (1561–1595)," in *Oxford Dictionary of National Biography* (Oxford: Oxford University Press, 2004). http://www.oxforddnb.com/view/article/26064 [Accessed November 29, 2018].
47 London, Inner Temple, Petyt Ms 538/10, fo. 25.

and furtherance of learning." He had been argued out of his Catholic recusancy and accepted back into the community of the Queen's church, his conscience corrected by right reasoning.[48]

Though conscience was claimed to license dissent, it was hard for Elizabethans to escape the providential nature of kingship. We can see this in how the theological parties responded to James VI's accession to the English throne. Conditioned to believe that the monarch had the ultimate authority in matters of religion, they lobbied their new king to use his supreme governorship over the church on their behalf. James, believing in the power of right reason, resorted to a conference to discuss the issues.

Puritans hoped that a Scots king would follow the Scottish Presbyterian precedent and grant them the sort of church order they wanted, free of irritating rituals, prayer books, and canon law. Therefore, they immediately presented him with the "Millenary Petition," begging him to reform the church: "we, to the number of more than a thousand of your majesty's subjects and ministers, all groaning as under a common burden of human rites and ceremonies, do with one joint consent humble ourselves at your majesty's feet, to be eased and relieved in this behalf."[49] The petitioners presented a list of things that wished James to change in the English church he had inherited. Attacking the worship and governance of the church, they were preparing legislation to dissolve the Elizabethan Settlement in James' first parliament.

The bishops of the established church, naturally, warned James of the evil in the hearts of Catholics, Puritans, and all who refused to conform to Elizabeth's church order. Though they recognized that their church, and their colleagues, were not perfect, they insisted on the importance of the church to the monarchy—a point James, having dealt long with Scottish Presbyterians, understood easily.

James called a meeting of Puritan leaders and English bishops at Hampton Court Palace in January 1604. He heard both sides out, trying hard to ensure everyone had his say, allowing a few small changes requested by the petitioners, and very importantly ordering a new translation of the Bible, in keeping with the latest scholarly knowledge. But he made it crystal clear that he, as Supreme Governor of the Church, was not going to undermine the bishops or give up control of the church. Like Elizabeth, God had given him responsibility to rule, and rule he would. Reminiscing about the trouble caused in Scotland by leaders of the kirk who presumed to know more than their monarch, he suggested that freedom of religious conscience drove men mad. Therefore, "I will have one doctrine, and one discipline, one religion in substance and in ceremony."[50]

---

48 BL Add. 11406, fos. 307, 315, 317, 321.
49 Henry Gee and William John Hardy, eds. *Documents Illustrative of English Church History* (New York: Macmillan, 1896), 508.
50 Barlow, *Conference*, 54.

The man who had replaced Elizabeth, Handmaiden of the Lord, understood his divinely granted authority to rule the church. He knew the enemies of the bishops were trying to use his supremacy against them, but he also knew that if gave them power, they would destroy his royal role: "I know what would become of my supremacy. No Bishop, no king."[51]

James declared of the religious dissenters, "I shall make them conform themselves, or I will harry them out of this land, or else do worse."[52] He was talking directly to Puritans in this instance, but he included Catholics and others in his view. Unfortunately, his force could not make dissenting consciences willfully obedient. Disagreements about the form and duty of a godly state and church would become more and more rancorous and nasty as the youngest Elizabethans grew to adulthood.

---

51 Ibid., 62.
52 Ibid., 63.

11

A Generation of Hearers

The new system of cultural values emerging in Elizabeth's reign focused on reading and hearing. Believing in the power of words, Elizabethans distrusted the visual, focusing on the Word of God as the source of all truth. Whether Elizabethans preferred hierarchical values of the old kind or believed in the power of conscience over community, they expressed their values in words, fearing the misleading power of the eyes, which channeled emotion to the heart rather than through the rational head. Elizabethans were connoisseurs of words. Words left less room for deceitful misunderstandings that led away from God and toward forbidden thoughts and actions.

Elizabethan religious leaders were deeply suspicious of the arts in religion, believing statues, paintings, painted glass, and ravishing music to be painted "whores," leading to spiritual fornication. They were especially dangerous for the uneducated. Since, in all churches and commonwealths, "the ignorant and weak are the greatest number, to whom images are hurtful and not profitable," the magistrates had to ban them. Rather than stirring the mind to devotion, they "distract the mind from prayer, hearing of God's word, and other godly meditations."[1]

Like so many things in the Elizabethan world, the rejection of the arts in worship raised hard boundary questions. When did the arts cross the line into idolatry? How pure must worship be? Could there be music? What kind of music? What about poetry? What about paintings or music for secular but not religious purposes? Working out these tensions stimulated an especially English kind of cultural renaissance.

Of course, this resistance to the arts in worship was based on Protestant rejection of Catholic practice. Leaders of the Catholic responses to Protestantism saw the important power of images to encourage introspective, imaginative, and sensory experiences that helped the individual subjugate his soul to God.[2] Ignatius of Loyola encouraged his Jesuits to use images as

---

1 *Parker Correspondence*, 85.
2 Moshe Sluhovsky, Becoming a *New Self. Practices of Belief in Early Modern Catholicism* (Chicago: University of Chicago Press, 2017), 19.

Being Elizabethan: Understanding Shakespeare's Neighbors, First Edition. Norman Jones.
© 2020 John Wiley & Sons, Inc. Published 2020 by John Wiley & Sons, Inc.

meditation aids, enriching the meaning of text, in his powerful *Spiritual Exercises*.[3] The Council of Trent declared in 1563:

> profit is derived from all sacred images, not only because the people are thereby admonished of the benefits and gifts bestowed upon them by Christ, but also because the miracles which God has performed by means of the saints, and their salutary examples, are set before the eyes of the faithful; that so they may give God thanks for those things; may order their own lives and manners in imitation of the saints; and may be excited to adore and love God, and to cultivate piety.[4]

The same Council recognized that human wits could not be raised to the contemplation of God without "external props," including music.[5]

This Catholic embrace of the sensual encouraged new artistic and intellectual expressions of interior sentiment in Catholic Europe in the Elizabethan era. St. Teresa of Avila (d. 1582) and St. John of the Cross (d. 1591) achieved new interiority through meditative, disciplined asceticism that encouraged subjugation to God. Tintoretto (d. 1594) was decorating the Scuola di San Roco and putting every saint he could find into his massive painting, "Paradise," a visual evocation of heaven. Michelangelo da Caravaggio (d. 1610) was painting ethereally lit faces of real people into biblical stories. In Rome, Giovanni Pierluigi da Palestrina (d. 1594) was composing a new Baroque polyphony, with intelligible texts, designed to ravish the heart through the ears. Claudio Monteverdi (1567–1645) was pioneering ecclesiastical *concertante*, madrigals, vespers, and operas. They were creating the European Baroque.

But in England, there was no great Baroque art, architecture, or mystical meditation. There, the Baroque was an affair of the ear, associated with masters of words—poets and playwrights such as William Shakespeare, Edmund Spenser, Philip Sydney, and Christopher Marlowe—and preachers like "Silver-Tongued" Henry Smith and John Donne. Henry Smith summed it up in a sermon when he proclaimed, "This is the generation of hearers."[6] "By the ear cometh knowledge."[7]

---

3 Gauvin Alexander Bailey, *Art on the Jesuit Missions in Asia and Latin America, 1542–1773* (Toronto: University of Toronto Press, 1999), 8.

4 *The canons and decrees of the sacred and oecumenical Council of Trent*, J. Waterworth, ed. and trans. (London: Dolman, 1848), 235. http://thesacredarts.org/newsite/knowledge-base/ from-the-holy-see/105-the-council-of-trent-on-the-invocation-veneration-and-relics-of-saints-and-on-sacred-images-1563 [Accessed November 29, 2016].

5 K.G. Fellerer and Moses Hadas, trans. "Church Music and the Council of Trent." *The Musical Quarterly* 1953; 39(4), 576–94. The quoted words come from Session 22, chapter 5 of the Council, quoted in 577 n. 9. http://www.jstor.org/stable/739857 [Accessed November 29, 2018].

6 Thomas Smith, ed. *The Works of Henry Smith*, 2 vols. (Edinburgh: James Nichol, 1866), I, 328.

7 Ibid., I, 318. Smith died in 1591. When people could not hear him, they read him. His collected sermons went through twenty-two editions between 1592 and 1676.

England was in the same intellectual milieu as other European nations, but its circumstances meant that the era produced a distinctive culture of words read, spoken, and sung, many of them tending toward poetry. Most of the cultural institutions that underwrote the great art of the early Baroque no longer existed in Protestant England. Lacking churches and monasteries to support art, music, and architecture, English energies went into more secular and less public forums, like the Court, or into the theaters, where there were paying customers.[8] Or else they went into the great verbal art forms that paid for specialist performances: sermons and prayers. Because so much of the population was illiterate, delivering the Word of God to everyone without the aid of pictures required the enforced listening and rote learning provided by worship using the *Book of Common Prayer* and skilled preaching. Reinforcing them was the new form of vernacular hymn singing, a pedagogical tool to teach theological lessons through pleasurable experience.

Words in Worship

The English culture of the word was a performance culture. Obviously, Elizabethans lived in the first great age of the English-speaking stage, but we should not start with Shakespeare. The performances most seen and appreciated by Elizabethans were sermons, written and delivered by ministers to the public. They formed the bedrock of communication, and ministers were thoughtfully prepared to deliver them. Equally, their audiences were prepared to consume them in ways it is hard for modern ears to grasp. Auditors were engaged in self-referential consumption of words, encouraged, as the prayer book puts it, to "hear ... read, mark, learn, and inwardly digest" their lessons. Rhetoric was a part of every educated person's training, and preachers were given advanced instruction about the special rhetorical forms and devices they were to use. The minister's job was to use carefully structured messages in God's service, expounding His Word in ways that awakened the hearers' faith, prompting and directing Christian lives.

All the manuals on rhetoric were concerned with effective performance, suitable to the seriousness of the message. Richard Bernard, author of a preaching manual, wanted "comely moderation," combined with a voice "so far lift up, as it may always be heard," well-modulated, "guided as the hearers not understanding the matter, may yet by the manner discern where about you are."

---

8 Alexander Marr, "Pregnant Wit: *Ingegno* in Renaissance England." *British Art Studies*, 1. https://doi.org/10.17658/issn.2058-5462/issue-01/amarr [Accessed November 29, 2018].

This meant matching voice to content, speaking sadly when the matter was lamentable and happily in causes of rejoicing.[9] Their purpose was straightforward, even if their art was not. Preachers practiced the art of homiletics, teasing out doctrine from Scripture, cutting it carefully, splicing the pieces together, and applying them to real situations, instructing and exhorting. The hearers learned both the doctrine and the use of the doctrine from the preacher. It took an educated man to do this, one skilled intellectually and rhetorically.[10]

In 1592, William Perkins, having set out a preaching style that used Ramist opposites to instruct ("To be or not to be" is a classic example of the method of combining startling oppositions), boiled preaching down to four actions:

1) To read the text distinctly, out of the canonical Scriptures.
2) To give the sense and understanding of it being read, by the Scripture itself.
3) To collect a few and profitable points of doctrine out of the natural sense.
4) To apply ... the doctrines rightly collected to the life and manners of men, in a simple and plain speech.

He declared the "sum of the sum" to be to "Preach one Christ by Christ to the praise of Christ."[11] As was typical of Perkins' style of instruction, he also reduced the whole art of preaching to a single graphic. About a third of the chart is about the intellectual construction of the sermon, but the largest part is the "uttering." The minister's speech must be spiritual but delivered with gestures and actions of the voice and body that will bind human wisdom.[12] As another author on preaching said, preachers must have the power of propounding sound doctrine while "moving and drawing minds."[13] A good preacher entertained as he taught, making his message clear. We do not have many descriptions of pulpit behavior, but in 1559, Dr. Cole is described as assailing his audience "having turned himself towards all quarters and into every possible attitude, stamping with his feet, throwing about his arms, bending his sides, snapping his fingers alternately elevating and depressing his eye brows."[14]

9 Quoted in Kate Armstrong, "Sermons in Performance," in Peter McCullough, Hugh Adlington, and Emma Rhatigan, eds. *The Oxford Handbook of the Early Modern Sermon* (Oxford: Oxford University Press, 2011), 129–30.
10 Greg Kneidel, "*Ars Praedicandi*: Theories and Practice," in McCullough, Adlington, and Rhatigan, *Early Modern Sermon*, 3–20.
11 William Perkins, *The arte of prophecying, or, A treatise concerning the sacred and onely true manner and methode of preaching...* (1607), 148. STC (2nd ed.)/19735.4.
12 Ibid., front matter.
13 Andreas Hyperius, *The practise of preaching, otherwise called the Pathway to the pulpet conteyning an excellent method how to frame diuine sermons, & to interpret the holy Scriptures according to the capacitie of the vulgar people. First written in Latin by the learned pastor of Christes Church, D. Andreas Hyperius.* Iohn Ludham, trans. (1577), fo. 5v. STC (2nd ed.)/11758.5.
14 Robinson, *Zurich Letters*, I, 14.

The preacher must break through to the hearts of his congregation. "Silver-Tongued" Henry Smith sketched the preacher's audience in the 1590's:

> Some come unto the service to save forfeiture [the fine for not attending church], and then they stay the sermon for shame; some come because they would not be accounted atheists; some come because they would avoid the name of papist; some come to please their friends. One hath a good man to his friend, and lest he should offend him, he frequents the preachers, that his friend may think well of him; some come with their masters and mistresses for attendance; some come with a fame; they have heard great speech of the man, and therefore they will spend one hour to hear him once, but to see whether it be so as they say; some come because they be idle; to pass the time they go to a sermon, lest they be weary of doing nothing; some come with their fellows: one saith, Let us go to the sermon; Content, saith he, and he goeth for company; some hear the sound of a voice as they pass by the church, and step in before they be aware; another hath some occasion of business, and he appoints his friends to meet him at such a sermon, as they do at Paul's. All these are accidental hearers.[15]

He goes on, reading the thoughts of his congregation:

> One is like an Athenian, and he harkeneth after news; if the preacher say anything of our armies beyond the sea, or council at home, or matters at court, that is his lure. Another is like the Pharisee, and he watcheth if anything be said that may be wrest to be spoken against persons in high place, that he may play the devil in accusing of his brethren ... Another smacks of eloquence, and he gapes for a phrase, that when he cometh to his ordinary [tavern] he may have one figure more to grace and worship his table. Another is malcontent, and he never pricketh up his ears till the preacher come to gird against some whom he spiteth, and when the sermon is done, he remebereth nothing which was said to him, but that which was spoken against others. Another cometh to gaze about the church; he hath an evil eye, which is still looking upon that from which Job did avert his eye [girls].[16] Another cometh to muse; so soon as he is set, he falleth into a brown study; sometimes his mind runs on his market, sometimes on his journey, sometimes of his suit, sometimes of his dinner, sometimes of his sport after dinner, and the sermon is done before the man thinks where he is. Another cometh to hear, but so soon

---

15 Smith, *Works of Henry Smith*, I, 326–7.
16 He is referring to Job 31:1, "I made a covenant with mine eyes; why then should I think upon a maid?"

as the preacher hath said his prayer, he falls fast asleep, as though he had been brought in for a corpse, and the preacher should preach at his funeral.[17]

Facing such an audience required the preacher to frame the message in ways that would make Scripture interesting and applicable.

If preaching was an art, so, too, was listening to sermons. Henry Smith preached two on the "Art of Hearing" in his London pulpit at St. Clements Danes in 1592, teaching even "the ancientist hearers in London" to understand sermons so they could recall them afterward. This new aural literacy became a hallmark of godly living. Paying attention, following an argument, and learning to perform homiletic analysis of Scripture made one a good student of God's Word. Good listeners could be transformed by God's grace as they followed the ping-pong match between scriptural references and contemporary applications.[18]

Good listening required close attention. A "godly hearer" focused on the preacher, not stirring, not smiling, making communal worship an individual act of discipline. The "vanity of the eye" was an especially difficult thing, since men and women sat together in church, and "our women wearing no manner of veil which in other countries is usual," prompted lust. One must stare at the preacher, or look down, to keep the mind on holy things.[19] This problem moved church-wardens to install high-walled box pews that prevented lascivious gawking.

Simonds D'Ewes recalled how he was taught as a school boy to take notes at sermons, becoming a "rational hearer." Unlike the "brute creatures" seated around him, he recorded what he heard on anything that came to hand, scribbling on scraps while attending multiple sermons each day. In this way, he "grew to a great measure of knowledge in the very body of divinity." This young rational hearer was the ideal godly audience for good preachers.[20]

If preaching required the clergy to untwist Scripture so it could be fitted to circumstance, they had to know the Bible. But they learned it, as befitted university-trained clerics, in Latin. They thought in Latin, and they prayed in Latin—in 1560, there was a Latin edition of the *Book of Common Prayer* produced for use in colleges and universities.[21] But when they got into the pulpit, they had to explain it in English.

---

17 Smith, *Works of Henry Smith*, I, 327.
18 Laura Feitzinger Brown, "Slippery Listening: Anxious Clergy and Lay Listeners' Power in Early Modern England." *The Sixteenth Century Journal* 2016; 47(1), 5.
19 George Hakewell, *The Vanitie of the Eie* (1608), quoted in Arnold Hunt, *The Art of Hearing. English Preachers and their Audiences* (Cambridge: Cambridge University Press, 2010), 67.
20 Simonds D'Ewes, *Autobiography and Correspondence … in Two Volumes*, James Orchard Haliwell, ed. (London: 1845), I, 95. J. Sears McGee, *An Industrious Mind. The Worlds of Sir Simonds D'Ewes* (Stanford: Stanford University Press, 2015), 38.
21 Norman Jones, "Elizabeth, Edification, and the Latin Prayer Book of 1560." *Church History* 1984; 53(2), 174–86.

The point of the preaching was to explicate the Bible, and the Word of God was available in English for those who could read. English editions were in the hands of readers beginning with William Tyndale's 1525 New Testament, completed by Miles Coverdale in the 1530's, bundled together in Henry VIII's Great Bible of 1539. When the *Book of Common Prayer* appeared in English in 1549, changing English worship from Latin to English, the Scriptures it quoted were in Tyndale's English.

In 1560, Protestant exiles in Geneva produced a new translation known as the Geneva Bible. Featuring the innovation of numbered verses and explanatory glosses, it was cheaper and smaller than the other translations, though not always as easy on the ear. This became the Bible available to most Elizabethans, though there were several other Protestant translations, culminating in the King James version of 1611.[22]

In 1582, Catholic exiles in Rheims published their own translation of the New Testament, with commentaries. In 1609–10, Catholic exiles produced a translation of the Old Testament to join the Rheims New Testament. Known as the Douay–Rheims Bible, it was designed to counter the English versions that supported Protestant theology, especially the Geneva Bible.

That there were several translations of the Bible in circulation does not mean that there was an agreed upon version for normal use. This welter of translations complicated the understanding of God's Word, since it forced scholars back to the original languages and encouraged slanted translations. When King James called the clergy together for the Hampton Court Conference in 1604, he learned that the lack of an authorized translation gave all the dissenters loop holes. They refused to subscribe to the *Book of Common Prayer* because the biblical passages it quoted were from "a most corrupted translation." Very well, said the King, and ordered a new translation "to satisfy our scrupulous brethren."[23] James made it very clear that his new translation would, unlike the Geneva Bible, underscore the necessity of obeying kings.[24] King James' authorized version of the Bible, published in 1611, did not end the quibbling, but it further increased the importance of the Word of God rightly understood by insisting there was only one allowable, best translation.

These arguments over translation, which were also arguments over interpretation, enhanced the value of preachers capable of teaching how to understand the complicated sacred book, which their hearers might own and read, but whose meanings they often found hard to grasp. People trying to make sense of Scripture devoted a great deal of time and energy to finding good preachers—"gadding to sermons," as their critics said.

---

22 Lori Anne Ferrell, "The Preachers' Bibles," in McCullough, Adlington, and Rhatigan, *Early Modern Sermon*, 21–33.
23 *The Holy Bible* (1611), "The translatours to the reader." STC (2nd ed.)/2216.
24 Barlow, *Conference*, 35.

Words in Prayer

Attending sermons, however, was only the beginning of the spiritual journey. The desire to understand Scripture and live accordingly required the performance of prayer. As Richard Greenham explained, "hearing the word with profit" required a disciplined process. Before going to the church, you were to be humble in prayer, so the preacher "may speak to your conscience." You should listen, said Henry Smith, like baby birds who lift their beaks to catch what their mother brings them. Afterward, immediately apply the "threatenings and promises and instruction" of the sermon "in heart" with a short prayer. Then, when you are home, change what you remember of the sermon into longer prayers and desire God to help you "remember it most when you should practice it."[25] This process of rehearsing sermons converted aural learning into oral yearning and, eventually, into interiorized guidance.

Prayer was both a controlled and democratic performance. As we have seen, scripted prayers were used in church, and in conjunction with all community events. There were printed prayers for all sorts of things, carefully designed to teach correct messages. But people also prayed extemporaneously. For some, this was the hallmark of true faith, since a prayer performed *ex tempore* was more heartfelt, more emotionally real, than one written by a third party and expressed generically. They felt that the *Book of Common Prayer* used "stinted prayers," rather than allowing fruitful "praying in the spirit."[26]

The Catholic Church had an ancient tradition of scripted prayer, usually performed in Latin, and its personal prayer was generally penitential. It was part of the process of paying for sin in preparation for purgatory. It had to done in the right forms and times. Personal piety was shaped by books of hours and sought the aid of saints and the Virgin Mary. These, the English reformers rejected. No more prayers for intercession should be offered, and a different sort of prayer of repentance was needed.

The Protestants redefined prayer. Drawing on the Fathers of the Church, the 1562 "Homily on Prayer" taught it was "a lifting up of the mind to God; that is to say, an humble and lowly pouring out of the heart to God." It was an "affection of the heart, and not a labor of the lips." So, true prayer consisted "not so much in the outward sound and voice of words, as in the inward groaning and crying of the heart to God."[27] It followed from this that no angel,

---

25 Kenneth L. Parker and Eric J. Carlson, *"Practical Divinity." The Life and Works of Revd Richard Greenham* (Aldershot: Ashgate, 1998), 138. Smith, *Works of Henry Smith*, I, 333.

26 Lancelot Andrewes, "One of the Sermons upon the Second Commandment, Preached in the Parish Church of St. Giles, Cripplegate, on the ninth of January, A.D. MDXCII," in *Ninety-Six Sermons* (Oxford: John Henry Parker, 1843), V, 70.

27 *Sermons, Or Homilies, Appointed to be Read in Churches in the Time of Queen Elizabeth of Famous Memory* (Oxford: Oxford University Press, 1840), 289.

saint, or Blessed Virgin could know the secrets of one's heart, so prayer should be addressed only to God.

Because God saved through faith, which was a gift, the homily instructed the faithful to pray for the opening of God's gifts in their souls through divine promptings:

> therefore we ought first of all to crave such things as properly belong to the salvation thereof [the soul]; as the gift of repentance, the gift of faith, the gift of charity and good works, remission and forgiveness of sins, patience in adversity, lowliness in prosperity, and such other like fruits of the Spirit, as hope, love, joy, peace, long-suffering, gentleness, goodness, meekness, and temperancy; which things God requireth of all them that profess themselves to be his children[28]

Having prayed for their own souls, the faithful were also to glorify God with prayer. This could be done by anyone, following Christ's injunction to pray without ceasing, but the Elizabethan homilies on prayer were very clear. It was especially important to keep the Sabbath (avoiding "filthy fleshliness") and to attend church. "Lift up pure hands, with clean hearts, in all places and at all times. But do the same in the temples and churches upon the sabbath-days also."[29]

Tied as it was to church attendance, the scripted prayer of the Elizabethan church was too Catholic for some. The prayer book itself was largely a translation of the Catholic mass, and its written prayers were "performed" by ministers and congregants, smacking of the formulaic religion of papal priests. It was also too unemotional. Reading from a book did not stir a believer's passion and invention the way heart-felt faith demanded. Many Elizabethans, Catholic and Protestant, took the interior experience of faith as the most important part of religious feeling. This feeling could not be expressed by people mumbling along with the minister, especially if they could not read.

Consequently, extemporaneous praying became an aural art with its own values and forms. It allowed a person to vent emotion, to speak to the community and God about particular issues. It worked as a meditative tool for the illiterate as well as the literate. The diary of the minister Richard Rogers describes how prayer and meditation supported one another. In January 1580, Rogers spent some time with John Knewstubs, Rector of Cockfield, Suffolk, profiting from his example. He was, says Rogers, unwearied in prayer, passing most days and nights praying. Knewstubs used prayer to acknowledge his sin, to recall God's marvelous love for everyone, and to remember God's bountiful liberality. These three things helped him to walk in the way of the Lord and

---

28 Ibid., 295.
29 Ibid., 307.

prevented him from being snared by the Devil. Rogers tried to emulate him. His daily regimen included an hour of reading, meditation to prepare for private prayer, private prayer, and group prayer and catechizing.[30]

Reading Rogers' diary, you find him, a clergyman, praying in all sorts of settings, always hoping God will close the gap between them. "Yesternight, by prayer late with myself and wife," he writes, "I ... commit myself to my God with a mind clearly enlightened with ample knowledge or comprehension of God."[31]

It is hard to know how he physically behaved during prayers. The *Book of Common Prayer* enjoined kneeling at certain points, but there are several biblically approved attitudes of prayer. Elizabethans who were concerned that their church was too Catholic preferred standing or kneeling with arms raised and palms turned to Heaven: the *orans* position of the primitive church. It was possible to stand or sit with head bowed, too. A few prostrated themselves before God, in an Old Testament manner. In short, the posture of prayer reinforced the words, and demonstrated a theological ideal.

Singing the Word

What all praying had in common was language, much of it poetic, composed with an ear to its emotional impact. It is not surprising that poetry was one of the great cultural products of the era. The forms it took were related to the religious values of its authors, which makes sense, since it was designed to express the interior experience of religious development. The metaphors for which it reached echoed theological presumptions and served as the grounds for religious meditation. If England had no mystics like St. Teresa or St. John of Cross, it had religious poetry that worked toward the same transcendent emotional effect in its very different milieu, culminating in poets like John Donne and his much younger contemporary, George Herbert.

Protestant theologians were not particularly friendly to poetry, but it was a scriptural way of speaking, and translating the Psalms, the Song of Solomon, and other Old Testament books required poetic skills in English. Even the New Testament contained poetic moments, such as the "Hymn of Mary," also known by its Latin name, "*Magnificat*." Found in Luke's Gospel (1:46–55), it is the Virgin Mary's song of praise to the Lord. Prosaic Protestants, fearing the manipulation of emotion, felt that the message was in the words, not seeing them as lyrics. But by the middle of the Elizabethan era, it was apparent to many that the devotional efficacy of the Psalms, in particular, depended on

---

30 M.M. Knappen, *Two Elizabethan Puritan Diaries by Richard Rogers and Samuel Ward* (Chicago: The American Society of Church History, 1933), 95–6.
31 Ibid., 96.

their poetic value, and so devotional poetry emerged as a valuable spiritual tool.[32] As Sir Philip Sidney observed in his *The Defense of Poesy*, poets like King David and King Solomon, the authors of the Psalms and the Song of Songs, imitated the "inconceivable excellencies" of God. In the New Testament, St. James counseled singing psalms when we feel merry or to console the dying. Poetry, Sidney argued, draws the mind more effectually and so teaches virtue most excellently. By doing this, the poet can exceed nature and give honor to the Maker of makers. "The poet is the food for the tenderest stomachs."[33]

Aspiring poet Michael Drayton found much more in the Bible that could be turned into English poetry. His first book was entitled *The Harmony of the Church*, in which he anglicized the "spiritual songs and holy hymns of godly men, patriarchs and prophets" for the solace and comfort of the godly.[34]

Elizabethans sang a lot of psalms in church. Congregational singing was one of the reasons people liked to go—it was a departure from the Catholic tradition of Latin music controlled by professional choirs. John Jewel reported only a year after the Elizabethan Settlement came in that hymn singing was helping the acceptance of the new worship. "You may sometimes see at Paul's Cross," he wrote, "after the sermon, six thousand persons, old and young, of both sexes, all singing together and praising God. This sadly annoys the mass-priests and the Devil. For they perceive that by these means the sacred discourses sink more deeply into the minds of men."[35]

Reformers saw hymns as didactic and did not want the music to overwhelm the words. They were a vehicle for teaching, not an act of holiness. Bishop Horne of Winchester made this obvious in 1571, when he ordered that in his cathedral, "no note shall be used in song that shall drown any word or syllable ... whereby the sentence cannot well be perceived by the hearers." He disliked polyphonic singing "whereby the sense may be hindered."[36]

By the middle of the reign, psalm singing had become a regular part of divine worship, and the metrical psalms complied by Thomas Sternhold and John Hopkins had become a common part of public religious experience, published in more than 160 Elizabethan editions (Figure 11.1).[37] The Sternhold and

---

32 Ramie Targoff, *Common Prayer. The Language of Public Devotion in Early Modern England* (Chicago: University of Chicago Press, 2001), 59.
33 Lewis Soens, *Sir Philip Sidney's Defense of Poesy* (Lincoln: University of Nebraska Press, 1970), 11, 19, 26. Brian Cummings, *The Literary Culture of the Reformation. Grammar and Grace* (Oxford: Oxford University Press, 2002), 267.
34 Michael Drayton, *The harmonie of the church. Containing, the spirituall songes and holy hymnes...* (1591). STC (2nd ed.)/7199.
35 John Ayre, ed., *The Works of John Jewel*, 4 vols. (Cambridge: Parker Society, 1845–50), IV, 230–1.
36 William Howard Frere, ed. *Visitation Articles and Injunctions of the Time of the Reformation*, vol. III, 1559–1575 (London: Longmans, 1910), 319.
37 Steven W. May, "Poetry," in Doran and Jones, *Elizabethan World*, 553.

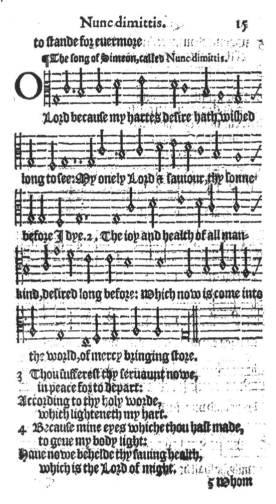

Figure 11.1 The *nunc dimittis* from the 1577 edition of Thomas Sternhold's and John Hopkins' metrical psalms, "to be sung of all the people together, in all churches." *The whole boke of Psalmes collected into Englishe…* (1577), fo. 15. STC / 2334:04. Henry E. Huntington Library and Art Gallery.

Hopkins tunes were clumsy, so by the 1590's, the eight-line melodies of the metrical psalms were being replaced by new four-line melodies, often named for English towns like "Oxford," "Winchester," "Hackney," and "Glastonbury." They became so familiar that they were known to rich and poor alike, easy to sing and easy to remember. These strophic metrical verses—the Book of Psalms translated into verse—were sung in unison with the rest of the congregation, becoming the "common tunes." It was, as Christopher Marsh remarks, "the sound of the church."[38] The hymns taught Scripture and theology in memorable ways.

In a religion stripped of most of its sensuality, music remained, expressing patriotism, thanksgiving, and religious joy, while providing meditative space in which to find comfort amidst religious anxiety.[39]

The singing of hymns was not limited to church. People sang them in private worship, and as part of their home entertainment. William Damon, an Italian recorder player employed by Elizabeth, turned the psalms sung in church into music for home use. In 1591, Damon's music was published in a "corrected" version by William Swayne, who divided it into parts. It was his intention, he said, to provide psalms for people who, "after the serious labor of their calling are desirous rather to recreate themselves in singing of Psalms, than in other exercises of less comfort, and evil mark."[40]

There was a booming market for music for the home. Madrigals had been introduced from Italy, and people like Thomas Whythorne began to write part music, hoping to profit from the demand. Whythorne's lyrics were deeply self-conscious, playing with the tension between self and divine duty. In one of his songs, the youthful mirth of a young man is betrayed, leading him to fall back on God, his only faithful friend.[41] In his *Duos*, the cantus sings: "Blessed are those that are undefiled in the way and walk in the law of the Lord"; the bass sings: "herewithall shall a young man cleanse his way, even by ruling himself after Thy word ... O Lord teach me thy statutes."[42]

Music for parish use was nothing like the great liturgical music we associate with Baroque composers such as Palestrina. The democratic aspect of English worship precluded the kind of professional musicianship available in the Cappella Julia in St. Peter's where Palestrina worked, or in St. Mark's in Venice where Monteverdi produced his gorgeous "Vespers of the Blessed Virgin" in 1610. But England did have venues in which complex religious music could be composed and performed. Professional choirs survived the Reformation in cathedral establishments, where singing God's praise was the primary

---

38 Nicholas Temperley, "'All skillful praises sing': how congregations sang the psalms in early modern England." *Renaissance Studies* 2015; 29(4), 531–53. Christopher Marsh, *Music and Society in Early Modern England* (Cambridge: Cambridge University Press, 2010), 407–15, 434.
39 Jonathan Willis, *Church Music and Protestantism in Post-Reformation England: Discourses, Sites and Identities* (London: Routledge, 2010), 241.
40 William Daman, *Bassus. The second booke of the musicke of M. William Damon, late one of her maiesties musitions conteining all the tunes of Dauids Psalmes, as they are ordinarily soung in the Church: most excellently by him composed into 4. parts. In which sett the highest part singeth the church tune. Published for the recreation of such as delight in musicke* (1591), "To the Reader." STC (2nd ed.)/6221.
41 Thomas Whythorne, *Triplex, of songes, for three, fower, and fiue voyces...* (1571), fos. 3–6v. STC 25584-1844.
42 Thomas Whythorne, *Cantus. Of duos, or songs for tvvo voices...* (1590), "Cantus." Sig. A2v; Bassus Aiiiv. STC 25583-1192.

function.[43] The music in Queen Elizabeth's Chapel Royal was of a high quality, often performed by continental professionals. In the royal world of competitive display, public music was important.

William Byrd held an appointment as organist of the Chapel Royal, and was a superb composer, taking the poetry of the Bible and of the secular poets and setting it to music. Byrd's first book, written with his equally talented elder colleague Thomas Tallis and published in 1575, neatly sums up the relationship between Scripture, poetry, and music. Designed to publicize his monopoly on music paper, it honored Elizabeth. It is a collection of songs with sacred subject matter, with lyrics on themes like "Lord have mercy on us."[44] His 1588 book *Psalms, Sonnets, and Songs of Sadness and Piety* followed suit. His friend Sir Philip Sidney, author of *The Defense of Poesie* and translator of the Psalms, gave lyrics to several of Byrd's compositions, such as "O Lord How Vain are our Frail Delights," a *contemptus mundi* meditation. In the same collection, though, we find Byrd setting sonnets from Sidney's pastoral *Astrophel and Stella*, blending the sacred and the profane.[45]

These musical compositions were not conceived just as music. In accord with the theory of the time, music ("proportion poetical") and poetry were both part of the same effort to move the feelings of the listener. They were a form of rhetoric that worked together to produce *enargia*, defined in 1599 by William Scott as "force, effectualness, or vigor, which is the character of passion, and life of persuasion and motion"; an audibly powerful description adding luster and light, as well as harmony, to improve the impact of an argument.[46]

Perhaps the light thrown on God's Word by setting divine poetry to music worked on William Byrd's soul, since he converted to Catholicism. By the early 1580's, he was frequently reported for attending Catholic masses and consorting with recusants. His wife Julia was first accused of recusancy in 1577; William himself was presented for it in 1584. But the records of the King Bench prove that Byrd was continually protected from prosecution. Frequently reported and indicted, he was never tried. He was granted a letter by the Privy Council ordering the Attorney General to stop processes against him, *per mandatum regine* (by order of the Queen).[47] He continued to write for the

---

43 Stanford E. Lehmberg, *The Reformation of Cathedrals. Cathedrals in English Society, 1485–1603* (Princeton: Princeton University Press, 1988), 182–3, 193–206.

44 William Byrd and Thomas Tallis, *Cantiones, quae ab argumento sacrae vocantur, quinque et sex partium* (1575), 34. STC (2nd ed.)/23666.

45 Gavin Alexander, "The Musical Sidneys." *John Donne Journal* 2006; 25, 70. Quoting William Scott, *The Modell of Poesye, An Original-Spelling Edition*, Gavin Alexander, ed. (Cambridge, 2013), fo. 18v. http://www.cambridge.org/gb/files/1713/7458/6256/Original_Spelling_Edition.pdf [Accessed November 29, 2018].

46 Philip Brett, *William Byrd and His Contemporaries. Essays and a Monograph*, Joseph Kerman and Davitt Moroney, eds. (Berkeley: University of California Press, 2007), 114–15.

47 David Mateer, "William Byrd's Middlesex Recusancy." *Music & Letters* 1997; 78(1), 11.

Chapel Royal in both English and Latin. Eventually, he withdrew to live near the powerful Petre family's seat at Ingatestone Hall in Essex, where he could more easily practice Catholicism, while still collecting his pay. Though he was excommunicated by the English church in 1598, and charged with "seducing" people to popery, he kept his appointment as a Gentleman of the Chapel Royal until his death in 1623.[48] Through these years, he was composing for both Protestant and Catholic services. His *Gradualia*, published in 1605–07 without title pages or dedications, contained settings for the Catholic mass, and may have been used by English Catholics in their worship.

Byrd moved in an artistic milieu that included the poetic Sidney family, other composers like Orlando Gibbons and John Dowland, and courtiers like Sir Philip's boyhood friend, Fulke Greville. When Sir Philip Sidney was killed at the Battle of Zutphen in 1586, Greville became his literary executor. But Greville did not agree with Sir Philip about poetry's ability to transcend. He knew that no imperfect person could know God; no poet could create like God. Humans could only understand the limitations of the human mind and reflect God's creation.[49] As He put it in his "Treatise on Religion":

> Then by affecting power, we cannot know Him;
> By knowing all things else, we know Him less;
> Nature contains Him not, Art cannot show Him;
> Opinions idols and not God express.
> Without, in power, we see Him everywhere;
> Within, we rest not till we find Him there.[50]

Greville knew that intervening grace that stirred the heart was the only knowledge of God that was possible. We can apprehend God in our hearts, not in reason, and no artist can show God to us; only God can reveal Himself.

Greville, though a poet, was suspicious of the muses, pagan daughters of Zeus. He feared they were being exalted above God, and he and his co-believers feared gross pleasures that distracted the mind from the proper contemplation of God. There was a lively battle in Protestant circles about the role of the arts in worship. Fearing Catholic idolatry, some were passionately opposed to art and music in church, as well as to secular poetry. Those expressions that did not keep the soul fixed on the Word of God were dangerous.

People of this school thought organs and bells should be removed from churches, alongside statues, paintings, and stained glass. The church should

---

48 Edward F. Rimbault, ed. *The Old Cheque-Book, or Book of Remembrance of the Chapel Royal, from 1561 to 1744* (London: Camden Society n.s., 3, 1872), 58, 62, 128, 189.
49 Cummings, *Literary Culture*, 271–3.
50 Fulke Greville, "A Treatise of Religion," in Alexander B. Grosart, *The Works in Verse and Prose of … Fulke Greville*, 4 vols. (1870), I, 241.

become a place of solemn reading and preaching where the Word was delivered without distraction. Naturally, there was a lively counter argument for music in worship.

John Case, a leading philosopher at Oxford, turned his neo-Aristotelian logic on the enemies of church music. In 1588, he published a Latin apology for instrumental, vocal, and mixed music in church. Pointedly, its title page bore quotations from the Psalms that proved that King David appointed priests to be "singers with instruments of music, psalteries and harps and cymbals, sounding, by lifting up the voice with joy."[51] But Case went beyond quoting Scripture. He developed a sophisticated argument about the effect of the *enargia* of music on the soul, its ability to decrease evil instincts and move the spirit to godliness. Our spirits heard heavenly music before we were born, he explained, and therefore they respond to it. Spirits are moved best when voices and instruments are mixed polyphonically, like Thomas Tallis did in *Spem in alium*, a motet in forty parts with eight choirs of five voices in each, written in the early 1570's. Since, said Case, the sound carries the words directly to the mind, it simultaneously stimulates the brain and all other parts of the body. Toes tap while the mind is moved toward God. The purpose of music, therefore, is to "express to the mind through various motions and sounds of the air many secrets of the future and of the celestial harmony from which it is sprung."[52]

Having argued against those who would remove art from worship, Case concluded that art imitates nature, in that nature provides the material for art, but art can, using that material, improve upon it. He suggested the analogy of medicine, which, using natural things, can change other natural things through the art of the physician. Case supported neither Sidney's nor Greville's position on the influence of human invention on divine creation, but was saving a role for human ingenuity that let it escape from theological sterility. He believed human change was possible and good; music can help us find God.[53]

Seeing versus Hearing

The tension between the different theories about art underscores another dominant note in Elizabethan self-expression: doubt and uncertainty. In France in 1576, Michel de Montaigne famously took as his motto, "*Que sais-je?*"— "what do I know?"—voicing the confusion of an era in which theological

---

51 John Case, *Apologia musices tam vocalis quam instrumentalis et mixtae* (1588). STC (2nd ed.)/4755.
52 Grantley McDonald, "Music, Spirit and Ecclesiastical Politics in Elizabethan England: John Case and his *Apologia Musices*," in Steffen Schneider, ed. *Aesthetics of the Spirits. Spirits in Early Modern Science, Religion, Literature and Music* (Göttingen: V&R Unipress, 2015), 488.
53 Charles B. Schmitt, *John Case and Aristotelianism in Renaissance England* (Kingston and Montreal: McGill-Queen's University Press, 1983), 193.

certainties could not be rationally resolved. If conscience was the judge, no one could know for certain which truth was absolute, compared to the truths everyone learned through experience and emotion.

Though Montaigne understood the classical skepticism of Sextus Empiricus, he and his English counterparts like Sir Francis Bacon were more influenced by their understanding of the probable as opposed to the improbable. They were taught by their schoolmasters to argue *in utramque partem*, on both sides, imitating Aristotle and Cicero. They had to see things pro and con to make their arguments work, and they were taught by Cicero that you did not need absolute proof to be comfortable in your preferences, you only needed to be more probably correct.

This internalization of truth could lead a mind in several directions. Sir Philip Sidney could confidently assert that a poet—like himself—can know what others cannot. Others could comfortably insist that men can know nothing certain unless God reveals it, but that their certainty, too, remains a matter of individual experience. The most direct way out of this conundrum of ignorance was empirical observation with the purpose of answering concrete questions. Empirical observation was linked to artistic representation, however, so Elizabethans were conflicted about how to "see" the world around them.

Empiricists like Sir Francis Bacon could divorce possible knowledge, based on empirical observation of the world, and impossible knowledge, which the human mind cannot acquire. Only possible knowledge could be tested for certainty; therefore, science should abandon the discussion of the empirically unknowable. Bacon, introducing his inductive scientific method in 1620, said:

> I propose to establish degrees of certainty, to retain the evidence of the senses subject to certain constraints, but mostly to reject ways of thinking that track along after sensation. In place of that, I open up a new and certain path for the mind to follow, starting from sense-perception.[54]

Knowing when to trust revelation, as opposed to sense perception and empirical observation, was hard—even harder than separating thinking from sensation, emotional knowledge from objective knowledge. New ways of knowing about the physical world were encroaching on God's revelation. This debate most famously included punishment of Galileo for promoting the heliocentric theory, based on observation that proved that the earth orbits the sun, not the other way around. In the Bible, the Lord made the sun stand still for an entire day so Joshua could slaughter the enemies of Israel. Therefore, the

54 Francis Bacon, *The New Organon: or True Directions Concerning the Interpretation of Nature*, Jonathan Bennett, trans. (2017), preface. http://www.earlymoderntexts.com/assets/pdfs/bacon1620part1.pdf [Accessed November 29, 2018].

heliocentric theory could not be correct theology. Which had more authority, human observation or divine action?

There was a generational divide over certainty. Elder Elizabethans believed that knowledge, used with a good conscience, could lead to certainty. Their children were not so sure. Maybe other stimulants were needed.

The frontispiece of Bacon's *Instauratio magna* shows a ship going beyond the Pillars of Hercules, where no man had gone before, signaling Bacon's rejection of previous knowledge and his quest for certainty based on observable truths.[55] He clearly chose a picture to make a point that would require a thousand words to explain.

Bacon knew there were no telescopes that could see into the soul. But could the soul be captured? Could it look out of its clay encasement and express itself? In words, it could; just as it could tangibly thrill to music. Was it licit to capture souls in art? A painting could let us see into a person, just as it could teach a moral. Were paintings invitations to idolatry, or instructive empirical observations?

Most Elizabethan portraits are flat, seemingly naïve. Generally, it is presumed that this was because of the Reformation, which stifled artistic expression through concern with preventing idolatry like that associated with Catholic images of saints. Accurate representation of the human body was discouraged, or used in highly metaphorical ways.

But what really happened is more interesting. Religious art was domesticated to teach the Word of God. Protestant reformers stripped idolatrous art from churches, but they approved biblical imagery outside them when used for civil and didactic purposes, just as they approved of private hymn singing, even if they believed only psalms could be sung in church. Images were good when representing acts of history, divine and human, in private places. People who wished to appear and act as good Christians liked pious imagery.[56] They even painted their religious heroes and slogans on dishes and pots.[57] If art reinforced the Word of God, and was not idolatrous, it was good. But to evoke God, it did not have to be highly realistic. It only needed to trigger the Platonic idea in the mind.

In such a world, a knowledge of the Word of God was a necessity. Prayer, biblical literacy, and exegesis became all important to artistic expression. Religious and artistic cultures interpenetrated one another, on walls, pulpits, and stages. Public places were decorated with pious art, such as the courtroom in Ledbury where a painted knot garden surrounds a quotation from Psalm 15:4,[58] or the

---

55 Francis Bacon, *Instauratio magna* (1620), frontispiece. STC (2nd ed.)/1163.
56 Tara Hamling, *Decorating the "Godly" Household. Religious Art in Post-Reformation Britain* (New Haven: Yale University Press, 2010), 3–5.
57 Alexandra Walsham, "Domesticating the Reformation: Material Culture, Memory, and Confessional Identity in Early Modern England." *Renaissance Quarterly* 2016; 69, 566–616.
58 "16th Century Painted Room." Ledbury Town Council. http://www.ledburytowncouncil.gov.uk/16th_Century_Painted_Room.aspx [Accessed November 29, 2018].

White Swan at Stratford, where the story of Tobit from the Apocrypha, complete with quotes, covers a wall.[59]

Pious, meditative decorations were used domestically, too, paint often imitating the tapestries of the richer sort. Lady Ann Bacon Drury, the daughter of Sir Nicholas Bacon and sister to Sir Francis, put her religion and learning together in her private oratory, the "closet," which was decorated with sixty-one small panel paintings, most with mottoes and verses. Apparently, it was a multi-media way of prompting meditation, both Christian and stoical. It was designed to help her come to terms with the disappointments and griefs of life.

The design was deeply influenced by Joseph Hall. Hall, educated at Cambridge, was a satirical poet in the 1590's, but after his ordination in 1600, he became Ann Bacon Drury's rector at Hawstead. Hall wrote *The Art of Divine Mediation*, a Protestant step-by-step guide to creating "compunction in the heart," stirring devotion by vividly remembering the life of Christ and other biblical stories. Though a relative of Jesuit meditational practice, Hall's tools were more individualized, and made room for written and visual props. As he said, "Divers paths lead oftimes to the same end; and every man aboundeth in his own sense." Nonetheless, "it is more impossible to live without an heart, than to be devout without meditation." Thus, Lady Ann's décor of paintings, mottoes, and quotes worked together to allow daily meditation on an ever-varying range of subjects as her needs arose.[60]

Other kinds of emotional meditations were aided by art, if you were rich and powerful. Nicholas Hilliard was the greatest portraitist of the Elizabethan era, but he painted miniatures for courtiers. His works are tiny, meant to be worn around the neck or kept in a private place. A liminer and goldsmith, he used the techniques of his craft to make jewel-like private, intimate, and highly detailed "counterfeits" of individuals. Patronized by the Earl of Leicester, Lord Burghley, and the Queen, his portraits were highly personal, seen by very few.[61] For their owners, they were treated as objects of pious devotion.

Sir James Melville of Halhill, the Scottish ambassador to Elizabeth, tells how portraits of this kind were used. In 1564, negotiating with Elizabeth about the possible marriage of Leicester to Mary Queen of Scots, he was taken by the Queen into her bed chamber. She opened a little desk, in which he saw "divers little pictures wrapped within paper, and their names written with her own hand upon the papers." She unwrapped two. One was of Mary, and the other of "my Lord," Leicester. When Sir James asked if he could take the portrait of

---

59 "Stratford's Elizabethan Wall Painting." The Shakespeare Blog. http://theshakespeareblog. com/2014/05/stratfords-elizabethan-wall-paintings [Accessed November 29, 2018].

60 H.L. Meakin, *The Painted Closet of Lady Anne Bacon Drury* (Farnham: Ashgate, 2013), 137–43. Joseph Hall, *The arte of diuine meditation...* (1606), 186–7, 192. STC (2nd ed.)/12642.

61 Elizabeth Goldring, *Robert Dudley, Earl of Leicester, and the World of Elizabethan Art. Painting and Patronage at the Court of Elizabeth* (New Haven: Yale University Press, 2014), 89–92.

Leicester to Mary, Elizabeth refused, "alleging that she had but that one picture of his." Then Elizabeth took Mary's portrait "and kissed it, and I kissed her hand, for the great love I saw she bore my mistress."[62]

Words of Players

To the public at large, the Word of God reached out from the walls, from printed woodcuts, from pulpits, and even from the stage. A good didactic story well acted, with a moral, could move the hearts and minds of playgoers. The early reformers knew this and used it to undermine Catholicism, grasping the power of the old morality plays to deliver the Christian message.

By the 1570's, however, concern about plays and pageants was on the rise as pressure for a reformation of manners mounted. In 1572, the Act for the Punishment of Vagabonds tried to shut down traveling theatrical troupes, classing actors, minstrels, bearwards, and other entertainers as people who deserved to be whipped and branded as vagabonds unless they were sponsored by a baron of the realm or other "personage of greater degree."[63] Philip Stubbes, biblical as usual, explained why plays and interludes were reprehensible. In plays, the Word of God was handled sacrilegiously, insulting God. "In the first of John," Stubbes wrote, "we are taught, that the word is God, and God is the word. Wherefore, whosoever abuseth this Word of our God on stages, in plays and interludes, abuseth the Majesty of God ... purchasing himself eternal damnation."[64]

Just as traveling actors were being repressed, the first public theaters were opening in London, with the aptly named "Theater" being the first, in 1576. These moved the performances into theatrical spaces and out of the courtyards of inns and other generic areas. Marking an important development in English culture, this expansion worried some people. Theaters sparked debates about whether plays helped people live the Word of God. Stubbes was careful to rebut the claim that you could learn as much morality from a good play as from a sermon. The theater's commercial popularity was new in Elizabeth's middle years, stimulated, ironically, by the very laws that were designed to abolish it. The barons and other great persons created professional companies, which in turn created a lively demand for plays. But many were unsure about the influence of these popular (in the sense that anyone who paid was let in) productions on public morality and order. Did seeing Juliet and Romeo disobeying their parents promote godly obedience, knowing clandestine marriages come

---

62 Gordon Donaldson, ed. *The Memoirs of Sir James Melville of Halhill* (London: Folio Society, 1969), 37.
63 14 Eliz. I, c. 5.5.
64 Stubbes, *Anatomy*, 199.

to bad ends? Or did it stimulate lust and a desire to throw off social conventions in the name of sinful romantic self-fulfillment? Did attending *The Massacre of Paris* teaching you to hate and fear Catholics, or did you just thrill with delighted horror at French savagery?

The opposition agreed that plays prompted lewdness, but there was a greater threat to morality caused by actors, who incited God's wrath. A pamphlet blowing a retreat from plays and theaters showed "the filthiness of plays in times past; the ... the abomination of theaters in the time present: both expressly proving that the common-weal is nigh unto the curse of God, wherein either players be made of, or theaters maintained."[65] This pamphlet is attributed to Anthony Munday, who, ironically, authored popular comedies like *John a Kent and John a Cumber*. He was the lead author of the unproduced play *Sir Thomas More*, on which it is believed he collaborated with William Shakespeare.

Munday was a hypocrite, but his scripts confirm many of Stubbes' anti-theatrical prejudices. A dramatized folktale, Munday's *John a Kent and John a Cumber* has a virtuous Englishman doing battle with a Scottish wizard using magic and disguises. Cumber disguises himself as Kent; Kent disguises himself as Cumber. They battle over two princesses who love two Welsh princes. Kent defeats Cumber (and the girls' father) and unites the girls with their lovers.[66] It is, as Stubbes would have said, full of devilish magic and incitements to lust and disobedience.

Besides stirring base feelings and divine wrath, plays, performed and printed, were capable of juxtaposing moral choices, presenting multiple perspectives that confused the Stubbeses of their world. As Elizabethans turned to conscience as the guarantor of their spiritual condition, actors could mirror their internal debates between public and private moralities.[67]

This mirroring property of the theater made it a vehicle of counsel, not only for individuals, but for society and rulers. The young men of the magisterial classes who attended schools like Eton, Oxford, Cambridge, and the Inns of Court were trained in moral reasoning through writing and acting academic plays. These plays modeled magistracy and good counsel, enacting good and bad examples, in a Plutarchian way.[68] This was especially true in the earlier part of the reign, when plays performed at the universities and the Inns of Court had political messages. Most famously, *Gorboduc*, a Senecan

---

65 *A second and third blast of retrait from plaies and theaters the one whereof was sounded by a reuerend byshop dead long since; the other by a worshipful and zealous gentleman now aliue: ... expresly prouing that that common-weale is nigh vnto the cursse of God...* (1580). STC (2nd ed.)/21677.

66 HEM HM 500.

67 Lawrence Manley, "Theatre," in Doran and Jones, *Elizabethan World*, 545.

68 Jessica Winston, *Lawyers at Play. Literature, Law, and Politics at the Early Modern Inns of Court, 1558–1581* (Oxford: Oxford University Press, 2016), 219. Paulina Kewes, "'Jerusalem thou dydst promyse to buylde up': Kingship, Counsel and Early Elizabethan Drama," unpublished article. My thanks to Dr. Kewes for sharing it with me.

tragedy in blank verse by Thomas Norton and Thomas Sackville, was acted in the Inner Temple in the Christmas of 1561. It urged Elizabeth to marry and prevent a civil war over the succession. It was best, it suggested, if her spouse was an Englishman—Sir Robert Dudley being the likely candidate—rather than Eric XIV of Sweden, who was then courting her. It was played at Court before the Queen, where she and the courtiers would have had a hard time missing its message.[69]

Significantly, Elizabeth understood and seems to have enjoyed plays. She also saw them as necessary to the reputation of her Court and as influencing public perceptions. She was aware of their importance in the "public sphere," where they might create trouble for the regime. Consequently, the Crown took control. In 1579, Edmund Tilney was appointed Master of the Revels, charged with providing professional theater for the Court. In 1581, he was granted a commission to "order and reform, authorize and put down" plays. In 1583, a theater troupe, The Queen's Men, was created under Tilney's authority and protection. Other companies were licensed by him. Under these circumstances, professional theater flourished, though playwrights had to be careful about too directly touching issues of religion and government. When James I came to the throne, he continued the system, making four royal companies, and in 1610, Sir George Buc succeeded as Master of the Revels, continuing the licensing, and adding printed plays to his domain.[70]

Some plays were stopped, such as *The Isle of Dogs*, a 1597 play by Thomas Nashe and Ben Jonson, closed after one performance for an unknown reason. Some had to be rewritten or modified to maintain pubic calm. After the publication of the *Martin Marprelate Tracts*, the actors burlesqued "Martin" so much that they were finally silenced because they were dealing with religion and policy, "unfit and undecent to be handled in plays."[71] The actors probably thought they were aiding the cause, since the preachers at Paul's Cross busied themselves with attacks on Martin, too.

Theater, in its established playhouses like the Globe, the Rose, and Blackfriars, in smaller travelling companies, in great houses and colleges, and in print was a booming business. Philip Henslowe, who owned the Rose Theater, left a diary that showed thirty to thirty-five plays in repertoire, rotating six days a week throughout the year. In October of 1594 alone, fifteen different plays were performed at the Rose, alternating between serious dramas, such as Christopher Marlowe's *Dr. Faustus* and *The Jew of Malta*, and lighter fare such as *A Pleasant and Conceited Comedy, called, The Knack to*

69 Norman Jones and Paul W. White, "*Gorboduc* and Royal Marriage Politics: An Elizabethan Playgoer's Report of the Premiere Performance." *English Literary Renaissance* 1996; 26, 3–17.
70 Richard Dutton, "Jurisdiction of Theater and Censorship," in Arthur F. Kinney, ed. *A Companion to Renaissance Drama* (Oxford: Blackwell, 2002), 223–36.
71 Black, *Martin Marprelate*, xlv.

Know an Honest Man,[72] whose themes of sexual jealousy, murder, and moral corruption turn it into a morality tale.[73]

The greatest of the playwrights were successfully treating the troubled minds of people who were caught up in the tug-of-war between personal conscience and external truths. Like ministers, they could awaken in a conscience the need of God's grace, making their public uncomfortable. Shakespeare's *Othello* or Marlowe's *Tamburlaine* could confront an audience with their own painful moral dilemmas and shameful moral lapses.

As Lawrence Chaderton taught future preachers at Cambridge, they should "rip up all the inward and secret corners" of their hearers' minds. Pietists (who linked individual, emotional faith with a rigorous Christian lifestyle) like Chaderton and his fellows sought to induce wretchedness, spreading displeasure and despair, and demanding individuals discover their inner sinfulness. Like Stubbes, with his critiques of behavior, they were highly critical of the popular theology that thought trying to be good was good enough.

To keep people from sliding into comfortable "good enough" Christianity, these champions of conscience insisted they should be in a constant state of self-examination and self-accusation. An uncomfortable conscience was a sign that God had chosen a person for salvation. This tension between comfortable assurance of salvation and a certainty of election created dramatic tension in the individual's relation to conscience, community, and God. Playwrights worked in that same tense zone of self-examination.[74] Ministers, players, and poets all used words to create critical self-awareness, recognizing sinners needed a sharp jolt.

Words Evoking the Word of God

John Donne, a great poet-preacher, writing in what became known as his "Holy Sonnets," expressed this need for God's violence to awake in us our consciousness of sin:

> Batter my heart, three-person'd God ; for you
> As yet but knock ; breathe, shine, and seek to mend ;
> That I may rise, and stand, o'erthrow me, and bend
> Your force, to break, blow, burn, and make me new.
> ...

72 W.W. Greg, ed. *Henslowe's Diary* (London: A.H. Bullen, 1904), 20–21.
73 John S. Farmer, ed. *The Knack to Know an Honest Man, 1596* (Toronto: Tudor Facsimile Texts, 1912).
74 Peter Iver Kaufman, *Prayer, Despair, and Drama. Elizabethan Introspection* (Urbana: University of Illinois Press, 1996), 41–3, 63.

> Take me to you, imprison me, for I,
> Except you enthrall me, never shall be free,
> Nor ever chaste, except you ravish me.[75]

Recognizing the need for an emotional experience that testified to one's salvation could induce despair in those who failed to gain a personal testimony. In Donne's case, we must ask if this ravishing of the heart represents his conversion experience.[76] Raised a Catholic and educated by Jesuits, Donne converted to Protestantism, going on to become Dean of St. Paul's. One of the English church's great preachers, Donne knew how to touch the emotions of his audience with words.

Reassuringly, Richard Hooker, not a pietist, took the position that a grieved spirit was no argument for faithlessness. He, like his pietist colleagues, thought that the experience of doubt and despair should be welcomed as a good sign, and so we should never lose hope. Christ was the anchor that kept people from drifting off into depression. Donne, in a poem addressed to George Herbert, explained that his family crest had been a sheaf of snakes, but he traded the poisonous serpents for a new seal, the anchor of faith in the cross. Playing with metaphors, he suggested that as the cross grew into an anchor, his faith was completed.[77] Translated by his young friend Sir Izaak Walton, the poem reads:

> Crucify nature then and then implore
> All grace from him crucify'd there before
> When all is cross and that cross anchor grown
> This seal's a catechism not a seal alone.[78]

Before the cross you bore turned into an anchor of hope, however, you had to struggle with despair. In Edmund Spenser's *The Faerie Queene* (1596), the Redcrosse Knight must do battle with the ragged figure of Despaire, who has just caused a suicide. He finds Despaire in his cave, surrounded by a blasted landscape in which the carcasses of suicides litter the ground and hang from dead trees. It is Despaire's special gift to convince people of the pointlessness of life, their sinfulness, and their immiserating fear, all of which could be ended by death:

> Then do no further go, no further stray,
> But here lie down, and to thy Rest betake,

75 John Donne, "Holy Sonnets," XIV in E.K. Chambers, ed. *Poems of John Donne* (London: Lawrence & Bullen, 1896), I, 165. http://www.luminarium.org/sevenlit/donne/sonnet14.php [Accessed November 29, 2018].

76 Cummings, *Literary Culture*, 365.

77 John Donne, "To George Herbert, Sent Him with One of My Seals of the Anchor and Christ," in Chambers, *John Donne*, I, 214. http://www.luminarium.org/sevenlit/donne/herbert.php [Accessed November 29, 2018].

78 Izaak Walton, "The Life of Dr. John Donne," in *John Donne. Devotions upon Emergent Occasions* (Ann Arbor: University of Michigan Press, 1959), 14.

Th' Ill to prevent, that Life ensuen may:
For, what hath Life, thee may it loved make,
And gives nor rather cause it to forsake?
Fear, Sickness, Age, Loss, Labour, Sorrow, Strife,
Pain, Hunger, Cold, that makes the Heart to quake;
And ever fickle Fortune rageth rife,
All which, and thousands more, do make a loathsom Life.

Despaire nearly convinces Redcrosse, but his companion Una intervenes just as he is about to strike himself with a dagger. She reminds him of God's love and grace.[79]

The Redcrosse Knight, shattered, is led to the "House of Holiness," where he is met by the heavenly virtues, convinced of his sins, undergoes repentance, and is taught from Lady Caelia's (Heaven's) book:

And that her sacred Booke, with blood ywrit,
That none could read, except she did them teach,
She unto him disclosed every whit,
And heavenly documents thereout did preach,
That weaker wit of man could never reach,
Of God, of grace, of justice, of free will,
That wonder was to heare her goodly speach:
For she was able with her words to kill,
And raise againe to life the hart that she did thrill.[80]

The epic adventures of the Redcrosse Knight lead him to glimpse the Heavenly City, the New Jerusalem, foreseen in the Book of Revelation. Strengthened by his chastened conscience, knowledgeable about God's plan, led to the Hill of Contemplation to meditate on God's goodness, he is prepared to fight a great battle with a devilish dragon name Errour. Putting on the whole armor of God, he fights for days against Errour. Each time the Knight appears dead, he is resurrected. Washed in the Well of Life, succored by the balm of the Tree of Life, he finally defeats Errour—Satan. A powerful poem, its complex allegories point to the need to fight God's fight, trusting that He will aid you in victory over the Devil, but not without suffering.

The Faerie Queene of Spenser's book is Gloriana, an obvious allegory of Queen Elizabeth. Spenser's whole poem is shot through with allegorical figures who can be identified as real people. It is, among many things, about the struggle of England's true religion against papist Errour. But the process by which

---

79 Edmund Spenser, Spenser's *The Faerie Queene, Book I*, George Armstrong Wauchope, ed. (New York: Macmillan, 1921), 1.9.14.388–96, 53.470–8.
80 Ibid., 1.10.19.163–171.

Redcrosse prepares to succeed in the battle against Errour reflects the battle in conscience to accept God's grace and enact godly virtue.

We find a similar story in Christopher Marlowe's *The Tragical History of the Life and Death of Dr. Faustus*. First performed in 1592, it, too, narrates the struggle in conscience between God and the Devil. Dr. Faustus, having sold his soul to the Devil for success and a beautiful woman, is too terrified of God to ask for Grace to escape the bargain. The Devil wins Faustus' soul. Despite the prompting of conscience, Faustus fails to accept responsibility for his weakness, blaming fate and fortune, unnerved by Satan's threats. He is dragged down to hell by serpents, leaving the viewer with the uncomfortable question of whether they are like him.[81]

The problem Shakespeare gives his hero in *Hamlet* is to choose between despair and action. In the graveyard scene of Act V, Hamlet confronts the reality that death comes to everyone, no matter their rank or virtue. But mollifying the certainty of death is the certainty of Divine Providence. A disturbed conscience leads to proper resolution:

> *Hamlet*: Sir, in my heart there was a kind of fighting
> That would not let me sleep. Methought I lay
> Worse than the mutines in the bilboes. Rashly—
> And praised be rashness for it: let us know
> Our indiscretion sometimes serves us well
> When our deep plots do fall, and that should learn us
> There's a divinity that shapes our ends,
> Rough-hew them how we will—[82]

Armed with this inevitability, Hamlet accepts an invitation to a duel knowing he may be killed. It is a speech in which he rejects superstition and puts himself in God's hands. Quoting Matthew 10:29–31, in plain speech rather than verse, recalling Jesus' parable about God knowing when even a sparrow falls, Hamlet says, "We defy augury. There's a special providence in the fall of a sparrow. If it be now, 'tis not to come. If it be not to come, it will be now. If it be not now, yet it will come—the readiness is all. Since no man of aught he leaves knows, what is 't to leave betimes? Let be."[83] Hamlet is no longer the irresolute man who debated with despair in the great "To be or not to be" soliloquy. He is armed to resolution by his realization of God's mysterious ways.

It is hard to know what those consuming and speaking such words felt. Certainly, different people found different things resonating within them. But they were all trying to navigate the same terrain, wondering how to know and

---

81 Kaufman, *Prayer, Despairn and Drama*, 89–91.
82 Shakespeare, *Hamlet*, V.2.4–11.
83 Ibid., V.2.191–5.

obey the Word of God, looking for a narrative that made sense of their lives. It was a puzzle as central to Elizabethan artistic expression as it was to theology and governance. Some arts, though not those that appealed to the sensuous eyes, could move the emotions toward pietistic experiences of God. Some could teach the obedient to understand their duty, and some could help them question that duty. Ideally, they worked both ways.

Many godly people feared that secular arts did not teach godliness; they merely stirred up emotions that inspired sin. They preferred their drama in the pulpit. Others preferred it in the playhouses. As a society, the Elizabethans were exploring the pain of this confusion like a tongue on a broken tooth, finding the keys to their emotions in poetry, theater, and music. They were a nation of hearers who obsessed about the power of words to give meaning to life.

12

Elizabethan Lives Lived

To be an Elizabethan was to live in a time of dissensions. The world, which was supposed to be static, was changeable. The Reformation attempt to return to the golden, primitive age of the church had not produced unity. Whether it was undefeated Satan, or just the existence of religious choice, the times threw people back on their own consciences. And those consciences had to navigate a quickly changing economic, social, and political world. The necessity of all this was eroding the traditional hierarchical social structures. In the last years of Elizabeth's reign, these tensions were becoming unavoidable; the new century brought them into stark relief.

By the early seventeenth century, England had started down the road that led to an increasingly secular culture that separated individual values from the larger world. For the Elizabethans, this did not mean loss of Christian faith, but it did mean a "spiritualization" or "individuation" of faith as distinctions grew between what one personally believed and what the broader community held to be true. They were inventing the self as the principal form of human identity, stressing an inward awareness of intention and judgment that gave value to daily life and called on conscience to ratify choice. They were beginning to dissolve their religious culture in favor of inward faith. The Elizabethans were the first English speakers to confront these ideas of self.[1] The community-based, static Christian ideal was being replaced by a fluid one in which fulfillment of individual Christian potential was the proper goal.

At the levels of individuals and families, these shifts caused intergenerational tensions as older Elizabethans, raised in the world of Henry VIII, found their values challenged and revised by their children, who had never known that world. What the young Elizabethans thought natural and good was a radical change to their elders.

---

1 C. Johan Sommerville, *The Secularization of Early Modern England. From Religious Culture to Religious Faith* (Oxford: Oxford University Press, 1992), 178. Charles Taylor, *Sources of the Self. The Making of Modern Identity* (Cambridge: Cambridge University Press, 2012), x.

Being Elizabethan: Understanding Shakespeare's Neighbors, First Edition. Norman Jones.
© 2020 John Wiley & Sons, Inc. Published 2020 by John Wiley & Sons, Inc.

These changes triggered responses in all levels of English society. Across four generations, the English people were forced to cope and adapt, assuming cultural responses that shaped the future of their society.

Elizabethans were becoming used to religious plurality in families and communities that downgraded common religious culture as the unifying force in England. Increasingly, they relied on their consciences to guide them in right, godly behavior. But that reliance took them in varied directions, though they shared a common cultural landscape. In the few lives we know well enough to document, the themes of this book keep recurring: whether male or female, gentle or common, religious or irreligious, Elizabethans acted their fleeting lives on the same stage.

Shakespeare's Macbeth saw lives as pointless: "Life's but a walking shadow, a poor player/That struts and frets his hour upon the stage/And then is heard no more."[2] But Macbeth's bloody cynicism dismisses the hard choices Shakespeare and his neighbors were forced to make as they picked their way through life. They had been cast in God's play, but they had to decide how to perform their roles. Their lives were not just tales told by an idiot, full of "sound and fury signifying nothing."[3] They were records of people struggling to live as best they could in a time of rapid transition.

If you were cast as a godly member of the gentry, how did you behave in life? Sir Edward (1542–1605) and Lady Susan Lewknor (1550–1605) exemplify the qualities and behaviors of what it meant to be Elizabethans of the ruling sort, living pious lives of duty and devotion. Members of the Sussex and Essex gentry, they were both second-generation Protestants. Having received educations proper to their stations and genders, they assumed the duties that went with them, and carried them out assiduously. They experienced at first hand the religious and political turmoil of the time, and they did their best to serve God as they understood God's requirements. They believed in the Word, and they supported preachers. When they died within a day of one another in 1605, they were celebrated for their status and for their virtues in sermon and in poetry.

Sir Edward Lewknor the younger was born in 1542 into an important Sussex family. His father, Edward senior, was raised in the Sussex gentry. Inheriting the family manor when he was nine, in 1528, Edward senior became a ward of Robert Wroth of Middlesex, who sent him to study law at Gray's Inn with his son, Thomas, and arranged his marriage to his daughter, Dorothy.

The Wroths and Edward senior became ardent Protestants, rising to prominence in the Court of Edward VI. When Mary Tudor restored Catholicism, Edward senior was imprisoned in the Tower, attainted for treason for his support of Lady Jane Grey. He beat the executioner by dying of disease in 1556.

---

2 Shakespeare, *Macbeth*, V.5ll.24–7.
3 Ibid., ll.27–8.

Taking pity on Dorothy Wroth Lewknor and her three sons and six daughters, Queen Mary returned some of the family lands forfeited under Edward's attainder. Dorothy's eldest son, Edward junior, had the manors settled on him as successor to his father when he was sixteen.[4] Restored in blood by Elizabeth's first parliament, young Edward matriculated at St. John's College, Cambridge along with his little brother, Edmund.[5] At St. John's, the incubator of many of the leaders of the Elizabethan regime, the young men were steeped in the humanist learning that made them godly magistrates and confirmed their radical Protestantism. Edward, elected a fellow of the college, was known for his Latin eloquence. In 1564, when Queen Elizabeth visited Cambridge, he was commissioned to write orations in praise of both the Queen and the Chancellor of Cambridge, Sir William Cecil.[6] After Cambridge, Edward went off to study law at the Middle Temple.

In 1569, Edward married Susan Higham, when she was in her teens and he was twenty-seven. They made their home in Denham, Suffolk, with Susan's ardently Puritan mother Martha Higham, who died in 1593. Martha had brought the Rev. Robert Pricke to the tiny village as her chaplain in about 1577. He was the spiritual guide of the Lewknor family until he died in 1608.[7]

When Sir Edward and Lady Susan died in 1605, their joint epitaph proclaimed they lived together "without a quarrel" for thirty-six years. Undoubtedly, this exaggerated domestic harmony was a product of their clear roles in the relationship: he the master, she the obedient wife.

Rev. Pricke had so often gone over these roles in his sermons to the Lewknors that his friends memorialized him by printing his exegesis of the Fifth Commandment, "honor thy father and thy mother."[8] As Pricke preached to the Denham congregation, everyone was in a hierarchy of subjection that began with God, descended through the monarch and his magistrates, and continued down to husbands, who were presumed to be masters. Wives and servants were

---

4 HPT sub Lewknor, Edward http://www.historyofparliamentonline.org/volume/1509-1558/member/lewknor-edward-151617-56 [Accessed November 29, 2018]. HPT sub Wroth, Robert. http://www.historyofparliamentonline.org/volume/1509-1558/member/wroth-robert-148889-1535 [Accessed November 29, 2018].

5 HPT sub Lewknor, Edward. http://www.historyofparliamentonline.org/volume/1558-1603/member/lewknor-edward-1542-1605; http://www.historyofparliamentonline.org/volume/1604-1629/member/lewknor-sir-edward-i-1542-1605 [Accessed November 29, 2018].

6 Elizabeth Goldring, Faith Eales, Elizabeth Clark, and Jayne Elisabeth Archer, eds. *John Nichols's The Progresses and Public Processions of Queen Elizabeth I: A New Edition of the Early Modern Sources Vol. I 1533–1571* (Oxford: Oxford University Press, 2012), 388 n., 419 n.

7 Patrick Collinson, "Magistracy and Ministry: A Suffolk Miniature," in R. Buick Knox, ed. *Reformation Conformity and Dissent* (London: Epworth Press, 1977), 81–2.

8 Richard Allen, "The Inscription Dedicatorie" and S. Egerton, "To the Christian Reader," in Robert Pricke, *The doctrine of superioritie, and of subiection, contained in the fift commandement...* (1608). STC (2nd ed.)/20337.

obedient to their husbands and masters, children subject to their parents, including their mothers, and their schoolmasters, who were an extension of their parents. Servants were subject to their masters. Male servants, when at home, were masters of their own wives and children. Carefully backed by scriptural references, Pricke asked them to return to this static, hierarchical, divine order.

Sir Edward and Lady Susan knew it was their joint duty to love and care for one another, according to their roles. He was to cherish her and supply her needs, recognizing that her weakness and inferiority demanded that he take care of her: "albeit she be a weak and frail vessel: yet is she an excellent gift of God, serving for many excellent ends and purposes: and therefore men are to deal with them [women] in a tender and chary manner: as men deal with glasses, and with tender vessels that are brittle."[9] He was to honor her, to govern her in a "reverend manner," preferring her over all others (including their children), remembering "that as she is not the head, so is she not the foot, but an excellent creature" of God.[10]

Lady Susan's role was to love and obey her husband, keeping him happy and helping him toward godly living. She should yield to his direction and discretion, keeping his commandments as God's commandments. Naturally, she should stay at home, only going out to attend sermons and perform acts of charity. In dress, she should be as modest as she was chaste, "according to the proportion of her husband's ability and estate."[11]

Between them, the husband and wife must raise godly, obedient children who knew their duties to all their superiors, making them useful members of the commonwealth. This they did. Sir Edward sent his eldest son, Edward, to Emmanuel College, Cambridge, ensuring he was raised in the bosom of Puritan theology. Timothy Pricke, Robert Pricke's son, also attended Emmanuel, his education paid by Martha Higham. Thus, the Lewknor–Pricke dynasty oversaw Denham for two generations, carrying out their inherited roles: Edward the master, Pricke the minister.

The Highams and Lewknors sought to make Denham into a godly community, using their God-given authority as masters and preachers to reform their servants' manners. They brought the light of the Gospel, as their epitaph declared, to "this tiny and obscure town."[12] The formal expressions of mourning included a dirge for Sir Edward and Lady Susan, spoken by the people of Denham, who declared their master and mistress "Too good for us, upright in heart and mind."[13]

---

9 Ibid., Sig. K4v.
10 Ibid., Sig. K4 [ii$_v$].
11 Ibid., Sig. K4 [iii]–L3.
12 Collinson, "Magistracy and Ministry," 80.
13 Edward Lewknor, *Threnodia in obitum D. Edouardi Lewknor Equitis, & D. Susannae coniugis charissimae. = Funerall verses vpon the death of the right worshipfull Sir Edvvard Levvkenor Knight, and Madame Susan his Lady With Deaths apologie, and a reioynder to the same* (1606), 34–5. STC (2nd ed.)/15561.

Addressing the Lewknors' servants, tenants, and dependents, Pricke explained that the master is of a higher degree than the servants, so the master, as their superior, must "stoop down" to them. That being so, the servants must honor the master and accept their inferiority. Since the master's authority comes "only from God himself," as proved by Scripture, "the servant cannot resist his master or condemn him."

This inequality presses weighty duties on to the master, since he has to take care of his inferiors, just as he has to care for his "fragile" wife. Representing the person of Christ, the Great Master, the master conveys to his servants what they need to live. Pricke preached that the master was to provide housing and work for his employees, protecting them from injuries. Without his wise direction, they would "run head long into miseries and destruction." Most importantly, the master was responsible for the eternal salvation of his servants' souls.[14]

In his eulogy, Pricke represented the Lewknors as fulfilling their responsibilities to their servants. The Lewknors' inferiors, he said, "have lost the government and direction of such a Master and Lady, as continually expressed no less love and care over them then if so be they had been their natural children: so that by their death, they are bereft of many sweet comforts and helps, which many a year, some of them enjoyed."[15]

As masters, the Lewknors were responsible for the poor of their community, too. Commanded by Christ to feed the hungry and cloth the naked, they apparently obeyed.[16] The Rev. Pricke cried out, "O ye poor and miserable of these parts, howl ye and cry out: seeing they are taken from you, whose hands in times past were always open to relieve your necessities."[17]

Striving as they were to create a godly community in Denham, the Lewknors probably did care for their servants and help the poor, within the prescribed limits of station and status. And they certainly looked after their charges' spiritual welfare, since they were deeply committed to the battle against Satan and the Pope.

Robert Pricke praised Sir Edward's religious values: "He bare a fervent love and zeal toward the truth, which he was ready at all times, to defend against *Papists, Atheists, and Heretics, &c.* as divers do well know, who have felt the force and weight of his arguments in disputation."[18] This comment emphasizes Lewknor's enthusiastic participation in the Elizabethan battle over religious truth acquired through reason. Lewknor publicly engaged in such disputes in parliament and without, demanding further reformation.

---

14 Pricke, *Subjection*, Sig. M3–M4.
15 Pricke, *Learned sermon.*
16 Lewknor, *Threnodia*, 35.
17 Pricke, *Learned sermon.*
18 Ibid.

An active member in every parliament from 1571 until 1604, Sir Edward used his influence in support of religious reform, aligning with those who wanted to purify the church. He was clearly in favor of Presbyterianism and the reformation of manners. He presented a petition against the abuses of the clergy, gathered from eastern Sussex, marking him as one of those who wanted a better educated, preaching ministry with high moral standards.[19] Archbishop Whitgift summed up Sir Edward's hostile opinion on church government: "speaking of bishops [he] said that they were rather deformers than reformers."[20] When Cope's "Bill and Book" was introduced in 1587, Edward ardently supported its proposed Presbyterian purification of the church. As a result, he was imprisoned for a spell in the Tower of London for transgressing the Queen's injunction against debating religion in parliament. That, however, did not change his religious opinion, and he conscientiously supported the ideals of the godly. Given his association with Cope, we can assume he did not favor May poles and church ales on his manor.

When James I came to the throne, Sir Edward participated in the movement for the Millenary Petition asking for church reform, and he supported the suppression of swearing, the regulation of ale houses, the control of apparel, the repression of recusants, and other causes connected with the reformation of manners.[21]

We know Sir Edward appreciated the Protestant histories that justified the reform of the church. When John Foxe's son was taken prisoner by pirates and held for ransom, he moved the House of Commons to raise a subscription to pay it because "Mr Fox had made the *Book of Martyrs* and was a man of famous memory."[22]

In 1594, Edward was appointed a justice of the peace for Suffolk, responsibly attending every meeting of the Quarter Sessions until his death in 1605.[23] As a member of parliament, he made the laws. As a justice, he enforced them against rogues and vagabonds, recusants and others, and made further laws concerning what to do with such people. He was serving as his honor required, and through service, his deservedness was manifested. Perhaps that is why James I knighted him in 1604. Lewknor knew, as Rev. Pricke told him, that magistrates were instituted by God for the peace of the commonwealth. They had to be learned and courageous. Most importantly, they had to do their duty with a true fear of God.

---

19 Hartley, *Proceedings*, II, 43.
20 Ibid., 53.
21 HPT sub Lewknor, Edward. http://www.historyofparliamentonline.org/volume/1558-1603/member/lewknor-edward-1542-1605; http://www.historyofparliamentonline.org/volume/1604-1629/member/lewknor-sir-edward-i-1542-1605 [Accessed November 29, 2018].
22 Hartley, *Proceedings*, III, 240.
23 Diarmaid MacCulloch, *Suffolk and the Tudors. Politics and Religion in an English County 1500–1600* (Oxford: Clarendon Press, 1986), Appendix I.

The fear of God restrained magistrates from evil and forced them to be scrupulous, "for he that truly feareth God, dareth not to fly from the things that do displease Him, and practice the duties which he hath commanded." He would have also known that fear of God's providential anger empowered him to reform his sinful neighbors.[24]

Sir Edward's virtuous attitude toward the world was proclaimed by his elder son's mourning poem. The smallpox that killed the couple was brought home by a friend of their sons. The boys had been away at school, and their parents, knowing the disease was raging, summoned them back. Their neighbor, fearing his son would infect the Lewknors, urged that he be sent on to his own home. Sir Edward apparently shrugged it off, putting his faith in God's providence, supposedly declaring: "Is death such ill, as is default in duty? No: God work his will."[25]

In a community that demonstrated its worth in words, the decision to publish a volume of poems honoring Edward and Susan Lewknor was not unusual. Versifying in multiple languages was part of the artistic arsenal of educated Elizabethans. Laudatory poems were included in books, collected by friends, and scribbled at the drop of a hat. They are often poor as poems, but they were assumed to convey emotion more effectively than prose. Though deeply Christian in purpose, they are full of classical allusions.

The opening poem of the Lewknors' memorial, *Threnodia*, invokes the Muses who dwell on Mt. Helicon, harkening back to the Greek poet Hesiod in the seventh century BCE. The muses are invited to come to Cambridge and Oxford, at the request of shepherd swains, to mourn the Lewknors. The reader was expected to appreciate this mingling of classical, Christian, and contemporary allusions. The poems are mostly in Latin, but sometimes—for the even more learned and discerning—they are in Greek or Hebrew. The authors are not generally named except by initials and the name of their Cambridge or Oxford college, though some can be identified. One is Andrews Downs, like Sir Edward a member of St. John's, who became Regius Professor of Greek in 1584. He was one of the translators of the King James Bible. Naturally, his poem to the Lewknors is in Greek.[26]

These poets make it clear that Sir Edward and Lady Susan were friends of the learned, supporting college students. The poetic references likening them to Maecenas, the great patron of Virgil and other Roman authors, are further proof of their commitment to godly learning. Pricke says, "Let students and favorers of Learning, join ... in mourning: seeing they shall all see them no more in this world, by whom ... they received comfort and encouragement in their studies."[27]

---

24 Pricke, *Subjection*, Sig. C3–C4.
25 Lewknor, *Threnodia*, 4.
26 Ibid., passim.
27 Pricke, *Learned sermon*, Sig., fo. 8.

Figure 12.1 Sir Edward and Susan Lewknor tomb, 1605, St. Mary's Church, Denham, Suffolk © Copyright Evelyn Simak and licensed for reuse under creativecommons.org/licenses/by-sa/2.0 http://www.geograph.org.uk/photo/2930989.

In death, Edward and Susan Lewknor were memorialized as ideal role models. These rulers of their little commonwealth in Denham were buried with the pride and aesthetic taste of the magisterial elite (Figure 12.1). Towering over their chest tomb, Corinthian columns bear a huge coat of arms, busy with quarterings that provide their impressive lineages. The overall artistic motif is neo-classical, influenced by Italian taste, with faux marble and a frieze of Greek keys. Beneath its canopy, Sir Edward and Lady Susan kneel bolt upright, hands together in prayer. Behind them in order of precedence kneel their two sons and six daughters, the epitome of an upright, godly family. Cartouches on the tomb narrate their lives and their godliness. Lords of their manor, they occupy a purpose-built mortuary chapel attached to Denham's medieval church. There, *saecula saeculorum*, their tomb testifies to all what it meant to be good Elizabethans. They occupied their places in a divinely ordered world and did their best to do their duty to God, family, and community by ruling according to godly virtue, with good taste.

The biographical threnody published by their son, Sir Edward, sums up the Elizabethan virtues of his father and mother:

> ... the State hath lost
> A Senator of many Parliaments:
> The Church may well account her loss is most
> Of such a son. The Country sad laments
> A wise and upright Justicer: The poor
> A worthy house keeper. O if no more
> Ye feel your own, yet others damage help deplore.
>
> And if how much he in your gifts surpassed,
> So much the Graces sweet his Lady graced:
> A right Susanna, virtuous, faire, and chaste,
> A lily bright though now by death effaced:
> If both in every part of virtue were
> A matchless match, a pair without compare:
> For Virtues sake weep while ye may not weep a tear.[28]

Elsewhere in the collection is this statement declaring God's providence, comforting the survivors with the warning their deaths delivered:

> But welcome Death, for thou art sent of God
> To them for joy, to us for smarting rod.[29]

Sir Edward and Lady Susan lived their lives within the values of their culture, assuming their stations and acting accordingly, like their ancestors. Unlike their ancestors, their choices were informed by their very Protestant understanding of what God expected of them. They may not have been as virtuous as their memorialization suggests, but they shared in the values expressed in it.

---

28 Lewknor, *Threnodia*, 3.
29 Ibid., 35.

For them, being Elizabethans meant reshaping their inner and outer worlds in accordance with their understanding of the Word of God.

The Suffolk Lewknors were shining examples of godly magistracy in Suffolk; their Lewknor cousins in Sussex exemplify other life choices. Among the Chichester side of the family were Catholics, even Jesuits, as well as men who were more concerned about profits and family than theology.

The Sussex Lewknors were clients of Anthony Browne, Viscount Montague, and his family. Montague was a powerful conforming Catholic who used his social station and the obedience it demanded to sway the politics of the region.[30] The Sussex Lewknors had to walk carefully, serving the Queen, Montague, and whatever their personal consciences demanded.

Thomas Lewknor of Tangmere and Selsey (c. 1538–96), Sir Edward's eldest cousin, was an adult before Elizabeth came to the throne. He studied law in the Middle Temple, and he became a justice of the peace in Sussex, but he only reluctantly conformed to the Queen's religion. Bishop Barlow put him down as a "misliker of Godly order" in 1564. In 1579, a church warden of his parish noted that Justice Lewknor had "never been at church but four times, and at Easter he received the communion." However, despite being called a "notorious papist" by Bishop Curteys, he and his brother Sir Richard did most of the judicial work in the Rape of Chichester, including prosecution of recusant Catholics. They might prefer Catholic theology, but they conformed to the will of their anointed queen.[31]

Sir Richard Lewknor of West Dean (1542–1616) made a successful career in the law, conforming in religion. He entered the Middle Temple in Mary's reign, rising to be a bencher and serjeant-at-law in the Inn, as well as the recorder of Chichester. First appointed a justice of the peace in 1573, he became presiding justice at the Chichester Quarter Session, where he sentenced four seminary priests to death for treason. He worked in Sussex until 1600, when Elizabeth appointed him Chief Justice in the counties palatine of Chester and Flint, and justice in Denbigh and Montgomery, based in Chester.[32]

Sir Richard Lewknor and Lord Zouche battled over precedence in the Welsh Marches, but Sir Richard had the Queen's confidence: her letter to the Lord President of the Council of Wales praised his legal skill and established his authority, ordering that "As Sir R. Lewknor is a man of learning and judgment, principal in trust after the president, and the learned men in the commission are not many, he is to be one of the quorum whenever present."[33] Moving to the

---

30 Michael Questier, *Catholicism and Community in Early Modern England* (Cambridge: Cambridge University Press, 2006), 57–60.

31 HPT sub Lewknor, Thomas. http://www.historyofparliamentonline.org/volume/1558-1603/member/lewknor-thomas-1538-96 [Accessed November 29, 2018].

32 HPT sub Lewknor, Richard. http://www.historyofparliamentonline.org/volume/1558-1603/member/lewknor-richard-1542-1616 [Accessed November 29, 2018].

33 TNA SP 12/274, fo. 234.

Welsh Border at age fifty-eight, he actively worked to calm Wales after the Essex rebellion. Clearly, he was a devoted legal servant of the Queen, if not of her church. He was known to be sympathetic to Catholics, including his brother George, who was an open recusant.

Thomas and Richard Lewknor had a long feud with Bishop Curteys of Chichester, which may have been encouraged by religious disparities, but was mostly about the bishop's attempts to control the Rape of Chichester. His interference with Thomas' export of grain to London was one of the thirty-four articles of complaint that Thomas and his colleagues alleged to the Privy Council in 1577. With extensive farms, Thomas found his business impeded by the bishop, who claimed regulatory authority which, it was charged, should have belonged to the entire commission of the peace. Richard was caught up in the fight over the enforcement of the law governing grain brokers. The Lewknors thought Curteys was trying to ruin them by preventing the sale of their wheat.[34]

Naturally, Bishop Curteys dismissed the Lewknors as dishonorable, unworthy, and indebted. He also called Thomas a "proud arrogant fool."[35] Clearly, battles about honor and business ethics were roiling Chichester. In a fight over money, the bishop resorted to his most stinging weapon, impugning their honor.

In retaliation, the Lewknors accused the bishop of licensing May games, implying Curteys was one of those corrupt, hypocritical clerics denounced by their puritanical cousin Sir Edward. Whether or not Richard and Thomas desired a godly reformation of manners, they protected their openly recusant brother George, who lived in Chichester. Their fourth brother, Edmund, may have gone to a continental seminary to be trained as a Catholic priest.

In the next generation, Thomas Lewknor's son Lewis (c. 1560–1627) was also educated at the Middle Temple, but he did not temporize over religion like his father. A Catholic, Lewis left England and took service with the Spanish army in the Low Countries. Severely wounded in 1587, he lost his captaincy. To support himself, he turned coats, spying on other English Catholics in Spanish service. In 1590, Lord Treasurer Burghley compiled, in his own hand, a list of Spanish pensions being received by English Catholics living abroad—information extracted from Lewknor's reports.[36]

Lewis' experiences as a Spanish soldier and spy were turned into a sensational book: his letters were published as *The Estate of English Fugitives Under the King of Spain*. Coming from one who had been "gentleman servant" of the King of Spain in the Low Countries, it warned those who fled there, "pretending

34 TNA SP 12/112, fo. 125.
35 Ibid., fo. 105.
36 TNA SP 12/233, fos. 58–59v.

matters of conscience" and "vain tickling humor," to beware the pagan, Moorish manners of the Spanish.[37]

After Lewis returned to England, he began publishing translations from Spanish and French. One, *The Resolved Gentleman*, has verses that summarize his experience of life:

> See, here, laid open to thy sight and sense,
> Th' Error, and Terror, of this wretched Life:
> Thy many Foes, the means for thy Defense;
> The glorious End, succeeding all this strife.
>
> Learn to redeem the precious Time here lent thee:
> Shun false allurements, and Courts subtlety:
> Resolve herein: Of thine amiss repent thee;
> So mayst thou vanquish Chance and Debility...
>
> **Epigraph:**
> *Le Temps s'en va.*[38]

That epigraph, "The times they are a-changing," catches some of the irony of his later life. Having been a Spanish Catholic soldier and then an English spy, he ended up living on Drury Lane, London, and working at King James' Court. Thanks to family connections and his facility with languages, James I knighted Lewis and granted him the office of Master of Ceremonies for life. Lewis' uncle, Sir Richard, secured him a seat in parliament in 1604. Despite Lewis' cooperation with the regime, his son, like his father, followed his Catholic conscience, fled to the Continent, and became a Jesuit.[39]

The Lewknors of Sussex were not atypical for their time. Puritans, Anglican conformists, recusants, Jesuits, farmers, judges, soldiers of fortune, their choices and allegiances were fluid. Loyal to the Crown, most of the men served in parliament and on the judicial bench, but they were ambivalent about the official religion. It was too Protestant for some, not Protestant enough for others. Farmers and merchants, they fought their bishop over control of the market for their grain using the Queen's law, modeling "proto-capitalist"

---

37 *A discourse of the usage of the English fugitives, by the Spaniard* (1595). STC (2nd ed.)/15563. Lewis Lewknor, *The estate of English fugitiues vnder the king of Spaine...* (1595), fos. 2–3. STC (2nd ed.)/15564.
38 Olivier de la Marche, *The resolued gentleman. Translated out of Spanishe into Englyshe, by Lewes Lewknor Esquier* (1594). STC (2nd ed.)/15139.
39 HPT sub Lewknor, Lewis. http://www.historyofparliamentonline.org/volume/1604-1629/member/lewknor-sir-lewis-1560-1627; http://www.historyofparliamentonline.org/volume/1558-1603/member/lewknor-lewis-1627 [Accessed November 29, 2018].

concepts of the market. Humanistically educated, they enjoyed the cosmopolitan culture of the Latinate, and they consumed and produced lots of words. The Lewknors were high on the social tree, knew it, and expected the deference that was their due.

John Smyth of Nottingham (c. 1570–1612) found that the Word of God liberated him from the assumed authority of people like the Lewknors. One of the founders of the Baptist church, Smyth came from a small town near Nottingham. Entering Christ Church College, Cambridge in 1589, he took his MA in 1593, studying with a man who was later expelled from his fellowship for his radical ideas. Smyth himself was ordained and became a fellow of the college, but he, too, had to resign in 1598 because he had doubts about the dress and liturgy of Elizabeth's church. He began a religious journey that would take him into radical separation from the Church of England and eventual exile in Holland.

Having been appointed Lecturer in Lincoln, Smyth developed a theology that led him to separation. Though he denied he was a separatist, in a 1605 defense of his sermons on the Lord's Prayer he declared, "Christians must stand fast in that liberty wherewith Christ hath made us free: and seeing that we are redeemed with a price, we must not be the servants of men, much less of times."[40] The absolute truth of the Word of God was not subject to loose interpretation or vacillation.

Smyth spoke with a prophetic voice, demanding that the magistrates support the ministers: "as Magistrates are called nursing fathers and mothers, so Ministers are called Gods fellow-workmen, builders, shepherds and such like: for that they feed the flock, build the city, and perform the work of the Ministry outwardly as God doth inwardly."[41] England's magistracy was not, in his considered opinion, supporting true worship, and Smyth eventually separated from the Queen's church, rejecting the authority of English bishops. He gathered his own small flock of believers, and they moved to Holland in 1607, where they might be free to practice the True Faith as Smyth understood it. He had convinced himself that authority rested in the congregation, which could only be composed of true believers. Rejecting all other authority, he re-baptized himself and his congregation. This self-baptism shocked even those radical religious communities in which he moved.

Smyth's faith in his own conclusions about duty to God began to slip after that, and he sought acceptance from the Waterlander Anabaptists before his death in 1612. By then, he had repented his bitter attacks and separation from other Christians. Realizing that his own conviction was met by others with equally certain consciences, he repented his "blind zeal, and preposterous

40 John Smyth, *A paterne of true prayer...* (1605), 6. STC (2nd ed.)/22877.1.
41 Ibid., 94–5.

imitation of Christ," admitting he had been too quick to judge others. Though the bishops of England "sit as Antichrist in the Temple of God, which is the conscience," he now recognized that not all who accepted their authority were to be condemned.[42] Demanding the right to follow God in his conscience, Smyth was forced to accept the right of others to do the same.

But not all Elizabethans were ardently conforming to this reformed biblical order. Simon Forman (1552–1611), writing in his egomaniacal autobiography, declared God was in direct control of his life and had big plans for him. Forman recalled, as a child of six in Wiltshire, dreaming visions of great mountains and waters falling on him, which he always survived. The dreams assured him that "God, the only defender of all that be His, would never let him be over thrown; but continually gave him always in the end the victory of all his enemies, and he overpaste [surpassed] all with credit by the help of God, to whom be praise for evermore! Amen!"[43]

An ambitious, intelligent man, Forman was self-educated, becoming a schoolmaster before setting up as a physician, alchemist, and astrologer. Along the way, he was kidnapped by pirates and then pressed by the Navy as a sailor for the second Essex Spanish campaign. His unlicensed medical practice caused him to be plagued by law suits from the College of Physicians. He was a social climber, a man who shunned the assigned roles of his society and was attacked for it. His autobiography celebrates his getting and spending money, his sexual experiences, and even his clothes. In 1600 alone, he spent the huge sum of £50 on clothing for his wife and himself. Dressing above his station, he consumed conspicuously and became a moneylender.[44]

In a world obsessed by proper station, dressing according to one's place, and accepting the authority of one's betters, Forman was untuning, if not breaking, the string of order.

He knew he could do this because God called him to his alchemical and medical work. A voluminous writer, he published a book on navigation and left extensive manuscripts on magic and medicine, an autobiography, and his case-books. Taken together, they describe a self-ordained expert who claimed his status through learning. He collected a respectable library. He was the sort of polymath who was possible in an age of cheap print and weak boundaries between professions.[45]

Forman dabbled in many things, believing God directed him. When, in 1591, he published a tract on longitude, it contained a justification of his God-given

---

42 John Smyth, *The Works of John Smyth, Fellow of Christ's College, 1594–8*, W.T. Whitley, ed. (Cambridge: Cambridge University Press, 1915), II, 752–4.
43 Simon Forman, *The Autobiography and Personal diary of Dr. Simon Forman, the celebrated astrologer...*, James Orchard Haliwell, ed. (London, 1849), 3.
44 Ibid., 31.
45 Eric H. Ash, *Power, Knowledge, and Expertise in Elizabethan England* (Baltimore: Johns Hopkins University Press, 2004), 11–12.

abilities: "Am I a monster degenerated from kind, or am I not a creature, made and formed by His divine will, and born into the world, and do live to show forth and speak of glory and power as well as others." All creatures manifest God's power and glory, each one in its kind and nature, and God has given each distinct abilities. Does not rhubarb cure choler? Did not God reveal the secrets of the seven liberal arts to Hermes Trismegistus? So why should not Simon Forman be called by God to explain how to find longitude? The time had come, and Simon Forman was God's instrument.[46]

Forman's belief that he was called to learn the secrets of nature demonstrates both his understanding of the divine order of creation and the leveling idea of vocation. His work on longitude is based on a set of observable certainties about the world that confirmed the fixed laws of the divine order that made knowledge possible.[47] This being so, it was possible for lowly Simon Forman to acquire knowledge and skill that others did not have, descrying the hidden qualities in all things. People should celebrate his inspired flaunting of the social order and reward him for his good works:

> consider with your selves, what God is, what his power containeth: what his gifts are, what his will is. Consider also what time bringeth to light, what Art and cunning skill is: and to what industry and travail attaineth: Lay all maliciousness apart, and envy nor infame none, nor condemn them that travail in any Art or Science for his country's wealth[48]

Forman acquired a reputation as a learned man, who, using astrology and seer stones, and calling on the help of angels, could diagnose and cure illness. He was on the cutting edge of health sciences, where alchemical research was taking on new importance because of the advances in Paracelsian medicine.[49] He attracted a large clientele, but an unsavory reputation. His critics said society ladies were pledging their souls to the Devil in exchange for his help with their romantic affairs.

By the early seventeenth century, Forman was well established in London, and he was attending plays. His manuscript, *The Book of Plays and Notes Thereof*, contains summaries of Shakespeare productions he saw at the Globe Theater. Forman watched for the secrets hidden within the stories, drawing the morals and taking warnings from them. "Rehearsing" what he had heard (just as Elizabethans did with sermons), Forman learned from *Richard II* to beware powerful people who asked astrologers to foretell their futures. In the play, when the Duke of Lancaster asked a "wise man" whether he would be king, he

---

46 Simon Forman, *The groundes of the longitude...* (1591). STC (2nd ed.)/11185.
47 Ibid.
48 Ibid.
49 Kassell, *Medicine and Magic*, 209–25.

learned he would not, but his son would. To keep the knowledge secret, Lancaster hanged his expert. Forman was incensed. "This was a policy in the commonwealth's opinion. But I say it was a villain's part and a Judas's kiss to hang the man for telling him the truth. Beware by this example of noble men and of their fair words and say little to them, lest they do the like by thee for thy good will."[50]

As a self-educated man, Forman's reading was eclectic and his style of learning eccentric, but he had extensive knowledge of the texts of his trade. He owned the staple works of astronomy and astrology, but he also read widely in more esoteric authors like Cornelius Agrippa.[51] Agrippa taught him to look for the hidden meanings in all things. Forman combined Agrippa's ideas with the medical theories of Paracelsus to derive an understanding of how natural magic and apothecary drugs worked together, giving a modern confirmation to the traditional belief that all creation worked in concert.[52]

Simon Forman was a self-made early Elizabethan. Those born nearer the end of the reign were educated in ways that emphasize the vast cultural change that occurred between the 1550's and the 1590's. Anne Clifford (1590–1676) exemplifies the younger generation of Elizabethans, growing up in a world in which individual conscience was cultivated. We know a great deal about her education thanks to her memorialization of it in a painting known as "The Great Picture" (Figure 12.2). In it, she had herself portrayed at the age of fifteen, in 1605, surrounded by her books. It is those books that give insight into what she was being taught, proving her education in the skepticism, poetry, and history on the cutting edge of Elizabethan intellectual life.

Anne had the painting done in 1646, representing her family history and her personal experiences up to the time she was fifty-six. Its left panel represents her at fifteen, when she inherited her father's title. The middle panel memorializes her parents and dead brothers, and the right-hand panel represents her as the mature Countess of Cumberland. Its backstory is a complicated battle with her uncle over her inheritance from her father, so the painting summarizes the evidence of her right to his title. At the same time, she used it to portray her education and her attitude toward religion and life.

Anne Clifford memorialized her education in the left-hand panel of the triptych. We see her surrounded by books and overseen by portraits of her governess, Mrs. Anne Taylor, "a religious and good woman," and her tutor, Samuel Daniel, "a man of upright and excellent spirit as appears by his works." We

---

50 Simon Forman, "*The Bocke of Plaies and Notes therof per forman for Common Pollicie* (1611). Bodl., Ashmole 208, fo. 201v. http://www.shakespearedocumented.org/exhibition/document/formans-account-seeing-plays-globe-macbeth-cymbeline-winters-tale [Accessed November 29, 2018].
51 Kassell, *Medicine and Magic*, 51–2.
52 Ibid., 196–7.

Figure 12.2 The Great Picture Triptych, Attributed to Jan van Belcamp, 1646. Abbot Hall Art Gallery, Kendal, Cumbria LA9 5AL. https://www.abbothall.org.uk/great-picture.

know little about Mrs. Taylor, but we know a great deal about Daniel, a poet and historian renowned for his artistry. He had travelled in France and Italy, spoke French and Italian, and was a cosmopolitan. He moved in Elizabethan intellectual circles with Sir Philip and Mary Sidney, Countess of Pembroke, living for a time in her household. He was just the man to introduce an earl's daughter to the latest intellectual trends.

Lady Anne's youthful education in navigation, history, literature, and alchemy may have evolved from her family's interests. Her father was George Clifford, Third Earl of Cumberland (1558–1605). Born just before Elizabeth acceded, George lost his father when he was twelve, in 1570. He was educated until then as a Catholic, but the Earl of Bedford, Francis Russell, bought his wardship and began educating him according to his own enthusiastic Protestant ideals. George's father had already negotiated to marry his boy to Russell's daughter Margaret, and their contract was completed in 1577. Their two sons died in childhood, so their daughter Anne was his sole heir.

George Clifford did not seem to take much interest in education, religion, and culture, pursuing more military ideals. Queen Elizabeth's official Champion, he carried her glove in jousts at Court, but his martial enthusiasm was more than decorative. Participating in the new war economy, he built ships and organized multiple privateering expeditions against the Spanish, served with distinction in the Armada crisis, and personally led an attack that captured San Juan, Puerto Rico. He lost money on most expeditions, but when the East India Company was organized, he was a charter member. He owned the first ship sent by the Company to the Indian Ocean. His maritime knowledge and wealth gave him an important role in England's entry into the globalizing economy. But to his contemporaries, his position at Court was more important, since, as an earl, the Court was his rightful place. Naturally, his daughter was prepared to serve there, too, just as her mother had, as a lady in waiting.

Anne never had much good to say about her father. A womanizer, the earl and her mother separated in 1600, and he willed his earldom to his brother to keep it in the male line, rather than to Anne, on whom, as his sole heir, it was entailed. She spent decades getting it back. Anne idolized her mother, who was highly educated, a patron of scholars, and a practicing alchemist and Paracelsian. Strikingly, the portrait of her parents in the center panel of the triptych only shows three books: the Bible, the works of Seneca in English, and "A written handbook of Alchemy Extractions, of Distillations, And Excellent Medicines." The manuscript book was inherited by Anne and survives. Analysis of the manuscript suggests that Margaret Clifford was moving in the scientific circles of people like John Dee and using many of the same books as Simon Forman.[53]

Lady Anne, therefore, was groomed for a place in Queen Elizabeth's Privy Chamber and given the education and social graces of a Court lady. Elizabeth's death ended that expectation, and Anne's diary of 1603 opens with Elizabeth's funeral and the uncomfortable transition of power to King James. Her mother and aunt feared civil war, so they were greatly relieved when the transition was peaceful, "my mother being all full of hopes every man expecting mountains and finding molehills." One of the changes she noted in the new king's Court was the filth. Visiting him for the first time at Theobalds, "we all saw a great change between the fashion of the Court as it is now and that in the Queen's time, for we were all lousy by sitting in the chamber of Sir Thomas Erskine [Captain of King James' guard]."[54]

Anne was thirteen years and three months old when Elizabeth died, and far advanced in the readings assigned to her by Samuel Daniel. By then, Daniel's poetry had won Edmund Spenser's praise and William Shakespeare had borrowed stories from him. Fulke Greville was trying to get him patronage, too— all of which points to a man well connected culturally, if not well paid. By the late 1590's, he was part of the thriving history-writing industry, working on a verse account of the Wars of the Roses, but it was his *stile dulce* poetry that got him his great patron, Anne's mother. In 1603, Daniel produced a poem, "Octavia," an epistolary piece voicing the anguish of Marc Antony's wife Octavia when he abandoned her for Cleopatra. It was a veiled reference to the story of the Cliffords' troubled marriage, and Lady Anne's mother took Daniel as a client. In exchange, he had to tutor her daughter.

---

53 Penny Bayer, "Margaret Clifford's Alchemical Receipt Book and the John Dee Circle." *Ambix* 2005; 52(3), 271–84.
54 D.J.H. Clifford, ed. *The Diaries of Lady Anne Clifford* (Stroud: Allen Sutton, 1990), 21–22.

Daniel complained that tutoring slowed his study of the fifteenth century, telling Sir Thomas Egerton, "whilst I should have written the actions of men ... I have been constrained to live with Children."[55] However, he and Lady Anne became friends, and remained so until he died in 1619, when she erected a tomb for him.

We can see in Lady Anne's painted libraries the ways Daniel shaped her early education and influenced the rest of her life. She is portrayed with a range of religious, philosophical, and historical works. They are all in English and French, so it is not certain whether she had any Latin, but we can see she was educated as a Protestant and a skeptic, while reading a great deal of contemporary poetry and history.

In the left panel of the painting, the books lying at her feet tell us a good deal. Cornelius Agrippa's *Of the Vanity of the Sciences* is there, teaching that Aristotle was wrong, and that if you wanted true knowledge, you must Platonically "descend into yourselves ... depart from the clouds of man's traditions, and cleave to the true light."[56] This instruction on internalized skepticism was joined on her floor by *The Feigned History of Don Quixote*. Historical study is exemplified by *Camdens Britannia*, and preparation for life in a global economy by *Abraham Ortelius His Mapps of the World*. A divider caliper rests against the volume of maps.

The skepticism popular among late Elizabethans is represented by the *Essays* of Michel de Montaigne, as well as *Don Quixote*.[57] Both inspire doubt about old, accepted truths. Notably, Montaigne, translated by John Florio, Samuel Daniel's brother-in-law, taught her to look within herself for certainty. This vein of French skepticism continued to attract Lady Anne throughout her life, as shown in the right panel, where we find the elder Anne's right hand resting on the Bible and Pierre Charron's *Book of Wisdom Translated out of French into English*. Charron was Montaigne's philosophical heir, carrying forward his skepticism. Though he was a Catholic priest, late in his life (he died in 1603) he concluded that the only way to attain true knowledge was to know yourself. This required a knowledge of the human condition, "as a preparative unto wisdom."[58] Recognized now as a father of secularism, Charron's position on religion was that all religious knowledge came from inward certainty, not outward

55 John Pitcher, "Daniel, Samuel (1562/3–1619)," in *Oxford Dictionary of National Biography* (Oxford: Oxford University Press, 2004). http://www.oxforddnb.com/view/article/7120 [Accessed November 29, 2018].
56 Heinriech Cornelius Agrippa, *Of the vanitie and vncertaintie of artes and sciences...* (1575), fo. 187. STC (2nd ed.)/205.
57 Michel de Montaigne, *The essayes or morall, politike and millitarie discourses of Lo: Michaell de Montaigne ... Iohn Florio* (1603). STC (2nd ed.)/18041.
58 Pierre Charron, *Of wisdome three bookes written in French by Peter Charro[n] Doctr of Lawe in Paris*, Samson Lennard, trans. (1608), preface. STC (2nd ed.)/5051.

opinion, in agreement with Agrippa. He warned that "religion and faith, which is but the opinion of man" was not to be confused with "grace and supernatural inspiration, which is proper to natural and moral virtue and action."[59] People should not, he said, confuse piety with probity, religion with honesty, devotion with conscience.[60] These lessons from late sixteenth-century skeptics were very popular with later Elizabethans.

Samuel Daniel would have known Charron's argument that there is a difference between piety and probity, teaching it is right in conscience to conform to the religion of the state, a *politique* position reminiscent of the earlier Elizabethan Nicodemites. Speaking of how to raise a child (like Lady Anne), Charron says good manners and honesty must be engrafted through fear of God, and that the child must learn "not to be over scrupulous in the mysteries and points of religion, but to conform himself to the government and discipline of the church."[61]

The internalization of religion taught by Daniel and the French skeptics was reinforced by much else that Lady Anne portrayed herself as reading. There is theology—what Elizabethan did not read theology?—but it takes the form of more internally focused teaching, both in prose and in poetry.

For instance, young Anne has Guillaume de Salluste Bartas' *Weeks and Works*. A French Protestant, Bartas wrote long meditative poems with lines like these:

> Who on this gulf would safely venture faine,
> Must not too-boldly hale into the Maine,
> But longst the shore with sails of faith must coast,
> Their star the bible, steersman the Holy Ghost.[62]

Not surprisingly, Josuah Sylvester's translation—the version on Anne's shelf—is prefaced by a laudatory poem by Samuel Daniel.

More moral philosophy came from France in the form of a translation of Pierre de La Primaudaye's *The French Academy*. A Protestant courtier, La Primaudaye combined moral instruction with the question vexing France, how to find civil peace. He believed philosophy could help people overcome the miseries of mankind, allowing them to lead pleasant, peaceable lives.[63]

---

59 Ibid.
60 Ibid., 287.
61 Ibid., 481.
62 Guillaume de Salluste Bartas, *Bartas: his deuine vveekes and works...*, Iosuah Sylvester, trans. (1605), 5. STC (2nd ed.)/21649.
63 Pierre de La Primaudaye, *The French academie wherin is discoursed the institution of maners, and whatsoeuer els concerneth the good and happie life of all estates and callings, by preceptes of doctrine, and examples of the liues of ancient sages and famous men...* (1586), "Author to the Reader." STC (2nd ed.)/15233.

Clearly, Lady Anne was taught to see the world through the lenses of late Elizabethan Protestant, self-reflective Christianity. Learning of her true nature through internal interrogation, her idea of duty to conscience was more liberal than that of predestinarians, since each conscience had to find its own way, but she also learned that the religion of the monarch should be obeyed. Spiritual conviction was separated from political duty.

As a preparatory to self-reflection, Daniel fashionably taught Anne to read history, placing herself and her society into historical perspective. Excitingly, there in her youthful collection of books is the work of Louis Leroy on the "interchangeability" of the world. First written in French, it appeared in English in 1594, and it is a fine example of what Americans might call a "world civ" text. It treats of all periods of history, includes non-European histories, and draws the conclusion that societies are always changing.[64] Leroy, the Professor of Greek at the College du France, was a noted translator of Plato from Greek into French, writing on history and politics. Lady Anne's book was an extended meditation on history ancient and modern, full of anecdotes and strange stories. But Leroy's moral was clear. The ancients were no better than the moderns, and more and better knowledge can be found today. As he traced the rise and fall of nations, he was using historical relativism to free people from slavish adherence to the classical past. Its presence in Lady Anne's model book shelf is a skeptical rejection of humanist devotion to the classics and of social conservatism, and even a challenge to the privileged biblical history.

Reading it, she imbibed historical skepticism through the histories of Islam, Chinese empires, Zoroastrians, and Africans. Leroy charts the rise and fall of empires all over the world, along with religions, without feeling the necessity to hark back to a more glorious classical or religious time. Things change—they are always changing—and it is the duty of people to struggle for the good in the face of this change. As Europe had been overrun by Goths, Huns, Lombard, Vandals, Saracens, "many strange nations, differing in fashions, colors and habits" could be expected to again burn its cities, churches, and libraries, changing languages and manners. Nature, too, would assault civilizations, according to its own laws, as directed by God's providence, with earthquakes, fires and floods. "Wherefore, men of good minds ought not to be amazed ... but ... take courage," each working in his vocation "to preserve ... so many goodly things lately invented, or restored; whose losses would be almost irreparable; and to deliver them over to such as come after us; as we have received them of our ancestors: and namely GOOD LETTERS."[65]

---

64 Louis Leroy, *Of the interchangeable course, or variety of things in the whole world...* (1594). STC (2nd ed.)/15488.
65 Ibid., fo. 126v.

What Lady Anne made of Leroy is not clear, but it is clear why Samuel Daniel thought she should read him. He conforms with what we know of Daniel's own attempts to makes sense of life and art. Daniel's long poem "Musophilus" versifies much of Leroy's argument, celebrating the importance of poetry in maintaining civilization.

Among Daniel's collected works are a series of verse "epistles," one of which is addressed to Lady Anne. Published in 1603, when she was thirteen, it catches the ideals held for a young aristocratic lady in the advanced intellectual circles of the Court. Her mother, reports the poet, was laboring to adorn the mansions of Anne's mind with furniture of worth, making her as highly good as highly born, to give her "virtues equal to your kind." In someone so aristocratic, honor must be carefully guarded, since the slightest stain would show. She must be kept from straying "into the private ways of carelessness." Daniel lapses astronomical, telling Anne that people of her rank bring order to the world, "for low in the'air of gross uncertainty, confusion only rules. Order sits high." Having been born a superior planet, she must see to her virtue: "...how careful must you be/To be yourself." Self-knowledge is the secret of virtue, since "within our hearts, the ambushment lies." By closely guarding her own ego, she could guard her family honor, and that of her children to come, setting an example for future generations in keeping with the example of her ancestors, "Since nothing cheers the heart of greatness more/Then th'Ancestors fair glory gone before."[66]

Daniel's epistle to Anne's mother sounds the same notes, stressing the need for self-knowledge and clear conscience in the face of her husband's bad behavior. Daniel was teaching a heart-centered conscience, a skeptical relationship with the world, the importance of station and order, and the danger of zealotry.

Lady Anne died in 1676, often recalling in her diary the events of sixty and seventy years before. Her favorite reading came from her youth, which taught her fierce devotion to her duty as the hereditary Countess and Sheriffess of Cumberland. Skeptic though she was, she was a devoted student of the Bible, generally ending each day's diary entry with a scriptural citation, framing her day's trials with quotations from Psalms, Job, or Ecclesiastes.[67] For her, the Elizabethan Age lasted a very, very long time.

Though they were only a few years apart in age, the training received by Lady Anne was not given to Sir Edward Lewknor the younger by his Puritan parents,

---

66 Samuel Daniel, "To the Ladie Anne Clifford," in *A panegyrike congratulatory deliuered to the Kings most excellent maiesty at Burleigh Harrington in Rutlandshire. By Samuel Daniel. Also certaine epistles. With a defence of ryme...* (1603). STC (2nd ed.)/6259.

67 Clifford, *Diaries*, 230. Charles G. Williamson, *Lady Anne Clifford, Countess of Dorset, Pembroke and Montgomery, 1590–1676. Her life, letters and work* (Kendal: Titus Wilson and Sons, 1922), 111, 306.

though a godly conscience was important to him, too. Anne was taught that the world waxes and wanes and nothing is constant; Lewknor was taught that there is one ancient truth that must be restored, overcoming historical corruption as it moves toward a godly stasis. As a godly magistrate, he was focused on the primitive church; she was focused on her duty to the commonwealth and her family according to her place of high degree. John Smyth was caught up in exact obedience to the Word of God, his conscience forcing him to break with every authority. Simon Forman, transgressing ideas of place and degree, was a "new man" rising from hard work and aspiration to become one who understood the heavens, cured sickness, talked with angels, and aggressively asserted his own value in a world in which expertise had currency.

They were all Christians, but with very different ideas about God. They disagreed about what it meant to obey Him in conscience, about the operations of God's providence, about social status and place, and about community and behavior. For Elizabethans, burgeoning knowledge of the natural and historical worlds fueled change and increased confusion. Such change created social tensions that resolved themselves in blood in the civil wars of the 1640's and produced new cultural norms very alien from those of the young Queen Elizabeth.

To be Elizabethan was to navigate a path through the cultural chaos of the later sixteenth century. But there were many routes and few trustworthy guides. This tangled delta of cultural streams created competition and conflict over how to make sense of life, fomenting huge change, contributing to a brilliant expansion of English literary culture, opening the way for global empire and capitalism, and creating a new religious order. The later Elizabethans stumbled out of a broad set of certainties into a world that was much less sure, much less able to agree on what was true, much more dependent on observation and internal analysis than that of their grandparents.

Primary Bibliography

Manuscripts

Cambridge

Cambridge University Library [CUL]
Luard 179a. Common place book of Francis Wilsford, c. 1581–88.
Mm.1.29
Corpus Christi College, Parker Library [CCCC]
Ms. 121
Trinity College
Ms. B.14/9

Ghent

University of Ghent. D'Heere, Lucas, *Théâtre De Tous Les Peuples Et Nations De La Terre Avec Leurs Habits Et Ornemens Divers, Tant Anciens Que Modernes, Diligemment Depeints Au Naturel Par Luc Dheere Peintre Et Sculpteur Gantois.* https://lib.ugent.be/catalog/rug01%3A000794288/ items/910000094764 [Accessed November 29, 2018].

Hatfield, Hatfield House

Cecil Papers [CP]
CP 2/97; 18/74; 22/96; 55/49; 88/19; 90/80; 162/73; 163/109; 167/102; 173/95; 177/14; 185/158; 186/57; 199/102; 251/39

Being Elizabethan: Understanding Shakespeare's Neighbors, First Edition. Norman Jones.
© 2020 John Wiley & Sons, Inc. Published 2020 by John Wiley & Sons, Inc.

Kew

The National Archives [TNA]
C66/1820
E 133/2
E178/469; E178/2004
PC 2
PROB 11, 56; 57; 92
SP 11/4
SP 12/13; 23; 26; 40; 42; 60; 85; 90; 112; 173.1; 176.1; 233; 224; 244; 255; 282
SP 15/12; 19
SP 46/26
SP 70/86; 121
SP 83/10

London

British Library [BL]
Additional Mss. 11406; 37419; 48023
Cotton, Vespasian D.18
Harley 290; 3638
Lansdowne 6; 7; 14; 26; 50; 58; 72; 82; 80; 101; 102
Stowe, 362
College of Arms
Ms. B 16
Guildhall
Ms. 20,845
Ms. 11588/1
Inner Temple
Petyt Ms 538/10

Oxford

Bodleian Library [Bodl.]
Ashmole 208, The Bocke of Plaies and Notes therof per forman for Common Pollicie
Ashmole 228
Jones, 17
Rawlinson D. 718
Top, C.14.

Northampton

Northamptonshire Libraries, Phillipps Ms. 2569

Nottingham

University of Nottingham Library, Mi LM 26 in Middleton Collection, MSS
Division

San Marino, CA

Henry E. Huntington Library [HEH]
EL 2219, 2579
HA Family Papers. Unindexed wills of Francis Hastings of Bosworth (c. 1580) and
Francis Hastings of North Cadbury (before 1596)
HA Religious Box 1
HA 5099
HAP Box 12
HM 8 Thomas Buttes commonplace book "A Boke of Verses named Aurum e
Stercore. Collectore R.O. Talbott
HM 160; 500; 1340; 35072

Washington, DC

Folger Shakespeare Library
V.b.375 "A Blazon of Arms"

Printed Works

Acontio, Jacobo. *Stratagematum Satanae Libri Octo* (Basil, 1565).
Acontio, Jacobo. *Satan's Strategies Books V–VIII.* Charles D. O'Malley, trans.
San Francisco: Sutro Branch, California State Library, Occasional Papers
English Series 5, part II, 1940. WPA Project No. 665-08-3-236.
Agrippa, Heinriech Cornelius, of Nettesheim. *The commendation of matrimony.*
Dauid Clapam, trans. (1540). STC (2nd ed.)/202.
Agrippa, Heinriech Cornelius, of Nettesheim. *A treatise of the nobilitie and
excellencye of vvoman kynde, translated out of Latine into englysshe by Dauid
Clapam* (1542). STC (2nd ed.)/203.
Agrippa, Heinriech Cornelius, of Nettesheim. *Of the vanitie and vncertaintie of
artes and sciences.* Ia. San., trans. (1575). STC (2nd ed.)/205.
Alabaster, William. *Alabaster's Conversion (1599).* Dana F. Sutton,
ed. (2012). http://www.philological.bham.ac.uk/alabconv/ (Accessed
November 30, 2018).
Alley, Hugh. *Hugh Alley's Caveat. The Markets of London in 1598*: Folger Ms.
V.a.318. Ian Archer, Caroline Barron, and Vanessa Harding, eds. London:
London Topographical Society, 1988.
Anon. *The Lamentations of Jeremie in Meeter. With apt notes to sing them withal*
(1587). STC/2108:10.

Averell, W. *A meruailous combat of contrarieties Malignantlie striuing in the me[m]bers of mans bodie, allegoricallie representing vnto vs the enuied state of our florishing common wealth: wherin dialogue-wise by the way, are touched the extreame vices of this present time. With an earnest and vehement exhortation to all true English harts, couragiously to be readie prepared against the enemie.* (1588). STC (2nd ed.)/981.

Aylmer, John. *An harborovve for faithfull and trevve subiectes, agaynst the late blowne blaste, concerninge the gouernme[n]t of vvemen. wherin be confuted all such reasons as a straunger of late made in that behalfe, with a breife exhortation to obedience. Anno. M.D.lix* (1559). STC (2nd ed)/1005.

Ayre, John, ed. *The Works of John Jewel,* 4 vols. Cambridge: Parker Society, 1845–50.

Bacon, Francis. *Instauratio magna* (1620). STC (2nd ed.)/1163.

Bacon, Francis. *The New Organon: or True Directions Concerning the Interpretation of Nature.* Jonathan Bennett, trans. (2017). http://www. earlymoderntexts.com/assets/pdfs/bacon1620part1.pdf [Accessed November 29, 2018].

Bacon, Francis. "Of Unity." http://www.westegg.com/bacon/unity.html [Accessed November 29, 2018].

Barlow, William. *The summe and substance of the conference, which it pleased His Excellent Majestie to have with the lords bishops, and others of his clergie (at which the most of the lords of the councill were present) in His Majesties privie-chamber, at Hampton Court, Jan. 14. 1603* (1804).

Baro, Peter. "Two Theames or Questions, handled and disputed openly in the Schooles at Cambridge, in the Latin tung, by P. Baro, Doctor of Diuinitye and Englished by I. L.," in Andreas Hyperius, *A speciall treatise of Gods prouidence and of comforts against all kinde of crosses and calamities to be drawne from the same With an exposition of the 107. Psalme. Heerunto is added an appendix of certaine sermons & questions, (conteining sweet & comfortable doctrine) as they were vttered and disputed ad clerum in Cambridge. By P. Baro D. in Diui.* I.L., trans. (1588). STC (2nd ed.)/11760.

Baro, Peter. "Summary of Three Opinions Concerning Predestination," in James Nichols, ed. and trans. *The Works of James Arminius,* 3 vols. London: 1825, I, 91–100.

Barron, Caroline, Christopher Coleman, and Claire Gobbi, eds. "The London Journal of Alessandro Magno 1562," *The London Journal* 1983; 9(2), 136–52.

Bartas, Guillaume de Salluste. *Bartas: his deuine vveekes and works...* Josuah Sylvester, trans. (1605). STC (2nd ed.)/21649.

Beard, Thomas. *The theatre of Gods iudgements: or, a collection of histories out of sacred, ecclesiasticall, and prophane authours concerning the admirable iudgements of God vpon the transgressours of his commandements. Translated out of French and augmented by more than three hundred examples...* (1597). STC (2nd ed.)/1659.

Beaumont, Francis and John Fletcher. *Beaumont and Fletcher*. A.R. Waller, ed. New York: Octagon, 1969.

Billingsley, Henry, trans. *The elements of geometrie of the most auncient philosopher Euclide of Megara ... Whereunto are annexed certaine scholies, annotations, and inuentions, of the best mathematiciens, both of time past, and in this our age. With a very fruitfull praeface made by M. I. Dee, specifying the chiefe mathematicall scie[n]ces, what they are, and wherunto commodious: where, also, are disclosed certaine new secrets mathematicall and mechanicall, vntill these our daies, greatly missed* (1570). STC (2nd ed.)/10560.

Bilson, Thomas. *The true difference betweene Christian subiection and unchristian rebellion wherein the princes lawfull power to commaund for trueth, and indepriuable right to beare the sword are defended against the Popes censures and the Iesuits sophismes vttered in their apologie and defence of English Catholikes: with a demonstration that the thinges refourmed in the Church of England by the lawes of this realme are truely Catholike, notwithstanding the vaine shew made to the contrary in their late Rhemish Testament* (1585). STC (2nd ed.)/3071.

Birch, Thomas. Memoirs *of the reign of Queen Elizabeth, from the year 1581 till her death. In which the secret intrigues of her court, and the conduct of her favourite, Robert earl of Essex, both at home and abroad, are particularly illustrated. From the original papers of... Anthony Bacon, esquire, and other manuscripts never before published*. London: 1754.

Black, Joseph L., ed. *The Martin Marprelate Tracts. A Modernized and Annotated Edition* (Cambridge: Cambridge University Press, 2008).

Bodin, Jean. *De la demonomanie des sorciers* (Paris: 1582). USTC 1699.

Bonner, Edmund. An honest godlye instruction and information for the tradynge, and bringinge vp of children, set furth by the Bishoppe of London co[m] maundyng all scholemaisters and other teachers of youthe within his diocese, that they neither teach, learne reade, or vse anye other maner of A B C, catechisme or rudimentes, then this made for the first instruction of youth (1556). STC (2nd ed.)/3281.

Booty, John, ed. *The Book of Common Prayer, 1559: The Elizabethan Prayer Book* (Washington, DC: Folger Shakespeare Library, 2005).

A brieff discours off the troubles begonne at Franckford in Germany Anno Domini 1554 Abowte the booke off off [sic] common prayer and ceremonies, and continued by the Englishe men theyre to thende off Q. Maries raigne, in the which discours, the gentle reader shall see the very originall and beginninge off all the contention that hathe byn, and what was the cause off the same (1574). STC (2nd ed.)/25442.

Ibid.

Bruce, John, ed. *Liber Familicus of Sir James Whitelocke, A Judge of the Court of King's Bench in the Reigns of James I. and Charles I* (London: Camden Society ser. 1, 70, 1858).

Bruno, Conrad. *Adversus Novam Historiam Ecclesiasticarum, quam Matthias Illyricus et eius Collegae Magdeburgici per centurias nuper edidterunt, ne quisque illis male fidei historicis novis fidat, admonitio Catholics* (Dillingen, 1565).

Bullein, William. *The gouernment of health: a treatise written by William Bullein, for the especiall good and healthfull preseruation of mans bodie from all noysome diseases, proceeding by the excesse of euill diet, and other infirmities of nature: full of excellent medicines, and wise counsels, for conseruation of health, in men, women, and children. Both pleasant and profitable to the industrious reader* (1595), 3. STC (2nd ed.)/4042.

Byfield, Nicholas. *The beginning of the doctrine of Christ. Or A catalogue of sinnes shewing how a Christian may finde out the euils, hee must take notice of in his repentance. With rules, that shew a course, how any Christian may be deliuered from the guilt and power of all his sinnes* (1619). STC (2nd ed.)/4209.5.

Byrd, William and Thomas Tallis, *Cantiones, quae ab argumento sacrae vocantur, quinque et sex partium* (1575). STC (2nd ed.)/23666.

Calendar of Patent Rolls Preserved in the PRO, Philip and Mary, Elizabeth, 9 vols. (London: Her Majesty's Stationery Office, 1937–66).

Calvin, John. *An admonicion against astrology iudiciall and other curiosities, that raigne now in the world:...* G.G., trans. (1561). STC (2nd ed.)/4372.

Calvin, John. *The Institution of the Christian Religion*, Thomas Norton, trans. (1574). STC (2nd ed.)/4418.

Campion, Edmund. *Ten Reasons Proposed to His Adversaries for Disputation in the Name of the Faith and Presented to the Illustrious Members of our Universities* (St. Louis: B. Herder, 1914).

Canons and decrees of the sacred and oecumenical Council of Trent. J. Waterworth. ed. and trans. (London: Dolman, 1848).

Carey, Robert. *The Memoirs of Robert Carey*. F.H. Markes, ed. (Oxford: Clarendon Press, 1972).

Casas, Bartolomé de las, *The Spanish colonie, or Briefe chronicle of the acts and gestes of the Spaniardes in the West Indies, called the newe world, for the space of xl. yeeres:...* M.M.S., trans. (1583). STC (2nd ed.)/4739.

Case, John. *Apologia musices tam vocalis quam instrumentalis et mixtae* (1588). STC (2nd ed.)/4755.

Cecil, William. *The Execution of Justice in England for Maintenaunce of publique and Christian peace, against certeine stirrers of sedition, and adherents to the traytors and enemies of the Realme, without any persecution of them for questions of Religion, as is falsely reported and published by the fautors and fosterers of their treason. Xvii. Decemb. 1583* (1583). [STC 4902.]

Ibid.

Charron, Pierre. *Of wisdome three bookes written in French by Peter Charro[n] Doctr of Lawe in Paris.* Samson Lennard, trans. (1608). STC (2nd ed.)/5051.

Clifford, D.J.H., ed. *The Diaries of Lady Anne Clifford* (Stroud: Allen Sutton, 1990).

Collins, Arthur, ed. *The Life of the Great Stateman William Cecil, Lord Burghley* (London, 1732).

Cooper, J.P., ed. *The Wentworth Papers 1597–1628* (London: Camden Society ser. 4, 12, 1973).

Corder, Joan, ed. *The Visitation of Suffolk 1561 made by Willaim Hervey Clarenceux King of Arms*, 2 vols. (London: The Harleian Society, 1984).

Cowell, John. *Institutiones iuris Anglicani ad methodum et seriem institutionum imperialium compositae & digestae. Opus not solum iuris Anglicani Romaniq[ue] in hoc regno studiosis, sed omnibus qui politeian & consuetudines inclyti nostri imperii penitius scire cupiunt, vtile & accommodatum....Cum duplice indice, quorum alter titulos ordine alphabetico, alter obscuras iruis Ang. dictiones earumq[ue] explicationem continet* (1605). STC (2nd. ed.)/5899.

Cowell, John. *The interpreter: or Booke containing the signification of words wherein is set foorth the true meaning of all, or the most part of such words and termes, as are mentioned in the lawe vvriters, or statutes of this victorious and renowned kingdome, requiring any exposition or interpretation...* (1607). STC (2nd ed.)/5900.

Craddock, Edward. *The shippe of assured safetie wherein wee may sayle without danger towards the land of the liuing, promised to the true Israelites: conteyning in foure bokes, a discourse of Gods prouidence, a matier very agreable for this time, vvherof no commo[n]ly knovven especiall treatise hath bene published before in our mother tong. What great varietie of very necessarie and fruitfull matier is comprysed in this worke, conuenient for all sortes of men, by the table of the chapters follovving after the pracface, ye may perceyue* (1572). STC (2nd ed.)/5952.

Cranmer, Thomas. "A Prologue or Preface Made by the Most Reverend Father in God Thomas Archbishop of Canterbury Metropolitan and Primate of England," in *The Byble in Englyshe that is to saye the conte[n]t of al the holy scrypture, both of ye olde, and newe testame[n]t... This is the Byble apoynted to the vse of the churches* (1540). STC (2nd ed.)/2071.

Cross, Claire, ed. *The Letters of Sir Francis Hastings 1574–1609* (Taunton: Somerset Record Society LXIX, 1969).

Crowley, Robert. *The Select Works of Robert Crowley.* J.M. Cowper, ed. (London: Early English Text Society extra series, 15, 1872).

Daniel, Samuel. *A panegyrike congratulatory deliuered to the Kings most excellent maiesty at Burleigh Harrington in Rutlandshire. By Samuel Daniel. Also certaine epistles. With a defence of ryme...* (1603). STC (2nd ed.)/6259.

Daman, William. *Bassus. The second booke of the musicke ... conteining all the tunes of Dauids Psalmes, as they are ordinarily soung in the Church: ... composed into 4. parts. In which sett the highest part singeth the church tune. Published for the recreation of such as delight in musicke* (1591). STC (2nd ed.)/6221.

Darel, John. *A true narration of the strange and greuous vexation by the Devil, of 7. persons in Lancashire, and VVilliam Somers of Nottingham Wherein the doctrine of possession and dispossession of demoniakes out of the word of God is particularly applyed vnto Somers, and the rest of the persons controuerted: togeather with the vse we are to make of these workes of God* (1600). STC (2nd ed.)/6288.

Davies, John. *The Complete Poems of Sir John Davies*. Alexander B. Grosart, ed. (London: Chatto and Windus, 1876).

Dent, Arthur. *The plaine mans path-way to heauen. VVherein euery man may clearly see, whether he shall be saued or damned. Set forth dialogue wise, for the better vnderstanding of the simple* (1601). STC (2nd ed.)/6626.5.

Dering, Edward. "A Sermon Preached before the Queenes Maiestie, the 25 day of februarie, by Maister Eward Dering. 1569," in *Maister Derings workes* (1590). STC (2nd ed.)/6675(a).

Dewar, Mary, ed. *A Discourse of the Commonweal of this Realm of England. Attributed to Sir Thomas Smith* (Charlottesville: Folger Shakespeare Library, University Press of Virginia, 1969).

D'Ewes, Simonds. *Autobiography and Correspondence*, 2 vols, James Orchard Haliwell, ed. (London: 1845).

Donaldson, Gordon, ed. *The Memoirs of Sir James Melville of Halhill* (London: Folio Society, 1969).

Donne, John. *Poems of John Donne*, vol. I. E. K. Chambers, ed. (London: Lawrence & Bullen, 1896).

Donne, John. *Devotions upon Emergent Occasions together with Death's Duel* (Ann Arbor: University of Michigan Press, 1959). http://www.gutenberg.org/files/23772/23772-h/23772-h.htm [Accessed November 29, 2018].

Downame, George. *A treatise vpon John 8. 36 concerning Christian libertie The chiefe points whereof were deliuered in a sermon preached at Pauls Crosse, Nouemb. 6. 1608* (1609). STC (2nd ed.)/7124.

Drayton, Michael. *The harmonie of the church Containing, the spirituall songes and holy hymnes, of godly men, patriarkes and prophetes: all, sweetly sounding, to the praise and glory of the highest. Now (newlie) reduced into sundrie kinds of English meeter: meete to be read or sung, for the solace and comfort of the godly* (1591). STC (2nd ed.)/7199.

Dyce, Alexander, ed. *The Works of Thomas Middleton in Five Volumes* (London: 1840).

Edwards, Richard. *The excellent comedie of two the moste faithfullest freendes, Damon and Pithias Newly imprinted, as the same was shewed before the Queenes Maiestie, by the Children of her Graces Chappell...* (1571). STC (2nd ed.)/7514.

Elizabeth I. *By the Queene. The excesse of apparel, and the superfluitie of unnecessary forreyne wares therto belongyng, nowe of late yeeres is growen by sufferance to suche an extremitie* (1574). STC (2nd ed.)/8066.

Elyot, Thomas. *The Book Named the Governor.* S.E. Lehmberg, ed. (New York: Dutton, 1970).

Ibid.

Fisher, John. *The copy of a letter describing the wonderful woorke of God in deliuering a mayden within the city of Chester, from an horrible kinde of torment and sicknes 16. of february 1564* (1565). STC (2nd ed.)/10910.

Fitzherbert, Anthony. *La Nouvelle Natura Brevium du Iuge tresreverend Monsieru Anthoine Fitzherbert dernierement renuse et corrigee...* (1560). STC 10960.

Fitzherbert, Anthony and Richard Crompton, *L'Office et Aucthoritie de Justices de Peace 1584* (London: Professional Books, 1972).

Forman, Simon. *The Autobiography and Personal diary of Dr. Simon Forman, the celebrated astrologer, from A. D. 1552, to A. D. 1602, from the unpublished manuscripts in the Ashmolean museum, Oxford.* James Orchard Haliwell, ed. (London, 1849).

Forman, Simon. *The groundes of the longitude with an admonition to all those that are incredulous and beleeue not the trueth of the same. VVritten by Simon Forman, student in Astronomie and Phisique. 1591* (1591). STC (2nd ed.)/11185.

Foster, Elizabeth Read, ed. *Proceedings in Parliament 1610, 2 vols.* (New Haven: Yale University Press, 1966).

A Fourme of Prayer, necessary for the present time (1588). STC/2010:07.

Foxe, John. *The Unabridged Acts and Monuments Online or TAMO* (1583 ed.) (Sheffield: HRI Online Publications, 2011). http://www.johnfoxe.org/index.php?realm=text&edition=1583&pageid=2158&gototype=modern#top [Accessed November 29, 2018].

Frere, William Howard, ed. *Visitation Articles and Injunctions of the Time of the Reformation, vol. III, 1559–1575* (London: Longmans, 1910).

Fulke, William. *A sermon preached at Hampton Court on Son[day] being the. 12. day of Nouember, in the yeare of our Lord. 1570. VVherin is plain[ly] proued Babylon to be Rome, both by Scriptures and doctors* (1570). STC (2nd ed.)/11449.5.

Furnivall, Frederick J., ed. *Child-Marriages, Divorces and Ratifications ... the Diocese of Chester, A.D. 1561–66* (Oxford: Early English Text Society, orig. ser., 108, 1897).

Gardiner, James, ed. *Three Fifteenth-century Chronicles, with Historical Memoranda by John Stowe* (London: Camden Society n.s., 28, 1880).

Gee, Henry and William John Hardy, eds. *Documents Illustrative of English Church History* (New York: Macmillan, 1896).

Grafton, Richard. *A chronicle at large and meere history of the affayres of Englande and kinges of the same deduced from the Creation of the vvorlde, vnto the first habitation of thys islande: and so by contynuance vnto the first yere of the reigne of our most deere and souereigne Lady Queene Elizabeth: collected out of sundry aucthors, whose names are expressed in the next page of this leafe* (1569). STC (2nd ed.)/12147.

Green, Robert. *A maidens dreame upon the death of the Right Honorable Sir Christopher Hatton knight, late Lord Chancellor of England* (1591). STC (2nd ed.)/1227.

Greg, W.W. ed. *Henslowe's Diary* (London: A.H. Bullen, 1904).

Greville, Fulke. *The Works in Verse and Prose of... Fulke Greville*, 4 vols. Alexander B. Grosart, ed. (1870).

Haliwell, James Orchard, ed. *The Autobiography and Personal diary of Dr. Simon Forman, the celebrated astrologer, from A. D. 1552, to A. D. 1602, from the unpublished manuscripts in the Ashmolean museum, Oxford* (London,1849).

Hall, Joseph. *The arte of diuine meditation profitable for all Christians to knowe and practise; exemplified with a large meditation of eternall life* (1606). STC (2nd ed.)/12642.

Hariot, Thomas. *A briefe and true report of the new found land of Virginia of the commodities and of the nature and manners of the naturall inhabitants...* (1590). STC (2nd ed.)/12786.

Harman, Thomas. *A caueat or warening, for common cursetors vulgarely called vagabones, set forth by Thomas Harman, Esquier, for the vtilitie and profit of his naturall countrey. Newly augmented and enlarged...* (1573). STC (2nd ed.)/12788.

Harrison, William. *Deaths aduantage little regarded, and The soules solace against sorrow Preached in two funerall sermons at Childwal in Lancashire at the buriall of Mistris Katherin Brettergh the third of Iune. 1601. The one by William Harrison, one of the preachers appointed by her. Maiestie for the countie palatine of Lancaster, the other by William Leygh, Bachelor of Diuinitie, and pastor of Standish. Whereunto is annexed, the Christian life and godly death of the said gentlevvoman* (1602). STC (2nd ed.)/12866.

Harrison, William. *The Description of England*, 2nd ed. Georges Edelen, ed. (Washington, DC: Folger Shakespeare Library, 1994).

Hartley, T.E., ed. *Proceedings in the Parliaments of Elizabeth I*, 3 vols. (Leicester: Leicester University Press, 1981–95).

Helmholz, R.H. ed. *Select Cases on Defamation to 1600* (London: Selden Society, 1985).

Hester, John. *The first part of the key of philosophie. Wherein is contained moste ex- [sic] excellent secretes of phisicke and philosophie, divided into twoo bookes.: In the firste is shewed the true and perfect order to distill ... In the seconde is shewed the true and perfect order to prepare, calcine, sublime, and dissolue all maner of mineralles.../First written in the Germaine tongue by the moste learned Theophrastus Paraselsus, and now published in the Englishe tongue by Ihon [sic] Hester practitioner in the arte of distillation...* (1580). STC (2nd ed.)/19181.5.

Historical Manuscripts Commission. *The Manuscripts of Rye and Hereford Corporations*, 13, Part 4.

Holland, Thomas. *Carmen funebre in mortem illustrissimi Comitis Leicestrensis, qui Corneburiae in agro Oxoniensi 4. Sept. 1588. vita defunctus est* (1588). STC (2nd ed.)/13595.5.

The Holy Bible conteyning the Old Testament, and the New: newly translated out of the originall tongues: & with the former translations diligently compared and reuised, by his Maiesties speciall co[m]mandement. Appointed to be read in churches (1611). STC (2nd ed.)/2216.

Hooker, Richard. "A Learned Discourse on Justification," in W. Speed Hill, ed. *Folger Library Edition of the Works of Richard Hooker, Vol. 5: Tractates and Sermons* (Cambridge, MA: Belknap Press of Harvard University Press, 1990), 105–70.

Hunnis, William. *A hyue full of hunnye contayning the firste booke of Moses, called Genesis. Turned into English meetre...* (1578). STC (2nd ed.)/13974.

Hyperius, Andreas. *The practise of preaching, otherwise called the Pathway to the pulpet conteyning an excellent method how to frame divine sermons, & to interpret the holy Scriptures according to the capacitie of the vulgar people.* John Ludham, trans. (1577). STC (2nd ed.)/11758.5.

Illyricus, Matthias Flacius. *Catalogus testivm Veritatis, Qvi ante nostram ætatem reclamarunt Papæ. Opus uaria rerum, hoc præsertim tempore scitu digniβimarum, cognitione refertum, ac lectu cum primus utile atq[ue] necessarium...* (Basil:1556). USTC 619735.

James VI & I, *Daemonologie in forme of a dialogue, diuided into three books* (Edinburgh: 1597). STC/239:13.

"A Joyfull newe ballad of the Royall entracnce of Quene E[lizabeth] in the Cetye of London the 24 of November in the 3i yere of hyr majesties Reigne to gyve god praise for the overhtrowe of the spanyardes," in Steven W. May and Arthur F. Marotti, *Ink, Stink Bait, Revenge, and Queen Elizabeth. A Yorkshire Yeoman's Household Book* (Ithaca: Cornell University Press, 2014).

Kassell, Lauren, Michael Hawkins, Robert Ralley, John Young, Joanne Edge, Janet Yvonne Martin-Portugues, and Natalie Kaoukji (eds.), 'Casebooks', The casebooks of Simon Forman and Richard Napier, 1596–1634: a digital edition, https://casebooks.lib.cam.ac.uk, accessed 26 January 2019.

Keating Clary, William, ed. *Liturgies and Occasional Forms of Prayer Set Forth in the Reign of Elizabeth* (Cambridge: Parker Society, 1847).

Kitchin, John. *Le Court Leete, et Court Baron, collect per Iohn Kitchin de Greys Inne un Apprentice in le Ley, et les cases et matters necessaries pur Seneshcals de ceux courts a scier, pur les Students de les measons de Chauncerie* (1580). STC (2nd ed.)/15017.

The Knack to Know and Honest Man, 1596, John S. Farmer, ed. (Toronto: Tudor Facsimile Texts, 1912).

Knappen, M.M., ed. *Two Elizabethan Puritan Diaries by Richard Rogers and Samuel Ward* (Chicago: American Society of Church History, 1933).

Knox, John. *The first blast of the trumpet against the monstruous regiment of women* (Geneva: 1558). STC/253:09.

La Marche, Olivier de. *The resolved gentleman.* Lewes Lewknor, trans. (1594). STC (2nd ed.)/15139.

Laneham, Robert. *A letter whearin part of the entertainment vntoo the Queenz Maiesty at Killingwoorth Castl in Warwik sheer in this soomerz progress 1575 is signified/from a freend officer attendant in coourt vntoo hiz freend a citizen and merchaunt of London* (1575). STC (2nd ed.)/15190.5

Larkin, James F. and Paul L. Hughes, eds. *Stuart Royal Proclamations, Vol. 1: Royal Proclamations of King James I 1603–1625* (Oxford: Oxford University Press, 1973).

Larkin, James F. and Paul L. Hughes, eds. *Tudor Royal Proclamations*, 3 vols. (New Haven: Yale University Press, 1964–69).

Leach, Arthur Francis, ed. *Educational Charters and Documents 598 to 1909* (Cambridge: Cambridge University Press, 1911).

Leadam, I.S., ed. *Select Cases in the Court of Requests 1497–1569* (London: Selden Society, 12, 1898).

Legate, Robert. *A briefe catechisme and dialogue betwene the husbande and his wyfe contaynynge a pyththy [sic] declaracyon of the Pater noster, Crede, and tene commaundementes, very necessary for all men to knowe. Ite[m] dyuerse other dialogues betwene the truthe and the unlearned man: wherein the truthe (which is Goddes worde) teacheth all symple and ignoraunte people what is necessary for them to knowe vnto their saluacyon* (1545). STC (2nd ed.)/4797.3.

Leroy, Louis. *Of the interchangeable course, or variety of things in the whole world and the concurrence of armes and learning, thorough the first and famousest nations: from the beginning of ciuility, and memory of man, to this present. Moreouer, whether it be true or no, that there can be nothing sayd, which hath not bin said heretofore: and that we ought by our owne inuentions to augment the doctrine of the auncients; not contenting our selues with translations, expositions, corrections, and abridgments of their writings.* R.A., trans. (1594). STC (2nd ed.)/15488.

Lewknor, Edward. *Threnodia in obitum D. Edouardi Lewknor Equitis, & D. Susannae coniugis charissimae. = Funerall verses vpon the death of the right worshipfull Sir Edvvard Levvkenor Knight, and Madame Susan his Lady With Deaths apologie, and a reioynder to the same* (1606). STC (2nd ed.)/15561.

Lewknor, Lewis. *A discourse of the usage of the English fugitives, by the Spaniard* (1595). STC (2nd ed.)/15563.

Lewknor, Lewis. *The estate of English fugitiues vnder the king of Spaine and his ministers Containing, besides, a discourse of the sayd Kings manner of gouernment, and the iniustice of many late dishonorable practises by him contriued* (1595). STC (2nd ed.)/15564.

Machyn, Henry. *The Diary of Henry Machyn Citizen and Merchant-Taylor of London (1550–1563).* J.G. Nichols, ed. (London: Camden Society, 1848).

Malynes, Gerard. *Consuetudo, vel lex mercatoria, or The ancient law-merchant Diuided into three parts: according to the essentiall parts of trafficke. Necessarie for all statesmen, iudges, magistrates, temporall and ciuile lawyers, mint-men, merchants, marriners, and all others negotiating in all places of the world* (1622). STC (2nd ed.)/17222.

Marcus, Leah S., Janel Mueller, and Mary Beth Rose, eds. *Elizabeth I. Collected Works* (Chicago: University of Chicago Press, 2000).

Martin, Dorcas. "An instruction for Christians, conteining a fruitfull and godlie exercise, as well in wholesome and fruitfull praiers..." in Thomas Bentley, ed. *The monument of matrones conteining seuen seuerall lamps of virginitie, or distinct treatises; whereof the first fiue concerne praier and meditation: the other two last, precepts and examples, as the woorthie works partlie of men, partlie of women; compiled for the necessarie vse of both sexes out of the sacred Scriptures, and other approoued authors* (1582). STC (2nd ed.)/1892.

May, Steven W. and Arthur F. Marotti. *Ink, Stink Bait, Revenge, and Queen Elizabeth. A Yorkshire Yeoman's Household Book* (Ithaca: Cornell University Press, 2014).

Mears, Natalie, Alasdair Raffe, Stephen Taylor, and Philip Williamson (with Lucy Bates), eds. *National Prayers. Special Worship Since the Reformation. Volume 1. Special Prayers, Fasts and Thanksgivings in the British Isles 1533–1688* (London: Church of England Record Society, 20, 2013).

Montaigne, Michel de. *The essayes or morall, politike and millitarie discourses of Lo: Michaell de Montaigne... The first booke...* John Florio, trans. (1603). STC (2nd ed.)/18041.

More Molyneux Family of Loseley Park, Historical Correspondence, vol. 8, 1564–1628 (Woking: Surrey History Centre). http://www.nationalarchives.gov.uk/a2a/records.aspx?cat=176-6729&cid=-1#-1 [Accessed November 29, 2018].

Mornay, Philippe de, seigneur du Plessis-Marly. *A woorke concerning the trewnesse of the Christian religion, written in French: against atheists, Epicures, Paynims, Iewes, Mahumetists, and other infidels.* Philip Sidney and Arthur Golding, trans. (1587). STC (2nd ed.)/18149.

Mulcaster, Richard. *Positions vvherin those primitiue circumstances be examined, which are necessarie for the training vp of children, either for skill in their booke, or health in their bodie* (1581). STC (2nd ed.)/18253.

Mulcaster, Richard. *The First Part of the Elementarie which Entreateth Chefelie of the right Writing of our English tung* (1582). STC (2nd ed.)/18250.

Muskett, J.J., ed. "The Diary of Adam Winthrop," in *The Winthrop Papers, Vol. I, 1498–1628* (Boston: Massachusetts Historical Society, 1929).

Nashe, Thomas. *The Works of Thomas Nashe*, 5 vols. Ronald B. McKerrow, ed. (London: Sidgwick & Jackson, 1910).

Nichols, John. *John Nichols's The Progresses and Public Processions of Queen Elizabeth I: A New Edition of the Early Modern Sources, Vol. I, 1533–1571.* Elizabeth Goldring, Faith Eales, Elizabeth Clark, and Jayne Elisabeth Archer, eds. (Oxford: Oxford University Press, 2012).

Nicholson, Brinsely, ed. *The Discoverie of Witchcraft by Reginald Scot* (London: Elliot Stock, 1886).

Nicholson, William ed. *The Remains of Edmund Grindal* (Cambridge: Parker Society, 1843).

Nostradamus, Michel. *The prognostication of maister Michael Nostredamus, doctour in phisick. In prouince for the yeare of our Lorde, 1559: With the predictions and presages of euery moneth* (1559). STC/2259.

Nowell, Alexander. *A Catechisme, or first instruction and learning of Christian religion. Translated out of Latine into Englishe* (1570). STC (2nd ed.)/18708

Nowell, Alexander, *A Catechism written in Latin by Alexander Nowell, Dean of St. Paul's; together with the Same Catechism translated in English by Thomas Norton*. G.E. Corrie, ed. (Cambridge: Cambridge University Press, 1853).

Parker, Kenneth and Eric C. Carlson, *"Practical Divinity." The Works and Life of Revd Richard Greenham* (Aldershot: Ashgate, 1998).

Parker, Matthew. *Correspondence of Matthew Parker, Archbishop of Canterbury*. Thomas T. Perowne, ed. (Cambridge: Parker Society, 1853).

Panvinio, Onofrio. *De primatu Petri et Apostolicae Sedis potestate libri tres ... contra Centuriarum auctores* (Venice: 1591). USTC 846557.

Peel, Albert, ed. *The Seconde Parte of a Register*, 2 vols. (Cambridge: Cambridge University Press, 1915).

Peele, James. *The maner and fourme how to kepe a perfecte reconyng after the order of the moste worthie and notable accompte, of debitour and creditour, set foorthe in certain tables, with a declaration thereunto belongyng, verie easie to be learned, and also profitable, not onely vnto suche, that trade in the facte of marchaundise, but also vnto any other estate, that will learne the same, 1553* (1554). STC (2nd ed.)/19547.

Peele, James. *The pathe waye to perfectnes, in th'accomptes of debitour, and creditour in manner of a dialogue, very pleasaunte and proffitable for marchauntes and all other that minde to frequente the same: once agayne set forthe, and verie muche enlarged...* (1569). STC (2nd ed.)/19548.

Perkins, William. *A golden chaine: or The description of theologie containing the order of the causes of saluation and damnation, according to Gods word... Hereunto is adioyned the order which M. Theodore Beza vsed in comforting afflicted consciences* (1600). STC (2nd ed.)/19646.

Perkins, William. *The first part of The cases of conscience Wherein specially, three maine questions concerning man, simply considered in himselfe, are propounded and resolued, according to the word of God* (1604), 43. STC (2nd ed.)/19668.

Perkins, William. *The arte of prophecying, or, A treatise concerning the sacred and onely true manner and methode of preaching first written in Latine by Master William Perkins; and now faithfully translated into English...* Thomas Tuke, trans. (1607). STC (2nd ed.)/19735.4.

Perkins, William. *The Second and Third Bookes of the Cases of Conscience in The whole treatise of the cases of conscience distinguished into three books... Newly corrected...* (1608). STC (2nd ed.)/19670.

Perkins, William. *The vvorkes of that famous and vvorthy minister of Christ in the Vniuersitie of Cambridge, Mr. William Perkins. The first volume: newly corrected according to his owne copies...* (1612–13). STC (2nd ed.)/19650.

Perkins, William. *The whole treatise of the cases of conscience distinguished into three bookes...* (1614), 284. STC (2nd ed.)/19671.5.

Perkins, William. *The Works of William Perkins*, Ian Breward, ed. (Appleford: The Sutton Courtney Press, 1970).

A petition directed to Her Most Excellent Maiestie wherein is deliuered 1. A meane howe to compound the ciuill dissention in the Church of England, 2. A proofe that they who write for reformation, do not offend against the stat. of 23. Eliz. c.2. and therefore till matters be compounded, deserue more fauour ...: here vnto is annexed, some opinions of such as sue for reformation ...: also, certayne articles vvherein is discouered the negligence of the bishoppes ...: lastlie, certayne questions or interrogatories dravvn by a fauourer of reformation... (1591). STC (2nd ed.)/1522a.

Pilkington, James. "A Confutacion of an Addition, with an Appologye Written and Cast in the Streets of West Chester, Against the Causes of Burnying Paule's Church in London...," in James Pilkington, *The Works of James Pilkington, B.D.* James Scholfield, ed. (Cambridge: Parker Society, 1842).

Pricke, Robert. *A verie godlie and learned sermon treating of mans mortalitie, and of the estate both of his bodie and soule after death. Preached at Denham in Suffolke. At the celebration of the solemne and mournfull funerals of the right orshipfull Sir Edward Lewknor Knight, and of the vertuous Ladie Susan, his wife, both at once. By M. Robert Pricke their beloued and faithfull minister: now also since that time (to the encrease of our sorow for the losse of so excellent a light) departed this life* (1608). STC (2nd ed.)/20338.

Primaudaye, Pierre de La. *The French academie wherin is discoursed the institution of maners, and whatsoeuer els concerneth the good and happie life of all estates and callings, by preceptes of doctrine, and examples of the liues of ancient sages and famous men: ... newly translated into English by T.B.* (1586). STC (2nd ed.)/15233.

Proffet, Nicolas. *Englands impenitencie under smiting, causing anger to continue, and the destroying hand of God to be stretched forth still ... preached before the Honourable House of Commons ... 1644.* (1645). Wing/P3647.

Rainolde, Richard. *A Booke Called the Foundacion of Rhetorike* (1563). STC (2nd edn)/20925a.5.

Rainolde, Richard. *A chronicle of all the noble emperours of the Romaines, from Iulius Caesar, orderly to this moste victorious Emperour Maximilian, that now gouerneth, with the great warres of Iulius Caesar, [and] Pompeius Magnus: setting forth the great power, and deuine prouidence of almighty God, in preseruing the godly princes and common wealthes* (1571). STC/393:05.

Rimbault, Edward F., ed. *The Old Cheque-Book, or Book of Remembrance of the Chapel Royal, from 1561 to 1744* (London: Camden Society n.s., 3, 1872).

Ramsay, G.D., ed. *John Isham Mercer and Merchant Adventurer. Two Account Books of a London Merchant in the Reign of Elizabeth I* (Northampton, Northamptonshire Record Society, 21, 1962).

"Regnans in Excelsis: Excommunicating Elizabeth I of England. Pope Pius V—1570." http://www.papalencyclicals.net/Pius05/p5regnans.htm [Accessed November 29, 2018].

Reynolds, William. *Calvino-Turcismus id est, Calvinisticae perfidiae cum Mahumetana collatio, et dilucida utriusque sectae confusio: quatuor libris explicata. Ad stabiliendam fidem orthodoxam.* William Gifford, ed. (Antwerp: 1597). USTC 402394.

Robinson, Hastings, ed. *The Zurich Letters*, 2 vols. (Cambridge: Parker Society, 1842–45).

Roma Gill, ed. *The Complete Works of Christopher Marlowe. Volume II. Dr Faustus* (Oxford: Clarendon Press, 1990).

Sander, Nicholas. *A briefe treatise of vsvrie* (1568). STC (2nd ed.)/21691.

Sanders, Nicholas. *The Rise and Growth of the Anglican Schism*, David Lewis, ed. (London: Burns and Oates, 1877).

Sandys, Edwin. *The sermons of Edwin Sandys, D.D., successively Bishop of Worcester and London and Archbishop of York.* John Ayre, ed. (Cambridge: Parker Society, 1841).

Scott, William. *The Modell of Poesye, An Original-Spelling Edition.* Gavin Alexander, ed. (Cambridge: 2013).

A second and third blast of retrait from plaies and theaters the one whereof was sounded by a reuerend byshop dead long since; the other by a worshipful and zealous gentleman now aliue: one showing the filthines of plaies in times past; the other the abhomination of theaters in the time present: both expresly prouing that that common-weale is nigh vnto the cursse of God, wherein either plaiers be made of, or theaters maintained. Set forth by Anglo-phile Eutheo (1580). STC (2nd ed.)/21677.

Selden, John. *The duello or single combat from antiquitie deriued into this kingdome of England, with seuerall kindes, and ceremonious formes thereof from good authority described* (1610). STC (2nd ed.)/22171.

Selden, John. *Iani Anglorum facies altera Memoriâ nempè à primulâ Henrici II. adusq[ue] abitionem quod occurrit prophanum Anglo-Britanniae ius resipiens succincto diegematikos connexum filo...* (1610). STC (2nd ed.)/22174.

Selden, John. *The historie of tithes that is, the practice of payment of them, the positiue laws made for them, the opinions touching the right of them : a review of it is also annext, which both confirmes it and directs in the vse of it* (1618). STC (2nd ed.)/22172.7.

Sermons, Or Homilies, Appointed to be Read in Churches in the Time of Queen Elizabeth of Famous Memory (Oxford: Oxford University Press, 1840).

Sidney, Phillip. *An apologie for poetrie* (1595). STC (2nd ed.)/22534.

A Skeltonicall salutation, or condigne gratulation, and iust vexation of the Spanish nation that in a bravado, spent many a crusado, in setting forth an armado England to invado (1589). STC (2nd ed.)/22620.

Smith, Henry. *The Works of Henry Smith*, 2 vols. Thomas Smith, ed. (Edinburgh: James Nichol, 1866).

Smith, Thomas. *De Republica Anglorum*, Mary Dewar, ed. (Cambridge: Cambridge University Press, 1982).

Smyth, John. *A paterne of true prayer A learned and comfortable exposition or commentarie vpon the Lords prayer: wherein the doctrine of the substance and circumstances of true inuocation is euidently and fully declared out of the holie Scriptures* (1605). STC (2nd ed.)/22877.1.

Smyth, John. *The Works of John Smyth, Fellow of Christ's College, 1594–8.* W.T. Whitley, ed. (Cambridge: Cambridge University Press, 1915).

Southwell, Robert. *An epistle of comfort to the reuerend priestes, & to the honorable, worshipful, & other of the laye sort restrayned in durance for the Catholicke faith* (1587). STC (2nd ed.)/22946.

Southwell, Robert. "Letter to Sir Robert Cecil," in *Nancy Pollard Brown, ed. Robert Southwell, S.J. Two Letters and Short Rules of a Good Life* (Charlottesville: University of Virginia Press for the Folger Shakespeare Library, 1973).

Spenser, Edmund. *Spenser's The Faerie Queene*, bk. I. George Armstrong Wauchope, ed. (New York: Macmillan, 1921).

Spenser, Edmund. *The Shepherds Calendar* in *The Yale Edition of the Shorter Poems of Edmund Spenser.* William A. Oram, Einar Bjorvand, Ronald Bond, Thomas H. Cain, Alexander Dunlop, and Richard Schell, eds. (New Haven: Yale University Press, 1989).

Stapleton, Thomas. *A fortresse of the faith first planted amonge vs englishmen, and continued hitherto in the vniuersall Church of Christ. The faith of which time protestants call, papistry* (Antwerp: 1565). STC (2nd ed.)/23232.

Stapleton, Thomas, trans. *The history of the Church of Englande. Compiled by Venerable Bede, Englishman* (Antwerp: 1565). STC 2nd ed./1778.

Sternhold, Thomas, John Hopkins, and William Whittingham, eds. *The whole boke of Psalmes collected into Englishe metre by T. Sternhold, W. Whitingham, I. Hopkins, and others: conferred with Hebrue, with apt notes. Newly set forth and allowed to be song of all the people together, in all churches, before and after morning and euening prayer: as also before & after the sermons, and moreouer in priuate houses, for their godly solace and comfort, laying apart all ungodly songes and balladdes, which tend onely to the nourishing of vyce and corrupting of youth...* (1577). STC (2nd ed.)/2448.

Strype, John. *The Life and Acts of the Most Reverend Father in God, John Whitgift, D.D.*, 3 vols. (London: 1718).

Strype, John. *The Annals of the Reformation*, 4 vols. (Oxford: 1824).

Stubbes, Phillip. *A christal glasse for christian women containing, a most excellent discourse, of the godly life and Christian death of Mistresse Katherine Stubs, who departed this life in Burton vpon Trent, in Staffordshire the 14. day of December. 1590. With a most heauenly confession of the Christian faith, which shee made a little before her departure: as also a wonderfull combate betwixt Sathan and her soule: worthie to be imprinted in letters of golde, and are to be engrauen in the tables of euery Christian heart. Set downe word for word, as she spake it, as neere as could be gathered...* (1592). STC (2nd ed.)/23382.

Stubbes, Phillip. *A motiue to good workes Or rather, to true Christianite indeede...* (1593). STC (2nd ed.)/23397.

Stubbes, Philip. *The Anatomie of Abuses*, Margaret Jane Kidnie, ed. (Tempe: Renaissance English Text Society, 2002).

Stubbings, Frank, trans. and ed. *The Statutes of Sir Walter Mildmay Kt Chancellor of the Exchequer and one of Her Majesty's Privy Councillors; authorized by him for the government of Emmanuel College founded by him* (Cambridge: Cambridge University Press, 1983).

Sutcliffe, Matthew. *De Turcopapismo: hoc est, De Turcarum & Papistarum aduersùs Christi ecclesiam & fidem coniuratione, eorumq[ue] in religione & moribus consensione & similitudine, liber unus : eidem praeterea adiuncti sunt, De Turcopapistarum maledictis & calumnijs, aduersus Gulielmi Giffordi ... volumen illud contumeliosissimum, quod ille Caluinoturcismus inscripsit, libri quatuor* (1599). STC (2nd ed.), 23460.

Sutcliffe, Matthew. *De pontifice Romano, eiusque iniustissima in Ecclesia dominatione, aduersùs Robertum Bellarminum, & vniuersum Iebusitarum sodalitium, libri quinque* (1599). STC (2nd ed.)/23457.

Sutton, Dana F., ed. *Unpublished Works by William Alabaster (1568–1640)* (Salzburg: University of Salzburg Studies in English Literature Elizabethan and Renaissance Studies, 126, 1997).

Taverner, Richard. *A catechisme or institution of the christen religion* (1539). STC (2nd ed.)/23709.

Travers, Walter. *A ful and plaine declaration of ecclesiastical discipline out of the Word of God, and of the declining of the Church of England from the same* (1588). STC (2nd ed.)/24185.

Travers, Walter. "A Supplication made to the Privy Counsel," in W. Speed Hill, ed. *Folger Library Edition of the Works of Richard Hooker, Vol. 5: Tractates and Sermons* (Cambridge, MA: Belknap Press of Harvard University Press, 1990), 189–210.

Turner, William. *The first and seconde partes of the herbal ... lately ouersene, corrected and enlarged with the thirde parte, lately gathered, and nowe set oute with the names of the herbes, in Greke Latin, English, Duche, Frenche, and in the apothecaries and herbaries Latin, with the properties, degrees, and naturall places of the same. Here vnto is ioyned also a booke of the bath of Bath in*

England, and of the vertues of the same with diuerse other bathes... (1568). STC (2nd ed.)/24367.

Turner, William. *A new boke of the natures and properties of all wines that are commonly vsed here in England with a confutation of an errour of some men, that holde, that Rhennish and other small white wines ought not to be drunken of them that either haue, or are in daunger of the stone, the revine, and diuers other diseases ... Whereunto is annexed the booke of the natures and vertues of triacles, newly corrected...* (1568). STC (2nd ed.)/24360.

Valades, Diego. *Rhetorica christiana: ad concionandi et orandi vsvm accommodata, vtrivsq[ue] facvltatis exemplis svo loco insertis* (Perugia: 1579). USTC 861655.

Vaughan, Lewis. *A new almanacke and prognostication, collected for the yeare of our Lord God. M.D.L.IX. Wherein is expressed the chaunge and full of the moone, with theyr quarters. The varietie of the ayre, and also of the windes throughout the whole yeare, with infortunate times to bie and sell, take medycine, sowe, plante, and iourney in, both by lande and by water, and other necessarye things...* (1558). STC (2nd ed.)/520.

West, William. *Symbolaeography which may be termed the art, description or image of instruments, extra-iudicial, as couenants, contracts, obligations, conditions, feffements, graunts, wills, &c. Or the paterne of praesidents. Or the notarie or scriuener* (1592). STC (2nd. ed.)/25267a.

Whetstone, George. *A Remembraunce of the Precious Vertues of the Right Honourable and Reuerend Iudge, Sir Iames Dier, Knight, Lord cheefe Iustice of the Common Pleas who disseased at great Stawghton, in Huntingdon shire, the 24. of Marche, anno. 1582* (1582). STC (2nd edn)/25345.

Whitaker, William. *A Disputation on Holy Scripture: Against the Papists, especially Bellarmine and Stapleton.* William Fitzgerald, ed. (Cambridge: Parker Society, 1849).

Whitelocke, James. *Liber Famelicus of Sir James Whitelocke.* John Bruce, ed. (London: Camden Society OS 70, 1858).

Whythorne, Thomas. *Songes for Three, Fower and Five Voyces* (1571). STC 25584-1844.

Whythorne, Thomas. *Cantus. Of duos, or songs for tvvo voices, composed and made by Thomas Whythorne Gent. Of the which, some be playne and easie to be sung, or played on musicall instruments, & be made for young beginners of both those sorts. And the rest of these Duos be made and set foorth for those that be more perfect in singing or playing as aforesaid, all the which be divided into three parts* (1590). STC 25583-1192.

Whythorne, Thomas. *The Autobiography of Thomas Whythorne.* James M. Osborn, ed. (Oxford: Oxford University Press, 1961).

Wilson, Thomas, trans. *The Three Orations of Demosthenes Chiefe Orator among the Grecians ... against king Philip of Macedonie: most nedefull to be redde in these daungerous dayes, of all them that loue their countries libertie, and desire to take warning for their better auayle, by example of others...* (1570). STC (2nd edn)/6578.

Wimbledon, Thomas. *A godly sermon no les fruitfull the[n] famous made in the yeare of our Lord God M.CCC.lxxxviij. and found out beyng hyd in a wall. Which sermon is here set forth by the old copy, with out adding or diminishing, saue the old [and] rude English here and there amended* (1575). STC (2nd ed.)/25827.5.

Wright, Louis B., ed. *Advice to a Son. Precepts of Lord Burghley, Sir Walter Raleigh, and Francis Osborne* (Ithaca: Cornell University Press for Folger Shakespeare Library, 1962).

Secondary Bibliography

Ailes, Adrian. "'A herald Kate? O put me in thy books.' Shakespeare, the Heralds' Visitations and a New Visitation Address," in Nigel Ramsay, ed. *Heralds and Heraldry in Shakespeare's England* (Donnington: Shaun Tyas, 2014), 105–24.

Alexander, Gavin. "The Musical Sidneys." *John Donne Journal* 2006; 25, 65–106.

Allen, Douglas. *The Institutional Revolution. Measurement and the Economic Emergence of the Modern World* (Chicago: University of Chicago Press, 2011).

Amussen, Susan D. "Social Hierarchies," in Susan Doran and Norman Jones, *The Elizabethan World* (London: Routledge, 2011), 271–84.

Appleby, Joyce. *Economic Thought and Ideology in Seventeenth-Century England* (Princeton: Princeton University Press, 1978).

Archer, Ian W. "Discourses of History in Elizabethan and Early Stuart London," in Paulina Kewes, ed. *The Uses of History in Early Modern England* (San Marino: Huntington Library, 2006), 201–22.

Armstrong, Kate. "Sermons in Performance," in Peter McCullough, Hugh Adlington, and Emma Rhatigan, eds. *The Oxford Handbook of the Early Modern Sermon* (Oxford: Oxford University Press, 2011), 120–36.

Ash, Eric. *Power, Knowledge and Expertise in Elizabethan England* (Baltimore: Johns Hopkins University Press, 2004).

Bailey, Gauvin Alexander. *Art on the Jesuit Missions in Asia and Latin America, 1542–1773* (Toronto: University of Toronto Press, 1999).

Baldwin, Frances Elizabeth. *Sumptuary Legislation and Personal Regulation in England* (Baltimore: Johns Hopkins Press, 1926).

Bayer, Penny, "Margaret Clifford's Alchemical Receipt Book and the John Dee Circle." *Ambix* 2005; 52(3), 271–84.

Birkholz, Daniel. "The Gough Map Revisited: Thomas Butler's 'The Mape off Ynglonnd,' c.1547–1554." *Imago Mundi* 2006; 58(1), 23–47.

Brett, Philip. *William Byrd and His Contemporaries. Essays and a Monograph*, Joseph Kerman and Davitt Moroney, eds. (Berkeley: University of California Press, 2007).

Being Elizabethan: Understanding Shakespeare's Neighbors, First Edition. Norman Jones.
© 2020 John Wiley & Sons, Inc. Published 2020 by John Wiley & Sons, Inc.

Brown, Laura Feitzinger. "Slippery Listening: Anxious Clergy and Lay Listeners' Power in Early Modern England." *The Sixteenth Century Journal* 2016; 47(1), 3–24.

Brown, Nancy Pollard. "Southwell, Robert [St Robert Southwell] (1561–1595)," in *Oxford Dictionary of National Biography* (Oxford: Oxford University Press, 2004). http://www.oxforddnb.com/view/article/26064 [Accessed November 29, 2018].

Carlson, Eric Josef. "Funeral Sermons as Sources: The Example of Female Piety in Pre-1640 Sermons." *Albion: A Quarterly Journal Concerned with British Studies* 2000; 32(4), 567–97.

Carruthers, Bruce G. and Wendy Nelson Espeland. "Accounting for Rationality: Double-Entry Bookkeeping and the Rhetoric of Economic Rationality." *American Journal of Sociology* 1991; 97(1), 31–69.

Charlesworth, Lorie. *Welfare's Forgotten Past: A Socio-Legal History of the Poor Law* (Oxford: Routledge, 2010).

Colbert, Carolyn. "'Mary hath chosen the best part': The Bishop of Winchester's Funeral Sermon for Mary Tudor," in Elizabeth Evenden and Vivienne Westbrook, eds. *Catholic Renewal and Protestant Resistance in Marian England* (Farnham: Ashgate, 2015), 273–92.

Collinson, Patrick. *The Elizabethan Puritan Movement* (London: Jonathan Cape, 1967).

Collinson, Patrick. "Magistracy and Ministry: A Suffolk Miniature," in R. Buick Knox, ed. *Reformation Conformity and Dissent* (London: 1977), 70–91.

Collinson, Patrick. *Archbishop Grindal 1519–1583. The Struggle for a Reformed Church* (Berkeley: University of California Press, 1979).

Cousin-Desjobert, Jacqueline. *La théorie et la pratique d'un éducateur élisabéthain. Richard Mulcaster c. 1531–1611* (Paris: Éditions SPM, 2003).

Cross, Clair. *The Puritan Earl. The Life of Henry Hastings Third Earl of Huntingdon 1536–1595* (London: Macmillan, 1966).

Cummings, Brian. *The Literary Culture of the Reformation. Grammar and Grace* (Oxford: Oxford University Press, 2002).

Cust, Richard. "Catholicism, Antiquarianism and Gentry Honour: The Writings of Sir Thomas Shirley." *Midland History* 1988; 23, 40–70.

Daniel, Richard Warren. "'Have a little book in thy Conscience, and write therein': Writing the Puritan Conscience, 1600–1650," in Jonathan Willis, ed. *Sin and Salvation in Reformation England* (Farnham: Ashgate, 2015), 245–58.

Dean, David. *Law Making and Society in Late Elizabethan England* (Cambridge: Cambridge University Press, 1996).

Dean, David and Norman Jones, eds. *The Parliaments of Elizabethan England* (Oxford: Basil Blackwell, 1990).

Dutton, Richard. "Jurisdiction of Theater and Censorship," in Arthur F. Kinney, ed. *A Companion to Renaissance Drama* (Oxford: Blackwell, 2002), 223–236.

Eden, Peter. "Three Elizabethan estate Surveyors: Peter Kempe, Thomas Clerke, and Thomas Langdon," in Sarah Tyacke, ed. *English Map-Making 1500–1650* (London: The British Library, 1983), 68–84.

Emmison, F.G. *Elizabethan Life: Morals and the Church Courts* (Chelmsford: Essex County Council, 1973).

Feingold, Mordechai. *The Mathematician's Apprenticeship. Science, Universities, and Society in England 1560–1640* (Cambridge: Cambridge University Press, 1984).

Fellerer, K. G. and Moses Hadas, trans. "Church Music and the Council of Trent." *The Musical Quarterly* 1953; 39(4), 576–94.

Ferrell, Lori Anne. "Transfiguring Theology: William Perkins and Calvinist Aesthetics," in Christopher Highley and John King, eds. *John Foxe and His World* (Aldershot: Ashgate, 2002), 160–79.

Ferrell, Lori Anne. "The Preachers' Bibles," in Peter McCullough, Hugh Adlington, and Emma Rhatigan, eds. *The Oxford Handbook of the Early Modern Sermon* (Oxford: Oxford University Press, 2011), 21–33.

Fletcher, Anthony. "Prescription and Practice: Protestantism and the Upbringing of Children, 1560–1700." *Studies in Church History* 1994; 31, 325–46.

Fox, Adam. "Remembering the Past in Early Modern England: Oral and Written Tradition." *Transactions of the Royal Historical Society*, 6th series, 1999; 9, 233–56.

Friedman, Alice T. "Portrait of a Marriage: The Willoughby Letters of 1585–1586." *Signs* 1986; 11(3), 542–55.

Gibson, Kenneth. "Downham, George (d. 1634)," in *Oxford Dictionary of National Biography* (Oxford: Oxford University Press, 2004). http://www.oxforddnb. com/view/article/7977 [Accessed November 29, 2018].

Goldring, Elizabeth. *Robert Dudley, Earl of Leicester, and the World of Elizabethan Art. Painting and Patronage at the Court of Elizabeth* (New Haven: Yale University Press, 2014).

Gordon, Andrew and Thomas Rist, eds. *The Arts of Remembrance in Early Modern England. Memorial Cultures of the Post Reformation* (Farnham: Ashgate, 2013).

Grafton, Anthony. *What Was History? The Art of History in Early Modern Europe* (Cambridge: Cambridge University Press, 2007).

Green, Ian. *The Christian ABC. Catechisms and Catechizing in England c. 1530–1740* (Oxford: Clarendon Press, 1996).

Greenslade, S.L. "The Faculty of Theology," in James McConica, ed. *The History of the University of Oxford. III. The Collegiate University* (Oxford: Oxford University Press, 1986), 295–334.

Griffiths, Paul. *Youth and Authority. Formative Experiences in England 1560–1640* (Oxford: Clarendon Press, 1996).

Griffith, William P. "Jesus College, Oxford, and Wales: the first half-century." *Transactions of the Honourable Society of Cymmrodorion, 1996, New Series, Vol. 3* 1997, 29–44.

Guinn-Chipman, Susan. *Religious Space in Reformation England: Contesting the Past* (London: Pickering and Chato, 2013).

Haigh, Christopher. *The Plain Man's Pathways to Heaven. Kinds of Christianity in Post Reformation England* (Oxford: Oxford University Press, 2007).

Hamilton, Sidney Graves. *Hertford College* (London: F.E. Robinson, 1903).

Hamling, Tara. *Decorating the "Godly" Household. Religious Art in Post-Reformation Britain* (New Haven: Yale University Press, 2010).

Haugaard, William P. "The Controversy and its Dissemination," in W. Speed Hill, ed. *The Folger Library Edition of the Works of Richard Hooker* (Cambridge, MA: Harvard University Press, 1990), V, 264–9.

Helmholz, R.H. *Roman Canon Law in Reformation England* (Cambridge: Cambridge University Press, 1990).

Hindle, Steve. "Hierarchy and Community in the Elizabethan Parish: The Swallowfield Articles of 1596." *The Historical Journal* 1999; 42(3), 835–51.

Hindle, Steve. *On the Parish? The Micro-Politics of Poor Relief in Rural England, c. 1550–1750* (Oxford: Oxford University Press, 2004).

Hindle, Steve. "'Bleeding Afresh'? The Affray and Murder at Nantwich 19 December, 1572," in Anglea McShane and Garthine Waler, eds. *The Extraordinary and the Everyday in Early Modern England* (London: Palgrave Macmillan, 2010), 224–45.

Hindle, Steve. "Poverty and the Poor Laws," in Susan Doran and Norman Jones, *The Elizabethan World* (2011), 301–15.

Houlbrooke, Ralph A. *The English Family 1450–1700* (London: Routledge, 1988).

Hutton, Ronald. *The Rise and Fall of Merry England. The Ritual Year 1400–1700* (Oxford: Oxford University Press, 1996).

Ingram, Martin. "Who Killed Robin Hood? Transformations in Popular Culture," in Susan Doran and Norman Jones, eds. *The Elizabethan World* (London: Routledge, 2011), 461–81.

Ingram, Martin. *Carnal Knowledge: Regulating sex in England, 1470–1600* (Cambridge: Cambridge University Press, 2017).

Jenkins, R. B. *Henry Smith: England's Silver-Tongued Preacher* (Macon: Mercer University Press, 1983).

Jensen, Freya Cox. *Reading the Roman Republic in Early Modern England* (Leiden, Boston: Brill, 2012).

Jones, H. Stuart. "The Foundation and History of the Camden Chair By the late H. STUART JONES Camden Professor, 1920–1927." *Oxoniensia* 1943–44, 169–92. http://oxoniensia.org/volumes/1943-4/jones.pdf [Accessed November 29, 2018].

Jones, Norman. "The Adaptation of Tradition: The Image of the Turk in Protestant England." *East European Quarterly East European Quarterly* 1978; 12(2), 161–75.

Jones, Norman. "Matthew Parker, John Bale, and the Magdeburg Centuriators." *The Sixteenth Century Journal* 1981; 12(3), 35–49.

Jones, Norman. *Faith by Statute. Parliament and the Settlement of Religion 1559* (London: Royal Historical Society, 1982).

Jones, Norman. "Elizabeth, Edification, and the Latin Prayer Book of 1560." *Church History* 1984; 53(2), 174–86.

Jones, Norman. *The Birth of the Elizabethan Age. England in the 1560s* (Oxford: Blackwell, 1993).

Jones, Norman. "Defining Superstitions: Treasonous Catholics and the Act Against Witchcraft of 1563," in Charles Carlton, ed. *State, Sovereigns and Society in Early Modern England in Honor of A.J. Slavin* (London: Sutton Publishing, 1998), 187–203.

Jones, Norman. *The English Reformation. Religion and Cultural Adaptation* (Oxford, Blackwell, 2002).

Jones, Norman. "David Lewis Founding Principal of Jesus College." *Jesus College Record* 2009; 33–42.

Jones, Norman. *Governing by Virtue. Lord Burghley and the Management of Elizabethan England* (Oxford: Oxford University Press, 2015).

Jones, Norman. "The Cambridge Connection and the Shaping of the Elizabethan State," in John McDiarmid, ed. *The Cambridge Connection in Tudor England: Humanism, Reform, Rhetoric, Politics* (Leiden: Brill, 2019).

Jones, Norman and Paul W. White. "*Gorboduc* and Royal Marriage Politics: An Elizabethan Playgoer's Report of the Premiere Performance." *English Literary Renaissance* 1996; 26, 3–17.

Jones, Peter Murray. "Thomas Lorkyn's Dissections, 1564/5 and 1566/7." *Transactions of the Cambridge Bibliographical Society* 1988; 9(3), 209–29.

Jones, William. "The Foundations of English Bankruptcy: Statutes and Commissions in the Early Modern Period." *Transactions of the American Philosophical Society* 1979; 69(3), 1–63.

Kallendorf, Hilaire. "Tears in the Desert: Baroque Adaptations of the Book of Lamentations by John Donne and Francisco de Quevedo." *Journal of Medieval and Early Modern Studies* 2009; 39.1, 31–42.

Kassell, Lauren. *Medicine and Magic in Elizabethan London* (Oxford: Oxford University Press, 2005).

Kastan, David Scott. *A Will To Believe. Shakespeare's Religion* (Oxford: Oxford University Press, 2014).

Kaufman, Peter Iver. *Prayer, Despair, and Drama. Elizabethan Introspection* (Urbana: University of Illinois Press, 1996).

Kaufman, Peter Iver. *Thinking of the Laity in Later Tudor England* (South Bend: University of Notre Dame Press, 2004).

Kaufman, Peter Iver. "The Godly, Godlier and Godliest," in Susan Doran and Norman Jones, eds. *The Elizabethan World* (London: Routledge, 2011), 238–253.

Kewes, Paulina. "Roman History, Essex, and Late Elizabethan Political Culture," in R. Malcolm Smuts, ed. *The Oxford Handbook of the Age of Shakespeare* (Oxford: Oxford University Press, 2016), 262–8.

Kneidel, Greg. "*Ars Praedicandi*: Theories and Practice," in Peter McCullough, Hugh Adlington, and Emma Rhatigan, eds. *The Oxford Handbook of the Early Modern Sermon* (Oxford: Oxford University Press, 2011), 3–20.

LaBouff, Nicole. "An Unlikely Christian Humanist: How Bess of Hardwick (ca. 1527–1608) Answered the 'Woman Question." *The Sixteenth Century Journal* 2016; 47(4), 847–82.

Lehmberg, Stanford E. *The Reformation of Cathedrals. Cathedrals in English Society, 1485–1603* (Princeton: Princeton University Press, 1988).

Levack, Brian P. "Cowell, John (1554–1611)," in *Oxford Dictionary of National Biography* (Oxford; Oxford University Press, 2004). http://www.oxforddnb.com/view/article/6490 [Accessed November 29, 2018].

Lewalski, Barbara K. "Re-writing Patriarchy and Patronage: Margaret Clifford, Anne Clifford, and Aemilia Lanyer." *The Yearbook of English Studies, Vol. 21, Politics, Patronage and Literature in England 1558–1658* 1991; 87–106.

Llewellyn, Nigel. *Funeral Monuments in Post-Reformation England* (Cambridge: Cambridge University Press, 2000).

MacCulloch, Diarmaid. *Suffolk and the Tudors. Politics and Religion in an English County 1500–1600* (Oxford: Clarendon Press, 1986).

MacCulloch, Dairmaid. *Thomas Cranmer* (New Haven: Yale University Press, 1996).

Manley, Lawrence. "Theatre," in Susan Doran and Norman Jones, eds. *The Elizabethan World* (London: Routledge, 2011), 531–49.

Manning, Roger B. *Religion and Society in Elizabethan Sussex: A Study of the Enforcement of the Religious Settlement, 1558–1603* (Leicester: Leicester University Press, 1969).

Marr, Alexander. "Pregnant Wit: *Ingegno* in Renaissance England." *British Art Studies* 2015; 1. https://dx.doi.org/10.17658/issn.2058-5462/issue-01/amarr [Accessed November 29, 2018].

Marsh, Christopher. *Music and Society in Early Modern England* (Cambridge: Cambridge University Press, 2010).

Marshall, Peter. "'The Map of God's Word': Geographies of the Afterlife in Tudor and Early Stuart England," in Bruce Gordon and Peter Marshall, eds. *The Place of the Dead. Death and Remebrance in Late Medieval and Early Modern England* (Cambridge: Cambridge University Press, 2000).

Mateer, David. "William Byrd's Middlesex Recusancy." *Music & Letters* 1997; 78(1), 1–14.

May, Steven W. "Poetry," in Susan Doran and Norman Jones, eds. *The Elizabethan World* (London: Routledge, 2011), 550–66.

McClain, Lisa. *Lest We Be Damned. Practical Innovation and Lived Experience among Catholics in Protestant England, 1559–1642* (London: Routledge, 2004).

McDonald, Grantley. "Music, Spirit and Ecclesiastical Politics in Elizabethan England: John Case and his *Apologia Musices*," in Steffen Schneider, ed.

Aisthetics of the Spirits. Spirits in Early Modern Science, Religion, Literature and Music (Göttingen: V&R Unipress, 2015), 477–98.

McGee, J. Sears. *An Industrious Mind. The Worlds of Sir Simonds D'Ewes* (Stanford: Stanford University Press, 2015).

McGrade, A. S. "Hooker, Richard (1554–1600)," in *Oxford Dictionary of National Biography* (Oxford: Oxford University Press, 2004). http://www.oxforddnb. com/view/article/13696 [Accessed November 29, 2018].

McInnes, Allan I. "The Multiple Kingdoms of Britain and Ireland: The 'British Problem,'" in Barry Coward, ed. *A Companion to Stuart Britain* (Oxford: Wiley-Blackwell, 2003), 3–25.

Meakin, H.L. *The Painted Closet of Lady Anne Bacon Drury* (Farnham: Ashgate, 2013).

Mitchell, Rose. "Maps in Sixteenth-Century English Law Courts." *Imago Mundi* 2006; 58(2), 212–19.

Morgan, Victor. "The Literary Image of Globes and Maps in Early Modern England," in Sarah Tyacke, ed. *English Map-Making 1500–1650* (London: The British Library, 1983), 46–56.

Moseley, C.W.R.D. "A Portrait of Sir Christopher Hatton, Erasmus and an Emblem of Alciato: Some Questions." *The Antiquaries Journal* 2006; 86, 373–9.

Muldrew, Craig. *The Economy of Obligation: The Culture of Credit and Social Relations in Early Modern England* (London: Macmillan, 1998).

Murray, Molly. *The Poetics of Conversion in Early Modern English Literature. Verse and Change from Donne to Dryden* (Cambridge: Cambridge University Press, 2009).

Newman, Kira L.S. "Shutt Up: Bubonic Plague and Quarantine in Early Modern England." *Journal of Social History* 2012; 45(3), 809–34.

Norton, David. *The King James Bible. A Short History form Tyndale to Today* (Cambridge: Cambridge University Press, 2011).

Oldridge, Darren. "Witchcraft and the Devil," in Susan Doran and Norman Jones, eds. The Elizabethan World (London: Routledge, 2011), 483–94.

Oldroyd, David. "John Johnson's Letters: The Accounting Role of Tudor Merchants' Correspondence." *Accounting Historians Journal* 1998; 25(1). http:// www.accountingin.com/accounting-historians-journal/volume-25-number-1/ john-johnsons-letters-the-accounting-role-of-tudor-merchants-correspondence/ [Accessed November 29, 2018].

Parker, Kenneth L. *The English Sabbath. A Study of Doctrine and Discipline from the Reformation to the Civil War* (Cambridge: Cambridge University Press, 1988).

Parker, Kenneth and Eric C. Carlson. *"Practical Divinity." The Works and Life of Revd Richard Greenham* (Aldershot: Ashgate, 1998).

Peck, Linda Levy. *Court Patronage and Corruption in Early Stuart England* (London: Routledge, 1993).

Pohl, Benjamin and Leah Tether. "Books Fit for a King: The Presentation Copies of Martin Bucer's *De regno Christi* (London, British Library, Royal MS. 8 B. VII) and Johannes Sturm's *De periodis* (Cambridge, Trinity College, II.12.21 and London, British Library, C.24.e.5)." *Electronic British Library Journal* 2015; 7, 1–35. https://www.bl.uk/eblj/2015articles/pdf/ebljarticle72015.pdf [Accessed November 29, 2018].

Pollock, Linda. *With Faith and Physic. The life of a Tudor Gentlewoman Lady Grace Mildmay* (London: 1993).

Popper, Nicholas. *Walter Ralegh's History of the World and the Historical Culture of the Late Renaissance* (Chicago: University of Chicago Press, 2012).

Porter, H.C. *Reformation and Reaction in Tudor Cambridge* (Hamden: Archon Books, 1972).

Questier, Michael. *Catholicism and Community in Early Modern England* (Cambridge: Cambridge University Press, 2006).

Ramsay, Nigel, ed. *Heralds and Heraldry in Shakespeare's England* (Donnington: Shaun Tyas, 2014).

Ramsay, Nigel. "'William Smith, Rouge Dragon Pursuivant' With an Edition by Ann Payne of Smith's MS Tract on Abuses Committed by the Painters and Others to the Detriment of the Heralds," in Nigel Ramsay, ed. *Heralds and Heraldry in Shakespeare's England* (Donnington: Shaun Tyas, 2014), 26–68.

Ramsey, P. "Some Tudor Merchants' Accounts," in A.C. Liulelon and B.S.Yamey, eds. *Studies in the History of Accounting* (London: Sweet & Maxwell, 1956), 185–201.

Richey, Esther Gilman. "'To Undoe the Booke': Cornelius Agrippa, Aemilia Lanyer and the Subversion of Pauline Authority." *English Literary Renaissance* 1997; 27.1, 106–28.

Rose, Elliot. *Cases of Conscience. Alternatives Open to Recusants and Puritans Under Elizabeth I and James I* (Cambridge: Cambridge University Press, 1975).

Ryan, John. "Historical Note: Did Double-Entry Bookkeeping Contribute to Economic Development, Specifically the Introduction of Capitalism?" *Australasian Accounting Business and Finance Journal* 2014; 8(3), 85–97.

Ryrie, Alec. "'Protestantism' as a Historical Category." *Transactions of the Royal Historical Society*, Sixth Series 2016; 26, 59–77.

Sacks, David Harris. "Commonwealth Discourse and Economic Thought. The Morality of Exchange," in Susan Doran and Norman Jones, eds. *The Elizabethan World* (London: Routledge, 2011), 389–410.

Schmitt, Charles B. *John Case and Aristotelianism in Renaissance England* (Kingston, Montreal: McGill-Queen's University Press, 1983).

Sharpe, J.A. *Sexual Defamation and Sexual Slander in Early Modern England: The Church Courts at York*, Borthwick Papers No. 58 (York: Borthwick Institute of Historical Research, 1980).

Sherlock, Peter. *Monuments and Memory in Early Modern England* (Aldershot: Ashgate, 2008).

Shuger, Deborah. "'Societie Supernaturall.' The Imagined Community of Hooker's *Lawes*," in Arthur Stephen McGrade, ed. *Richard Hooker and the Construction of Christian Community* (Tempe: MRTS, 1997), 307–29.

Shuger, Debora. *Censorship and Cultural Sensibility. The Regulation of Language in Tudor-Stuart England* (Philadelphia: University of Pennsylvania Press, 2006).

Slack, Paul. *The Impact of Plague in Tudor and Stuart England* (Oxford: Clarendon Press, 1990).

Sluhovsky, Moshe. *Becoming a New Self. Practices of Belief in Early Modern Catholicism* (Chicago: University of Chicago Press, 2017).

Smuts, Malcolm. "Varieties of Tacitism," forthcoming in Paulina Kewes, ed. *Ancient Rome and Early Modern England: History, Literature, and Political Imagination*. My thanks to Prof. Smuts for allowing me to see this pre-publication.

Snow, Vernon F., ed. *Parliament in Elizabethan England, John Hooker's Order and Usage* (New Haven: Yale University Press, 1971).

Soens, Lewis. *Sir Philip Sidney's Defense of Poesy* (Lincoln: University of Nebraska Press, 1970).

Sommerville, C. Johan. *The Secularization of Early Modern England. From Religious Culture to Religious Faith* (Oxford: Oxford University Press, 1992).

Stuckey, Michael. "'…this Society tendeth…': Elite Prosopography in Elizabethan Legal History." *Prosopon: The Journal of Prosopography* 2006; 1, 1–58.

Targoff, Ramie. *Common Prayer. The Language of Public Devotion in Early Modern England* (Chicago: University of Chicago Press, 2001).

Taylor, Charles. *Sources of the Self. The Making of Modern Identity* (Cambridge: Cambridge University Press, 2012).

Temperley, Nicholas. "'All Skillful Praises Sing': How Congregations Sang the Psalms in Early Modern England." *Renaissance Studies* 2015; 29(4), 531–53.

Tillyard, E.M.W. *The Elizabethan World Picture* (London: Chatto and Windus, 1943).

Tittler, Robert. *Townspeople and Nation. English Urban Experiences 1540–1640* (Stanford: Stanford University Press, 2001).

Tittler, Robert. *The Face of the City. Civic Portraiture and Civic Identity in Early Modern England* (Manchester: Manchester University Press, 2007).

Tittler, Robert. "Social Aspiration and the Malleability of Portraiture in Post-Reformation England: the Kaye Panels of Woodsome, Yorkshire, c. 1567." *Northern History* 2015; 52(2), 182–99.

Tutino, Stefania. *Shadows of Doubt. Language and Truth in Post-Reformation Catholic Culture* (Oxford: Oxford University Press, 2014).

Underdown, David. *Fire from Heaven Life in an English Town in the Seventeenth Century* (New Haven: Yale University Press, 1994).

Walsham, Alexandra. "'Frantick Hacket': Prophecy, Sorcery, Insanity, and the Elizabethan Puritan Movement." *The Historical Journal* 1998; 41(1), 27–66.

Walsham, Alexandra. "Inventing the Lollard Past: The Afterlife of a Medieval Sermon in Early Modern England." *Journal of Ecclesiastical History* 2007; 58.4, 628–55.

Walsham, Alexandra. "Domesticating the Reformation: Material Culture, Memory, and Confessional Identity in Early Modern England." *Renaissance Quarterly* 2016; 69, 566–616.

Whitehead, Bertrand T. *Brags and Boasts. Propaganda in the Year of the Armada* (Stroud: Allan Sutton Publishing, 1994).

Williams, Penry. *The Council the Marches of Wales Under Elizabeth I* (Cardiff: University of Wales Press, 1958).

Williams, Richard L. "The Visual Arts," in Susan Doran and Norman Jones, eds. *Elizabethan World* (London: Routledge, 2011), 567–86.

Williamson, Charles G. Lady *Anne Clifford, Countess of Dorset, Pembroke and Montgomery, 1590–1676. Her Life, Letters and Work* (Kendal: Titus Wilson and Sons, 1922).

Willis, Jonathan. *Church Music and Protestantism in Post-Reformation England: Discourses, Sites and Identities* (London: Routledge, 2010).

Winston, Jessica. *Lawyers at Play. Literature, Law, and Politics at the Early Modern Inns of Court, 1558–1581* (Oxford: Oxford University Press, 2016).

Wood, Andy. *The Memory of the People. Custom and Popular Senses of the Past in Early Modern England* (Cambridge: Cambridge University Press, 2013).

Wooding, Lucy. "Remembrance in the Eucharist," in Andrew Gordon and Thomas Rist, eds. *The Arts of Remembrance in Early Modern England. Memorial Cultures of the Post Reformation* (Farnham: Ashgate, 2013), 19–36.

Woolf, Daniel. *The Idea of History in Early Stuart England. Erudition, Ideology, and "The Light of Truth" from the Accession of James I to the Civil War* (Toronto: University of Toronto Press, 1990).

Woolf, Daniel. *The Social Circulation of the Past. English Historical Culture 1500–1730* (Oxford: Oxford University Press, 2003).

Wootton, David. "Scott, Reginald (d. 1599)," in *Oxford Dictionary of National Biography* (Oxford: Oxford University Press, 2004). https://doi.org/10.1093/ref:odnb/24905 [Accessed November 29, 2018].

Wrightson, Keith. "The 'Decline of Neighbourliness' Revisted," in Norman Jones and Daniel Woolf, eds. *Local Identities in Late Medieval and Early Modern England* (Houndsmill: Palgrave Macmillan, 2007).

Zollinger, Cynthia Wittman. "'The booke, the leafe, yea and the very sentence': Sixteenth-Century Literacy in Text and Context," in Christopher Highley and John N. King, eds. *John Foxe and his World* (Aldershot: Ashgate, 2002), 102–16.

Index

Page numbers in *italics* refer to figures.

Being Elizabethan: Understanding Shakespeare's Neighbors, First Edition. Norman Jones.
© 2020 John Wiley & Sons, Inc. Published 2020 by John Wiley & Sons, Inc.

tobacco 112
tolerance, religious 163, 246–247, 294
Tollemache, Lionel 24, 26
tomatoes 110, 116
Topcliff, Richard 180, 244, 245, 250
Topsell, Edward 112–113
Tragical History of the Life and Death of Dr. Faustus, The (Marlowe) 278
transubstantiation 52
travel, restrictions on 119
Travers, Walter 167, 176–177
Treatise of Treasons against Queen Elizabeth, A 242
"Treatise on Religion" (Greville) 267
Tremaine, Edward 216
Troilus and Cressida (Shakespeare) 66
Turner, William 45–46
Twelfth Night (Shakespeare) 7, 182
Twyford, Francis 210
Tyndale, William 51, 259

u

Union of two noble and Illustrious families of Lancaster and York (Hall) 137
universities *see* Cambridge University; Oxford University
Ussher, James 119
usury 202–203, 215, 221–225, 226, 227

v

Vaughan, Lewis 38, 40, *40*
Vermigli, Peter Martyr 53, 240
Vesalius, Andreas 6, 120
Vestiarian Controversy 241
Virginia, America 110
virtue
  for Catholics 174, 175–176
  changing ideas about 17, 18–19
  in classic writings 139–140
  commemorated in portraits 22–24, *23, 25*
  conscience *see* conscience, individual
  of the dead *see* obituaries and commemorations in words
  defamation of 189–190
  defined by Bible 4–5

defined by *Book of Common Prayer* 174
differences in attitudes 14, 16, 174, 181–182, 194–198, *194*, 199
dress 184–188, *185*
education in 82, 85, 87
lack of secular or church guidance 172
in magistrates 238–239
meanings of 13–14, 236–237, 238–239
in men 19, 20, 24, *25*
obedience *see* obedience
for Protestant extremists 173–174, 180–182
religious conversion 178–180
self-prescriptions 19, 20
Travers—Hooker debate 177–178
vs. vices 7–8
in women 4, 11–13, 17–18, 20–21, *21*, 23–24, *23*

w

wages 72
Wales 290–291
Wallington, Nehemiah 137
Walsingham, Sir Francis 78, 158
Walton, Sir Izaak 276
wars 9, 79, 151, 158, 159–160, 205, 217, 244
Waterhouse, Agnes 164
wealth; *see also* economics; greed
  to be used for God's purposes 59, 60, 63, 76–77, 151, 229
  disparity of 9, 67
  and dress 184
  gift from God 76
  and social mobility 228
  tied to social standing 67
Weeks and Works (Baras) 300
Wentworth, Sir William 136–137
West Indies 112
Westminster School 84–85
Wheatlye, Richard 197
Whitaker, William 126–127
White, John 110, *111*, 198
White, Rev. Dr. 175–176